ITALIAN REGIONAL COOKING

OLD and NEW

ITALIAN REGIONAL COOKING

OLD and NEW

Anna Martini

C

CENTURY PUBLISHING
LONDON

The publisher thanks the following for their collaboration:

Rinaldo Baraldi, *La Casalinga*, Verona; Peck, Milan; SPE-GA, Verona; Ugolini Import-Export, Verona; Sipa, Potenza; APM Rome/Palermo; The Italian Oenological Institute, Verona; Giovanni de Marchi; Giovanna Bianchi; Marcella Pedone, Milan; Agenzia Marka, Milan.

Drawings by Vittorio Salarolo
Photographs by Luca Steffenoni
Translated from the Italian by Sara Harris

First published in Great Britain
by Century Publishing Co. Ltd.,
76 Old Compton Street, London W1V 5PA

Printed and bound in Italy by Officine Grafiche, Arnoldo Mondadori Editore, Verona

Contents

Foreword

In the days when traveling from one part of Italy to another was still considered an adventure, the differences between the various regions were immediately apparent to the traveler. Each province had an atmosphere special to itself which was due not solely to its climate and landscape but also to the physical appearance and customs of its inhabitants and countless other contrasting facets of daily life. One of the most obvious and pleasurable aspects of travel was the changing food. The cooking of each region was based on certain staple products, often very limited in range but which the countryside was able to produce successfully and in large quantities. Eventually a region's name would become synonymous with excellence in certain foods and its fame would spread throughout Italy. Thus the stuffed pig's foot (trotter) or zampone was to Modena what beans were to Lamon and sausages to Norcia. These specialities have stood the test of time and certain dishes are still associated with a particular town or province.

Nowadays, however, it is more difficult to tell where one is merely by the dishes being served. In order to compile a gastronomic guide to Italy, one has to delve back into the past and collect the traditional local recipes. These are the pointers to geographical and historical boundaries which have long since vanished.

The growth of tourism and the increased mobility of labor mean that each area has gradually become less "typical." Where cooking is concerned, the most significant factor in this trend is the ease with which today's quick and efficient transportation systems can distribute the products of each region throughout the country, so that the population's diet is far more varied today than it used to be. Nowadays a type of household bread which originated in Apulia and mozzarella cheese from Piana del Volturno find their way onto the table of the average family in Milan, while the agricultural worker in Lucca consumes his share of the canned and packaged goods manufactured by Northern Italy's large food industry.

This book is a collection of recipes based on recipes which have been handed down from a preindustrial era. When researching these "classic" recipes, it became obvious that however fascinating they were from an historical and sociological standpoint, it was necessary to select and sometimes adapt them so that they were practical and easily mastered by the modern cook.

Today's gourmets will appreciate a revival of yesterday's good cooking, but allowances have to be made for the fact that eating habits have changed and less time can be devoted to the preparation of everyday meals. It is fascinating to read the recipes of the great Italian gastronome, Artusi, but even the most assiduous students of classic cookery might be put off by lengthy processes and large quantities of foods high in cholesterol needed to achieve such culinary sophistication. The recent trend toward low-fat, unadulterated food has been taken into consideration in this collection of dishes. Not so long ago, many of these recipes were dismissed as "peasant" cooking, but this so-called poor man's cuisine is now appreciated for its simplicity and wholesome qualities. The great strength of traditional Italian food is that it makes the most of pure basic ingredients and is relatively straightforward to prepare. It is hoped that this book will help to lure those who enjoy good cooking away from convenience foods.

The realization that the staple foods of each region in past centuries could often be counted on the fingers of one hand might lead to the mistaken assumption that the cooking of each area must have been very dull, with the same dishes recurring with monotonous frequency. One has only to read the recipes which have been compiled here to see what amazing variety was achieved by blending and contrasting the flavors of superb raw materials, by the subtle addition of herbs and spices, and by cooking certain foods in wine. In much of today's cooking there is often a depressing sameness of taste due to the ubiquitous monosodium glutamate, present in bouillon cubes and extracts added to dish after dish. This is in stark contrast to the days when flavors were far more distinctive: the true taste of each ingredient was enhanced by such unlikely but inspired combinations as fish with meat (anchovies and tuna with veal, for example, in vitello tonnè*).*

The main objective of this book is to provide a sound basis for the enthusiastic cook who wants to acquire expertise in traditional regional cooking of Italy. There is always room for improvement. New variations can be created and experiments attempted, just as has been the case with generations of wise and inventive cooks from all over Italy whose recipes are gathered here.

A well-known expert on cooking used to suggest to aspiring chefs that they should choose four or five dishes and concentrate on perfecting them in order to gain the reputation of being outstanding cooks. Some restaurants adopt this philosophy to attract their clientele who come to savor a limited repertoire of specialty dishes. This is a totally impractical solution for most cooks, and in compiling this cookbook, the aim has been to give those who use it a wide choice from which to select the recipes which appeal to them. Cooked with care and enjoyment, these dishes will make memorable meals for those lucky enough to be invited to share them.

Note. *All of the recipes in this book make 4 servings unless otherwise indicated. Measurements are given in American, imperial and metric. Measurements given are working approximations, therefore to avoid error never mix, but use either American, imperial or metric for each recipe. In cases where only one measure is given, it is valid for all three systems.*

General Hints and Basic Recipes

The preparation of fresh pasta plays an important role in Italian regional cooking. In some regions fresh pasta is still made every day, an intrinsic part of the daily routine. This is particularly true in the Emilia-Romagna region despite a plentiful supply of manufactured pasta. Cooks in this area still consider, quite rightly, that commercially prepared products never equal the genuine article.

The following directions are intended as guidelines rather than hard and fast rules, since experience and acquired skill will teach the cook the "ideal" method.

Sfoglia
Egg Pasta

For 4 portions, allow 2½ cups (10½ oz/300 g) all-purpose (plain) flour, 3 eggs, and a pinch of salt. In some regions a few drops of oil or milk are added to the eggs, in others the flour is worked with water only, using a combination of white all-purpose (plain) flour and semolina or durum wheat flour or whole-wheat (wholemeal) flour.

Since different types of flour vary in absorbency, either more or less than the above quantity of flour will be needed. The less flour used, the more yielding and easily rolled the dough will be. If the proportion 1⅛ cup (4½ oz/130 g) flour to each egg is exceeded, the pasta will become too stiff and dry. Hand-kneaded and rolled pasta dough is usually lighter and softer than pasta made in a machine (these machines can either be hand-operated or electric). If a machine is

used to roll out the dough, it should not be kneaded too much; the machine's rollers will smooth and even it out.

Sift the flour onto a pastry board or working surface, shaping into a mound and forming a well in the center. Break one egg into the well, add a pinch of salt, and, using a fork, incorporate the flour into the egg very gradually. Knead thoroughly until the dough is smooth and elastic (if cut in half at this stage the dough will reveal evenly distributed air bubbles which have been incorporated during kneading). Leave the dough wrapped in a lightly floured pastry cloth to rest for 15 minutes. Divide the dough in half (leaving the other portion wrapped in the floured cloth) and roll out with a rolling pin, working outward from the center and rotating a quarter turn each time so the sheet formed is circular. Do not press hard against the board, but concentrate on rolling the dough out and away from you. When

the dough is very thin and as even as possible, leave it until it is dry but not brittle (15 to 30 minutes). This will prevent the dough from sticking when it is rolled up and cut into tagliatelle, fettuccine, and maltagliati. (See illustration, page 12.) The more quickly the dough is rolled out and stretched, the thinner it will be, since after a short time it will start to dry out and become more likely to tear and split.

If the pasta dough is to be used for stuffed pastas such as tortellini, agnolotti, ravioli, or cannelloni, etc., do not leave it to dry but follow the instructions given in these specific recipes.

Pasta Ripiena
Stuffed Pasta

Follow the instructions for egg pasta, kneading well to make a firm, smooth dough, using eggs, flour, salt, and, if

Left: Making tagliatelle by hand.

desired, a few drops of olive oil. Roll out two thin sheets of dough and arrange the fillings in small, evenly spaced heaps on one of these (allow about ¼ teaspoon of filling for each portion). Brush the spaces between the filling with a mixture of egg and water to help seal the ravioli tightly. Carefully place the second sheet of pasta dough over the first one, pressing down gently but firmly with the fingertips around each heap of filling. Using a fluted pastry wheel, cut vertically and horizontally between the portions of filling to form small square pillows of pasta—ravioli. For agnolotti, cut into circles.

To make tortellini and cappelletti, cut out disks of pastry with a 2-inch (5-cm) pastry or cookie cutter (or an inverted glass). Place ¼ teaspoon of the filling in the center of each circle. Moisten the edges with beaten egg and water or milk and fold in half to form semicircles. The top edges should stop about ⅛ inch (3 mm) short of the lower edges. Press firmly together. Pinch the ends of the semicircles together (see instructions for individual recipes).

The illustrations on pages 14 and 15 show the method for making various types of stuffed pasta.

Pastafrolla
Italian Short Pastry

This type of pastry can be used for both sweet and savory dishes. For four portions allow the following quantities: 3½ cups/14 oz/400 g all-purpose (plain) flour; scant 1 cup/7 oz/200 g butter; 1 cup/7 oz/200 g sugar (if the recipe calls for a sweet egg pastry); 4 eggs; ½ tsp grated lemon rind; salt. Other ingredients may be added as directed in the individual recipes.

Mix the flour with the eggs, salt, grated lemon rind, and sugar (if used). Add the softened butter and work in evenly with a wooden spoon. The pastry should be quite firm; but if it is too firm, add a little ice-cold water or milk.

Pastafrolla should not be elastic or

aerated. In other types of dough the presence of small air bubbles is a good sign, but not in Italian short pastry.

Wrap the pastry in a cloth or plastic wrap and leave it in the refrigerator for a while—preferably overnight. This will greatly improve the consistency of the pastry.

A variation of this recipe uses only the yolks of 4 eggs. This gives a more delicate and lighter texture. When preparing the pastry this way, work with the fingertips rather than a wooden spoon.

The illustration on page 37 shows the preparation of Italian short pastry. The illustration on page 16 shows how to line a flan tin when baking an unfilled shell.

Pasta Millefoglie o Sfogliata
Italian Puff Pastry

Puff pastry is not used very much in Italian cookery, except in some parts of northern Italy, because it can only be really successful when prepared at a cool temperature. It should therefore not be attempted in hot weather except in an air-conditioned kitchen.

Quantities for four people are as follows: $3\frac{1}{2}$ cups/14 oz/400 g all-purpose (plain) flour; $1\frac{3}{4}$ cups/14 oz/400 g butter; $\frac{3}{4}$–1 cup/6–8 oz/1.8–2.4 dl ice-cold water. The amount of water needed will vary according to the type of flour used.

Mix two-thirds of the sifted flour with the water and add a pinch of salt. This is best done by heaping the flour on a marble or other working surface, making a well in the center and putting the salt into it. Work with the fingers of one hand, pour the water with the other, very gradually, into the center. Work the flour and water together just until the dough no longer sticks to the fingers. Roll the dough into a ball and let it rest for 30 minutes in the refrigerator. Work the remaining flour with the butter, pat it into an oblong slope, and leave it in the refrigerator to rest.

Dust the working surface very lightly

Right: Making tagliatelle using a pasta machine.

Above: To make round stuffed pasta, use a pastry cutter.

Below: How to cut, fill, and shape tortellini.

with flour and roll out the flour-and-water dough into an oblong shape just large enough to envelop the butter-and-flour mixture taken from the refrigerator (do not roll it too thin). Place the rectangle of butter and flour near one end of the rolled-out dough. Fold the other end over, completely encasing the butter.

Next comes the most delicate stage of making puff pastry: rolling out the pastry without the butter breaking through the encasing flour mixture. With gentle, deft strokes, working from the fold of the dough, roll out the pastry to form a long rectangle. Do not press too hard. Always roll this pastry away from you, never return the rolling pin toward you. When the pastry has doubled in length, fold the third nearest you toward the center and cover with the other third, forming three layers like a letter. Wrap the dough in plastic wrap or foil and refrigerate for 30 minutes. Then working from the narrow end, roll out as before. Repeat this chilling and rolling at least five or six times. Handle the pastry as little as possible and sprinkle as little flour as possible on the working surface and rolling pin, since the more flour used, the less the pastry will rise. The puff pastry is now ready for baking. Puff pastry can be wrapped in plastic wrap or foil and frozen for future use.

Puff pastry should be baked in a hot oven (450°F/230°C/mk 8). Do not open the oven while the pastry is cooking, otherwise it will not rise in the paper-thin layers which give it its Italian name—*mille foglie* (a thousand leaves). Once cooked, the pastry can be returned to the oven, garnished with cheese or other toppings which need browning. It can also be used for pastry such as *vol au vent* and *bouchée* cases for a wide variety of dishes from hors d'oeuvres to desserts.

Ready-made frozen puff pastry is available in most food stores. It saves a great deal of time and gives excellent results.

Pasta da Pane
Bread Dough

Leftover bread dough was often used for making pizzas; the easiest method is that used for making French bread but it should not be left to rise for a second time. Where differing quantities are given for ingredients in particular recipes, this method can be used as a general guide only. For four portions allow:

3¾ cups/1lb/450 g all-purpose (plain) flour; 2 envelopes active dry or 1 cake compressed yeast /1oz/25 g fresh yeast dissolved in 1 tbsp milk; ¼ cup/2 fl oz/60 ml oil; ¼ cup /2 fl oz/60 ml milk; 1 tsp salt. Warm all the milk to lukewarm and dissolve the yeast in 1 tablespoon of it. Allow to rest for 5 to 10 minutes and then add to the remaining warmed milk. Sift the flour and salt into a large mixing bowl and make a well in the center; pour in the yeast and milk mixture, amalgamated with the oil (which should be at room temperature). Sir thoroughly and knead for 20 minutes – the dough will be soft. Cover with a damp cloth and set in a warm place to rise for three hours. Pat

Below: Use a ravioli mold and roller for homemade stuffed square pasta.

Left: How to make short pastry and line a flan tin when baking an unfilled shell.

or roll the dough into the requisite number of large or smaller circles and then proceed to make the pizza according to the directions given for each individual recipe.

Polenta
Cornmeal

Polenta is made with cornmeal (maize flour) cooked in salted water. It is best cooked in a copper pan (not tinned) over a gentle heat or in a double boiler. (In days gone by, polenta was always cooked in a large cauldron suspended over the wood fire in the family kitchen.) Proportions are roughly 70 percent water to 30 percent cornmeal (maize flour). The absorbency of the flour will vary according to whether it is recently processed and whether it is finely or coarsely ground. Care must therefore be taken to adjust the quantities to avoid too heavy or too runny a consistency. In the region considered the home of polenta, from Bergamo to eastern Veneto, tastes vary. In Bergamo a very coarse grain cornmeal (maize flour) is preferred; in Verona a slightly less coarse grain is used; and in Vicenza, Padua, and Venice, finely ground cornmeal (maize flour) is considered best. The presentation of polenta when made and turned out onto the special round wooden board, called a *panara*, used for serving, also varies. The very thick, compact slab of polenta of Bergamo and Trent changes to a slightly thinner layer in Verona and to a very thin layer in Vicenza. In Venice white cornmeal (maize flour) is the most sought after, whereas in other regions yellow cornmeal (maize flour) is used.

There are some basic rules to remember when cooking polenta. Pour the cornmeal (maize flour) into the water as soon as it reaches the boiling point, in a slow, steady flow while stirring constantly in a clockwise direction with a wooden spoon to prevent lumps. Polenta is usually cooked for about 45 minutes in an ordinary saucepan, or for about 1½ hours in a double boiler. When the mixture comes away from the sides of the pan cleanly, it is done. It is possible to buy a special boiler equipped with an electrically powered beater for cooking polenta. This saves standing over the polenta and stirring while it cooks. For various polenta dishes, refer to the recipes given.

Right and overleaf: Some of the infinite variety of shapes and names of commercially available dried pasta manufactured in Italy. The names of these pastas vary from one manufacturer to another and some of the names are known only in certain regions of Italy. This makes it difficult to translate and neatly classify the names of pastas!

1 *capellini*
2 *sopracapellini*
3 *spaghettini*
4 *spaghetti*
5 *bucatini*
6 *linguine*
7 *mezzezite*
8 *fusilli*
9 *capellini a matassa*
10 *penne lisce*
11 *sigarette*
12 *denti di cavallo*
13 *pennette lisce*
14 *cellentani*
15 *sedanini*
16 *sedani*
17 *diavolini rigati*
18 *tortiglioni*
19 *eliche*
20 *penne rigate*
21 *fischioni mezzani rigati*
22 *quick macaroni*
23 *millerighi*
24 *conchiglie*
25 *farfallette*
26 *nocciole*
27 *semi di mela*
28 *avemaria rigate*
29 *semini*
30 *occhi di lupo*
31 *puntine*
32 *avemaria lisce*
33 *peperini*
34 *corallini*
35 *grattata mezzana*
36 *stellettine*
37 *conchigliette*
38 *anellini*
39 *tripolini trinati*
40 *grandine bucata*
41 *funghini trinati*

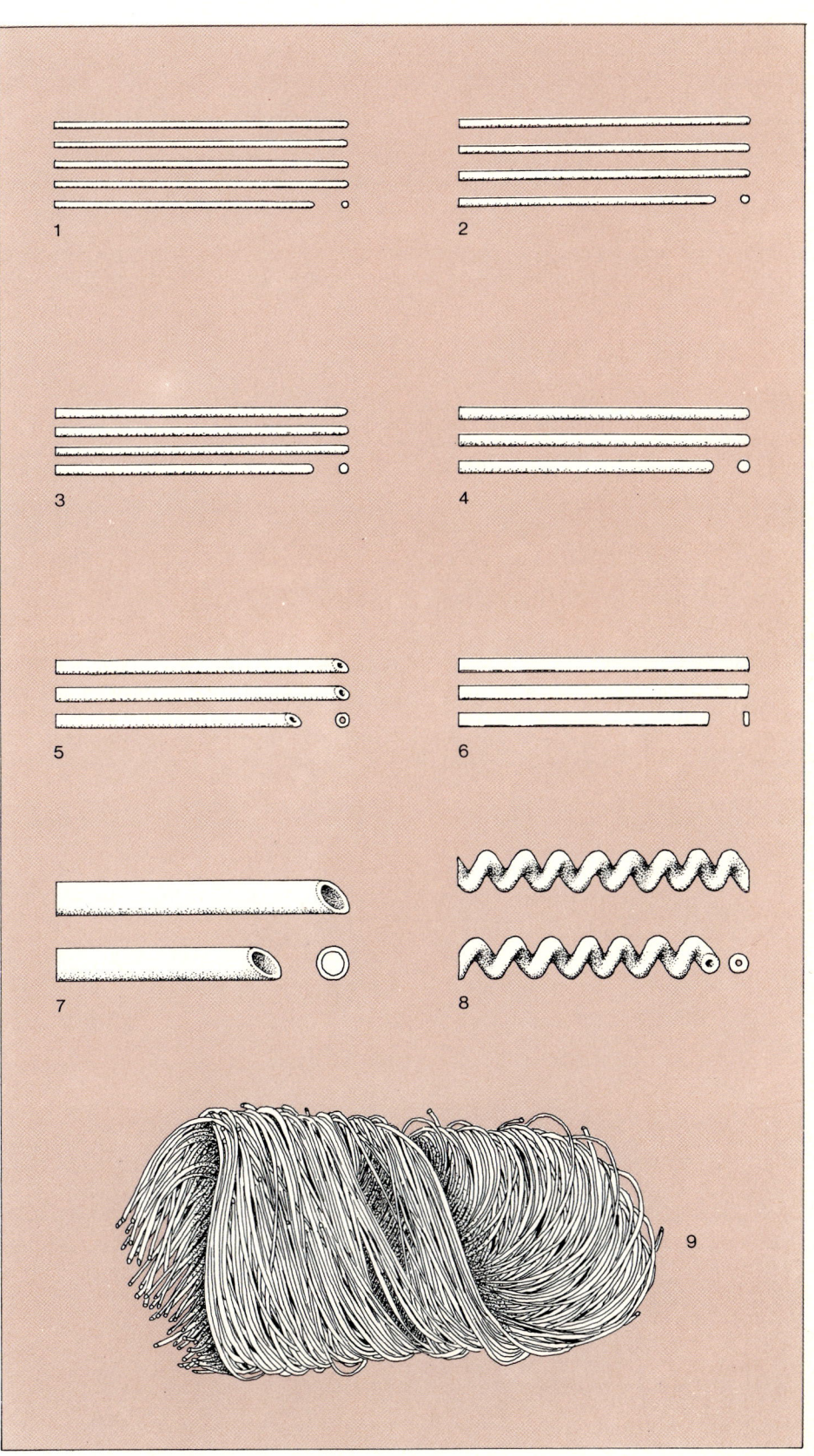

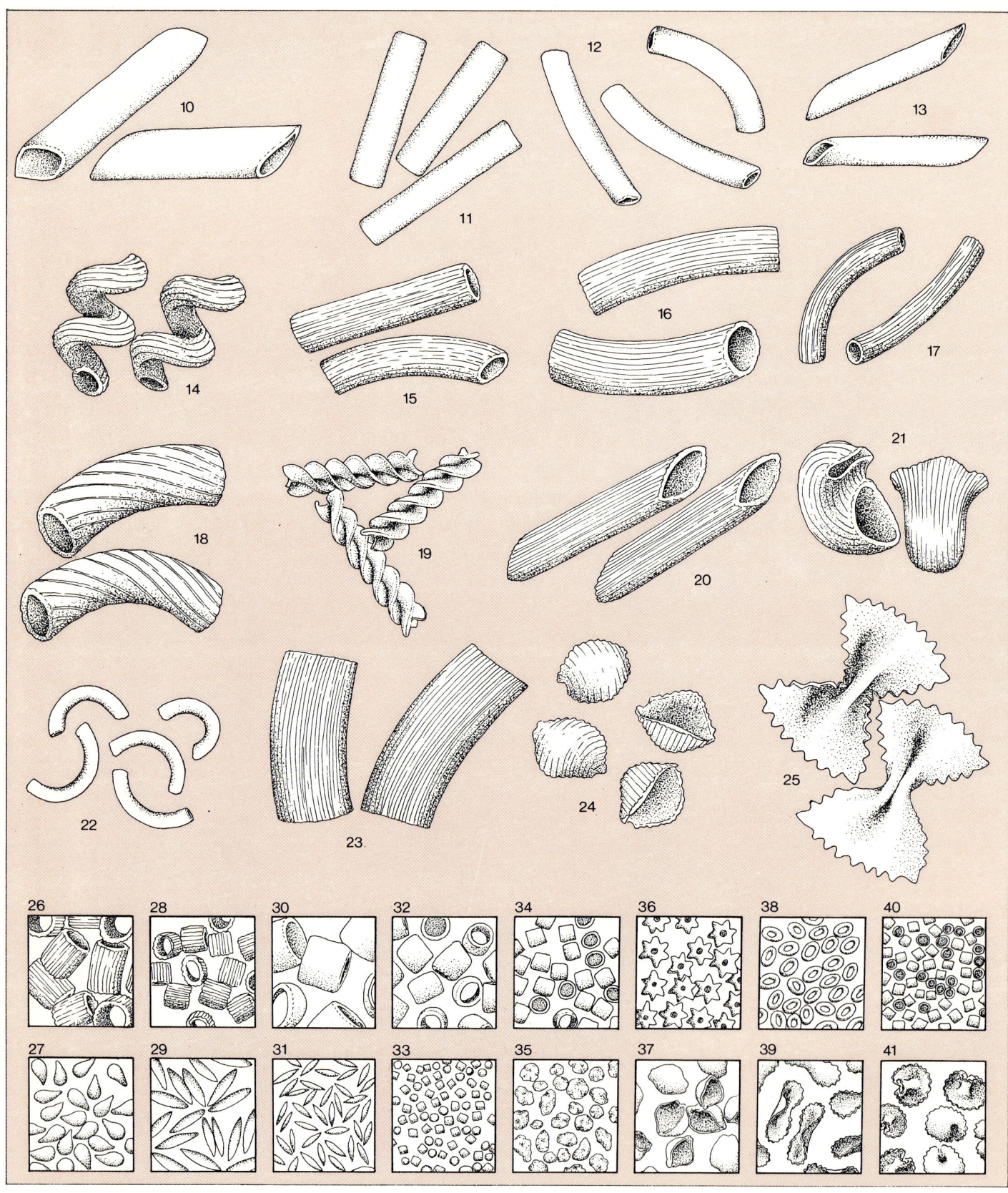

PIEDMONT AND

AOSTA

NOVARA

VERCELLI

TURIN

ASTI

ALESSANDRIA

CUNEO

VAL D'AOSTA

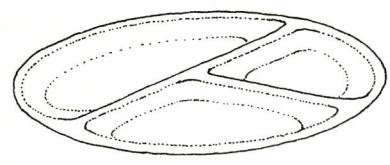

Fonduta
Piedmontese Cheese Fondue

1¾ c/7 oz/200 g Fontina cheese
½ c/4 fl oz/125 ml lukewarm milk
3 egg yolks
4 Tbsp/2 oz/50 g butter
freshly ground white pepper
1 Piedmontese (white) truffle (optional)
slices of freshly made toast

This fondue is an extremely popular winter treat. It should be served with slices of freshly made toast.

Remove the rind from the cheese, dice, and cover with milk. Leave to steep, preferably in an earthenware dish, for several hours. The cheese will absorb most of the milk. Using a wooden spoon, stir in the egg yolks and melted butter. Transfer the mixture to a double boiler and cook, stirring continuously. Do not boil. As soon as the mixture becomes smooth and creamy, remove from heat and stir in freshly ground white pepper to taste. Scatter slivers of raw white truffle, if desired, on top and serve immediately.

Piedmontese white truffles are, in fact, pale beige to light brown. Fresh truffles are imported by specialty food shops. They are extremely expensive but well worth trying for their unforgettable flavor. They should be washed and scraped or brushed before cooking. The canned variety is a pale echo of the fresh and will probably prove very disappointing. Even a very small fresh truffle can perfume a whole dish with its unmistakable aroma.

Bagna Cauda
Hot Dip

7 Tbsp/4 oz/100 g butter
5 Tbsp/3½ Tbsp/50 g oil
4 large cloves garlic
12 anchovy fillets
1 white truffle (optional)

Salted whole anchovies are used for this dish in Piedmont, but canned fillets chopped into very small pieces will do just as well.

Place the butter, oil, and very finely chopped garlic in a fondue dish (preferably earthenware) and heat gently until the garlic has shrunk but not colored. Remove from heat and add the anchovies, mashing them into the oil and butter with a fork until blended into a paste. Return to the heat and add the truffle (if used), cut very thin. Simmer, mixing well until the ingredients have combined smoothly. Serve at once.

Bagna cauda should be kept hot in much the same way as a fondue, over a spirit lamp or candle in the middle of the table, so that everyone can dip pieces of raw vegetables in the sauce. Celery, cardoons, and peppers are the most popular in Piedmont.

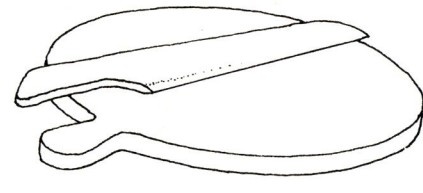

Agnolotti alla Piemontese
Piedmontese Stuffed Pasta

1lb/1lb/500g agnolotti (see recipe on
*   pages 11–12)*
5½ Tbsp/2¾ oz/80 g butter
¼c/2 oz/50 g grated Parmesan cheese
salt
1 white truffle (optional)

Cook the agnolotti in plenty of boiling salted water until they are tender but firm (al dente). Drain and place a layer in a heated serving dish; stir in a little melted butter and sprinkle with some of the grated Parmesan. Place another layer of pasta on top of this and sprinkle with more melted butter and grated Parmesan. Repeat the process until all the stuffed pasta has been used. Cover the top layer with wafer-thin slices of raw truffle (optional).

Bake in a 400°F (200°C/mk 6) oven for a few minutes and serve without delay.

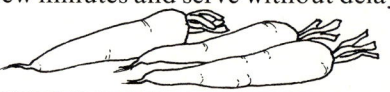

Panissa di Vercelli
Vercelli Rice and Bean Soup

1 c/7 oz/200 g dried borlotti beans (dried
*   white navy or haricot beans may be*
*   substituted)*
salt
3–4 oz/3–4 oz/100 g fresh pork rind
3 Tbsp/2 Tbsp/2 Tbsp oil
1 Tbsp/butter
1 c/5 oz/150 g Italian pork sausage meat
3–4 Tbsp/2 oz/50 g lard or fresh pork fat
*   (crushed)*
1 onion
1½ c/10½ oz/300 g Arborio rice
freshly ground pepper
grated Parmesan cheese

Soak the beans in water overnight. Boil them with the pork rind in at least 4 cups (1½ pt/1 liter) lightly salted water.

Put the oil, butter, sausage meat, fat, and very finely chopped onion in a large pan. Place over a low heat and mix with a wooden spoon until the onion is translucent but not colored. Add the rice, mixing and turning so that all the grains are coated with fat. Pour in a generous ⅔ cup (¼ pt/150 ml) of the liquid in which the beans were cooked, adding more, a little at a time, as the rice absorbs the liquid.

When the rice is nearly done, add the beans, pepper to taste, and, if necessary, a little more salt. Turn off the heat, sprinkle with grated Parmesan, mix once more, and serve immediately.

Tortino di Polenta e Fontina
Polenta Cake with Cheese

*3½ c/14 oz/400 g finely ground cornmeal
  (maize flour)*
salt
5–6 oz/5–6 oz/150 g Fontina cheese
2 Tbsp/1 oz/1 Tbsp melted butter
freshly ground white pepper

Bring 2 quarts (4 pt/2 liters) lightly salted water to a boil in a large pot. Gradually add the cornmeal (maize flour), stirring constantly. If too much flour is added at one time, the mixture will be lumpy. Reduce the heat and simmer, stirring very frequently for up to 45 minutes or until the polenta is thick and comes away from the sides of the pan easily. Taste to be sure that there is enough salt.

Turn onto a wooden platter or board and allow to cool. When cold, cut into ½-inch-thick (1-cm) slices. Cut the Fontina into thin slices. In a buttered ovenproof dish, arrange alternate layers of polenta and cheese, sprinkling each layer with a little white pepper. Finish with a layer of polenta and drizzle a little melted butter on top.

Bake in a hot oven (450°F/230°C mk 8) until the top layer is crisp and golden brown.

Lasagne al Sangue
Lasagne with Pork Sauce

4 oz/4 oz/100 g pork sweetbreads
½ onion
1 small bunch parsley
2 Tbsp/¾ oz/20 g butter
3 Tbsp/2 Tbsp/2 Tbsp olive oil
1 c/7 oz/200 g fresh pork sausage meat
*1 recipe/10½ oz/300 g fresh lasagne (see
  egg pasta recipe, page 11) or
  ½ lb/8 oz/225 g commercial lasagne*
1¼ c/½ pt/3 dl pig's blood
⅓ c/3½ fl oz/1 dl milk
¼ c/2 oz/50 g grated Parmesan cheese

Blanch the sweetbreads in lightly salted water: simmer for 1 minute, plunge into cold water, and remove membrane and any bloody tissue. Chop the onion and parsley finely. Heat the butter and oil in a saucepan until they begin to color. Add the chopped onion and parsley, the sausage meat and the chopped sweetbreads. Cover and cook over a low heat for about 30 minutes.

Below: Bagna Cauda is dialect for "hot bath." This aromatic hot dip can be served with raw vegetables.

Cook the lasagne in boiling salted water until half-done. Drain. Pour the pig's blood and milk into a wide skillet and heat gently (do not allow to boil at any stage or the mixture will curdle). When warm add the lasagne and mix carefully over a fairly low heat until the liquid becomes creamy in consistency and turns brown. Add the meat and onion from the saucepan; then remove from heat before adding the grated Parmesan. Stir once more and serve immediately.

Tagliatelle al Sugo
Tagliatelle with Tomato Sauce

2 Tbsp/1 oz/25 g grated Parmesan
    cheese
3 c/12¼ oz/350 g all-purpose (plain)
    flour
2 eggs
2 egg yolks
1 slice of cooked ham ¼ in (½ cm) thick
1 stalk celery
1 small carrot
4 Tbsp/2 oz/50 g butter
1 lb/1 lb/500 g canned tomatoes
salt
pepper

Mix the grated Parmesan with the flour and work in the eggs and egg yolks to form a very firm, elastic dough. Roll out into a very thin sheet. Allow to dry and cut into strips about 1¼ inches (3 cm) wide. (When the pasta sheet assumes a crinkly, leathery surface, it can be cut out and handled easily without much danger of sticking.) Place a few of these "ribbons" on top of each other, and cut them crosswise into ¼-inch (½-cm) widths. The tagliatelle noodles will thus be approximately ¼ inch (½ cm) wide and 1¼ inches (3 cm) long.

Dice the ham into small pieces and chop the celery and carrot very finely. Place half the butter in a skillet and sauté the chopped vegetables and ham. When the onions are soft but not brown, add the sieved tomatoes. Season with a little salt and pepper to taste and simmer over a low heat until the sauce has reduced and thickened somewhat.

Cook the tagliatelle in a large pot of boiling, salted water until it is al dente. Drain and transfer to a heated serving dish. Dot with small pieces of the remaining butter and cover with sauce. Serve more grated Parmesan separately.

Tagliatelline con la Fonduta
Tagliatelline with Cheese Fondue

2 c/7 oz/200 g thinly sliced Fontina
    cheese
½ c/4 fl oz/125 ml lukewarm milk
2 Tbsp/¾ oz/20 g butter
3 egg yolks

1 recipe fresh tagliatelline (see egg pasta
    recipe, page 11) or
½ lb/8 oz/225 g dried small ribbon
    noodles
salt
pepper
1 white truffle (optional)

Place the cheese in a bowl and pour the milk over it. Allow to stand for at least 2 hours.

Melt the butter in a double boiler over a low heat; add the cheese and 2 tablespoons of the milk in which it has steeped (most of the milk will have been absorbed). Beat gently with a wire whisk until the cheese has completely melted. Turn the heat up very slightly and add the egg yolks one at a time, beating vigorously to blend evenly and avoid curdling. Season with salt and pepper. Keep warm over a very low heat.

Cook the tagliatelline in plenty of boiling salted water; drain and turn into a heated serving dish. Pour the fondue sauce over the noodles and mix. Top with slivers of white truffle (optional).

Tajarin all'Albese con Fegatini
Tajarin with Chicken Livers

2½ c/10½ oz/300 g all-purpose (plain)
    flour
3 eggs
3 Tbsp/1½ oz/40 g butter

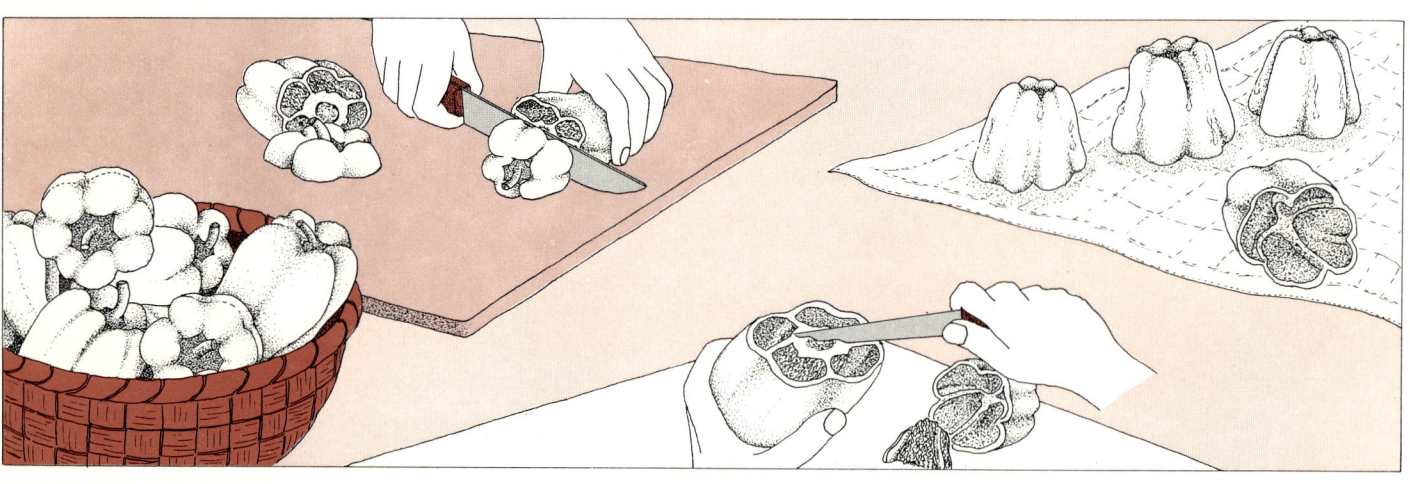

½ c/4 oz/100 g chicken livers
½ c/4 fl oz/125 ml stock or ½ tsp meat
    extract dissolved in ½ c/4 fl oz/125 ml
    hot water
salt
nutmeg (optional)
pepper
¼ c/1½ oz/40 g grated Parmesan cheese
1 white truffle (optional)

Prepare the pasta for these little ribbon noodles by combining the flour and eggs on a pastry board. Knead until the dough is soft and pliable and then roll out into a very thin sheet (divide the pasta in two sheets if the working surface is not large enough to handle one large sheet easily). Let dry a little and then cut out into *tajarin*, which should be about ¼ inch (½ cm) wide.

Heat the butter in a small saucepan and, as soon as it begins to froth, add the washed and trimmed chicken livers cut into thin slices. Sauté for 2 to 3 minutes. Add the chicken stock or meat extract. Season with salt and a pinch of grated nutmeg (optional). Simmer over a moderate heat until reduced.

Cook the noodles in plenty of boiling salted water until they are tender but still firm. Drain them and turn into a heated serving dish. Season with pepper and grated Parmesan cheese and add the sauce. Mix well and top with very thin slices of white truffle. (For decorative purposes, sliced button mushrooms can be substituted, but obviously nothing can replace the flavor of the raw truffles.)

Gnocchi alla Piemontese
Gnocchi Piedmont Style

1¾ lb/1¾ lb/800 g potatoes
1¾ c/7 oz/200 g all-purpose (plain) flour
salt
4 Tbsp/2 oz/50 g butter
4–5 fresh sage leaves or
    ¼ tsp dried sage

Peel the potatoes and cook them in a tightly covered saucepan with only a small amount of water so that they are steamed rather than boiled. When they are tender drain off any remaining water and return the pan to the heat, uncovered, for 15 seconds to get rid of excess moisture. Mash or put through a potato ricer or sieve immediately and heap into a mound on the pastry board or working surface.

Make a well in the middle of the potatoes and gradually work in the flour and a little salt. Knead the mixture well until it is smooth and pliable. Break off portions of the dough and shape into sausagelike rolls the thickness of a finger. Cut these into approximately 1¼-inch (3–cm) lengths. These can then be given the typical gnocchi shape by pressing each piece with the fingers against the concave side of a cheese grater or the tines of a fork (see illustration, page 55). These little dumplings should have the appearance of a shell, with a pronounced hollow on one side.

Cook the gnocchi in batches in plenty of rapidly boiling water. They cook very quickly and are done when they rise to the top. Remove them with a slotted spoon. Place on individual heated plates and cover with melted butter in which the sage leaves have been browned. Top with grated Parmesan cheese.

The amount of flour needed to hold the gnocchi together in the boiling water will vary depending on the type of potatoes used. Until you become familiar with the dough, it is a good idea to test one before shaping all of them. If the test piece falls apart, add a little more flour.

Gnocchi alla Bava
Gnocchi with Cheese

1¾ lb/1¾ lb/800 g potatoes
1¾ c/7 oz/200 g all-purpose (plain) flour
salt
5 oz/5 oz/150 g Fontina cheese
4 Tbsp/2 oz/50 g butter

Boil the potatoes; peel them and mash them or put them through a ricer or sieve, mounding them on a pastry board. (Never allow the potatoes to cool before putting them through the ricer or sieve, or the dough will not be smooth.)

Below and opposite: Preparing Peperoni Farciti alla Torinese (con Riso) (Stuffed Peppers Turin Style).

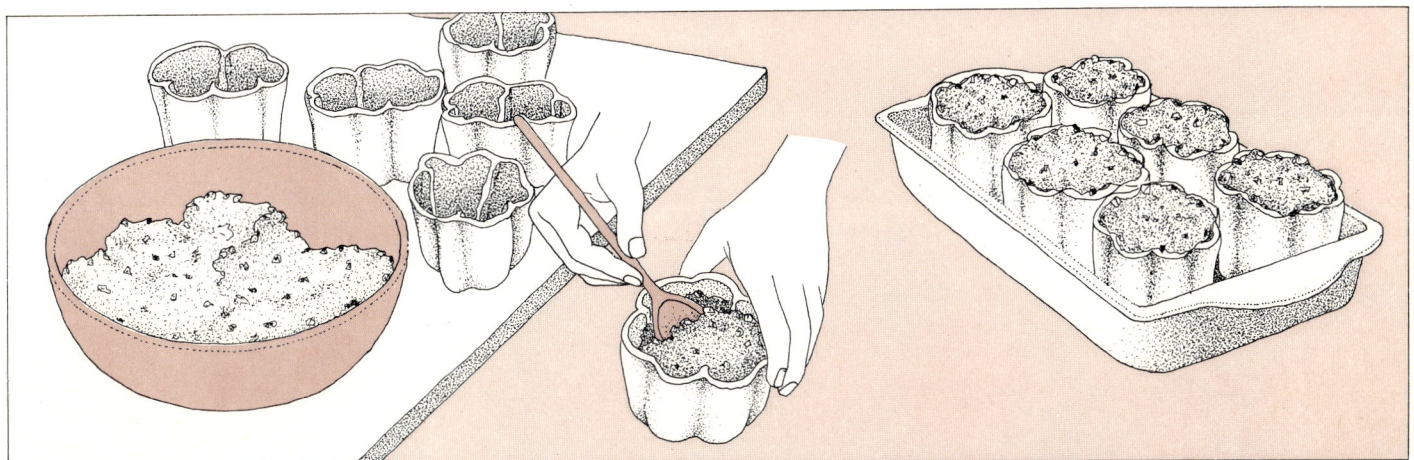

When the potatoes have cooled, work in the flour and a teaspoon of salt. Knead well to give a soft smooth dough. Roll out into long sausagelike rolls the thickness of a finger, cut into pieces approximately ¾ inch (2 cm) long. Press each little cylinder against the concave side of a cheese grater or the tines of a fork so that the gnocchi are crescent-shaped (see illustration, page 55).

Cook in plenty of boiling salted water in a large pan for about 10 minutes or until they float to the top. Remove with a slotted spoon, allow to drain well, and arrange in layers in a buttered oven-proof dish, placing a layer of the thinly sliced Fontina cheese between each layer of gnocchi. Sprinkle each layer of gnocchi with melted butter. Place in a 400°F (200°C/mk 6) oven for about 10 minutes, until the top starts to turn golden brown. Serve at once.

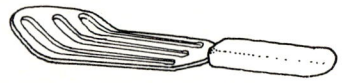

Peperoni Farciti alla Torinese (con Riso)
Stuffed Peppers Turin Style

4 large green or yellow peppers
⅔ c/5 oz/150 g rice
8 anchovy fillets
2 Tbsp/1 oz/25 g butter
6 Tbsp/4 Tbsp/5 Tbsp olive oil
1 clove garlic
1 small bunch parsley
salt

These stuffed peppers are equally delicious served hot or cold.

Cut the peppers in half horizontally, remove the membrane and seeds, and scald in boiling water for 2 to 3 minutes to loosen the thin outer skin. Peel.

Cook the rice in 2 cups (16 fl oz/4.75 dl) of boiling salted water. While it is cooking, chop the anchovy fillets finely. Heat the butter and 1 tablespoon of oil in a small pan and sauté the anchovies and the very finely chopped garlic over a low heat, working the anchovies with a fork until they dissolve to form a thin paste. When the rice is al dente, sprinkle

with 2 tablespoons of oil and the finely chopped parsley. Fill the pepper halves with the rice mixture and place them in an oiled ovenproof dish, topping each with anchovy sauce. Bake in a 350°F (180°C/mk 4) oven for 30 minutes.

Risotto coi Tartufi
Risotto with Truffles

1 small onion
4 Tbsp/2 oz/50 g butter
1¾ c/12¼ oz/350 g Arborio rice
5 c/2 pt/1¼ l stock
1 black or white truffle
¼ c/2 oz/50 g grated Parmesan cheese

The success of this dish depends largely on balancing the flavors of the Parmesan cheese and the truffle; more or less cheese may be needed in order to complement but not overwhelm the delicate aroma of the truffle.

Chop the onion very finely and put into a large heavy pan with two thirds of the butter. Sauté gently until pale gold. Add the rice (the round-grained Arborio variety is the best for risotto) and mix well so that each grain will become coated with butter. Bring the stock to a boil, simmer and pour into the rice, a cupful at a time, as the rice absorbs the moisture, adding water if no stock is left.

Just before the rice is done, add the remaining butter which will help to give the risotto the correct creamy consistency. Transfer the rice onto a warm serving platter and scatter wafer-thin slices of raw, fresh truffle on top. Sprinkle with grated Parmesan.

Riso in Cagnôn
Rice with Cheese

1¾ c/12½ oz/350 g rice
4 Tbsp/2 oz/50 g butter
scant ½ lb/7 oz/200 g Fontina or Bel Paese cheese (diced)

Cook the rice in 5 cups (2 pt/1¼ l) of boiling salted water. When it is tender but still firm, transfer to a double boiler or bain marie in which the butter has been heated. Stir constantly, adding the diced cheese. Keep the heat low, since the rice and melted cheese will stick to the bottom of the pan if the heat is too high.

Serve as soon as the rice is thoroughly coated with cheese.

Tartine di Carne Cruda
Italian Veal Tartare

1 lb/1 lb/500 g ground (minced) lean veal (such as the noisette cut from the leg)
1 clove garlic
2 anchovy fillets
salt
6 Tbsp/4 Tbsp/4 Tbsp oil
3 lemons
1 truffle (optional)

Put the veal, garlic, and anchovy through a food processor or blender or pound in a mortar with a pestle until reduced to a smooth paste. Transfer to a bowl, add a little salt to taste, and gradually blend in the oil and lemon juice with a wooden spoon.

Shape into four patties and serve on individual plates garnished with very thin slices of fresh raw truffle (optional).

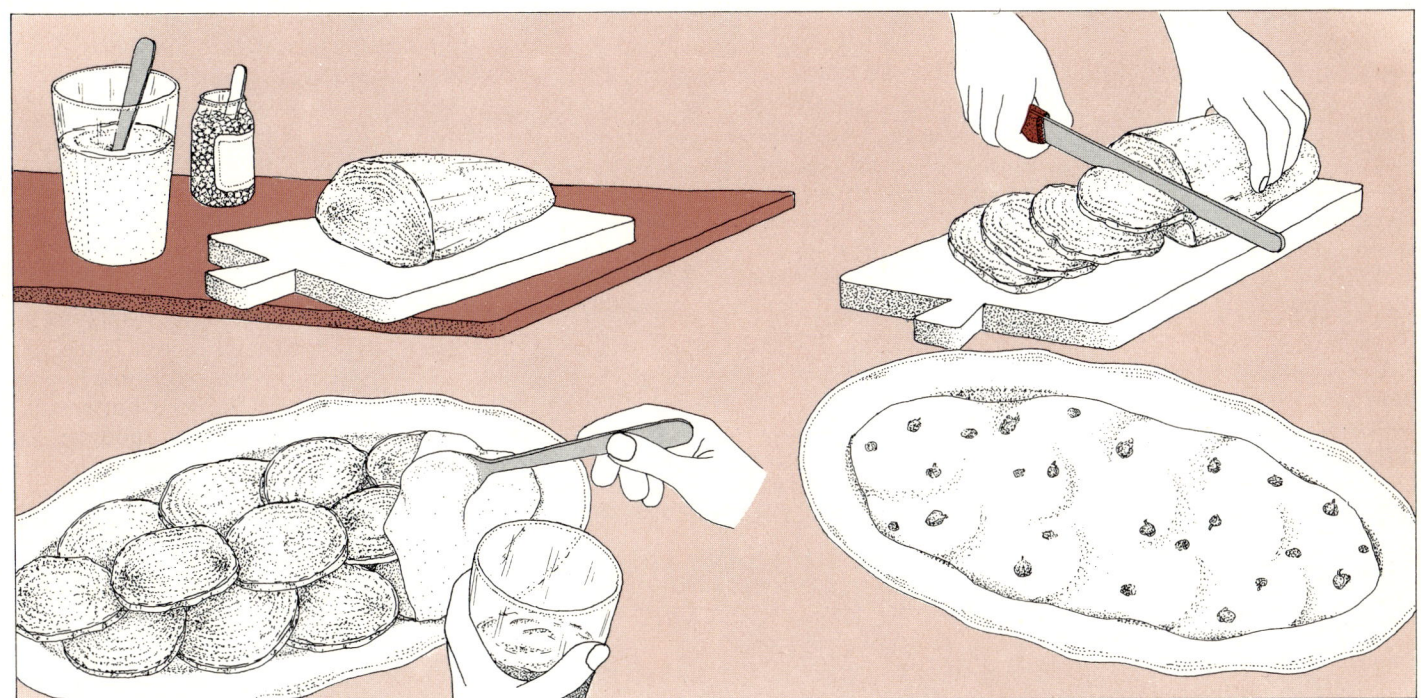

Manzo Brasato al Barolo
Beef Braised in Barolo Wine

1 bottle Barolo or other dry, full-bodied
    red wine
1 onion
1 stalk celery
1 carrot
freshly ground black pepper
salt
1 bay leaf
2 lb/2 lb/1 kg thick cut rib of beef
2 Tbsp/1 oz/25 g butter
2 Tbsp/1 oz/25 g fat from prosciutto (raw
    ham) or unsmoked bacon (minced)
1¼ tsp/1 tsp/1 tsp potato flour

This method of preparation will make
almost any cut of beef tender. It will take
about 2 hours to cook. The meat must
be simmered very gently.

Pour the wine into a pan just large
enough to accommodate the beef. Add
the finely chopped onion, celery, and
carrot, a little freshly ground black
pepper, a little salt, and the crushed bay
leaf. Place the meat in the wine and
marinate for at least 24 hours, turning
the beef several times. Before cooking

the meat, drain it, reserving the marinade, pat it dry, and tie it up neatly so
that it will keep its shape.

Melt the butter and fat in a pan and
brown the meat gently on all sides.
Meanwhile, reduce the marinade over a
high heat. When it is reduced by nearly
half, pour it over the beef. Add a little
salt. Cover the pan tightly and simmer
gently over a low heat until the beef is
very tender. Transfer the meat to a
serving dish and keep warm.

Mix the potato flour with a little water
and add to the wine sauce in which the
meat has cooked. Cook for a few
minutes over a low heat. Pour the sauce
over the beef and serve piping hot.

Vitello Tonnè
Veal with Tuna

about 1½ lb/1½ lb/600 g veal roast cut
    from the fillet end of the leg
1 bottle of dry white wine
1 Tbsp vinegar
1 bay leaf
2 cloves
1 stalk celery
½ onion

*Above: Vitello Tonnè (Veal with Tuna Sauce) is
an extremely popular dish in northern Italy.*

salt
1 6½ oz can/7 oz/200 g tuna packed in
    olive oil
2 hard-boiled eggs
8 anchovy fillets
⅓ c/3½ fl oz/1 dl oil
1 Tbsp capers

This dish is delicious served hot or cold
(the latter is more popular in Italy). It
makes an excellent first course when
accompanied by thick slices of toasted
French bread and is usually served with
a light dry red wine such as Grignolino.

The veal should be tied so that it will
retain its shape. Put it in a large, heavy
enamel pot with the wine, vinegar,
crushed bayleaf, cloves, and finely
chopped celery and onion. Marinate for
about 24 hours, turning occasionally to
ensure that the meat absorbs the flavors
evenly.

Remove the veal, strain the marinade,
and return both to the pot, making sure
that the liquid completely covers the
meat. Season with a little salt and bring
to a boil. Cook, uncovered, for about 45
minutes over a low heat. When the meat

is done, the cooking liquid should have reduced considerably.

Flake the tuna and pound into a paste with the hard-boiled eggs and anchovies. Place these ingredients in a fine strainer (sieve) and pour the cooking liquid through them. Stir gently while gradually adding the oil and finally the capers.

When the veal has completely cooled, remove the string, and, using a very sharp knife, cut it into even slices about $\frac{1}{4}$ inch ($\frac{1}{2}$ cm) thick. Arrange side by side or slightly overlapping on a large platter and cover with the sauce. Extra capers can be served separately for those who like a more pronounced taste.

An alternative sauce can be substituted. Put the tuna, some capers, and an anchovy fillet through a blender until you obtain a smooth sauce. Fold the sauce into 1 cup (8 fl oz/2.5 dl) mayonnaise, adding a few more capers if desired. This second version is a good standby for last-minute preparation.

Faraona alla Campagnola
Country Style Guinea Hen (Fowl)

2 2 lb/2 lb/1 kg guinea hens (squabs or Cornish hens may be used)
salt
freshly ground pepper
6 Tbsp/4 Tbsp/4 Tbsp oil
2 carrots
2 stalks celery
1 bunch parsley
2 sprigs fresh rosemary or
    $\frac{1}{2}$ tsp dried rosemary
7 Tbsp/4 oz/100 g butter
$\frac{3}{4}$ c/7 fl oz/2 dl dry white wine
1 white truffle (optional)

Clean the guinea hens (fowl) thoroughly, reserving the liver and the heart. Season inside and out with salt and pepper and place in a heavy roasting pan. Baste with oil and roast for about 1 hour at 350°F (180°C/mk 4), turning and basting with their juices from time to time.

Mince the vegetables and herbs (using only the leaves of the rosemary) together with the liver and the heart. Sauté in the butter until the vegetables are soft. Add the white wine together with a little water and simmer until somewhat reduced. Push the sauce through a strainer (sieve). It should be thickish; if it is too thin, return it to the saucepan and reduce for a few minutes more, stirring constantly.

When the guinea hens (fowl) are done, cut in half with poultry shears and then in quarters. Try to avoid splintering the bones when cutting, if the hens (fowl) are cleanly jointed, they will be much easier to eat. Arrange the portions on a heated serving platter and moisten with the sauce. Decorate with paper-thin slices of raw white truffle (optional).

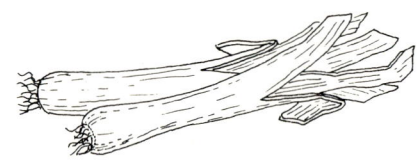

Rôstida
Pork and Variety Meat (Offal) Fricassee

scant 1 lb/14 oz/400 g pork variety meats
    (offal) (see instructions)
scant $\frac{1}{2}$ lb/7 oz/200 g loin of pork
4 Tbsp/2 oz/50 g butter
3 large ripe or canned tomatoes
salt
freshly ground pepper

In Italy the heart and lungs, used when still very fresh and carefully trimmed, would be considered best for this dish. However, pork liver, kidneys, and/or sweetbreads may also be used.

Slice the variety meats (offal) and the pork loin and brown lightly in the butter. Put the tomatoes through a food mill and add to the meat. Cover and cook slowly until the meat is very tender, stirring occasionally and adding a little water when necessary to obtain a fairly thick sauce.

This flavorful dish is best complemented by hot, freshly made polenta.

Costolette alla Valdostana
Veal Chops Valdostana

4 veal chops, 1–1$\frac{1}{2}$ inches (3–4 cm) thick
5–6 oz/5–6 oz/150 g Fontina cheese
4 slices prosciutto (raw ham)
salt
freshly ground pepper
2 Tbsp/1 Tbsp/1 Tbsp all-purpose
    (plain) flour
1 egg
bread crumbs
4 Tbsp/2 oz/50 g butter

Make a pocket in each chop, cutting toward the bone, which will form the bottom of the pocket. Cut the cheese into thin strips, divide into 4 equal portions and wrap each batch in a slice of prosciutto (raw ham). Flatten these "packets" slightly and insert inside the chops. Pound the edges of the chops together so that they will stay closed during cooking. Season both sides of each chop with salt and pepper, coat with flour, shaking off excess gently, and then dip in the beaten egg. Coat well with bread crumbs.

Melt the butter in a skillet large enough to take all the chops and sauté them over a low heat until golden brown and sufficiently cooked for the Fontina to melt inside the chop.

Serve at once accompanied by a fresh salad.

Trota alla Piemontese
Piedmont Style Trout

$\frac{1}{3}$ c/2 oz/50 g seedless white raisins
    (sultanas)
2 1$\frac{1}{2}$–1$\frac{3}{4}$ lb/1$\frac{1}{2}$–1$\frac{3}{4}$ lb/700–800 g trout
1 onion
1 sprig fresh rosemary or
    $\frac{1}{4}$ tsp dried rosemary
3–4 fresh sage leaves or
    $\frac{1}{4}$ tsp dried sage
1 stalk celery

1 clove garlic
⅓ c/3½ fl oz/1 dl oil
vinegar
grated rind of ½ lemon
2¼ c/1 pt/5 dl fish stock or very light
    meat or poultry stock
salt
freshly ground pepper
1 Tbsp butter
1¼ tsp/1 tsp/1 tsp all-purpose (plain)
    flour

Soak the raisins (sultanas) in lukewarm water for about 30 minutes. Gut and clean the trout thoroughly. Mince the onion, rosemary leaves, sage, celery, and garlic.

Heat the oil in a skillet, preferably oval, large enough to hold the whole trout lying flat. Sauté the chopped vegetables and herbs until soft but do not brown them. Place the trout in the skillet, sprinkle with a little vinegar and the grated lemon rind. Add the drained raisins (sultanas) and the fish stock. Season with salt and pepper, cover, and cook gently until done.

Place the fish on a heated serving platter and carefully remove the skin.

Work the butter into the flour (this is called beurre manié) and add to the cooking liquid in the skillet. Return to the heat, stirring continuously, for a few minutes until the sauce becomes creamy and smooth. Pour over the trout and serve immediately.

Peperoni alla Bagna Cauda
Peppers in Bagna Cauda Sauce

1 recipe Bagna Cauda (see recipe, page
    20)
4 large peppers
3 large ripe tomatoes
4 anchovy fillets
1 clove garlic

Prepare the Bagna Cauda as directed on page 20 and keep warm.

Place the peppers in a hot oven or broil (grill) them for a few minutes, turning frequently, to loosen their thin outer skins. Peel, cut lengthwise, remove membranes and seeds, and cut into thin strips. Place them in a heated serving dish, cover with skinned, seeded tomatoes cut into strips. Sprinkle with chopped anchovy fillets and the very finely chopped clove of garlic. Pour the prepared bagna cauda over the mixture and serve.

(Tomatoes are quickly and easily skinned if blanched in boiling water for 1 or 2 minutes to loosen their skins.)

Funghi Trifolati
Sautéed Mushrooms

1 lb/1 lb/500 g large mushrooms + 3
    Tbsp imported dried mushrooms such
    as cèpes or 1 lb/1 lb/500 g fresh cèpes
3 Tbsp/2 Tbsp/2 Tbsp oil
1 Tbsp butter
1 large clove garlic
1 small bunch parsley
salt
freshly ground pepper

This recipe is a very important one in Italian regional cooking. It is served as a dish on its own, as a marvelous flavoring in pasta or risotto, or as an accompaniment to veal or poultry. It also goes well with steak and roast meat.

Using some dried imported mushrooms will add flavor to commercially grown fresh mushrooms. Soak the dried mushrooms in warm water for 30 minutes, drain, and chop. If you are lucky enough to find fresh cèpes in specialty food shops, you will not need the dried variety. Clean and wash the cèpes very thoroughly, pat dry, and cut into thin slices.

Heat the oil and butter in a frying pan and add the mushrooms along with the finely chopped garlic and parsley. Season with salt and pepper. Cover the pan and cook gently for about 10 minutes (if fresh cèpes are used, cook for 20 to 30 minutes) stirring occasionally. When the mushrooms are nearly cooked, take the lid off the pan, raise the heat, and cook for a couple of minutes to reduce the juices.

Patate Tartufate
Truffled Potatoes

1¼ lb/1¼ lb/600 g potatoes
4 Tbsp/2 oz/50 g butter
1 truffle
¼ c/2 oz/50 g grated Parmesan cheese
salt
freshly ground pepper
½ lemon

Parboil the potatoes. Drain. When they have cooled, peel and cut into thin slices.

Grease a narrow, high-sided baking dish, such as a loaf pan, with butter and arrange the potatoes in layers, alternating them with layers of paper-thin truffle slices sprinkled with grated Parmesan. Season with salt and pepper and sprinkle each layer with melted butter. Top with a layer of potato slices brushed with melted butter.

Bake in a moderate (350°F/180°C/ mk 4) oven for about 45 minutes. Shortly before removing from the oven, sprinkle the juice of half a lemon over the potatoes. Serve very hot.

Salsa Tartufata
Truffle Sauce

1 small onion
1 clove garlic
1 small bunch parsley
2 Tbsp/1 oz/25 g butter
½ c/4 fl oz/125 ml dry white or Marsala
    wine
1¼ tsp/1 tsp/1 tsp all-purpose (plain)
    flour
salt
freshly ground pepper
½ c/4 fl oz/125 ml stock
1 white truffle

This sauce should be served very hot with chops, steak, or almost any roast meat.

Chop the onion, garlic, and parsley very finely and sauté in butter until they are soft. Blend the white or Marsala wine with the flour in a small bowl and add to the sautéed mixture, stirring constantly with a wooden spoon. Season to taste with salt and pepper. When the sauce has thickened add the stock ($\frac{1}{2}$ teaspoon of meat extract or $\frac{1}{2}$ bouillon cube dissolved in $\frac{1}{2}$ cup (4 fl oz/125 ml) hot water may be substituted) and simmer for a few minutes more. Add the truffle, sliced wafer-thin, and remove from heat.

Bicciolani
Spice Cookies

1$\frac{3}{4}$ c/10$\frac{1}{2}$ oz/300 g finely ground cornmeal
 (maize flour)
$\frac{1}{2}$ c/4 oz/100 g granulated sugar
1 pinch each ground cinnamon,
 coriander, white pepper, and nutmeg
1 c/7 oz/200 g butter
2 egg yolks
1–2 drops vanilla extract (essence)

Sift the flour with the sugar and spices into a bowl. Add the butter and vanilla extract (essence), and mix well. Blend in the egg yolks with a wooden spoon. Knead very briefly into a smooth dough. Wrap in a slightly dampened pastry cloth or dish towel and allow to rest in the refrigerator for about 5 hours.

Roll out the dough on a pastry board into a sheet no thicker than $\frac{1}{4}$ inch ($\frac{1}{2}$ cm) and cut into rectangles measuring approximately 1$\frac{1}{2}$ × 4 inches (4 × 10 cm) using a fluted pastry wheel. Grease a baking sheet and space the cookies evenly on it. Bake in a moderate oven (350°F/180°C/mk 4) for 10 to 15 minutes or until the cookies are golden brown.

LOMBARDY

VARESE

COMO

SONDRIO

BERGAMO

MILAN

BRESCIA

PAVIA

CREMONA

MANTUA

Pizzoccheri della Valtellina
Buckwheat Noodle and Vegetable Casserole

scant 2 c/7 oz/200 g fine buckwheat flour
scant 1 c/4 oz/100 g all-purpose (plain) flour
1 egg
⅓ c/3½ fl oz/1 dl milk
3 medium potatoes
6–8 savoy cabbage leaves
3–4 young, fresh sage leaves or ¼ tsp dried sage
4 Tbsp/2 oz/50 g butter
1 c/4 oz/100 g low-fat Valtellina or Taleggio cheese
freshly ground pepper

Sift the two types of flour together into a large mixing bowl, add the egg and the milk and mix together well, adding a little water, if necessary, to make a firm dough. Roll out into a fairly thin sheet and cut into noodles about 2½ inches (6 cm) long and about ½ inch (1 cm) wide.

Peel the potatoes and cut into pieces; boil them in plenty of salted water together with the cabbage leaves cut into strips. When the cabbage is almost done, add the pizzoccheri noodles and boil over a high heat. When the potatoes are tender but still firm, drain the vegetables and noodles in a colander. Sauté the sage gently in the butter; then remove the sage leaves. In a heated baking dish, alternate layers of noodles and vegetables with layers of sliced cheese sprinkled with sage butter. Season with pepper to taste.

Preheat the oven to 400°F (200°C/mk 6); place the dish in the oven and turn off heat. Remove after 5 to 10 minutes and serve.

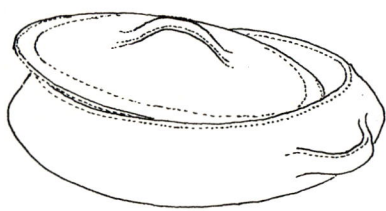

Gnocchi di Zucca Mantovani
Pumpkin Gnocchi Mantua Style

1 piece of pumpkin weighing about 1 lb/1 lb/500 g
1⅓ c/5 oz/150 g all purpose (plain) flour
salt
5 Tbsp/2½ oz/70 g butter
⅓ c/2½ oz/70 g grated Parmesan cheese

Peel and seed the pumpkin and pare off all traces of green underneath the skin. Cut the flesh into large pieces and boil in lightly salted water. When very tender, drain well and put through a food mill, food processor, or sieve.

Mix the resulting paste with the flour and a pinch of salt. Transfer to a board and knead very thoroughly until the dough is soft and pliable. It is best to add the flour gradually. The amount needed to produce a dough that is soft but not sticky will depend on how floury the pumpkin flesh is. Break pieces off the dough and roll into sausage shapes about ½ inch (1 cm) in diameter; cut into 1 inch (2 cm) lengths. Form these little cylinders into gnocchi as shown in the illustration on page 55. Boil a few at a time in a large pan of salted water. If too many are cooked at once they may stick together. As the dumplings rise to the top, remove with a slotted spoon. Toss generously with melted butter and top with the grated Parmesan. Serve while hot.

Tortelli di Zucca
Tortelli with Pumpkin Stuffing

1 pumpkin weighing 1½ lb/1½ lb/700 g
1 recipe egg pasta dough (see page 11)
½ c/2 oz/50 g almond macaroons
2 Tbsp/2 oz/50 g Cremona mustard (an Italian sweet pickle available in the U.S. and U.K.)
1 pinch sugar
½ c/4 oz/100 g grated Parmesan cheese
1½ Tbsp/1 Tbsp/1 Tbsp bread crumbs

1½ Tbsp/1 Tbsp/1 Tbsp grappa (or marc)
salt
4 Tbsp/2 oz/50 g butter

Slice off the top of the pumpkin, scoop out the seeds, and replace the top. Stand the pumpkin in a little water in a baking pan and bake in a moderate oven (375°F/190°C/mk 5) until it is tender. This will take 1½ to 2 hours. Add more water if too much evaporates. While the pumpkin is cooking, make egg pasta dough as directed on page 11, but do not cut into strips. Scoop out the pumpkin flesh, and put it through a food processor or food mill or mash it and put through a sieve. Mix in the crushed macaroons, the finely chopped Cremona mustard pickle, the sugar, half the grated Parmesan, the bread crumbs and the grappa. Stir thoroughly and add salt to taste.

Divide the pasta dough in half and roll each half into a thin sheet. On one sheet space out small heaps of the filling about 4 inches (10 cm) apart. Cover carefully with the second sheet of dough, pressing the two sheets together with the fingers between the little heaps of filling. Cut the sheet into squares with a fluted pastry wheel or sharp knife, so that each mound is in the center of its square—like a little pillow—with the edges tightly sealed. Boil the stuffed pasta in a large pan of boiling salted water until al dente. Drain and sprinkle with melted butter and grated Parmesan.

If Cremona mustard is unavailable, Bahamian mustard can be substituted with the addition of 1 tablespoon very finely chopped candied citron.

Casonsèi di Bergamo
Tortellini Bergamo Style

⅔ lb/11 oz/300 g spinach
1 clove garlic
¼ onion
4 Tbsp/2 oz/50 g butter
salt
freshly ground pepper
2 Tbsp/1 Tbsp/1 Tbsp finely chopped

parsley
scant 1 lb/14 oz/400 g potatoes
*3 Tbsp/2 Tbsp/2 Tbsp bread crumbs
  from stale bread*
⅓ c/4 oz/100 g grated Parmesan cheese
4 eggs
*⅔ c/5 oz/150 g Italian pork sausage
  (removed from casing)*
*2¾ c/10½ oz/300 g all-purpose (plain)
  flour*

The filling for this stuffed pasta is better if prepared a day in advance.

After washing the spinach thoroughly, boil it in ½ inch (1 cm) of water. Drain well and chop very finely. Meanwhile, sauté the very finely chopped garlic and onion in about 1 teaspoon of butter. Add the chopped spinach, season with salt and pepper, remove from heat, and add the parsley. Peel and boil the potatoes and put through a ricer or sieve into a mixing bowl. Mix in the bread crumbs, half the grated Parmesan, the spinach mixture, a beaten egg, and the sausage meat worked to a paste with a fork. Adjust seasoning and blend all these ingredients very thoroughly. Cover and refrigerate overnight.

Make an egg pasta dough, following the instructions on page 11. Knead well until soft and elastic and roll out to a thin sheet. With a round pastry cutter (or a glass) cut out disks of pastry about 2 inches (5 cm) in diameter and place ½ tablespoon of the filling in the middle of each. Fold the disk in half, enclosing the filling; the upper edge should be ⅛ inch (3 mm) inside the lower edge. Press down firmly to seal. Bring the two "corners" of the semicircle together around your index finger and pinch firmly together. As the dumplings are made, arrange them on a dry clean towel taking care that they do not touch each other or they may stick. Boil the *casonsèi* in plenty of salted water for about 5 minutes, drain, and put onto individual plates, sprinkling with the remaining grated Parmesan cheese and the rest of the butter, melted.

The scraps of pasta dough left over can be trimmed to form *maltagliati*— literally, "badly cut"—excellent in clear soup or served with sauce.

Riso alla Pilota
Winnowers' Risotto

1¾ c/12¼ oz/350 g Arborio rice
*1 c/7 oz/200 g Italian pork sausage meat
  (removed from casing)*
4 Tbsp/2 oz/50 g butter
¼ c/2 oz/50 g grated Parmesan cheese

This easy and appetizing dish takes its name from the men who winnow the rice grown in the region near Mantua.

Bring 3½ cups (1⅓ pt/7.5 dl) lightly salted water to a boil in a large saucepan; pour in the rice. Cook for about 5 minutes. Remove from heat, cover very tightly, and wrap the pan in a large heavy cloth. This will provide insulation and allow the rice to continue to cook, even though it is away from direct heat. This will take about 30 minutes, but the time will vary slightly depending on the quality of rice. Almost all the moisture should be absorbed.

While the rice is cooking, mash the sausage (or grind it finely) and sauté it in the butter. When the rice is al dente pour the sausage and butter mixture over it and sprinkle with the grated Parmesan. Mix vigorously and serve immediately.

Zuppa alla Pavese
Poached Eggs in Broth

4 Tbsp/2 oz/50 g butter
4 slices stale French bread
4 eggs
4 Tbsp grated Parmesan cheese
*4½ c/2 pt/1 l stock (canned consommé
  may be substituted if necessary)*

Melt the butter in a frying pan and fry the slices of bread over a fairly high heat until they are golden brown and crisp on both sides. Place one piece each in heated soup plates, break an egg onto each piece of toast, and sprinkle with a tablespoon of grated Parmesan.

Bring the stock to a boil. Pour a quarter of the boiling stock carefully into each dish; this will lightly poach the egg. It is best to bring the stock back to a fast boil before pouring it into each plate.

Riso con le Rane
Rice with Frogs' Legs

½ lb/8 oz/225 g frog's legs
½ onion
1 stalk celery
2 Tbsp butter
2 Tbsp oil
3 c/1¾ pt/1 l stock
1 c/7 oz/200 g rice
1 small bunch parsley

Wash the frogs' legs. Sauté the minced onion and celery in the butter and oil in a large pan. When onions and celery are translucent, add the frogs' legs and fry gently for a few minutes. Pour in the hot stock (a little meat extract dissolved in water can be used as long as it has a delicate flavor). When this has come to a boil, add the rice. Cook over moderate heat, stirring frequently. Before serving, sprinkle with the chopped parsley.

Two cloves of chopped garlic can be substituted for the onion in this recipe. Another variation, popular in Italy, is to cook the frogs' legs in a little salted water, remove the flesh from the bones, and use the cooking liquid in place of some of the stock when cooking the risotto.

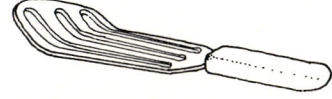

Risotto con la Zucca
Pumpkin Risotto

1 pumpkin weighing about 1 lb/1 lb/500 g
½ onion
6 Tbsp/4 Tbsp/4 Tbsp oil
1½ Tbsp/1 Tbsp/1 Tbsp butter
1½ c/10½ oz/300 g Arborio rice
1 tsp meat extract
salt
pepper
grated Parmesan cheese

Wash the pumpkin, peel, remove the seeds and membrane, and dice. Chop the onion finely. Heat the oil in a large, heavy pan and sauté the onion and pumpkin over a low heat for a few minutes, stirring with a wooden spoon. Keep some water simmering and add a little from time to time to keep the pumpkin moist. When the pumpkin becomes tender, add the rice, the meat extract, and salt to taste. Cook the risotto, adding water, a cup at a time, at intervals as the rice absorbs the moisture. When the rice is done, season with a little pepper if desired. Remove from heat and sprinkle with grated Parmesan, mixing once more. The risotto should have a creamy consistency.

Risotto alla Milanese

4 Tbsp/2 oz/50 g butter
1½ Tbsp/1 Tbsp/1 Tbsp bone marrow
½ onion
⅓ c/3½ fl oz/1 dl dry white wine
1½ c/10½ oz/300 g Arborio rice
4½ c/1¾ pt/1 l stock
salt
½ tsp saffron
4 Tbsp/2 oz/50 g grated Parmesan cheese

Melt the butter and the bone marrow gently in a large, heavy pan. Using a fork, pick out any small bits of beef fat which do not dissolve. Add the finely chopped onion and cook until it is translucent. Pour in the wine and reduce over a high heat. Lower the heat, stir in the rice, and sauté gently for a few minutes, mixing well to make sure that the rice grains are coated with the butter and marrow.

Add 1 cup stock, preferably homemade, but a bouillon cube dissolved in boiling water will do if necessary. Add salt to taste. Keep the stock simmering and add, a little at a time, to the rice as it absorbs the moisture. When the rice is nearly done, mix in a final ½ cup of stock in which the saffron has been dissolved. When the rice is tender but not mushy or sticky, turn off the heat and add the rest of the butter, stirring in gently. This will give the rice added sheen and the correct creamy taste. Sprinkle with grated Parmesan and serve at once.

Malfatti

Spinach and Cheese Gnocchi

1 lb/1 lb/500 g spinach
7 Tbsp/4 oz/100 g butter
½ onion
1 c/5 oz/150 g ricotta cheese
⅓ c/2½ oz/70 g grated Parmesan cheese
nutmeg
salt
freshly ground pepper
2 whole eggs
1 egg yolk
1¾ c/7 oz/200 g all-purpose (plain) flour

Trim and wash the spinach very thoroughly. Boil with no added water (enough will cling to the leaves after washing) and salt very lightly. Drain, squeeze it out well, and chop finely. Sauté the coarsely chopped onion in 2 tablespoons (1 oz/25 g) butter. When the onion starts to color, remove it from the pan and discard. Sauté the spinach in the onion-flavoured butter for a few minutes, mixing well. When the spinach has absorbed the butter, remove from heat and allow to cool. When cold, stir in the ricotta (which has been forced through a strainer or worked a little with a wooden spoon), half the grated Parmesan, a pinch of ground nutmeg, and salt and pepper to taste. Add the two eggs and the extra yolk and all but one tablespoon of the flour. Blend all these ingredients together thoroughly with a wooden spoon. Roll into several sausage shapes, about ¾ inch (2 cm) in diameter, and cut into 1-inch (3 cm) lengths. Shape them into gnocchi as shown on page 55. Drop them, a few at a time, into plenty of rapidly boiling, lightly salted water. As they rise to the top (after about 6 to 8 minutes), remove them with a slotted spoon and place them in a heated ovenproof dish. Melt the remaining butter, sprinkle it over the gnocchi together with the remainder of the grated Parmesan, and place in a fairly hot oven for 5 minutes. Serve.

Büsêca

Tripe Milanese

2 lb/2 lb/1 kg precooked light honeycomb tripe (preferably calf tripe)
4 Tbsp/2 oz/50 g butter
⅓ c/2½ fl oz/80 ml oil
2–3 slices/2 oz/50 g pancetta (fat bacon)
1 onion
1 stalk celery
4 fresh sage leaves or ½ tsp dried sage
1 carrot
salt
pepper
nutmeg (optional)
ground cloves (optional)
4 large ripe or canned tomatoes

Tripe is usually sold partially cooked. If it has not been precooked it will require careful scrubbing; it should then be soaked in cold water for several hours and blanched in salted water. It will also require far longer cooking—up to 12 hours or even more over a slow heat.

Cut the tripe into strips ½ inch (1 cm) wide and about 2 inches (5 cm) long. Mince the onion, celery, sage, and carrot. Heat the butter, oil, and pounded pancetta (fat bacon) in a large pan. Sauté lightly, stirring continuously. When the onion begins to color, add the tripe and sauté for about 10 minutes; season with salt and pepper and, if desired, a pinch each of nutmeg and ground clove. Put the fresh or canned tomatoes through a food mill or sieve and add to the tripe. Simmer until the sauce begins to thicken; then add a cup of hot water. Continue to add a little water at intervals if necessary until the tripe is very tender. Precooked calf tripe

***Opposite:** Bread has always been one of the most vital and valued staple foods in Italy.*

***Overleaf:** A selection of Sicily's superb citrus fruits surround a basket of realistic marzipan fruits for which the island is equally famous.*

will take about 2 hours and beef tripe about 3 hours.

In Milan this dish is often eaten with slices of bread fried in butter until golden brown.

As a variation, 1 cup (5 oz/150 g) Spanish or white lima beans can be cooked separately and added to the tripe about 15 minutes before it is ready. Even added this late in the cooking process, the beans will absorb the delicious flavors of the *büsêca*.

For another variation, add a heaped tablespoon of pearl barley, which has been soaked in water overnight, along with the tomatoes. It will cook perfectly in the long, slow period needed for the tripe.

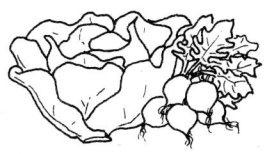

Piccate di Vitello
Veal Piccata

4 ¼-inch (½ cm) thick veal escalopes, cut
*   from the round*
1 tsp all-purpose (plain) flour
salt
1½ Tbsp/1 Tbsp/1 Tbsp butter
juice of ½ lemon
1 small bunch parsley

Place the veal escalopes between two sheets of wax paper and pound them with a mallet, or the flat side of a meat cleaver, or a skillet to a thickness of ⅛ inch (3 mm). Remove any gristle or membrane and dust lightly with the flour and a pinch of salt. Melt the butter in a skillet and sauté the veal slices on both sides over a fairly high heat; this will only take about 2 minutes for each side. Turn off the heat, sprinkle with the lemon juice and the chopped parsley, and serve at once.

Ossobuco alla Milanese
Veal Shanks Milanese

4 Tbsp/2 oz/50 g butter
4 veal shanks
2 Tbsp/1 Tbsp/1 Tbsp all-purpose
*   (plain) flour*
salt
pepper
⅓ c/3½ fl oz/1 dl dry white wine
1 c/7 oz/200 g canned tomatoes
1 clove garlic
1 small bunch parsley
grated rind of ½ lemon
1 anchovy fillet (optional)

Heat the butter in a large, heavy pan. Dredge the veal shanks lightly with flour. The pieces are sawed across the bone by the butcher and therefore consist of bone and marrow surrounded by meat. Brown the veal evenly in the butter, turning carefully to avoid disturbing the marrow. Season with salt and pepper. Moisten with the wine, adding a little at a time. When the wine has reduced, add the tomatoes, which have been put through a food mill or forced through a sieve. Cover tightly and cook gently until the meat is so tender that it seems almost ready to fall off the bone—this will take 1 to 1½ hours. If necessary, add a little water during cooking; the sauce should, however, be fairly thick.

The traditional topping for ossobuco is gremolada: a mixture of minced garlic, finely chopped parsley, and grated rind of ½ lemon (sometimes a pounded anchovy fillet is added). When the ossobuco is ready, remove the lid of the pan, sprinkle an equal amount of the gremolada on top of each piece, and simmer, uncovered, for a further 5 minutes without turning.

Ossobuco should be served very hot with Risotto alla Milanese (see recipe, page 32) or on top of mounds of plain boiled rice.

Rane Fritte
Fried Frogs' Legs

1 lb/1 lb/500 g frogs' legs
1 c/8 fl oz/¼ l dry white wine
2 eggs
a few Tbsp milk
salt
all-purpose (plain) flour
oil for frying
1 lemon

Wash and dry the frogs' legs. Place in the wine for a few hours to marinate. Beat the eggs, milk, and salt together and add enough flour to make a fairly thick coating batter. Let stand while the frogs' legs marinate. Remove the frogs' legs from the wine and pat dry. Heat sufficient oil to cover the frogs' legs in a large frying pan. When it is very hot, dip the frogs' legs one by one in the batter and place carefully in the hot oil. When they are crisp and golden brown, remove with a fork or slotted spoon and drain on paper towels. Serve while still hot and crisp. Garnish with lemon wedges.

Uccellini Scappati
Lombardy Kebabs

scant ½ lb/7 oz/200 g calf or pork liver
scant ½ lb/7 oz/200 g calf kidneys
¼ lb/4 oz/100 g calf sweetbreads
5–6 oz/5–6 oz/150 g pancetta (fat bacon)
*   or parboiled salt pork (thinly sliced)*
fresh sage leaves
4 Tbsp/2 oz/50 g butter
salt
freshly ground pepper

Cut the liver, kidneys, and sweetbreads into cubes about ½ inch (1 cm) thick. Thread skewers in the following order: pancetta (bacon), sage leaf, liver, kidney, pancetta (bacon), sage, sweetbread, kidney, liver, sage, pancetta (bacon).

Melt the butter in a large pan which can accommodate the skewers easily, place the skewers of meat side by side and season with salt and pepper. Sauté, turning frequently so that the meat cooks evenly. Take care not to overcook or the liver and kidneys will become hard and tough. Cooking should only take 5 to 10 minutes, depending on the size of the cubes.

This is a very tasty dish, but it is really outstanding if each skewer is served on a slice of hot toasted polenta.

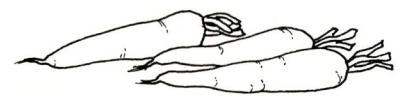

Carpione in Umido
Braised Carp

1 carp weighing about 2 lb/2 lb/1 kg
1 onion
4 Tbsp/2 oz/50 g butter
3 Tbsp/2 Tbsp/2 Tbsp oil
2 Tbsp/1 Tbsp/1 Tbsp all-purpose
*   (plain) flour*
⅓ c/3½ fl oz/1 dl dry white wine
1½ Tbsp/1 Tbsp/1 Tbsp vinegar
salt
freshly ground pepper
1 small bunch parsley
1 lemon

Have the carp cleaned and scaled. Wash well and cut into 4 sections. Sauté the finely chopped onion lightly in the oil and butter in a large heavy pan. Add the pieces of fish and the flour which has been mixed into a cup of water. Then add the wine. Cook until the liquid has reduced somewhat, stirring gently and making sure that the fish does not stick to the pan. Add the vinegar diluted in ½ cup water and season to taste with salt and pepper. Cover tightly and simmer slowly for about 30 minutes, stirring gently from time to time, taking care not to break up the fish. Shortly before serving, sprinkle with very finely chopped parsley.

Arrange the carp on a heated serving platter, pour the cooking liquid over it, and garnish with lemon wedges.

Asparagi con le Uova
Asparagus Milanese

2 lb/2 lb/1 kg tender young asparagus
¼ c/2 oz/50 g grated Parmesan cheese
4 very fresh eggs
4 Tbsp/2 oz/50 g butter
salt

Wash the asparagus thoroughly. If an asparagus steamer is not available, divide the asparagus into bundles of 8 spears each and tie up with string. This makes it easier to lift the spears out of the pot when they are done without damaging them. Stand the bundles in a deep pot with a small amount of water in the bottom. Cover tightly and steam until done. They should be tender but still retain their texture. When the asparagus is done, arrange it on a heated serving platter with the tips pointing toward the center leaving space for the eggs in the middle. Sprinkle with Parmesan cheese. Fry the eggs in the butter, sprinkle with a little salt, and transfer carefully to the center of the platter. Serve at once.

Polenta Taragna
Polenta Valtellina Style

3½ c/14 oz/400 g buckwheat flour
2 Tbsp finely ground cornmeal (maize
*   flour)*
⅔ c/5 oz/150 g butter
1½ c/7 oz/200 g Valtellina or Taleggio
*   cheese*

This dish is a specialty of the Valtellina district and has become popular throughout Lombardy.

Sift the buckwheat flour with the cornmeal (maize flour) and prepare the polenta as directed on page 16. Just before removing it from the heat, add the butter, cut up into small pieces, and the diced cheese. Mix for 7 to 8 minutes and then turn out onto a heated platter or polenta board, and serve without delay.

Polenta in Fiur
Milk Polenta

This is another traditional dish of the Valtellina region. The polenta is prepared like an ordinary polenta (see page 16) but with buckwheat flour instead of cornmeal (maize flour) and using milk instead of water. It is a good idea to cook it in a double boiler which will prevent its burning or sticking. Before removing it from the heat, stir in 1½ cups (7 oz/200 g) diced low-fat cheese.

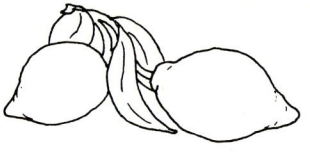

Salsa Verde
Italian Parsley Sauce

1 hard-boiled egg
2 anchovy fillets
1¼ tsp/1 tsp/1 tsp capers
1 bunch parsley (1 cupful when chopped)
3 Tbsp/2 Tbsp/2 Tbsp fine fresh bread
*   crumbs soaked in 3 Tbsp/2 Tbsp/*
*   2 Tbsp white wine vinegar*
olive oil or mixed olive and vegetable oil
salt

This sauce is used a great deal in Italy since it goes extremely well with cold or hot (usually boiled) meats and poached or steamed fish.

Chop the hard-boiled egg, anchovy fillet, capers, and parsley very finely. Squeeze the bread crumbs to get rid of any excess vinegar. Place all ingredients in a bowl and blend very well together. Beat in olive oil a little at a time until the sauce has a creamy consistency. Add salt to taste and let stand for at least 2 hours.

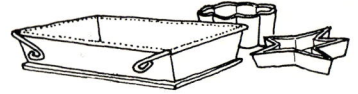

Crema al Mascarpone
Mascarpone Cream

2 whole eggs (separated)
1 egg yolk
⅔ c/5 oz/150 g granulated sugar
1 c/7 oz/200 g fresh Mascarpone cheese
1 Tbsp rum or brandy
4–8 cats' tongues or ladyfingers (boudoir biscuits)

Mascarpone is a snow-white creamy cheese made entirely with fresh, sweet cream during the autumn and winter in Italy.

Beat the three egg yolks with the sugar; add the mascarpone and mix very well. Stir in the rum or brandy; then fold in the two egg whites, which have been beaten until stiff but not dry. When the mixture is evenly blended, turn into four cocotte dishes or sherbet glasses. Accompany with thin, dry cookies such as cats' tongues or ladyfingers (boudoir biscuits).

Pastafrolla alla Marmellata
Italian Jam Tart

4 egg yolks
2¼ c/9 oz/250 g all-purpose (plain) flour
½ c/4 oz/100 g granulated sugar
grated rind of 1 lemon or orange
5 Tbsp/2½ oz/70 g butter
3 Tbsp/1½ oz/40 g lard
1 jar fruit preserves of your choice (apricot, cherry, etc.)

Mix the egg yolks, flour, sugar, and grated lemon rind. Add the softened butter and the lard. Blend the ingredients together to form a thick, soft dough, handling as little as possible.

Right: The procedure for mixing the basic Pastafrolla (Italian Short Pastry), of which there are several variations.

(The shortening (fat) can be cut in with a knife.) Too much handling will make the dough tough. Wrap the dough in a pastry cloth or foil and allow it to rest in the refrigerator for several hours or overnight.

Butter and lightly flour a shallow baking pan. Roll out the dough into a sheet about $\frac{1}{4}$ inch ($\frac{1}{2}$ cm) thick. Line the pan, taking care not to stretch the pastry, and trim off round the edges. Fill with fruit preserves and cover with a lattice top made from the pastry trimmings, adding a decorative border if desired. Place in a preheated oven and bake at 350°F (180°C/mk 4) for about an hour. Remove when the pastry is golden brown.

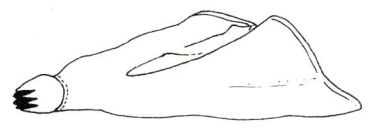

Laciaditt
Lombardy Apple Fritters

$1\frac{3}{4}$ c/7 oz/200 g all-purpose (plain) flour
salt
1 egg
$1\frac{1}{4}$ c/$\frac{1}{2}$ pt/3 dl milk mixed with an equal
    amount of water
2–4 firm, tart cooking apples
grated rind of $\frac{1}{2}$ lemon
shortening (fat) for frying (lard or
    vegetable oil)
4 Tbsp/2 oz/50 g granulated sugar

In a large bowl, mix the sifted flour, salt, and egg together with enough of the milk and water mixture to form a fairly runny coating batter. Let stand for 30 minutes or longer. Peel, quarter, and core the apples and cut them into thin slices. Add to the batter together with the grated lemon rind.

Heat plenty of lard or oil to 350°F (180°C), and fry spoonfuls of the apples and batter until the fritters are a pale amber color. Drain the fritters briefly on paper towels, sprinkle with sugar, and serve.

Pan de Mej
Sweet Buns

2 envelopes active dry or 1 cake
    compressed yeast/1 oz/25 g fresh yeast
scant 1 c/3$\frac{1}{2}$ oz/100 g all-purpose (plain)
    flour
scant 1 c/5 oz/150 g finely ground
    cornmeal (maize flour)
$\frac{1}{2}$ c/4 oz/100 g coarsely ground cornmeal
    (maize flour)
$\frac{1}{3}$ c/2$\frac{3}{4}$ oz/80 g granulated sugar
7 Tbsp/4 oz/100 g butter
salt
3–4 Tbsp vanilla sugar*

Mix the yeast with a little lukewarm water and incorporate the all-purpose (plain) flour. Wrap loosely in a lightly floured pastry cloth and leave to rise in a warm place for about 30 minutes. When the dough has doubled in volume, punch down and work in the sifted fine and coarse cornmeal (maize) flours, the sugar, and the softened butter. Add the salt and enough milk to form a soft but workable dough. Shape into small buns, making a crisscross incision on top of each, and arrange them on a buttered baking sheet. Allow to rise in a warm place for about 30 minutes. Bake in a preheated 400°F (200°C/mk 6) oven for about 30 minutes. Remove from oven and glaze with the vanilla sugar dissolved in 1 tablespoon boiling water and cool, or glaze by brushing with egg yolk before baking and sprinkle with vanilla sugar as soon as the buns are removed from the oven.

*Vanilla sugar is easily made by splitting two vanilla beans (pods) and cutting them in 1-inch (3 cm) lengths. Mix with 2 pounds (2 lb/1 kg) granulated or confectioners' (icing) sugar; pour into a jar with a tight-fitting cover. Allow to stand for 3 days before using. Half this quantity can be made if preferred. If you do not have vanilla sugar on hand, add a drop or two vanilla extract (essence) to the boiling water in which the glazing sugar is dissolved.

Fritelle di Riso
Rice Fritters

$2\frac{1}{4}$ c/18 fl oz/$\frac{1}{2}$ l milk
scant $\frac{1}{2}$ c/4 oz/100 g round-grain rice
$1\frac{1}{2}$ Tbsp/$\frac{1}{2}$ oz/1 Tbsp sugar
1 Tbsp/$\frac{1}{2}$ oz/1 Tbsp butter
salt
1 tsp grated lemon rind
3 eggs (separated)
4 Tbsp/2 oz/50 g all-purpose (plain)
    flour
1 Tbsp Jamaican rum
oil for frying
vanilla sugar (see previous recipe)

Bring the milk to a boil and add the rice; simmer for 10 minutes, stirring frequently. Add the sugar, butter, salt, and grated lemon rind. Continue cooking until the rice is very tender. Remove from heat, turn into a bowl, and allow to cool. Add the egg yolks, the flour, and the rum. Heat about 3 inches (7 cm) of oil in a heavy pan. Beat the egg whites until stiff but not dry. Fold the egg whites gently into the rice with a metal spoon. Drop tablespoonfuls of the mixture into the boiling oil, a few at a time, and remove them when they are golden brown. Drain on paper towels, then transfer to a heated serving platter, and dredge with vanilla-flavored confectioners' (icing) sugar.

TRENTINO-ALTO ADIGE

BOLZANO

TRENT

Canèderli
Tyrolean Dumplings

4 eggs
¾ c/7 fl oz/2 dl milk
salt
½ lb/8 oz/225 g stale bread (crusts
*   removed)*
2 oz/2 oz/50 g pancetta (fat bacon)
2 slices salami (about 2 oz/2 oz/50 g)
1 medium onion
1 small bunch parsley
⅓ c/1½ oz/40 g all-purpose (plain) flour
freshly ground pepper
grated Parmesan cheese

Break the eggs into a bowl and beat vigorously with the milk and a little salt. Cut the bread into small squares and soak in the egg mixture for about 20 minutes, stirring frequently with a wooden spoon to make sure that the bread has absorbed the liquid evenly. Dice the pancetta (bacon) and salami and sauté with the chopped onion and parsley. Add this to the eggs and bread and gently stir in the sifted flour a little at a time. Season to taste.

Bring a large pan of salted water to a boil and drop the dumplings in one by one. The dumplings can be shaped in two ways: either rinse the hands in cold water, take a rounded tablespoonful of the mixture, and roll it into a ball by hand or press a tablespoon filled with the mixture against the inside of a soup ladle's bowl (see illustration right). The latter method will give the more typical egg-shape to the dumplings. Before shaping all the dumplings it is wise to test the texture and cohesiveness of the dough by boiling one dumpling on its own. If it disintegrates in the boiling water, add one or two more tablespoons of flour to the mixture.

When the dumplings are cooked, remove with a slotted spoon, transfer to individual plates, and top with melted butter and Parmesan. Some people prefer these dumplings served in a good clear homemade broth, a light bouillon which will complement the delicate flavor of the *canèderli*.

Tagliatelle Smalzade

Tagliatelle with Veal and Cream Sauce

2½ c/10½ oz/300 g all-purpose (plain) flour
3 eggs
salt
4 Tbsp/2 oz/50 g butter
1 lb/1 lb/500 g veal chunks
1 medium onion
⅓ c/3½ fl oz/1 dl white wine
⅓ c/3½ fl oz/1 dl stock
freshly ground pepper
⅓ c/3½ fl oz/1 dl heavy (double) cream

Reserving 1 tablespoonful of flour, mix the rest with the eggs and a pinch of salt. Knead well until the dough is smooth and pliable and little air bubbles start forming all over the surface of the dough. If it is too firm, add a little lukewarm water. Roll out into an even but not too thin sheet; allow to dry a little, then roll up and cut into tagliatelle strips about ⅛ inch (3 mm) wide.

Lightly dust the veal with the reserved flour. Heat the butter in a skillet until it starts to turn color, add the veal and the sliced onion. When the veal is lightly browned all over, pour in the wine and cook until it has completely evaporated. Moisten the veal with a little stock (if no homemade stock is available, use half a bouillon cube dissolved in hot water). Just before the veal is done, season with salt and pepper and add the cream.

Cook the tagliatelle in a large pan of boiling, salted water, drain, and transfer to a heated serving platter. Pour the sauce from the veal over the noodles and serve immediately. The veal chunks can be served as a main course with a salad, although some people prefer that the meat be served with the noodles and sauce.

For a lighter dish, omit the cream and use a little more stock.

***Opposite: Step-by-step preparation of Canèderli. Their name comes from the Tyrolean German dialect word for dumplings—*knöderl.**

Crauti e Lucanica Trentina

Sauerkraut and Trent Sausage

7 Tbsp/4 oz/100 g fresh ham fat
1¾ lb/1 lb 12 oz/800 g sauerkraut
1¼ tsp/1 tsp/1 tsp meat extract
salt
scant 1 lb/14 oz/400 g lucanica sausage

Lucanica trentina is a lightly flavored, mild sausage made from pork and beef.

Pound the ham fat and heat it in a large, heavy pan. Add the sauerkraut (see note below) with enough water to cover. If a less acid taste is preferred, rinse the sauerkraut in plenty of water before cooking. Add the meat extract dissolved in hot water. Season with a little salt if needed. Cover the pan tightly and cook for 4 hours, stirring at intervals and adding a little hot water if too much has evaporated. After about 3 hours, add the sausages and, when these are done, serve with fresh polenta.

If you use commercially prepared sauerkraut buy it in plastic bags or jars, not cans. Homemade sauerkraut prepared in the Italian manner, however, has a far more subtle taste. Trim a large Savoy or white cabbage and shred finely, pack into a large earthenware or glass jar, cover with wine vinegar and leave for at least 48 hours. Drain well before using.

Manzo Brasato alla Vecchia Trento

Trent Braised Beef

1 beef rump roast or top round (topside) weighing up to 1½ lb/1½ lb/600 g
½ onion
4 Tbsp/2 oz/50 g butter
1 sprig fresh rosemary or ¼ tsp dried
⅓ c/3½ fl oz/1 dl vinegar
⅓ c/3½ fl oz/1 dl heavy (double) cream
1 c/8 fl oz/¼ l milk
salt
freshly ground pepper
1–2 c/8–16 fl oz/¼–½ l stock

Lard the meat and tie up neatly. Sauté the finely chopped onion in the butter (preferably in a large fireproof earthenware cooking pot, although an enameled cast-iron pan will do). Place the beef sprinkled with flour in the pan with the rosemary and brown evenly for 5 to 10 minutes over a moderate heat, turning frequently. Pour in the vinegar and turn up the heat slightly so that it will evaporate. Add the cream and milk, lower the heat, and season with salt and pepper. Cover tightly and cook over a low heat, simmering for 1 hour or more, until the meat is very tender. Moisten from time to time with a little boiling stock when the sauce reduces too much. Shortly before the meat is done, remove it from the pan and strain the sauce. Return both sauce and meat to the pan and finish cooking. Carve the meat into fairly thick slices and coat with the sauce. Serve immediately with piping-hot fresh polenta.

Lepre alla Trentina

Jugged Hare Trentina

1 hare weighing about 3¼ lb/3¼ lb/1½ kg
1 bottle dry red wine
cinnamon
1 Tbsp sugar
2 Tbsp seedless raisins (sultanas)
1¼ Tbsp/½ oz/1 Tbsp pine nuts
rosemary
fresh sage leaves
1 bay leaf
juniper berries
peel of 1 lemon
⅓ c/3½ fl oz/1 dl vinegar
4 Tbsp/2 oz/50 g butter
4 Tbsp/2 oz/50 g lard
½ onion
salt
freshly ground pepper

Clean the hare thoroughly, joint it, and reserve the giblets (heart, liver, and lungs). Pour ½ of the wine into a bowl, add a pinch of cinnamon, the sugar, raisins (sultanas), pine nuts, and the ground (minced) giblets. Place the pieces of hare in another bowl, cover with the rest of the wine, and add the rosemary, a few fresh sage leaves, the crumbled bay leaf, 4 or 5 juniper berries, the lemon peel, and the vinegar. Marinate for at least 48 hours.

Heat the butter and lard in a large, heavy pan and sauté the finely chopped onion until it starts to color. Add the marinated hare and brown (reserve the marinade). Pour in the wine and spice mixture; season with salt and pepper; and cover tightly. Braise over a low heat, stirring from time to time, until the meat is tender. This will take about 2 hours. Strain the marinade in which the pieces of hare were steeped and add a little to the pan during cooking when needed.

The mixture of sweet and piquant flavors in this dish makes it particularly appetizing, and it is best eaten with fresh polenta. An old, tough hare will do very well as the exceptionally long marinating tenderizes even the stringiest meat.

Profezéni (Cervella in Carrozza)
Fried Brain Croûtes

1 pair calf brains
2 eggs
½ c/4 fl oz/125 ml milk
salt
3 Tbsp/1 oz/25 g all-purpose (plain) flour
8 slices toast
oil for frying
bread crumbs

Blanch the calf brains in boiling water for a few minutes. Carefully remove the membrane that surrounds them. Simmer the brains in a little salted water for 5 minutes. Drain, transfer to a bowl, and cream with a fork.

Beat the eggs and milk together. Add a little salt and the sifted flour a little at a time, taking care that no lumps form. The resulting batter should be quite thin. Spread one side of each piece of toast evenly with the brains. Heat enough oil to deep-fry the slices in a skillet. Dip the toast spread with the

brains in the batter and then coat evenly with bread crumbs. When the oil is very hot, fry the toast until crisp and golden brown on both sides. Drain briefly on paper towels and serve at once.

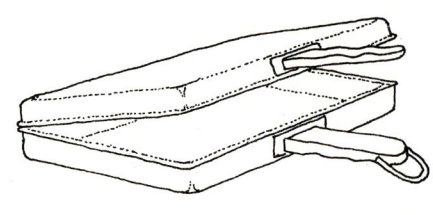

Pollo Farcito
Stuffed Chicken

1 roasting chicken about 3 lb/3 lb/1½ kg
¼ c/3 oz/90 g fresh bread crumbs
⅓ c/3½ fl oz/1 dl milk
¼ c/1 oz/25 g walnuts
½ c/2 oz/50 g pine nuts
¾ c/5 oz/150 g chicken livers
¼ c/2 oz/50 g grated Parmesan cheese
1 egg
nutmeg
salt
freshly ground pepper

Rinse and dry the chicken well. Soak the bread crumbs in lukewarm milk. Blanch the walnut kernels in boiling water for 2 minutes and remove the thin skin. Put them along with the pine nuts through a nut grinder or pound in a mortar until fine. Remove the thin skin from the chicken livers and trim them. Mince or chop them very finely and mix with the soaked bread crumbs from which the excess milk has been squeezed. Place the chicken liver and bread-crumb mixture, the pounded nuts, the grated Parmesan, the egg, and a pinch of grated nutmeg in a bowl. Season with salt and pepper to taste and mix well, blending all the ingredients thoroughly.

Bone the chicken as described on page 190; stuff it loosely and sew up. Wrap it in cheesecloth to help it retain its shape and poach in lightly salted water for about 1¼ hours. Remove from pan, unwrap cheesecloth, and drain. Carve

into slices, working along the chicken from front to back so that each slice will consist of stuffing surrounded by chicken meat.

Rollato di Spinaci
Spinach Roll

1 lb/1 lb/500 g spinach
⅔ c/5 oz/150 g butter
½ onion
4 oz/4 oz/100 g cooked smoked ham
salt
freshly ground pepper
nutmeg (optional)
7 Tbsp/4 oz/100 g all-purpose (plain) flour
¼ c/2 fl oz/3 Tbsp oil

Trim and wash the spinach in several changes of water. Boil with no extra water—enough will cling to the leaves after washing. When done, drain well and squeeze out all excess moisture by hand. Chop very finely. Heat 1 tablespoon butter in a pan and sauté the finely chopped onion, approximately one-third of the ham, finely diced, and the chopped spinach. Season with salt and pepper to taste, adding a pinch of nutmeg if desired.

Make a dough with the flour, 2 tablespoons of oil, a pinch of salt, and a little water. Knead well until elastic and soft enough to roll out into an oblong-shaped sheet about ⅛ inch (3 mm) thick. Spread the spinach mixture evenly over the sheet of pasta, sprinkle with the remainder of the chopped ham, and roll up like a large strudel. Wrap carefully in cheesecloth, tie up each end like a salami, and simmer in salted water for about 30 minutes. Lift the roll out of the water, remove the cheesecloth with care, and slice.

These slices can be arranged, over-lapping slightly, on a heated serving dish and sprinkled with the rest of the butter, which has been melted, and grated Parmesan cheese, or they can be served directly onto individual plates and dressed with the melted butter and grated cheese.

Trote alla Trentina
Trout Trentina

¼ c/2 oz/50 g seedless white raisins
  (sultanas)
4 small trout
2 Tbsp all-purpose (plain) flour
¾ c/7 fl oz/2 dl oil
1 sprig fresh rosemary or ¼ tsp dried
3–4 fresh sage leaves or ¼ tsp dried
½ onion
1 clove garlic
1 bunch parsley
2 lemons
1 c/8 fl oz/¼ l white wine vinegar
salt

Soak the raisins (sultanas) in lukewarm water for 20 minutes. Gut and wash the trout thoroughly, pat it dry, and coat lightly with flour. Heat half the oil in a skillet with the rosemary and sage and, when very hot, remove and discard the herbs. Fry the fish, turning frequently. Remove from heat.

Sauté the sliced onion, preferably in an earthenware or enameled cast-iron fireproof casserole, until it is translucent. Add the very finely chopped garlic and parsley, the grated rind of 1 lemon, the vinegar, a little salt, and finally, the raisins (sultanas) squeezed to get rid of excess moisture. Simmer this marinade for a few minutes. Arrange the trout in a large casserole dish, lying side by side in a single layer, and pour the marinade over them. Cover and allow to stand for about 24 hours.

To serve, lift the trout out of the marinade, arrange on a serving platter.

Frittata alla Trentina

4 very fresh eggs (separated)
4 Tbsp all-purpose (plain) flour
salt
milk
¾ c/7 fl oz/2 dl oil

Right: Rollato di Spinaci (Spinach Roll) is a delicious specialty from the Trentino.

Beat the egg yolks in a bowl and add the sifted flour a little at a time, making sure that there are no lumps in the mixture. Add a little salt and then dilute gradually with the milk, stirring constantly, until the batter is thin and just coats the back of a wooden spoon. Beat the egg whites separately, add to the batter, and fold in gently and evenly.

Heat about one-quarter of the oil in a round omelet pan, and, when it is very hot, pour in a quarter of the batter. Lift the edges gently to allow any excess batter to spread evenly and, when the underside is pale golden brown, turn and brown the other side. Tip the frittata onto paper towels to absorb any excess oil and keep warm. Repeat the operation, pouring more oil into the pan before cooking the remaining three frittatas. When the excess oil has been absorbed, fold the frittata in thirds.

Serve with a fresh green or mixed salad.

The frittatas can be filled with chopped anchovy fillets and parsley or sautéed mushrooms or finely diced soft cheese before being folded.

Polenta di Patate
Potato Polenta

2 lb/2 lb/1 kg potatoes
½ c/4 oz/100 g smoked pancetta (fat bacon)
½ c/4 oz/100 g pork fat
1 onion
⅓ c/3½ fl oz/1 dl oil
2 Tbsp all-purpose (plain) flour
4 oz/4 oz/100 g salami
salt
freshly ground pepper

Peel and boil the potatoes and mash them or put them through a potato ricer while still very hot. Transfer them to a large pan or polenta kettle. Sauté the diced pancetta (bacon) and pork fat and the minced onion in the oil, stirring constantly until the onion turns golden brown. Stir in the flower with a wooden spoon and blend well. Add this mixture to the potatoes in the large pan together with the salami, cut into thin strips.

Season with salt and pepper to taste. Cook the potato mixture over a fairly high heat, stirring all the time, until the potato leaves the sides of the pan cleanly. Turn out onto a round polenta board or platter and serve with Italian vegetable preserves and pickles, a cucumber salad, or a fresh green salad.

This potato dish keeps well and is just as delicious heated up and eaten the next day. To reheat, fry, turning once, until both sides are crisp and brown or place under the broiler (grill) for a few minutes on each side.

Polenta Smalzada Trentina
Baked Polenta

2¼ c/9 oz/250 g cornmeal (maize flour) or buckwheat flour
10 anchovy fillets
¼ c/2 oz/50 g grated Parmesan cheese
4 Tbsp/2 oz/50 g butter (melted)

Bring 6 cups (2½ pt/1½ liters) of water to a boil in a large pot and add the flour gradually while stirring constantly with a wooden spoon. Continue to cook over a lower heat for up to 45 minutes, mixing well to prevent the polenta from sticking to the bottom of the pan and burning. The polenta may not take this long to cook; it is done when it comes away from the sides of the pan easily. The lengthy cooking gets rid of any bitter taste. Traditionally polenta is stirred in a clockwise direction, but this is just a custom. In Italy electric polenta pans and beaters are available to ease this somewhat laborious task. When the polenta is ready, turn into a buttered pie dish, smooth and level the surface, sprinkle with finely chopped anchovy fillets and grated Parmesan, and spoon the melted butter evenly over the surface. Bake in a very hot oven (450°F/230°C/mk 8) for 5 to 10 minutes and serve immediately.

Polpettine di Fagioli
Bean Patties

scant 1 lb/14 oz/400 g white navy (haricot) beans
¼ c/2 oz/50 g grated Parmesan cheese
salt
pepper
nutmeg
2 eggs
bread crumbs
⅓ c/3½ fl oz/1 dl oil

Boil the beans in salted water until soft and mash or push through a sieve or ricer into a mixing bowl. If dried beans are used, soak them overnight. Add the grated Parmesan, a pinch of salt, pepper, and a pinch of grated nutmeg. Stir in the eggs to bind the mixture. Mix in about 1 tablespoon of bread crumbs to stiffen the mixture and, if it is still not firm enough to hold its shape well, add more bread crumbs. Taking a tablespoon at a time, shape the patties by hand and coat with bread crumbs. Heat the oil in a skillet until very hot and fry the patties until golden brown.

Smacafam
Polenta with Sausages

2¼ c/18 fl oz/½ l milk
1¾ c/7 oz/200 g buckwheat flour
salt
freshly ground pepper
½ onion
4 Tbsp/2 oz/50 g lard or diced pork fat
1 lucanica or other mild pork and beef sausage

Pour the milk into a heavy pan and heat gently until lukewarm. Add the sifted flour gradually, stirring continuously to prevent lumps. Season with salt and pepper to taste. Sauté the finely chopped onion in a small pan with the diced pork fat; when the onion has colored evenly,

Opposite: Preparing Strudel, the famous Austrian dessert.

add to the milk-and-flour mixture and stir well. Turn the batter into a greased pie dish large enough for the batter to form a layer no more than ½ inch (1 cm) thick. Top with thick slices of sausage and bake in a moderate oven (350°F/180°C/mk 4) until golden brown.

Diced or grated cheese can be added to the batter to enrich an otherwise simple but tasty dish.

Strudel

Dough:
1⅓ c/5 oz/150 g all-purpose (plain) flour
1 egg
2 Tbsp/⅔ oz/20 g sugar
2 Tbsp/1 oz/25 g butter (melted)
salt

Filling:
¼ c/1 oz/25 g seedless raisins (sultanas)
¼ c/1 oz/25 g almonds or pine nuts
1 lb/1 lb/500 g apples
⅔ c/2 Tbsp/2 Tbsp fine bread crumbs
2 Tbsp/1 oz/25 g butter
4 Tbsp/2 oz/50 g sugar
grated rind of 1 lemon
½ c/2–3 Tbsp/2–3 Tbsp fruit preserves (optional)
butter to grease the baking dish
confectioners' (icing) sugar

Sift the flour into a large bowl. Make a well in the center and in it place the egg, sugar, melted butter, and the salt dissolved in a little warm water. Work the flour into the center of the well and mix and knead until a fairly stiff dough is obtained. If it seems too firm or a little crumbly, add a little more water. Gather the dough into a ball and place it on a lightly floured pastry board; knead well for 20 minutes or until it is perfectly smooth; then cover it with a warm bowl and let it rest for 45 minutes.

While the dough is resting, prepare the filling. Soak the raisins (sultanas) for a few minutes in lukewarm water; then drain and dry them. Blanch, skin, and chop the almonds if they are being used. Peel, core, and slice the apples very thin.

Heat the bread crumbs slowly in the butter, stirring well. Remove them from the heat as soon as they start to color (if they brown too much they will impart a bitter taste to the filling).

Cover a table at least 36 inches (1 meter) square with a clean tablecloth, dust the cloth lightly with flour. Place the dough in the center of the cloth and roll out with a floured rolling pin into a square sheet as thin as possible. Dust the rolling pin lightly with flour at frequent intervals to keep the pastry from sticking to it.

Spread the apples, bread crumbs, raisins (sultanas), chopped nuts, sugar, and grated lemon rind over the sheet of dough, stopping $\frac{1}{2}$ inch (1 cm) short of the edges. Smear a little jam over the filling if desired. Flip the bare strip of dough around the edges inward. Then taking the cloth in your hands, gently roll up the dough by lifting the cloth gradually higher and higher; this forms a loose roll and avoids too much handling. Press the ends together to make sure that no filling oozes out during baking. Slide the roll carefully onto a lightly buttered baking sheet, seam side down. Bake in a 350°F (180°C/mk 4) oven for about 30 to 40 minutes. Allow the strudel to cool for about 10 minutes, sprinkle with confectioners' (icing) sugar. Serve.

Pinza di Pane
Sweet Pizza

6–8 slices/5 oz/150 g stale bread (crusts removed)
2 c/$\frac{3}{4}$ pt/4 dl lukewarm milk
4 Tbsp/2 oz/50 g granulated sugar
$\frac{1}{3}$ c/2 oz/50 g seedless raisins (sultanas)
2 eggs
grated rind of $\frac{1}{2}$ lemon
2 Tbsp all-purpose (plain) flour
$\frac{1}{4}$ c/1 oz/25 g pine nuts
$1\frac{1}{2}$ Tbsp/$\frac{3}{4}$ oz/20 g butter

Break the bread into pieces and place in a bowl; pour in the lukewarm milk. Add the sugar and mix well so that the bread is evenly moistened. Let stand for 1 hour. Soak the raisins (sultanas) in warm water, drain, and squeeze out excess moisture. Stir the bread-and-milk mixture until it is smooth and soft. Then add the eggs, grated lemon rind, sifted flour, raisins (sultanas) and pine nuts. Grease a cake pan and pour in the mixture (the pinza should be about $1\frac{1}{2}$ inches (4 cm) thick). Dot the surface with small pieces of butter and bake in the oven at about 350°F (180°C/mk 4) for 30 minutes.

Krapfen
Doughnuts

$2\frac{1}{2}$ c/$8\frac{3}{4}$ oz/250 g cake (very fine) flour
1 cake compressed/1 oz/25 g fresh yeast
$\frac{1}{3}$ c/$3\frac{1}{2}$ fl oz/1 dl milk
4 Tbsp/2 oz/50 g butter
3 egg yolks
salt
$\frac{1}{4}$ c/2 oz/50 g sugar
pastry cream or fruit preserves for filling
oil or lard for deep frying

Mix 1 tablespoon of flour, the crumbled yeast, and a small quantity of milk into a soft dough ball. Wrap in a pastry cloth and leave to double in volume in a warm place away from drafts. Combine the remaining flour and the butter, which has been melted over hot water, in a fairly large mixing bowl. Mix in the egg yolks one at a time. Incorporate the dough ball which should be full of air bubbles, followed by the salt, sugar, and enough milk, added a little at a time, to form a smooth, firm dough. Knead briefly until the dough is soft and pliable but do not work more than absolutely necessary. Sprinkle with flour, wrap in a pastry cloth, and allow to rise.

When the dough has doubled in bulk, place on a lightly floured board and roll out into a sheet no thicker than $\frac{1}{2}$ inch (1 cm). Cut out disks of dough at least 2 inches (5 cm) in diameter with a pastry or cookie cutter. Place a teaspoonful of preserves or pastry cream in the middle of half the disks. Moisten the edges with a finger dipped in milk and place the remaining circles on top, pressing the edges down gently but firmly so that they are tightly sealed. Dampening with milk gives a good seal and the filling is unlikely to ooze out during frying.

Let the doughnuts stand in a warm place for about 20 minutes to rise. Deep-fry 1 or 2 at a time until they are a light brown color. Drain on paper towels.

Chifelini alla Confettura
Jam Crescents

$\frac{1}{2}$ lb/9 oz/250 g potatoes
2 c/9 oz/250 g all-purpose (plain) flour
$\frac{1}{2}$ c/4 oz/100 g sugar
salt
scant 1 c/7 oz/200 g butter (melted)
2 eggs
grated rind of 1 lemon
1 cake compressed/1 oz/25 g fresh yeast
2–3 Tbsp lukewarm milk
jam or pastry cream for filling
1 egg yolk

Peel and boil the potatoes and mash them or put them through a potato ricer or sieve while they are still very hot. Mix the potatoes, sifted flour, sugar, salt, melted butter, the 2 whole eggs, grated lemon rind, and yeast (previously dissolved in the lukewarm milk). Knead the resulting dough thoroughly until it is smooth and elastic (if it is too firm, add a little more lukewarm milk). Place in a lightly floured mixing bowl, cover with a cloth, let rise for about 1 hour.

When the dough has doubled in volume, roll it out into a sheet about $\frac{1}{8}$ inch (3mm) thick. Cut into 4- to 6-inch (12–15 cm) squares. Place a teaspoon of jam or pastry cream in the middle of each square. Fold the squares diagonally to form triangles, taking care that the jam stays in the center. Fold over again and bend to form a crescent shape.

Arrange the crescents, well spaced out, on a buttered and lightly floured baking sheet, cover with a cloth, and let rise once more, until the Chifelini have doubled in volume. Using a pastry brush, glaze each roll with beaten yolk of egg. Bake in a hot oven (400°F/200°C/mk 6) for about 20 minutes.

VENETO

Granséola alla Veneziana
Venetian Crab

4 live hard-shell crabs
vinegar
salt
freshly ground pepper
olive oil
1 lemon
1 small bunch parsley

Place the crabs in boiling salted water acidulated with a few drops of vinegar. Boil for 10 to 15 minutes, depending on size; remove from water and allow to cool. Clean carefully, taking care not to damage the upper shell, to which the crab meat will be returned. Remove the claws and legs and extract all the meat from them. Grasp the "apron" at the back of the crab's underbelly firmly, using a knife to help pry it up if necessary, and pull the two halves of the crab apart, exposing the flesh. Remove the inedible portions such as the spongy gills and intestine, but use all the rest of the contents, including the delicious coral roe or creamy part which is the crab's liver. Discard the eggs and any tough leathery bits and pick out any splinters of shell. Place the crab meat in a bowl and add salt and pepper, olive oil, and lemon juice to taste. Mix well and return in 4 equal portions to the cleaned, dried shells. Sprinkle with finely chopped parsley.

Bìgoli co'le Sardèle
Bìgoli with Sardine Sauce

scant 1lb/14 oz/400 g fresh bìgoli or
  scant ¾ lb/10½ oz/300 g commercial
  whole-wheat (wholemeal) spaghetti
3 canned sardines
scant ¼ c/2 fl oz/50 g oil

To make fresh bìgoli:
scant 2 c/9 oz/250 g whole-wheat
  (wholemeal) flour
2 eggs
salt

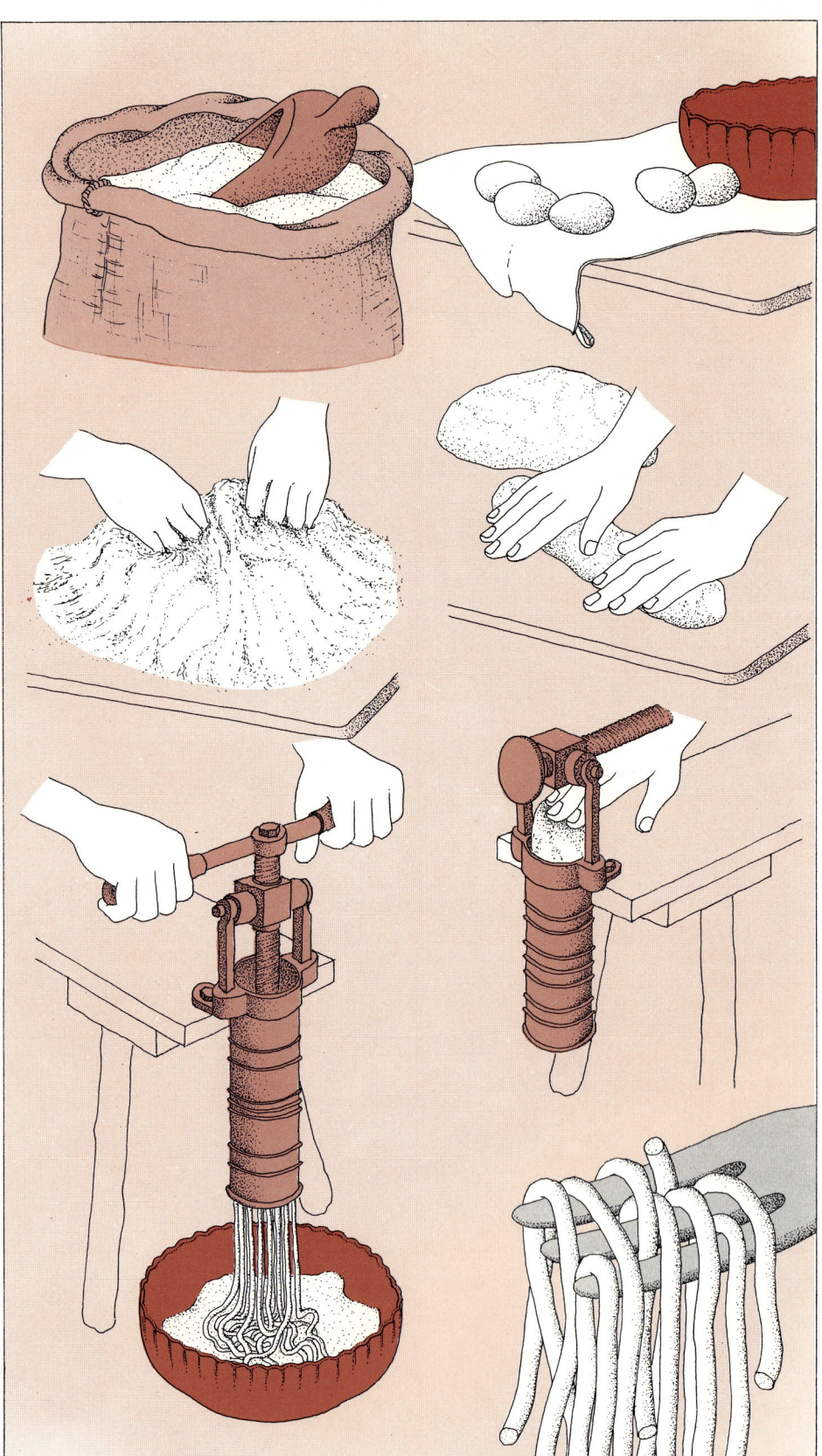

Make a firm, smooth dough with the flour, eggs, a pinch of salt and a little water. When the dough has been well-kneaded, put through the "bìgolaro" (see illustration opposite). These bìgoli form the basis of many Venetian dishes.

To make the sauce for the pasta, pat sardines dry of excess oil with paper towels, remove bones and mash well with a fork. (If the sardines are the salted variety, wash well to remove salt; this can also be done by rubbing them gently with a fresh lemon wedge.)

Blend the sardines with the oil with a fork to form a smooth, creamy paste and heat in a small saucepan over moderate heat.

Bring a large pan of lightly salted water to a boil and add the bìgoli. If manufactured hard pasta has been substituted for homemade bìgoli, it will require considerably longer cooking time compared with the seconds needed for absolutely fresh pasta.

When the pasta is al dente drain, turn onto a heated serving platter, and top with the sardine sauce. Grated Parmesan cheese is not served with this particular dish.

Bìgoli in Salsa
Bìgoli with Anchovy Sauce

1 medium onion
8 anchovy fillets
¼ c/2 oz/50 g olive oil
1 small bunch parsley
freshly ground pepper
scant 1 lb/14 oz/400 g bìgoli (see
* preceding recipe) or*
* scant ¾ lb/10½ oz/300 g commercial*
* whole-wheat (wholemeal) spaghetti*
salt

Chop the onion and the anchovies very finely. Place in a small pan with the olive oil and a little water. Cover tightly and simmer for about 10 minutes or until the onion is very soft. Shortly before remov-

Opposite: Bìgoli, specialty of the Veneto, are made
with a special hand-operated press, the bigolaro.

ing the sauce from the heat, add the parsley, chopped very finely, and some freshly ground pepper. The sauce is ready when all the ingredients can be blended into a smooth, creamy consistency. Cook the bìgoli (or commercial pasta) in plenty of boiling, slightly salted water (dry pasta will take much longer to cook than fresh), drain, and top with the anchovy sauce. Grated Parmesan cheese is not served with this dish.

Bìgoli coi Rovinazzi
Bìgoli with Giblets

½ c/4 oz/100 g chicken gizzards and
* hearts*
½ c/4 oz/100 g chicken livers
4–6 fresh sage leaves or ¼ tsp dried sage
4 Tbsp/2 oz/50 g butter
chicken stock
scant 1 lb/14 oz/400 g homemade bìgoli
* (see recipe above) or*
* scant ¾ lb/10½ oz/300 g commercial*
* whole-wheat (wholemeal) spaghetti*
salt
¼ c/2 oz/50 g Parmesan cheese

In Venice *rovinazzi* would include not only hearts and gizzards, but also such parts as the wing tips and the feet, etc.

Clean and trim the gizzards, hearts, and livers and cut into small pieces. Melt the butter in a small pan, add the sage leaves, and sauté lightly. Add the gizzards and hearts (not the livers at this stage) and cook for about 30 minutes over a moderate heat, adding a few tablespoons of chicken stock from time to time when the mixture needs moistening. Add the chicken livers about 4 to 5 minutes before removing the pan from the heat, so that they will remain moist and tender and will not be overcooked.

Cook the bìgoli in plenty of boiling salted water until al dente. Drain, turn into a hot serving dish, and pour the sauce over them. Sprinkle with grated Parmesan cheese and serve while still piping hot. If commercial pasta is used, start cooking it before the chicken livers are added to the sauce, as it will take longer to cook.

Bìgoli co'l'Ànara
Bìgoli and Duck

2 young ducklings (or 1 large duck)
1 onion
1 stalk celery
1 small carrot
4–6 fresh sage leaves or ½ tsp dried
4 Tbsp/2 oz/50 g butter
chicken stock
salt
pepper
scant 1 lb/14 oz/400 g fresh bìgoli (see
* recipe for Bìgoli co' le Sardèle above)*
* or*
* scant ¾ lb/10½ oz/300 g commercial*
* whole-wheat (wholemeal) spaghetti*
¼ c/2 oz/50 g grated Parmesan cheese

Clean and wash the duck thoroughly, setting aside the giblets. Poach the duck in plenty of lightly salted water in a large cooking pot together with the onion, carrot, and celery. Sauté the finely chopped sage leaves or dried sage in the butter until soft; add the very finely chopped or ground (minced) giblets. Moisten with 3 to 4 tablespoons of stock, season with salt and pepper, and simmer for about 15 minutes over a low heat.

Skim or strain the liquid in which the duck has been poached and use it to boil the bìgoli. Keep the duck warm in a covered dish in the oven. When the pasta is cooked but still firm, drain, turn on to a heated serving platter, and add the sauce. Sprinkle with grated Parmesan and mix gently.

Serve the duck as the main course, accompanied by Salsa Verde (page 36) or Salsa al Dragoncello (page 110).

For a lighter and less fatty sauce skin the duck before poaching, since the skin contains most of the fat.

Paparèle e Fegatini
Pappardelle with Chicken Livers

¾ c/5 oz/150 g chicken livers
2¼ c/9 oz/250 g all-purpose (plain) flour
3 eggs
salt
2 Tbsp butter
freshly ground pepper
4 c/1¾ pt/1 l chicken, or a mixture of beef and chicken, stock
¼ c/2 oz/50 g grated Parmesan cheese

Wash and trim the chicken livers, removing the membrane and any discolored parts. Cut into small pieces.

Mix the flour, eggs, and a pinch of salt and work the dough until smooth and elastic. Roll out fairly thin and allow to dry for a few minutes; then cut into strips about ¼ inch (½ cm) wide (see illustration on page 12).

Heat the butter in a small pan and, when it begins to foam, add the chicken livers, season with salt and pepper, and sauté for 2 to 3 minutes, mixing and turning the chopped liver to ensure even cooking. Meanwhile, bring the stock to a boil. Add the chicken livers and the noodles. By the time the noodles are done they should have absorbed nearly all the stock. This dish should be moist but not overly liquid since this is not a soup. Serve with grated Parmesan on the side.

Pasta e Fasioi
Pasta and Beans

1 onion
¾ c/7 fl oz/2 dl oil
2 c/14 oz/400 g Lamon beans or white navy (haricot) beans
8 c/3½ pt/2 l chicken stock
1 c/7 oz/200 g canned tomatoes or 1–2 Tbsp tomato paste diluted with water
salt
freshly ground pepper
scant ½ lb/7 oz/200 g tagliatelle
¼ c/2 oz/50 g grated Parmesan cheese

The best beans for this very tasty soup come from Lamon, just to the north of Feltre. Not only do they have a wonderful flavor, they also have such tender skins that the whole bean melts in the mouth when cooked. If dried beans are used, soak them overnight or for several hours in lukewarm water.

The tagliatelle or ribbon noodles used in the Veneto region are made with durum wheat flour and water. They are relatively thick and cut fairly wide, making this soup robust and hearty.

Sauté the finely chopped onion in the oil in a large pan until translucent; add the beans and cover with boiling stock. Cover tightly and cook over a very low heat until tender—about 1 hour. Add the tomatoes, which have been put through a food processor, food mill, or sieve, or the diluted tomato paste and simmer, covered, for a further 2 hours. Remove about one-third of the beans from the pan with a slotted spoon and rub them through a fine sieve straight back into the pan to thicken the soup. It should have an almost creamy texture. If the soup has reduced too much and is no longer sufficient for 4 people, add a little more stock. Season with salt and pepper to taste. Add the tagliatelle and cook until they are al dente. Remove from the heat, add the grated Parmesan, and serve. This soup can be allowed to stand in individual bowls for up to 10 minutes, since its flavor is enhanced when it is served warm rather than hot.

Gnocchi alla Veneta
Gnocchi with Tomato Sauce

1¾ lb/1¾ lb/800 g baking potatoes
1¼ c/5 oz/150 g all-purpose (plain) flour
2 eggs
salt
1 lb/1 lb/500 g ripe or canned tomatoes
4 Tbsp/2 oz/50 g butter
grated Parmesan cheese

Peel, boil, and mash the potatoes. Sift the flour into a large bowl and add the still hot mashed potatoes. Beat the eggs lightly with a generous pinch of salt and combine with the potato and flour mixture. Place the dough on a lightly floured board and knead until soft and smooth. Divide the dough into several portions and roll these into long sausagelike shapes about ½ inch (1 cm) in diameter. Cut these "sausages" into pieces approximately 1 inch (2 cm) long. Using your little finger, make a dent in the middle of each dumpling, causing it to curl into a shell shape. Alternatively, press the gnocchi against the concave side of a cheese grater or the tines of a fork (see page 55 for illustration). Keep the dumplings separate and do not pile them up as you make them or they will stick to each other.

Put the tomatoes through a food processor, food mill, or sieve and heat with butter and a pinch of salt. Simmer, uncovered, so that the sauce will reduce and become fairly thick.

Gnocchi alla Veronese

1¾ lb/1¾ lb/800 g baking potatoes
1¾ c/7 oz/200 g all-purpose (plain) flour
6 Tbsp/3 oz/80 g butter
¼ c/2 oz/50 g grated Parmesan cheese
½–1 tsp cinnamon
1 tsp sugar
salt

Using the potatoes and flour, prepare the gnocchi according to the previous recipe. Cook them in plenty of boiling salted water (this will take about 3 minutes for each batch), removing them with a slotted spoon as they float to the surface. Drain the gnocchi and transfer them to heated individual dishes. Melt the butter until it is golden brown; drizzle about 2 tablespoons over the gnocchi in each plate. Season each serving with a pinch of sugar and a pinch of cinnamon; sprinkle with plenty of grated Parmesan.

***Opposite:* At Vieste in the Gargano on the Adriatic coast, the hot summer sun plays a vital part in the processing of next winter's supply of tomato paste.**

***Overleaf:* At Lula in Sardinia, lambs are spit-roasted on St. Francis's feast day.**

Boil the gnocchi (in several batches if necessary) in a large pan of salted water, removing them with a slotted spoon as they rise to the surface. Transfer them to a heated serving dish. The gnocchi will take about 3 to 5 minutes to cook. Serve into individual dishes and top each portion with 2 generous tablespoons of the tomato sauce. Sprinkle each with about 1 tablespoon grated Parmesan.

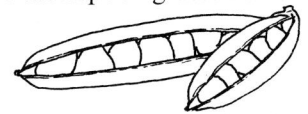

Risi e Bisi
Rice with Peas

5 Tbsp/2 oz/50 g pancetta (fat bacon)
1 small bunch parsley
1 large shallot or ½ onion
4 Tbsp/2 oz/50 g butter
2 lb/2 lb/800 g young, tender peas or
    frozen baby peas (petits pois)
sugar
1 tsp meat extract + 1 bouillon cube or
    4 c/1¾ pt/1 l light stock
1¼ c/9 oz/250 g rice
salt
freshly ground pepper
¼ c/2 oz/50 g grated Parmesan cheese

Chop the pancetta (bacon) parsley, and shallot finely and sauté in half the butter in a heavy pan. Add the peas, approximately 1 cup (½ pint/¼ liter) of water, and a pinch of sugar. Cover tightly and cook for about 5 minutes or until the peas are just tender. Add about 4 cups (1¾ pt/1 liter) boiling stock or equivalent quantity of boiling water with the cube and the meat extract dissolved in it. As soon as the mixture returns to a boil, add the rice and season with salt and a little pepper to taste. When the rice is done add the remaining butter and the grated Parmesan. The authentic Venetian Risi e Bisi is like a thick soup, the liquid being almost gelatinous with a consistency described as *all'onda*: when the soup plate is tilted, the contents slip gently toward the edge. Venetians often eat this "soup" with a fork.

This soup can be made even more flavorful if, when fresh peas are used, their pods are boiled and the cooking liquid is then used to cook the peas.

Risotto di Bisato
Eel Risotto

1 medium-sized eel
1 onion
6 Tbsp/4 Tbsp/4 Tbsp oil
2 Tbsp/1 oz/25 g butter
1¾ c/¾ lb/350 g rice
½ tsp meat extract
1 bouillon cube
salt
freshly ground pepper
1 small bunch parsley

Clean the eel thoroughly but do not skin. Cut crosswise into pieces, starting about 3 inches (7 cm) below the head so as not to penetrate the gall bladder which lies close to the head. Sauté these pieces and the finely chopped onion in the oil and butter in a heavy pan. Add a ladleful of hot water, cover, and leave to cook over a low heat for about 1 hour, moistening with a little more hot water when necessary. Remove the pieces of eel, skin them, and remove the spinal column or backbone. Set the eel aside on a heated dish.

Strain the cooking liquid into a large pan, add enough boiling water to cook the rice, and bring to a boil. Add the rice and, if it absorbs the liquid, add a little light stock, made from the meat extract and cube dissolved in water. Add a ladleful at a time, so that the rice is neither soupy nor too dry. Season with salt and pepper. When the rice is al dente, add the eel pieces. Mix well, sprinkle with chopped parsley, and serve immediately.

Riso e Lugànega
Rice with Treviso Sausage

4 c/1¾ pt/1 l stock
4 Tbsp/2 oz/50 g butter
½ onion
1½ c/10½ oz/300 g Arborio rice
⅓ c/3½ fl oz/1 dl dry white wine
salt
5–6 oz/5–6 oz/150 g Lugànega (Treviso
    sausage)
¼ c/3 Tbsp/3 Tbsp grated Parmesan
    cheese

Lugànega, the famous homemade pure pork sausage of Treviso, can be substituted with best quality commercially made pork sausages.

Bring the stock to a boil; reduce heat to simmering point.

Melt 2 tablespoons (1 oz/25 g) of the butter in a large pan or skillet and sauté the finely chopped onion in it until translucent and beginning to color slightly. Pour in the rice and stir well so that each grain is coated. Pour in the wine, turn up the heat and allow to evaporate. Reduce the heat and add some of the stock, seasoning with salt. As the liquid is absorbed by the rice, add more stock, about ¼ cup at a time.

When the rice is half cooked, add the finely chopped sausage meat. When the rice is al dente remove from heat, add the remaining butter to give the risotto a good sheen and a creamy consistency. Add the grated Parmesan; mix through gently but thoroughly; and serve.

Risotto con gli Asparagi
Asparagus Risotto

2 lb/2 lb/1 kg fresh, tender asparagus
1 bouillon cube
½ tsp meat extract
4 Tbsp/2 oz/50 g butter
1 onion
1¼ c/10½ oz/300 g rice
⅓ c/3½ fl oz/1 dl dry white wine
salt
freshly ground pepper
¼ c/2 oz/50 g grated Parmesan cheese

Rinse the asparagus well (if they have thick stalks, peel them) and cut off the tips, reserving these. Boil the asparagus in a little salted water for slightly longer than usual and when they are tender, rub them through a strainer (sieve), returning the resulting paste to the liquid in which they were cooked. Add the bouillon cube and the meat extract and keep warm over a gentle heat.

Melt 3 tablespoons (1½ oz/40 g) of the butter in a large, heavy pan, add the very finely chopped onion and sauté for a few minutes. Add the rice and mix well with a wooden spoon to ensure that each grain is coated with the butter. Pour in the wine, turn up the heat, and cook until the wine has evaporated. Reduce the heat. Add the asparagus liquid a little at a time as it is absorbed by the rice. Add a pinch of salt if necessary. When the rice is firm but tender, remove it from the heat, add the rest of the butter and the grated Parmesan, mix well but gently, and serve.

The reserved asparagus tips can be used in some other dish as needed or steamed and sprinkled on the risotto.

Risotto Nero

Risotto with Baby Cuttlefish

1¾ lb/1¾ lb/ 800 g very small cuttlefish or squid
1 clove garlic
½ onion
1 small bunch parsley
¼ c/3 Tbsp/3 Tbsp oil
⅓ c/3½ fl oz/1 dl dry white wine
4 c/1¾ pt/1 l fish stock
1 Tbsp tomato paste
1¼ c/10½ oz/300 g rice
salt
freshly ground pepper

Remove the ink sacs very carefully from the little cuttlefish and reserve (when the cuttlefish are very tiny small sharp scissors can facilitate this operation). Remove all the inedible parts such as the eyes, long central bone, yellowish deposit under the head, and anal and mouth portion. Wash, dry, and cut into thin strips.

Chop the garlic, onion and parsley very finely and sauté in the oil in a large heavy skillet over low heat. Add the cuttlefish and sauté lightly, turning and mixing. Pour in the white wine and the ink from the ink sacs. Simmer for 20 minutes, adding a small quantity of fish stock from time to time as the liquid reduces.

Dilute the tomato paste with a few tablespoons of hot water or fish stock and pour into the pan. Add the rice and stir continuously until it is firm but tender, moistening with fish stock as the rice absorbs the liquid. Season to taste.

Gnocchi alla Pastissada

Baked Gnocchi

1¾ lb/1¾ lb/800 g baking potatoes
1¾ c/7 oz/200 g all-purpose (plain) flour
salt
4 Tbsp/2 oz/50 g butter
1 Tbsp olive oil
2 c/14 oz/400 g tender lean beef, such as rump, diced small
¾ c/7 fl oz/2 dl dry red wine
1 lb/1 lb/500 g ripe or canned tomatoes
2 onions
grated Parmesan cheese
freshly ground pepper
cinnamon

Peel and boil the potatoes and mash or put through a potato ricer while still hot to prevent lumpy gnocchi. Turn onto a pastry board or working surface and work in the flour and a pinch of salt. Knead for 3 to 4 minutes or until the dough is smooth and light. Use just enough flour to bind the potatoes into a dough which will hold together when boiled (the amount will vary depending on the type of potatoes used). Divide the dough into several portions and roll these into long sausagelike shapes about ½ inch (1 cm) in diameter. Cut in lengths of approximately 1 inch (2 cm). Shape the gnocchi by pressing them against the concave side of a cheese grater or the tines of a fork to give them their characteristic curled shape and textured backs. (See illustration, page 55.) As the gnocchi are completed, place on a pastry cloth or dish towel, well spaced out so that they will not stick to one another.

Heat the butter and oil and add the diced meat. Sauté over a fairly high heat for a few minutes to seal the meat, turning so that it browns evenly. Add the wine and reduce. Add the skinned, seeded tomatoes together with the finely sliced onions. Cover tightly and simmer over a low heat for 3 to 4 hours. At the end of this cooking time the small pieces of meat should be so tender that they can be cut with a fork.

Cook the gnocchi in small batches in a large pot of boiling salted water, removing them with a slotted spoon as they rise to the top. Place on individual heated plates and cover with meat sauce. Some grated Parmesan, a little freshly ground pepper, and a pinch of cinnamon can be added to each serving to heighten the flavor.

Polenta Pastissada

Polenta with Veal and Giblets

2⅓ c/14 oz/400 g finely ground cornmeal (maize flour)
1½ Tbsp dried mushrooms
⅔ c/5 oz/150 g butter
2⅓ c/14 oz/400 g chicken giblets
salt
freshly ground pepper
½ onion
1 stalk celery
1 carrot
2 oz/2 oz/50 g pancetta (fat bacon)
2 Tbsp oil
½ lb/8 oz/225 g veal chunks
⅓ c/3½ fl oz/1 dl dry white wine
½ lb/8 oz/225 g canned or fresh ripe tomatoes
grated Parmesan cheese

Bring 10 cups (4¼ pt/2½ liters) of water to a boil in a large pot. Add salt and pour in the cornmeal (maize flour) slowly, stirring continuously to avoid lumps. Reduce the heat slightly and cook for about 45 minutes, stirring frequently. When the mixture is done, turn out into a shallow pan or onto a board. The consistency should be firm enough to hold its shape without being too thick. Let the polenta cool; then cut it into slices about 1 inch (2 cm) thick.

Meanwhile, place the dried mushrooms in a bowl of lukewarm water and let them soak and soften for about 20 minutes. Rinse them, then squeeze out any excess moisture in a paper towel, and chop them finely. Melt a third of the butter, add the mushrooms, and sauté for a few minutes over a moderate heat. Add the cleaned, trimmed, and chopped chicken giblets, a little salt and pepper to taste, and cook for about 5 minutes while stirring over a low heat. Remove from heat and set aside.

Sauté the chopped onion, celery, carrot, and pancetta (bacon) in the oil and a tablespoon of butter, in a separate pan. Stir continuously until the mixture starts to color. Raise the heat and add the veal chunks. Moisten with the wine. When the wine has reduced, add the sieved or puréed tomatoes and season with salt and pepper. Lower the heat, cover tightly, and simmer for about 1 hour, adding a little water from time to time if necessary. When the meat is very tender and the sauce has become quite thick, remove it from the heat. Grease a baking dish with butter and cover the bottom with a layer of polenta. Then cover with some of the veal and a few tablespoons of tomato sauce and cover with another layer of polenta slices, followed by some of the mushroom-and-chicken-giblet mixture sprinkled with a little Parmesan cheese. Repeat the operation, ending with a layer of polenta. Sprinkle some grated Parmesan on top and dot with small pieces of butter. Place the dish in a moderate oven (350°F/180°C/mk 4) for about 30 minutes and serve very hot.

Preparing potato gnocchi Veneto style.

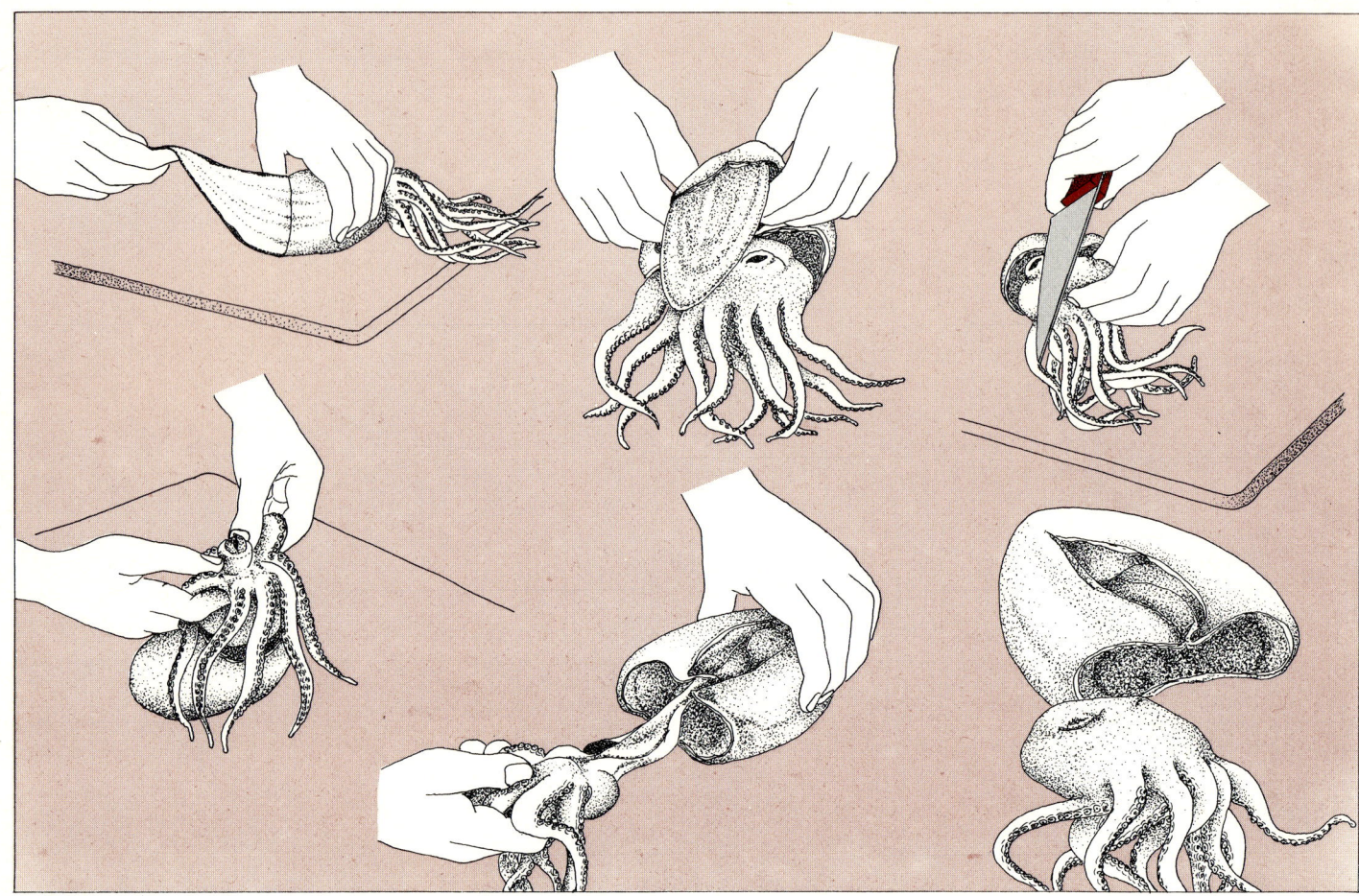

Above: Cleaning and preparing cuttlefish (or squid) for Seppie alla Veneziana (Venetian Style Cuttlefish).

Paéta (Tacchina) alla Melagrana
Turkey with Pomegranates

1 young turkey weighing approximately
4½ lb/4½ lb/2 kg
3 pomegranates
¼ lb/4 oz/100 g very thin slices of pancetta
(fat bacon)
⅓ c/3½ fl oz/1 dl oil
salt
freshly ground pepper

Clean and wash the turkey and reserve the giblets. Lard with the pancetta (bacon), especially over the breast, so that the turkey will not be dry when roasted. Roast in a fairly shallow baking dish for about 1½ hours in a moderate oven (350°F/180°C/mk 4), turning frequently and basting the turkey with its own juices. Halfway through the cooking time, baste the turkey with the juice of the crushed seeds of two pomegranates (these take time to pick out of their surrounding membrane), or 2 tablespoons bottled pomegranate juice.

Heat the oil in a small pan, add the very finely chopped giblets (the liver, gizzard, and heart), a little salt, and the juice from the seeds of the third pomegranate or 1 tablespoon bottled pomegranate juice. Cook slowly until the sauce has reduced and begun to thicken.

When the turkey is done remove the pancetta (bacon), carve, and place on a serving platter. Pour the giblet sauce over it and serve immediately.

Bovoloni
Snails in Garlic and Wine

1¾ lb/1¾ lb/800 g live snails or 12 canned
snails
⅓ c/3½ fl oz/1 dl oil
5 cloves garlic
1 small bunch parsley
¾ c/7 fl oz/2 dl dry white wine
salt
freshly ground pepper

If live snails are used, place them in a loose bag of bran or oatmeal for 5 to 6 days or place them in a wicker basket with the loose leaves of 2 heads of lettuce and several slices of bread which have been soaked in water and wrung dry. Cover the basket and allow it to stand for 3 days. By eating the lettuce and bread or the oatmeal or bran, the snails are purged of all poisonous vegetation that they might have ingested and are now perfectly safe to eat. Wash them under running water, then soak them for 2 hours in a large enamel pot of cold water acidulated with 1 cup vinegar and a handful of coarse salt. Drain them and put them through several changes of cold water until the water is absolutely clear. Drain again and discard any snails whose heads are not out of the shell. Remove the snails from their shells, place them in a pot, cover with cold water, and bring slowly to a boil over moderate heat. Simmer for 5 minutes, then drain in a colander. Cut off the tips of the heads and the black part on their tail ends. Pat dry with paper towels.

Place the oil and the whole garlic cloves in a small fireproof casserole dish (preferably earthenware) together with the coarsely chopped parsley; place the snails on top of this mixture; and *then* turn on the heat. Cover and simmer very slowly for about 4 hours, moistening with the wine, and, when this has all been used, adding a little water when necessary. Half way through the cooking time, season with salt and pepper.

Fegato alla Veneziana
Liver Venetian Style

1 lb/1 lb/500 g very young, tender calf
  liver
2 large onions
1 small bunch parsley
3 Tbsp/1¼ oz/40 g butter
¼ c/3 Tbsp/3 Tbsp oil
salt

Remove any membrane from the liver and, using a very sharp knife, cut into wafer-thin slices. Slice the onions into very thin rings; chop the parsley; and sauté these gently in the butter and oil in a large skillet until the onion is translucent. Remove from heat and allow to cool a little before the liver slices are added. This will help prevent the liver from toughening or becoming hard. Return to the heat and cook, allowing about 1 minute for each side. Remove

from heat and season with a little salt. Prepared this way, the liver will be moist and very tender. Serve immediately.

Sardèle in Saór
Marinated Sardines

1 lb/1 lb/500 g fresh sardines, red mullet
  (salt-water variety), or small sole
all-purpose (plain) flour
olive oil for frying
salt
⅓ c/3½ fl oz/1 dl olive oil for marinade
2 large onions
1 c/8 fl oz/¼ l white vinegar

Trim and gut the fish. Wash well and coat with flour. Fry in a large skillet in plenty of olive oil until they are well browned on both sides. Remove with a slotted spatula and place on absorbent paper to drain. Season with salt. (The olive oil used for frying can be strained through a fine strainer and, when cool, stored in a jar and used again for frying fish. The best olive oil should always be used.)

Clean the frying pan and pour in ⅓ cup (3½ fl oz/1 dl) of fresh oil. Slice the onions into thin rings and sauté in the oil over a low heat until they are golden brown. Add the vinegar and simmer until the liquid is somewhat reduced and has thickened slightly.

Place a layer of sardines in a small, deep dish (preferably earthenware or enamel; never stainless steel or copper). Pour over some of the marinade; then arrange another layer of sardines in the dish and cover with the remaining marinade. The fish should be completely submerged in the liquid. Cover and leave in a cool place for at least 48 hours.

In days gone by the dish was often more highly flavored, with pine nuts, seedless white raisins (sultanas), cinnamon, and other spices sprinkled on the layers of fish before the addition of the marinade.

Frittata di Gamberetti
Shrimp Frittata

scant ½ lb/7 oz/200 g fresh shrimp
  (prawns)
1 Tbsp butter
5 very fresh eggs
¼ c/3 Tbsp/3 Tbsp oil
freshly ground pepper
salt
1 small bunch parsley

If the shrimp (prawns) are raw, cook them for 5 to 10 minutes in very little salted water, effectively steaming them. Drain, allow to cool a little, shell, and devein. Melt the butter over a low heat and add the shrimps with a little salt. Cook for a few minutes, stirring and turning so that each shrimp is coated with butter.

Break the eggs into a bowl and beat them together lightly, adding a little pepper and salt. Pour the oil into a frying pan and, when it is very hot, pour in the beaten eggs and immediately stir with a fork in a circular motion 3 or 4 times. Lift the set eggs lightly from the sides, to allow uncooked egg to run underneath. Quickly sprinkle the shrimps over half the omelet and, when the eggs seem almost cooked (an ideal omelet is *baveuse* or very creamy in the center), use a spatula to fold the other half of the omelet neatly over the shrimp (prawns), forming a neat semi-circle. Slide immediately onto a warm serving dish, garnish with parsley, and serve without delay.

Cape Sante
Scallops Sautéed in Garlic

2 dozen/2 dozen/24 sea scallops
¾ c/7 fl oz/2 dl olive oil
1 small bunch parsley
1 clove garlic
salt
freshly ground pepper
4 clean scallop shells
juice of 1 lemon

Cape sante is Venetian dialect for scallops and these are usually sold already prepared and cleaned with the sac and beard removed. Wash them well, pat dry, and place in a frying pan with the olive oil and the finely chopped parsley and garlic. Season with salt and pepper and sauté over a low heat for a few minutes, turning a couple of times. Remove from heat and divide into 4 scallop shells. Sprinkle each portion with lemon juice and serve.

Baccalà alla Vicentina
Vicenza Style Stockfish

1¼ lb/1¼ lb/600 g stockfish or dried cod
2 large onions
1 clove garlic
¾ c/7 fl oz/2 dl oil
4 anchovy fillets
1 small bunch parsley
1¼ c/8 fl oz/¼ l milk
3 Tbsp grated Parmesan cheese

Although this dish is called "Baccalà" it is made with stockfish—cod which has been dried in the sun and not salted or packed in brine as a means of preserving it. It can equally well be made with ordinary dried salt cod.

Take the piece of stockfish and pound it well to help soften it. It must then be soaked in water in an enamel or earthenware bowl (never a metal container) for 2 or 3 days, with the water being changed every 24 hours. (It can sometimes be bought pre-soaked.) Once the fish has softened and plumped up, open it up by continuing the slit which has been made to gut it, lay it out flat, and dredge it lightly with flour and grated Parmesan. Sauté the chopped onions in half the oil, add the whole clove of garlic, and, when this has turned brown, remove and discard it. Chop the anchovy fillets and the parsley very finely, add to the sautéed onions and oil, and mix well with a wooden spoon. Spread half of this mixture over the inside of the fish, close the two sides of the fish together again and cut into steaks about 1½–2 inches (4–5 cm) thick.

Place these side by side in a baking dish (preferably earthenware) and sprinkle the remaining mixture over the stuffed fish steaks. Pour the milk and the remaining oil over the fish, which should be covered by the liquid, and cook for about 3 hours over a very low heat with the lid on.

This dish is delicious if eaten right away but, if anything, it improves if kept for 24 hours and reheated gently.

Seppie alla Veneziana
Venetian Style Cuttlefish

8 cuttlefish or squid
1 clove garlic
½ onion
⅔ c/¼ pt/150 ml oil
1 small bunch parsley
¾ c/7 fl oz/2 dl dry white wine
freshly ground pepper
fish stock or 1 bouillon cube dissolved in hot water
½ lemon
salt
toasted slices of polenta (see recipe, page 16 (polenta must be thick for slicing))

This dish should be accompanied by toasted slices of polenta.

Clean and trim the cuttlefish, removing the eyes, long central bone, and the yellowish deposit under the head as well as the ink sacs which should be reserved. Wash well and cut into strips. Sauté the clove of garlic whole with the finely chopped onion in 6 tablespoons of the olive oil. When the onions begin to turn golden brown, discard the garlic clove and add the pieces of cuttlefish and the chopped parsley. Pour in the wine and reduce over a high heat. Turn down the heat and add as much of the ink from the ink sacs as desired. Add pepper to taste, but do not salt. Cover, and cook over a low heat for about 30 minutes. If necessary, moisten with a little fish stock or light meat stock. Toward the end of the cooking time, add two more tablespoonfuls of oil and the juice of half a lemon. Season with salt to taste at this point, not before.

Verze Sofegae
Cabbage Veneto Style

1 large cabbage
4 Tbsp/2 oz/50 g chopped pork belly or ham fat
¼ c/3 Tbsp/3 Tbsp oil
1 clove garlic
1 sprig fresh rosemary or a pinch of dried
⅓ c/3½ fl oz/1 dl dry white wine
salt
freshly ground pepper

Discard the tough outer leaves of the cabbage. Wash well and slice into fine strips. Dice the pork belly or ham fat very finely and heat in a large pan or fireproof casserole, adding the oil, the crushed clove of garlic, and the rosemary. When the garlic has browned, discard together with the rosemary. Add the cabbage and season with salt and pepper to taste. Cover tightly and cook over a low heat, stirring frequently to prevent the cabbage from burning or sticking to the bottom of the pan. When the cabbage begins to wilt, add the dry white wine. Cook until the cabbage is tender but still firm.

Fondi di Carciofo alla Veneta
Artichoke Hearts Veneto

8 large artichokes
1 clove garlic
1 small bunch parsley
salt
pepper
⅔ c/¼ pt/150 ml olive oil
½ bouillon cube

Break all the leaves off each artichoke, one by one, by bending them outward until they snap off. When only the whitish inner core of the leaves remains, cut it off with a sharp knife and remove the choke. Plunge the heart immediately into a bowl of acidulated water to prevent its turning black.

Chop the garlic and parsley very finely. Drain the artichoke hearts well and arrange side by side in a shallow enameled pan or fireproof earthenware dish in which you have poured ¾ cup (7 fl oz/2 dl) of water (never use a metal pan as this will turn the artichokes gray). Top each artichoke heart with some of the garlic and parsley, sprinkle with salt and pepper, and gently drizzle a tablespoon of oil onto each, taking care not to dislodge the topping. Cook over a low heat without a lid. Once the water is simmering, crumble in the half bouillon cube, sprinkling it into the water between the hearts. Simmer until the hearts are tender (about 30 minutes), loosening the artichoke hearts if they show signs of sticking to the bottom of the pan and adding a little more water when necessary. Serve in the cooking dish without allowing them to cool.

If you like anchovies, a small strip of anchovy fillet (about 1 inch/2.5 cm long) can be placed on top of each artichoke heart before covering with the minced or chopped garlic and parsley. In this case less salt will be needed.

In the Veneto region risotto or tagliatelle are often served with this dish.

Fasoi Bogonadi
Beans Simmered in Tomato Sauce

2 c/14 oz/400 g white navy beans
(haricot) beans
⅓ c/3½ fl oz/1 dl olive oil
¼ c/4 oz/100 g tomato paste
1 small bunch parsley
1 clove garlic
salt
pepper

Boil the beans in unsalted water so that they will soften as they cook; if salt is added too soon, they will be hard. When dried beans are used, they should be soaked overnight in lukewarm water.

Heat the oil in a fireproof casserole or heavy skillet. Add the tomato paste diluted with a little water and the finely chopped parsley and garlic; when it comes to the boil, season with salt and pepper and add the cooked, drained beans. Mix well, cover tightly, and leave over a very low heat for about 10 minutes so that the beans will absorb the tomato sauce's flavor.

These beans must be served while still piping hot.

Radicchio alla Vicentina
Radicchio (Red Treviso Chicory) Vicenza Style

¾ lb/¾ lb/350 g radicchio rosso (red
Treviso chicory)
4 Tbsp/2 oz/50 g ham fat or pork belly
salt
freshly ground pepper
vinegar

Radicchio rosso is now imported, but if it is not available, chicory (green curly endive) or even fresh crisp spinach could be used instead, although the flavor will not be quite the same.

Wash and dry the chicory. Place in a bowl. Sauté the very finely chopped ham fat or pork belly and, when it is a good golden brown, add salt and pepper and then the vinegar, turning up the heat to evaporate the vinegar. Pour this hot dressing over the chicory, mix quickly, and serve at once. It is a good idea to heat the individual plates a little before serving.

Radicchio Rosso Fritto
Fried Red Radicchio (Red Treviso Chicory)

¾ lb/¾ lb/350 g radicchio rosso (red
Treviso chicory)
¼ c/1 oz/2 Tbsp all-purpose (plain) flour
1 egg
bread crumbs
oil
salt
freshly ground pepper

Discard the older, outer leaves of the radicchio (chicory). Wash, dry, and cut each head of raddichio (chicory) in half lengthwise. Heat enough oil to deep-fry the radicchio (chicory) in a deep, heavy pan. Roll each head in the flour, dip in beaten egg, and then coat with bread crumbs. When the oil is really hot, fry for a few minutes. The radicchio (chicory) should be golden brown on the outside. Drain off excess oil on paper towels, season with salt and pepper, and serve immediately.

Pearà
Pepper Broth

1 tsp butter
¼ c/1 oz/25 g bone marrow
1½ c/4 oz/100 g grated stale bread
8–10 c/3½–4 pt/2–2.5 l homemade stock
salt
freshly ground pepper

This soup is often served as a first course before boiled meats, using the liquid in which the meat has been boiled for the stock.

Melt the butter and marrow in a saucepan or, preferably, an earthenware cooking pot, removing any small pieces of marrow fat which do not dissolve after heating. Add the bread crumbs and stir for 2 to 3 minutes with a wooden spoon over a moderate heat. Add about 8 cups (3¼ pt/2 liters) homemade stock. Season with salt and plenty of pepper (*pearà* is a Venetian dialect corruption of the word *pepe*, "pepper"). Mix well; reduce the heat to very low and simmer for 2 to 3 hours, adding more stock if necessary.

Peverada
Venetian Savory Sauce

2 slices Venetian sopressa (mixed beef
and pork sausage), about 3½ oz/3½ oz/
100 g
¾ c/5 oz/150 g chicken livers
2 anchovy fillets
1 small bunch parsley
1 clove garlic

juice and grated rind of 1 lemon
⅔ c/¼ pt/150 ml olive oil
⅓ c/3½ fl oz/1 dl dry white wine or
  6 Tbsp/4 Tbsp/4 Tbsp wine vinegar
salt
freshly ground pepper

Chop or grind the sausage and the cleaned, trimmed chicken livers finely. Chop the anchovy fillets, the parsley, and the garlic very finely. Mix all these ingredients with the grated lemon rind. Sauté this mixture in the oil in a small pan, seasoning with a very little salt and some freshly ground pepper. Add the lemon juice and the wine (or wine vinegar).

This sauce makes an excellent accompaniment for roast chicken or guinea hen, heightening and enhancing the flavor of the meat.

Baìcoli Veneziani
Doge's Cookies

½ cake compressed/15 g/½ oz fresh
  yeast ¾ c/7 fl oz/2 dl milk
3½ c/14 oz/400 g all-purpose (plain)
  flour
5½ Tbsp/2 oz/50 g sugar
salt
1 egg white
scant 6 Tbsp/2¾ oz/80 g butter

Soften the yeast in ⅓ cup (3½ fl oz/1 dl) lukewarm milk in a small bowl. Sift about one-quarter of the flour onto the pastry board. Make a well in the center and pour in the yeast mixture; work in the flour gradually, adding a little more if necessary to make a firm dough. Knead briefly, form into a ball and place in a large lightly floured mixing bowl covered with a damp cloth. Make a crisscross incision in the top, and allow to rest for about 30 minutes. The dough should double in volume. Sift the rest of the flour with the sugar and a pinch of salt onto the pastry board. Make a well in the center, put the raised dough ball in the center together with the white of egg and the soft but not melted butter. Work

all these ingredients together and knead gently for 10 minutes, adding a little lukewarm milk from time to time. The dough should be soft and elastic, of much the same consistency as bread dough. Break off pieces of the dough and roll by hand into cylinder or sausage shapes about 4 inches (10 cm) long. Place on a greased baking sheet, cover with a cloth, and leave in a warm place for about 2 hours to rise. Bake in a moderate oven (350°F/180°C/mk 4) for approximately 15 minutes. Remove from oven, cover with a cloth, and leave in a warm place to "set" for up to 2 hours. Cut the long thin rolls slantwise into very thin slices. Arrange on the baking sheet and return to the oven (still at a moderate setting) until the cookies are golden brown.

When cool, store in an airtight container. Stored like this, these cookies will keep for months.

Zaleti
Yellow Diamonds

⅔ c/4 oz/100 g seedless white raisins
  (sultanas)
1¾ c/7 oz/200 g finely ground cornmeal
  (maize flour)
scant 1 c/3½ oz/100 g cake flour (very
  fine flour)
salt
grated rind of 1 lemon
3 eggs
scant ½ c/3½ oz/100 g granulated sugar
⅔ c/5 oz/150 g butter (melted)
½ c/2 oz/50 g pine nuts
3 Tbsp rum
confectioners' (icing) sugar

Soak the raisins (sultanas) in lukewarm water for about 20 minutes to soften and plump them out; then drain them and squeeze them free of excess water. Sift the flours and salt onto a pastry board or into a mixing bowl and mix in the grated lemon rind. Beat the eggs together with the granulated sugar and the melted butter; add the raisins (sultanas), pine nuts, and the rum. Shape the flour mixture into a mound on the pastry

board, make a well in the center, and pour in the egg mixture. Work together carefully; the dough should be very soft, pliable, and easy to work but should hold its shape. If it is too firm, moisten with very little lukewarm milk.

Break off small pieces of dough and shape into small, oval rolls 1½–2 inches (4–5 cm) high. Place on a lightly greased baking sheet and bake in a moderate oven (350°F/180°C/mk 4) for 30 minutes. Remove from oven, arrange on a serving dish, and dust with confectioners' (icing) sugar.

Galani
Carnival Cakes

2½ c/10½ oz/300 g all-purpose (plain)
  flour
1 tsp vanilla sugar (see instructions for
  Pan de Mej, page 38)
1½ Tbsp granulated sugar
1 egg
1 egg yolk
3 Tbsp white wine
lard or oil for frying
vanilla-flavored confectioners' (icing)
  sugar (see above)

Sift the flour, vanilla sugar, and granulated sugar onto the pastry board and form into a mound. Make a well in the center and mix in the egg, the egg yolk, and the wine, working to form a smooth, springy dough. Cover with a pastry cloth and let rest about 1 hour. Roll out into as thin a sheet as possible without tearing and cut out rectangles, diamonds, or other shapes as desired with a fluted pastry wheel. Fry the cookies in plenty of very hot oil until golden brown. Lift out with a slotted spatula (fish slice) and drain on paper towels. Transfer to an oval serving dish, dust with vanilla-flavored confectioners' (icing) sugar and serve when cool.

FRIULI-VENEZIA GIULIA

PORDENONE

UDINE

GORIZIA

TRIESTE

Minestrone d'Orzo
Barley Soup

*1 c/7 oz/200 g dried white navy (haricot)
  beans
scant 1 cup/7 oz/200 g pearl barley
2 oz/2 oz/50 g smoked pancetta (fat
  bacon)
1 clove garlic
1 small bunch parsley
1 small smoked Italian pork sausage
2 medium-sized potatoes
salt
freshly ground pepper*

Soak the beans in lukewarm water for 12 hours. Drain and place in a large saucepan with the barley and the chopped pancetta (bacon), garlic, and parsley. Pour about 9 cups (4 pt/ 2 liters) water into the pan, add salt and pepper, and bring to a boil. Reduce the heat, cover the pan, and simmer for about 2 hours. Add the chopped pork sausage and the diced potatoes. When the potatoes are done, remove the pan from the heat and leave it, still covered, to cool for a little while. This soup is best served warm rather than hot.

(In order to be sure that the cooking time of the pearl barley will synchronize with that of the beans, it too can be soaked overnight in water.)

Pane Indorato
Batter-fried Bread

*¼ c/1 oz/25 g all-purpose (plain) flour
1 Tbsp sugar
grated rind of ½ lemon
salt
1 c/½ pt/2½ dl milk
2 eggs
1 small loaf stale French bread, sliced
  thick
butter or lard for frying*

Mix together the flour, sugar, grated lemon rind, and a pinch of salt. Slowly add the milk and the eggs, stirring constantly. Dunk the slices of bread in the batter. Make sure they are permeated with the batter, but do not let them get too soggy, or they will disintegrate.

Heat some butter or lard in a frying pan, and fry the batter-dipped bread slices until they are golden brown on both sides. Remove with a slotted spatula and place briefly on paper towels to drain. Serve while still hot.

Rambasicci
Stuffed Cabbage Leaves

*1 lb/1 lb/500 g ground (minced) pork
  and beef
1 small bunch parsley
1 clove garlic
1 Tbsp grated Parmesan cheese
1 tsp paprika
salt
8 small, tender cabbage leaves
1 onion, sliced thin
2 Tbsp butter
¼ c/2 fl oz/60 ml oil
2 c/¾ pt/4 dl stock
3 Tbsp bread crumbs*

Place the ground (minced) meat, chopped parsley and garlic, grated Parmesan, paprika and a generous pinch of salt together in a bowl and mix well until the ingredients are fully blended.

Cook the cabbage leaves in plenty of boiling salted water for 3 to 4 minutes. Remove the cabbage very carefully from the pan and spread out on a cloth to drain. Place a little of the meat mixture in each of the cabbage leaves and fold over into little rectangular parcels, tying them up with some raffia or soft string or securing with cocktail sticks.

Sauté the onion for a few minutes in the butter and oil. Then arrange the stuffed cabbage side by side in the pan, cover, and fry gently for 15 minutes, moistening with a little stock from time to time. Remove the lid, sprinkle the stuffed cabbage with the bread crumbs, and simmer for a few minutes more so the juices can reduce and thicken. Serve without delay.

Paparòt
Hearty Country Spinach Soup

*1½ lb/1½ lb/700 g fresh spinach
1 clove garlic
4 Tbsp/2 oz/50 g butter
oil
6 c/3½ pt/1½ l stock or 2 bouillon cubes
  dissolved in 6 c/3½ pt/1½ l water
½ c/2¾ oz/80 g coarsely ground cornmeal
  (maize flour)
⅓ c/2 oz/50 g all-purpose (plain) flour
freshly ground pepper
salt*

Trim the spinach and wash very thoroughly in several changes of water. Cook with no other water than that which clings to the leaves after washing, steaming it in a pan with the lid on until it is tender (never cook spinach in an aluminum pan). This will take 5 minutes for young spinach. Drain the spinach, chop very finely, and then sauté gently with the finely chopped garlic for a couple of minutes in the butter and a tablespoon or two of oil.

Pour the stock into a large heavy pan (if no stock is available, dissolve 2 bouillon cubes in the liquid drained off the spinach and make up the required quantity with boiling water). Add the spinach and bring to a boil. Mix the cornmeal (maize flour) with the flour in a bowl. Moisten with the stock, mixing in a little at a time, and stir with a wooden spoon very thoroughly so that no lumps form. Pour this batter gradually into the sautéed spinach in the pan, stirring well. Season with pepper and salt and simmer for at least 20 minutes, stirring frequently. Ladle the soup into individual plates and serve piping hot.

Gulasch alla Triestina
Trieste Style Goulash

2 oz/2 oz/50 g salt pork (parboiled for 10
    minutes) or fat bacon
4 Tbsp/2 oz/50 g lard or vegetable oil
1¼ lb/1¼ lb/600 g onions
1¼ lb/1¼ lb/600 g lean beef cut in 1 in
    (3 cm) cubes
salt
paprika
1 sprig fresh rosemary or ¼ tsp dried
    rosemary
2 bay leaves
½ c/7 oz/200 g tomato paste

Dice the salt pork or bacon finely and
heat with the lard or vegetable oil in a
heavy pan. Add the finely sliced onions
and sauté over a very low heat until they
are translucent. Add the beef cubes, turn
up the heat, and brown the meat well on
all sides, turning frequently. Season with
salt and with as much paprika as desired
and add the rosemary and the bay leaves
tied together in a bunch or, better still,
tied loosely in a small piece of cheesecloth
(muslin) so that the rosemary leaves
do not break off in the sauce. Pour in
the tomato paste diluted with 2 cups
(¾ pt/½ liter) boiling water. Cover the pan
and simmer, slowly until the meat is
very tender and the onions have almost
dissolved, blending into the juices and
making a delicious sauce. Add a little
hot water during the cooking if the
liquid reduces too much. When the
meat is done, remove the herbs and
serve the goulash very hot.

Boiled or steamed potatoes or fresh
polenta are ideal accompaniments to
this dish.

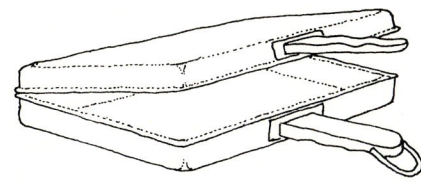

Jota
Bean and Sauerkraut Soup

scant ½ lb/7 oz/200 g dried white navy
    (haricot) beans
3–4 oz/3–4 oz/100 g pork belly
⅓ c/3 Tbsp/3 Tbsp oil
1 Tbsp all-purpose (plain) flour
2 oz/2 oz/50 g chopped salt pork or
    unsmoked fat bacon
1 clove garlic
½ onion
1 small bunch parsley
4–6 fresh sage leaves or ¼ tsp dried sage
2 rounded Tbsp coarsely ground
    cornmeal (maize flour)
2 oz/2 oz/50 g smoked pancetta (fat
    bacon)
scant ½ lb/7 oz/200 g sauerkraut. (For
    homemade sauerkraut, see the recipe
    for Crauti e Lucanica Trentina on
    page 41. Otherwise, buy packaged, not
    canned, sauerkraut.)
salt

Soak the beans in water overnight. Boil
them in 6 cups (3½ pt/1½ liters) of unsalted water with the diced pork belly.

Heat the oil in a small pan, remove
from heat, add the white flour, mix well,
and return to the heat, stirring continuously until the mixture turns light
brown. Then add this to the beans in
their cooking liquid.

Chop or mince the salt pork or bacon
very finely, heat in the same pan used to
cook the oil and flour mixture, and sauté
together with the finely chopped garlic,
onion, parsley, and sage. Add the
cornmeal (maize flour) and cook over a
low heat for a few minutes stirring
constantly. Then add this mixture to the
slowly simmering bean soup. Cut the
pancetta into thin strips and sauté these,
again in the same small pan. Add the
sauerkraut and cook slowly, stirring
gently.

Shortly before serving remove the
bean soup from the heat and add the
sauerkraut and pancetta. Mix, adjust
seasoning, and serve very hot.

Risotto di Gamberi
Shrimp Risotto

scant 1 lb/14 oz/400 g fresh shrimp
1 clove garlic
1 generous bunch parsley
½ onion
⅓ c/3½ fl oz/1 dl oil
1¾ c/¾ lb/350 g Arborio rice
⅓ c/3½ fl oz/1 dl dry white wine
freshly ground pepper
salt
1 Tbsp butter

Rinse the shrimp, boil them in a little
salted water for 3 to 4 minutes, and
allow them to cool a little before
removing the shells. Boil the shells in 6
cups (3½ pt/1½ liters) of water as you
proceed with preparing this dish. Strain
this liquid and use it as stock to cook the
rice.

Chop the garlic and onion very finely
and sauté in the oil in a large pan, mixing
with a wooden spoon. Add the rice and
turn and stir so that the grains are
coated with the oil. Pour in the wine and
turn up the heat to allow it to evaporate.
Add the shrimp and season with pepper
and a very little salt. Add approximately
1 cup (⅓ pt/2½ dl) stock, stirring while
cooking over a moderate heat until the
rice absorbs the liquid and "wipes" the
sides of the pan as you stir. Add a little
more stock at intervals when needed
until the rice is tender but firm. When
cooked, the rice in a risotto should be
creamy and smooth but not glutinous.
Add plenty of finely chopped parsley
and the butter to give the risotto a sheen.
Mix once more and serve without delay.

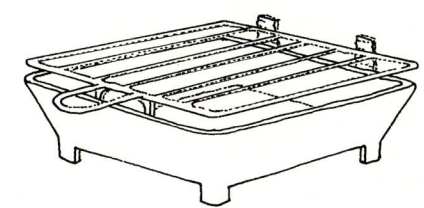

Culatta di Manzo alla Triestina
Trieste Braised Beef

2 lb/2 lb/800 g round (topside) of beef
1 thick 2 oz/2 oz/50 g slice prosciutto
   (raw ham) with fat
6 Tbsp/4 Tbsp/4 Tbsp oil
2 Tbsp/1 oz/25 g butter
½ onion
1 carrot
1 stalk celery
2–3 cloves
salt
freshly ground pepper
1 c/7 fl oz/2 dl dry white wine
3 c/1⅓ pt/¾ l homemade stock or
   1 bouillon cube and ½ tsp meat extract
   dissolved in boiling water

Lard the beef with the prosciutto (raw ham), tying to secure. Sauté the beef in the oil and butter over a fairly low heat, turning frequently for even browning. Add the finely chopped onion, the carrot and celery diced small, and the cloves. Season with salt and pepper and pour in the wine. (The beef should be cooked in a dutch oven or fireproof casserole just large enough to accommodate it and the cooking liquid comfortably.) Simmer, tightly covered, for about 1½ hours, moistening with a little hot water from time to time if necessary.

When the meat is tender, take it out of the pot, place it on a board or platter and allow it to cool slightly before carving it into slices. Arrange these slices on a heated serving platter. Quickly reduce the cooking liquid over a high heat until you have a thickish sauce. Pour it over the carved slices of beef.

If a smoother sauce is desired, strain the cooking juices, add a teaspoon of flour or arrowroot, and return the liquid to the pan, stirring over a moderate heat until it thickens and becomes creamy.

Creamed or mashed potatoes go very well with this dish.

Preparing and cooking Bastoncini di Patate (Potato Croquettes).

Granséole alla Triestina
Crabs au Gratin

4 live blue (ordinary) crabs
2 cloves garlic
1 bunch parsley
salt
freshly ground pepper
oil
juice of 1 lemon
bread crumbs

Put the crabs in a large pot of water and bring to a boil. As soon as the water boils, take out the crabs and extract all the edible portions, being careful to leave the upper shell intact (for more detailed instructions, see the recipe for Granséola alla Veneziana on page 48).

Chop the crab meat and the garlic and parsley. Mix well in a bowl with salt, pepper, oil, lemon juice, and two tablespoons of fresh bread crumbs. Return this mixture to the washed shells, sprinkle some more bread crumbs on top, and bake in a preheated oven at 325°F (170°C/mk 3) for about 20 minutes. Serve immediately.

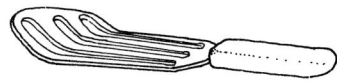

Filetti di Merluzzo
Cod Fillets with Piquant Sauce

1 onion
1 clove garlic
1 small bunch parsley
6 Tbsp/4 Tbsp/4 Tbsp oil
1 lb/1 lb/500 g cod or hake fillets
salt
1 Tbsp capers
4 anchovy fillets
1 rounded tsp all-purpose (plain) flour
*1 very small chili pepper or just the tip of
   a larger chili*
juice of 1 lemon

Mince the onion, garlic and parsley and sauté in oil for a few minutes, stirring frequently. Add the cod fillets, season with salt, and reduce the heat. Sauté, turning carefully with a spatula so that the fish cooks evenly but does not break up. Remove the cod and place in a heated covered serving dish.

Add the coarsely chopped capers to the juices in the pan. Mash the anchovies to a paste with a fork, and blend them into the liquid. Mix the flour thoroughly with ⅓ cup (3½ fl oz/1 dl) cold water and incorporate into the sauce. Lastly, add the chili pepper. Simmer for 5 minutes. Discard the chili pepper, add the lemon juice, and pour the hot sauce over the cod fillets. Serve at once.

Bastoncini di Patate
Potato Croquettes

1¾ lb/1¾ lb/800 g baking potatoes
3 egg yolks
3 Tbsp/1½ oz/40 g butter
nutmeg
*¼ c/1½ oz/3 Tbsp all-purpose (plain)
   flour*
1 egg
bread crumbs
sunflower seed oil for frying

Wash and peel the potatoes and cut into large cubes. Rinse them under running water and then boil them in plenty of lightly salted water. Drain well. Place the potatoes in a slow oven, so that they can dry out without coloring or hardening. Mash them well or put them through a ricer while still hot. Let the potatoes cool a little; then add 3 egg yolks, beating these in very briskly so they do not set before they are incorporated into the potatoes. Add the butter and transfer to a heavy pan, stirring over a low heat for a few minutes with a wooden spoon. Remove from the heat and add the nutmeg. When the potato mixture is cool enough to handle, oil your hands lightly, break off portions of potato, and roll out by hand into long, even sausage shapes about ¾ inch (2 cm) in diameter. Cut these into 1½–2 inch (4–5 cm) lengths. Roll these little cylinders in the flour, dip them in the lightly beaten egg, and coat them well with bread crumbs (toasted bread crumbs can be used for this recipe).

Fry the croquettes in plenty of hot oil (or deep fry) and when they are crisp and golden brown on the outside, remove them with a slotted spoon. Drain on paper towels and serve immediately.

Patate con la Cipolla alla Triestina
Potatoes with Onions Trieste Style

1¾ lb/1¾ lb/800 g yellow waxy potatoes
*2 oz/2 oz/50 g salt pork (parboiled 10
   minutes) or fat bacon*
2 Tbsp butter
1 large onion
salt
freshly ground pepper

This is a tasty, unpretentious dish which is very quick to prepare and goes very well with roast meats and with steaks.

Boil the potatoes, remove the skins (they should peel off easily), and slice thickly. Heat the butter and the very finely diced salt pork or fat bacon in a large frying pan, preferably a heavy cast-iron one, and cook the onion, sliced into rings, until it is translucent, moistening with a little water from time to time. Add the potatoes, season with salt and pepper, and cook over a moderately high heat, turning frequently with a spatula. Be careful that the potatoes do not break up and that the onion rings do not catch and burn on the bottom of the pan.

Frittata alle Erbe
Herb and Vegetable Frittata

*1¾ lb/1¾ lb/800 g mixed vegetables
   (spinach, leeks, Swiss chard, and
   onions)*
6 Tbsp/4 Tbsp/4 Tbsp oil
1 sprig fresh sage or a pinch of dried sage
6 fresh basil leaves
4 eggs
salt
freshly ground pepper

Wash the vegetables very thoroughly (both spinach and leeks are apt to be gritty if not well rinsed in several changes of water). Cut the leeks and onions into very thin rings, and boil the vegetables together in 1 cup salted water. When cooked, drain and squeeze out the excess water gently.

Heat the oil in a pan; add the vegetables and the very finely chopped herbs and sauté gently over a low heat for about 5 minutes, mixing well with a wooden spoon or spatula.

Beat the eggs and a pinch of salt and pepper with a fork or a wire whisk in a fairly large bowl. Add the cooked vegetables and herbs and stir well. The vegetables and herbs should be evenly blended with the eggs.

Heat a little oil in an omelet pan until very hot. Pour in the egg and vegetable batter; smooth the top surface over with a spatula; and, when the underside is crisp, turn and fry the second side until firm and golden brown. The frittata can be turned carefully with a spatula, or better still, place an oiled plate on top of the omelet pan; invert the pan so the frittata drops on to the plate; and then slide the frittata off the plate back into the pan. The inside of the frittata should be very soft, almost creamy; hence the importance of cooking over a high heat.

This frittata may be eaten hot or cold.

Kugelhupf

1 cake compressed/1 oz/25 g fresh yeast
milk
2½ c/10½ oz/300 g all-purpose (plain)
  flour
⅓ c/2 oz/50 g white seedless raisins
  (sultanas)
⅓ c/2 oz/50 g almonds
5 Tbsp/2 oz/50 g sugar
2 whole eggs
1 egg yolk
4 Tbsp/2 oz/50 g butter (melted)
grated rind of 1 lemon
salt
2–3 Tbsp rum
bread crumbs
confectioners' (icing) sugar

Dissolve the yeast in a little lukewarm milk and add enough sifted flour to form a dough of the same consistency as bread dough. Form into a dough ball and make a crisscross incision in the top of the ball and leave it, covered with a floured pastry cloth, in a warm place to rise.

Soak the raisins (sultanas) in lukewarm water in a small bowl. Blanch the almonds in nearly boiling water and skin.

When the dough has doubled in volume, sift the remaining flour on to a pastry board. Shape into a mound, form a well in the center, and blend in the sugar, the risen dough, the eggs and extra egg yolk, the melted butter, grated lemon rind, a pinch of salt, the rum and a little milk. Add more milk, a little at a time, if necessary. The dough should be very soft but not too soft or sticky to handle easily. Knead the dough for at least 30 minutes, then add the drained and dried raisins. Form into a ball, wrap in a floured pasty cloth, and leave to rise in a warm place away from drafts for at least 1 hour.

Grease a fluted ring mold or rum baba mold with butter, coat the sides with bread crumbs, line the bottom evenly with almonds and arrange the dough in the mold. The mold should be half filled. Cover with a damp cloth and let rise. Bake in a preheated oven at 350°F (180°C/mk 4) for just under 1 hour. Remove the Kugelhupf from the oven, allow it to cool, remove it from the mold and dust it liberally with confectioners' (icing) sugar.

Perseghini di Cividale
Cookie Rings

3½ c/14 oz/400 g all-purpose (plain)
  flour
1 c/9 oz/250 g butter
scant ⅓ c/2¾ oz/80 g sugar
salt
1½ tsp baking powder
confectioners' (icing) sugar

Sift the flour onto a pastry board or working surface and shape into a

mound with a well in the center. Mix in the butter melted slowly or softened over hot water, together with the sugar, a pinch of salt and the baking powder. Knead thoroughly until the dough is smooth and elastic. Break off small portions and shape into little rolls. Join up the two ends of each roll to form a ring. Sprinkle with a little confectioners' (icing) sugar and arrange on a buttered baking sheet. Bake in a preheated oven (350°F/180°C/mk 4) for 20 to 30 minutes.

Torta di Castagne
Chestnut Cake

scant 1 lb/14 oz/400 g chestnuts
⅔ c/4 oz/100 g almonds
4 eggs, separated
1 c/7 oz/200 g sugar
6 Tbsp/3 oz/85 g butter
grated rind of 1 lemon
confectioners' (icing) sugar

Boil the chestnuts in 4 cups of water for 5 minutes. Working quickly remove the hard outer casing and the thin inner skin (a pair of household gloves will be helpful). While the chestnuts are still hot, or at least warm, put them through a potato ricer or sieve into a large mixing bowl and set aside. Blanch, skin and chop the almonds very finely.

Place the 4 eggs in a bowl with the sugar and beat until frothy and increased somewhat in volume. Add the butter, which should have been gently melted or softened over warm water. Mix in the grated lemon rind, the finely chopped almonds and the sieved chestnuts. Mix with a wooden spoon until all the ingredients are well blended. Beat the egg whites until stiff but not dry and fold them in gently.

Spread the mixture evenly into a greased and lightly floured cake pan. Bake in a preheated oven at 350°F (180°C/mk 4) for about 40 minutes or until a cake tester comes out clean. Turn out onto a cake stand or dish and sprinkle with confectioners' (icing) sugar.

LIGURIA

Piccagge al Sugo
Lasagne with Veal and Tomato Sauce

2½ c/10½ oz/300 g all-purpose (plain)
    flour
3 eggs
salt
¼ c/1 oz/25 g dried mushrooms
4 Tbsp/2 oz/50 g butter
1 onion
¾ lb/10½ oz/300 g lean veal, cut in chunks
4 ripe (or canned) tomatoes
freshly ground pepper
¼ c/2 oz/50 g grated Parmesan cheese

Reserving a scant tablespoon of the flour, mix the rest with the egg and a pinch of salt to make a firm dough. Knead until smooth and elastic. Roll out into a fairly thin sheet. Leave to dry out a little (10 minutes should suffice) and then cut the sheet into the broad lasagne (about 3–4 inches/7½–10 cm wide) which are called *piccagge* in Genoese dialect. Spread the piccagge out on a pastry board or pastry cloth, spaced out so that they will not stick together.

Soak the dried mushrooms in a little hot water. Heat the butter in a large pan. Sauté the finely chopped onion and brown the veal on all sides, stirring and turning continuously over a low heat. When the veal has colored evenly, add the skinned, seeded and chopped tomatoes (if canned tomatoes are used, put through a food mill or sieve into the pan). Drain and squeeze out the mushrooms, chop them, and add them to the meat and tomatoes. Season with salt and pepper, cover and simmer for about 15 minutes. In a separate small saucepan, cook the remaining flour in a little butter until brown, stirring constantly. Add this to the veal and tomato sauce, mixing very well (you may wish to remove the pan from the heat). Add more water if necessary. Cover and simmer until the meat is tender.

Cook the piccagge in a large pan of boiling water until al dente. Drain and turn onto a heated serving platter. Pour on nearly all the sauce and top with the grated Parmesan. Carve the veal into thin slices and moisten with the remaining sauce. If escalopes are used, they will have enough sauce clinging to them and will not need this extra coating.

The meat, served with a fresh salad, makes an excellent main course to follow the first course of piccagge in sauce. However, some people prefer to serve the pasta, sauce, and meat together, topped with grated Parmesan.

Maccheroni Arrosto
Baked Macaroni

2 cloves garlic
1 sprig fresh rosemary or ¼ tsp dried
4 Tbsp/2 oz/50 g butter
scant ½ lb/7 oz/200 g lean ground
    (minced) veal or beef
1 Tbsp all-purpose (plain) flour
⅓ c/3½ fl oz/1 dl dry white wine
4 ripe (or canned) tomatoes
salt
freshly ground pepper
¾ c/7 fl oz/2 dl stock or 1 tsp meat
    extract dissolved in boiling water
¾ lb/12 oz/350 g macaroni
¼ c/2 oz/50 g grated Parmesan cheese

Chop the garlic and rosemary leaves. Heat 3 tablespoons (1½ oz/40 g) of the butter in a heavy pan and add the ground (minced) meat, stir in the flour and the chopped garlic and rosemary. Sauté over a moderate heat, mixing well. Turn up the heat, pour in the wine, and stir until the wine has evaporated.

Peel and seed the tomatoes and chop roughly (if canned tomatoes are used, put them through a food mill or sieve). Add them to the mixture in the saucepan and season with salt and pepper. Pour in the stock, stir well, cover, simmer gently until the sauce thickens and becomes creamy.

Cook the macaroni in plenty of boiling salted water, drain while still very firm (it will finish cooking in the oven). Arrange the pasta in layers in a buttered baking dish, alternating with layers of meat and tomato sauce and some grated Parmesan. Dot the top layer with small pieces of butter and bake in a moderate oven (350°F/180°C/mk 4) for about 20 minutes. Serve.

Corzetti alla Polceverasca
Corzetti Polcevera Style

2½ c/10½ oz/300 g all-purpose (plain)
    flour
3 eggs
salt
1 onion
¾ lb/10½ oz/300 g lean veal or beef
    (round (topside) or rump)
4 Tbsp/2 oz/50 g butter
4 ripe (or canned) tomatoes
freshly ground pepper
¾ c/7 fl oz/2 dl stock or 1 tsp meat
    extract dissolved in boiling water
¼ c/2 oz/50 g grated Parmesan cheese

Work the sifted flour, eggs, and a pinch of salt together to form a firm dough; knead until smooth and pliable. Instead of rolling the dough into a thin sheet as for lasagne, divide the dough into small hazelnut-sized pieces, roll into balls, and pinch each one between the thumbs and forefingers to give it the shape of a filled-in figure-eight. These *corzetti* or "figure-eights" are great Genoese favorites and a specialty of the region. Leave the pasta spread out on a pastry cloth to dry and prepare the meat sauce.

Chop the onion finely and dice the meat into very small pieces. Sauté the meat and onion for 5 minutes in the butter. Blanch, skin, and chop the tomatoes (if canned tomatoes are used, put them through a food mill or sieve). Add them to the meat and onion, season with salt and pepper, cover, and simmer gently for 45 minutes to 1 hour, adding a little stock to moisten whenever necessary. The very small pieces of veal or beef should be so tender that they

Opposite: Manzo Brasato al Barolo (Beef Braised in Barolo Wine) and Agnolotti alla Piemontese (Piedmontese Stuffed Pasta).

Overleaf: One of Lombardy's most famous dishes, Ossobuco alla Milanese (Veal Shanks Milanese), served on a bed of Risotto alla Milanese.

almost dissolve into the sauce. Allow the sauce to cool slightly; then liquify it in a blender or force it through a sieve. Return the sauce to a very low heat to keep warm while the pasta is cooking.

Cook the corzetti in a large pan of boiling, salted water until al dente. Transfer them to a heated serving dish, mix in the grated Parmesan, and top with the meat sauce.

This pasta is similar to other home-made egg pasta, and the name corzetti is also used for the rectangles and disks of egg pasta which are made in special molds.

Gasse al Sugo
Gasse with Veal and Tomato Sauce

2¼ c/10½ oz/300 g all-purpose (plain) flour
3 eggs
1 onion
4 Tbsp/2 oz/50 g butter
¾ lb/12 oz/350 g lean veal, cut in chunks
4 ripe (or canned) tomatoes
½ c/1 oz/25 g dried mushrooms
¼ c/2 oz/50 g grated Parmesan cheese
salt
freshly ground pepper

The main difference between this dish and Piccagge al Sugo (page 68) is the shape of the pasta. Instead of cutting the rolled out sheet of pasta dough into large lasagne, the rectangular piccagge, it must be cut into strips just under ½ inch (1 cm) wide and about 4 inches (10 cm) long. The two ends of these strips are then pressed firmly together to form a large loop or ring—*gasse* means loops in Genoese dialect. Work quickly so that the dough is still moist enough for the two ends to stick together and not come apart when cooked (a little beaten egg or milk can be used if necessary to secure them).

Follow the directions for Piccagge al Sugo, since the method of preparation is exactly the same.

Vermicelli con Spinaci
Baked Spinach and Noodles

1 lb/1 lb/500 g spinach
4 anchovy fillets
1 clove garlic
1 small bunch parsley
6 Tbsp/4 Tbsp/4 Tbsp olive oil
½ c/1 oz/25 g finely chopped pine nuts
scant 1 lb/14 oz/400 g vermicelli

Boil the well washed spinach in a little salted water and drain, reserving the cooking liquid. Chop the anchovies finely with the garlic, the parsley, and the spinach. Sauté this mixture for 2 to 3 minutes in the olive oil in a small pan. Add the chopped pine nuts and cook for a few minutes longer, pouring in a little of the spinach water so that the sauce is not too thick.

Boil the vermicelli in lightly salted water until half cooked. Drain well and transfer to a shallow baking dish (an ovenproof earthenware lasagne dish is ideal). Pour the sauce over the noodles and bake in a hot oven (400°F/200°C/mk 6) for about 15 minutes. The noodles will finish cooking in the sauce and absorb its flavor. Grated Parmesan is not served with this dish.

Trofie al Pesto
Trofie with Pesto

3 c/12 oz/350 g all-purpose (plain) flour
1 clove garlic
1 Tbsp lightly toasted pine nuts
4 Tbsp fresh basil leaves
6 Tbsp/4 Tbsp/4 Tbsp olive oil
¼ c/2 oz/50 g grated Parmesan and Pecorino cheese
salt

Work together the flour, a pinch of salt and enough water to form a firm dough. Knead this stiff dough very thoroughly. Break off small pieces (about the size of a cherry) and roll with the palm of the hand into short cylindrical shapes with tapering ends. Wind each length into a

spiral around the handle of a wooden spoon. Boil these *trofie* in plenty of salted water for a minute or two at most if cooked right away—test after about 30 seconds—and drain when al dente. Cover with pesto sauce (see Pesto alla Genovese, page 77).

Lasagne al Sugo
Lasagne with Meat and Tomato Sauce

2½ c/10½ oz/300 g all-purpose (plain) flour
3 eggs
salt
1 onion
1 stalk celery
1 small carrot
1 small bunch parsley
4 Tbsp/2 oz/50 g butter
scant 1 lb/14 oz/400 g lean veal or very tender beef
⅓ c/3½ fl oz/1 dl dry white wine
4 ripe (or canned) tomatoes
freshly ground pepper
¾ c/7 fl oz/2 dl meat stock (or 1 tsp meat extract dissolved in boiling water)
¼ c/2 oz/50 g grated Parmesan cheese

Reserve 1 tablespoon of the flour for later use. Work the rest of the flour, the eggs and a pinch of salt together to form a smooth, pliable dough. Roll out into a thin sheet and cut into squares measuring 2–2½ inches (5–6 cm) (in Genoa this particular shape of pasta is known as *lasagne*).

Chop the onion, celery, carrot, and parsley very finely and sauté gently in the butter with the finely diced veal or beef for about 5 to 6 minutes, or until the onion is translucent. Pour in the wine, turn up the heat, and cook uncovered until the wine has evaporated.

Blanch and peel the tomatoes, remove the seeds, and chop coarsely (if canned tomatoes are used, put them through a food mill or sieve). Add them to the meat and vegetable mixture. Season with salt and pepper, cover tightly, and simmer for about 15 minutes. Brown the reserved tablespoon of flour in a stainless steel or aluminum pan, mixing constantly with a wooden spoon until it turns a golden brown color (be careful not to let it burn). Remove it from the heat and mix in the hot meat stock gradually, stirring briskly and continuously. Add to the meat and vegetable sauce. Stir in well, cover the saucepan and simmer until the meat is very tender, and the sauce has thickened.

Cook the lasagne in plenty of salted water until tender but still firm. Place a layer of lasagne in a fairly deep preheated serving dish, cover with a layer of the sauce, and sprinkle with grated Parmesan cheese. Continue to alternate the layers in this manner until all the ingredients have been used. Serve immediately.

Minestrone col Pesto
Minestrone with Pesto

scant ½ lb/7 oz/200 g fresh, canned, or
  dried borlotti beans, or white navy
  (haricot) beans
2 potatoes, diced
2 ripe tomatoes, skinned and seeded
2 carrots, diced small
2 small zucchini (courgettes)
1 onion, thinly sliced
1 leek, cut into small rings
3 stalks celery, diced
1 small bunch borage (optional)
½ c/5 oz/150 g soup pasta (pennette, or
  fresh tagliatelle)
6 Tbsp/4 Tbsp/4 Tbsp oil
3 Tbsp/2 Tbsp/2 Tbsp grated Parmesan
  cheese
2 Tbsp/1 Tbsp/1 Tbsp grated Pecorino
  cheese
1 Tbsp pesto (see Pesto alla Genovese,
  page 77)
salt

Shell the beans or, if dried beans are used, soak them overnight in cold water. Wash, trim, and prepare the vegetables. Bring about 2 quarts (3½ pt/2 liters) of water to a boil in a fireproof earthenware or heavy cast-iron cooking pot, add salt and the prepared vegetables together with 3 tablespoons (2 Tbsp/2 Tbsp) oil. Cover and simmer until the

soup has reduced and thickened considerably but do not overcook the vegetables. If borage is used, chop the leaves and add them about half way through cooking the vegetables—they will add a subtle yet distinctive flavor.

When the vegetables are almost done, add the pasta and continue cooking. Dilute the pesto sauce in about ⅓ cup (3½ oz/1 dl) water and stir into the soup just before removing it from the heat. Before serving, add 3 tablespoons (2 Tbsp/2 Tbsp) oil and the grated Parmesan and Pecorino cheeses. (For a milder flavor, use all Parmesan.)

Spaghettini al Basilico Tritato
Spaghettini with Basil and Tomato Sauce

1 lb/1 lb/500 g fresh (or canned)
  tomatoes
4 Tbsp/2 oz/50 g butter
1 Tbsp finely chopped onion
salt
freshly ground pepper
¾ lb/¾ lb/350 g spaghettini (thin
  spaghetti)
1 bunch fresh basil leaves, finely chopped
3 Tbsp/1 oz/25 g grated Parmesan
  cheese

Cut or simply tear the tomatoes in half by hand; place in a saucepan and simmer for about 30 minutes (if canned tomatoes are used the entire contents of the can may be emptied into the saucepan). When they are done, put them through a food mill or sieve and set aside. Melt the butter in a small heavy pan and, when it starts to foam, add the finely chopped onion and cook until the onion shrinks and starts to become transparent. Pour in the tomatoes, season with salt and pepper, and simmer over a moderate heat for approximately 10 minutes.

Bring a large pan of salted water to a boil and cook the spaghetti until it is al dente. When it is done, transfer it to a heated serving dish, dot with small pieces of butter, and sprinkle with the

chopped basil and half the grated Parmesan cheese. Cover with the tomato sauce, mix well, and serve. Serve additional Parmesan separately.

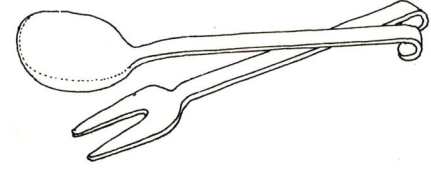

Pansoòti
Ravioli with Walnut Sauce

5 eggs
½ lb/8 oz/225 g beet greens, Swiss chard,
  or spinach
3 c/¾ lb/350 g all-purpose (plain) flour
2 Tbsp/1 Tbsp/1 Tbsp dry wine
½ c/4 oz/100 g grated Parmesan cheese
salt
Salsa di Noci (see recipe, page 77)

Hard-boil 2 eggs. Boil the beet greens or other greens in salted water, drain well when tender, and chop finely. Work the flour, the remaining 3 eggs, the wine, and a pinch of salt together on a pastry board or in a mixing bowl and leave covered with a pastry cloth to rest.

Mash the hard-boiled eggs with a fork and blend in the chopped greens, half the grated cheese, and a pinch of salt.

Roll the dough out into a thin sheet and cut into pieces measuring about 3 inches (8 cm) square. Then cut each of these squares in half diagonally to form two triangles of equal dimensions. Place a small portion of stuffing in the very middle of each triangle and fold the triangles in half to enclose the filling in a small, bulging triangular packet, (Pansoòti means "pot-bellied" in dialect). Be careful, however, not to overfill the ravioli and be sure to press the edges very firmly together so that they do not separate when boiled. Cook the pansoòti in a very large pan of gently boiling salted water (they will not take long if cooked immediately after being made), drain, turn into a warmed earthenware dish, and top with the walnut sauce and the remaining grated Parmesan.

Lasagne al Sugo di Funghi
Lasagne with Mushroom Sauce

4 large tomatoes
scant ¼ lb/7 oz/200 g fresh cèpes,
    (boletus edulis), or field mushrooms
    or
    scant ½ lb/7 oz/200 g large cultivated
    mushrooms + 1–2 Tbsp imported dried
    mushrooms
1 Tbsp oil
½ onion
1 clove garlic
1 small bunch parsley
salt
freshly ground pepper
¾ lb/¾ lb/350 g commercial lasagne
3 Tbsp/1½ oz/40 g butter
¼ c/2 oz/50 g grated Parmesan cheese

Blanch and peel the tomatoes; then open them up by hand and remove the seeds and excess watery juice. Clean the mushrooms. If field mushrooms are used, simply wipe with a damp cloth; if fresh cèpes are available, wash, scrape and trim them very thoroughly as they are often gritty. Dried mushrooms should be softened in warm water for 20 minutes (they add flavor to cultivated mushrooms.) Slice the mushrooms. Heat the oil in a pan and add the finely chopped onion, garlic, and parsley, and the tomatoes cut into thin strips. Add the mushrooms and season. Cover and simmer gently for up to 30 minutes or until the juices reduce and become creamy.

Bring a large pan of salted water to a boil and cook the lasagne until tender but firm. Drain, turn into a heated serving dish, and dot with small pieces of butter. Top with the mushroom sauce and sprinkle with grated Parmesan cheese.

Pesto, or Basil Sauce, is made with fresh basil leaves, olive oil, garlic and Pecorino and Parmesan cheese. At the lower right is an illustration of trenette.

Trenette al Pesto
Trenette with Pesto

¼ c/3 Tbsp fresh basil leaves
1 Tbsp lightly toasted pine nuts
1 clove garlic
¼ c/2 oz/50 g grated Parmesan and
    Pecorino cheese
4 Tbsp olive oil
1 medium-sized potato
¾ lb/¾ lb/350 g trenette or linguine

Using a pestle and mortar (preferably a marble mortar) pound the basil leaves together with the pine nuts and the garlic into a paste (this can be done in a blender, but the result is not always totally satisfactory). Turn the paste into a bowl and add the grated Pecorino and Parmesan cheese, mixing well with a wooden spoon and adding the oil a very little at a time. Allow the pesto sauce to stand for at least one hour.

Boil the peeled and diced potato in plenty of salted, boiling water, and, when it is half-cooked, add the *trenette* (long, flat ribbon noodles; the Genoese variety are made from whole-wheat (wholemeal) flour and take longer to cook. Drain while they are still very al dente, reserving a small quantity of the cooking liquid. Turn into a preheated serving dish, and top with the pesto sauce diluted with a little of the reserved hot liquid.

Ravioli ai Funghi
Ravioli with Mushrooms

scant 1 lb/14 oz/400 g fresh spinach
4 Tbsp/2 oz/50 g butter
3 c/¾ lb/350 g all-purpose (plain) flour
salt
6 eggs
1 c/7 oz/200 g very fresh ricotta cheese
4 oz/4 oz/100 g cooked ham
¼ c/2 oz/50 g grated Parmesan cheese
mushroom sauce (see the recipe for
    Lasagne al Sugo di Funghi on page 73
    or for Funghi Trifolati on page 27

Another method of preparing homemade ravioli: A serrated pastry wheel is used to cut out the squares of stuffed pasta.

Steam the spinach and, when it is tender, squeeze out all excess moisture and put it through a sieve or food mill. Return to a gentle heat until absolutely dry.

Make an egg pasta dough with the sifted flour, a little salt, 4 eggs, and the spinach purée. Knead the dough well and then roll out into a thin sheet.
Filling:

Mix the ricotta cheese with 2 eggs, the very finely ground (minced) ham, the grated Parmesan cheese, and a pinch of salt.

Using a fluted pastry cutting wheel, cut the sheet of dough into 2½-inch (6 cm) squares and place a small heap of filling in the center of half the squares. Place the other squares on top of the stuffing and press the edges together. Cook the ravioli in plenty of salted water and drain well when tender. Sprinkle with melted butter and grated Parmesan cheese, mix very gently, and top with the mushroom sauce. Serve more grated Parmesan cheese separately.

Riso col Preboggión
Rice with Mixed Herbs and Pesto

2 bunches mixed herbs (see instructions)
scant ½ lb/7 oz/200 g Arborio rice
3 Tbsp/2 Tbsp/2 Tbsp oil
3 Tbsp/2 Tbsp/2 Tbsp pesto sauce (see
    Pesto alla Genovese, page 77)
½ tsp meat extract
salt

Preboggión are bunches of edible wild herbs and plants found in the country-side surrounding Genoa and which are sold in the markets. As a substitute, spinach with a mixture of such fresh herbs as parsley, marjoram, basil, chervil, mint, or savory can be used.

Wash the spinach and herbs carefully. Boil them, tied in bunches, in 1½ quarts (3 pt/1½ liters) salted water. When they are nearly cooked, add the rice and cook until just tender. Remove spinach and herbs from the water before adding the rice and have on hand an additional quantity of fresh, chopped herbs to sprinkle onto the rice when it is done. Just before removing the rice from the heat, add the oil and 3 tablespoons (2 Tbsp/2 Tbsp) pesto sauce diluted in a little hot stock made with the meat extract and boiling water. Add salt to taste, mix well, and serve accompanied by a small bowl of grated Parmesan cheese.

Gnocchi di Castagne
Chestnut Gnocchi

¾ lb/¾ lb/350 g chestnut flour
2½ c generous/10½ oz/300 g all-purpose
    (plain) flour
1 Tbsp shelled walnuts
1 generous Tbsp pine nuts
2 cloves garlic
1 small bunch parsley
⅓ c/3½ fl oz/1 dl oil
⅓ c/3 oz/80 g Parmesan cheese

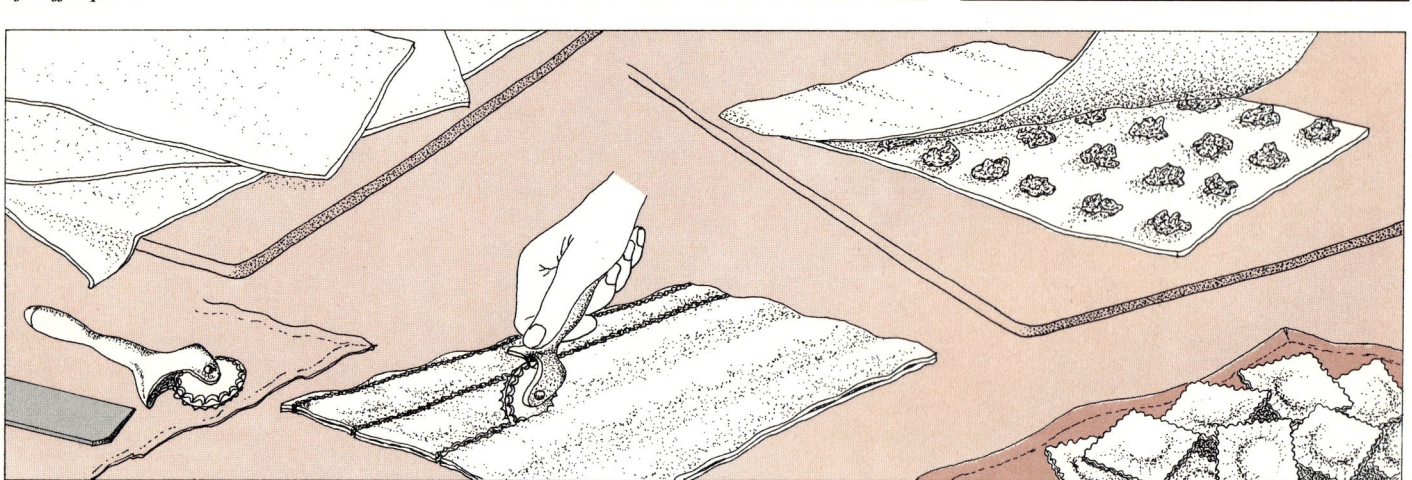

Sift the two types of flour together and add enough water to form a soft dough. Knead well until the dough is smooth and pliable. Divide the dough into portions roughly the size of small oranges and roll these with the palms of the hands against the board or working surface into long rolls about the thickness of a finger. Cut these long rolls of dough into 1 inch ($2\frac{1}{2}$ cm) lengths and form into gnocchi by pressing against the concave surface of a grater or the tines of a fork (see illustration page 55). Space them out well on a pastry cloth or board so they do not stick to each other.

Blanch the walnuts in boiling water for 3 to 4 minutes to loosen the thin, inner skins and remove these. Toast the pine nuts lightly in the oven. Place the walnuts and the pine nuts in a mortar and pound well. Sauté the finely chopped garlic and parsley in 4 tablespoons oil. Add the pounded walnuts and pine nuts and cook for 2 to 3 minutes, stirring constantly. Beat the remainder of the oil with enough boiling water to produce a smooth, creamy liquid. Remove sautéed mixture from heat and add the oil and water.

Cook the gnocchi in plenty of boiling, salted water (they will take about 7 to 8 minutes). Remove them with a slotted spoon as they rise and transfer onto heated individual plates. Cover each with some sauce and grated Parmesan.

Torta Pasqualina

Genoese Easter Pie

5 c/$1\frac{1}{4}$ lb/600 g all-purpose (plain) flour
$\frac{1}{2}$ c/6 Tbsp/6 Tbsp oil
2 Tbsp/1 oz/25 g butter
1 lb/1 lb/500 g very small artichokes or spinach
juice of $\frac{1}{2}$ lemon
$\frac{1}{2}$ onion
$\frac{1}{4}$ c/2 oz/50 g grated Parmesan cheese
$1\frac{1}{2}$ c/$10\frac{1}{2}$ oz/300 g fresh ricotta cheese
4 eggs
$\frac{1}{3}$ c/$3\frac{1}{2}$ fl oz/1 dl milk
marjoram (preferably fresh)
salt
freshly ground pepper

Sift the flour onto a pastry board or smooth working surface. Form into a mound and make a well in the center. Place in it $\frac{1}{4}$ cup (2 fl oz/60 ml) oil and a generous pinch of salt. Work gradually into the flour, adding water, if necessary. Knead well until smooth. Allow the dough to rest for about 30 minutes in a warm bowl covered with a cloth. Then divide it into 6 or 7 equal portions, form these into balls, place them on a lightly floured cloth, and cover them with a dampened cloth. Leave for 15 minutes.

Wash the vegetables in lightly salted water, trim and pick over, and rinse well. If artichokes are used, remove outer leaves, drop into water acidulated with juice of $\frac{1}{2}$ lemon to prevent their discoloring. Sauté the finely chopped onion together with the chopped vegetables in the remaining oil (if artichokes are used, slice them fairly thinly vertically). Season with salt and cook over a moderate heat for a few minutes, stirring well. Place the ricotta cheese in a mixing bowl, add a pinch of salt and the milk, and blend together thoroughly.

Roll the first ball into a circle large enough to line and overhang the inside of an oiled deep springform (spring-release) cake tin. Brush this first sheet of dough very lightly with oil. Roll out the second dough ball into a circle just large enough to fit snugly inside the pan, and brush it lightly with oil, dotting very small pieces of butter at intervals near the edges. Follow this with a third and fourth layer, oiling the third but not the fourth layer. Spread the vegetables gently and evenly over the fourth layer. Roll out a fifth circle of dough and place it on top of the vegetables. Spread the ricotta on this layer thickly. Make four evenly spaced oval wells in the ricotta, place a very small piece of butter in each and break each of the four eggs neatly into its own well. Season each egg with a little salt and pepper, chopped marjoram, and grated Parmesan. Cover with the remaining circle or circles of dough, brushing each layer with oil. Fold the overlap from the bottom layer over the edges of the top layer, thus sealing it. Oil and prick the top layer. Bake in a preheated oven (about 400°F/200°C/mk 6) for 45 minutes.

Tortino di Alici alla Vernazzana

Anchovy Mold

1 lb/1 lb/500 g fresh anchovies or 2 cans of anchovy fillets
1 lb/1 lb/500 g yellow, waxy potatoes
$\frac{1}{2}$ onion
1 clove garlic
1 small bunch parsley
4–5 fresh basil leaves
2 ripe (or canned) tomatoes
3 Tbsp oil
salt
freshly ground pepper

Split anchovies and remove backbones and heads. Peel the potatoes and slice thinly. Chop the onion, garlic, parsley, and basil very finely. Peel and chop the tomatoes. Oil a casserole and line the bottom with a layer of potato slices; cover with a layer of anchovy fillets, sprinkle with a little of the chopped herb mixture, and season with salt and pepper. Continue layering in this way until all the ingredients are used up, ending with a layer of potato slices: brush these with plenty of oil and bake in a hot oven (400°F/200°C/mk 6) for about 30 minutes. Unmold and serve immediately.

Bagnùm

Quick Fish Soup

$1\frac{3}{4}$ lb/$1\frac{3}{4}$ lb/800 g fresh anchovies or 3 cans of anchovy fillets
$\frac{1}{2}$ onion
2 cloves garlic
1 small bunch parsley
3 Tbsp oil
$\frac{1}{4}$ c/3 Tbsp/3 Tbsp dry white wine
1 lb/1 lb/500 g ripe tomatoes
salt
freshly ground pepper
8 slices of stale bread
1 Tbsp butter

Split anchovies and remove backbones and heads.

Fry the finely chopped onion, garlic, and parsley gently in the oil. When the onion is just beginning to color, pour in the wine, turn up the heat, and allow the wine to evaporate. Reduce the heat, add the peeled, seeded, and chopped tomatoes and mix well. Season to taste and simmer over a low heat for about 15 minutes. Pour in approximately 2 cups ($\frac{3}{4}$ pt/$\frac{1}{2}$ liter) of water and, when the liquid has come to a boil again, add the anchovies. Simmer gently for 15 to 20 minutes.

While the anchovies are cooking, fry the slices of stale bread in the butter until golden brown. Place two slices in each soup plate and pour the fish soup over them.

Pesce Marinato
Marinated Fish

$1\frac{1}{4}$ lb/$1\frac{1}{4}$ lb/600 g fresh fish selected according to availability (see instructions)
oil
1 clove garlic
1 sprig fresh rosemary or a pinch of dried rosemary
4 c/$1\frac{3}{4}$ pt/1 l vinegar
salt

In Italy the fish would include anchovies, freshwater or sea eels, sardines, whiting, and mackerel.

Clean and trim the fish. Deep fry. When well browned, place on paper towels to drain and sprinkle with salt.

Gently fry the garlic and rosemary in 2 or 3 tablespoons of oil for 2 to 3 minutes in a large, heavy pan (do not use aluminum). Pour in the vinegar, add a pinch of salt, bring to a boil, and then simmer for 2 minutes. Remove the pan from the heat, allow to cool, and then strain the liquid. Place the fish in an earthenware bowl and pour the cooled marinade over them.

The fish are most flavorful if they are allowed to marinate for 24 hours, and they keep very well for several days in a hermetically sealed jar stored in a cool place.

Frittata di Gianchetti
Frittata with Roe

$\frac{3}{4}$ lb/$\frac{3}{4}$ lb/350 g hard roe (anchovy, sardine, cod, or shad)
4 very fresh eggs
salt
freshly ground pepper
1 clove garlic
1 small bunch parsley
oil
3 Tbsp/2 Tbsp/2 Tbsp grated Parmesan cheese

Remove the outside membrane and any small blood vessels from the roe but do not wash. Beat the eggs very well with a wire whisk; season with pepper and salt. Stir in the roe and the very finely chopped garlic and parsley. Mix well and pour into a large omelet pan or frying pan containing enough hot oil to fry the frittata. When the mixture has set on the bottom, turn and cook the other side, taking care not to overcook. The inside of the frittata should still be creamy. Serve the minute the frittata is ready.

Minestra di Gianchetti
Fish Soup with Roe

1 qt/$1\frac{3}{4}$ pt/1 l strained fish fumet or stock made from fish trimmings or from the court bouillon in which a fish has been poached
$\frac{1}{2}$ lb/$\frac{1}{2}$ lb/225 g shelled fresh (or frozen) peas
1 c/7 oz/200 g hard roe (anchovy, sardine, cod, or shad)
generous $\frac{1}{4}$ lb/5 oz/150 g vermicelli
1 egg

A fish fumet, the seasoned water in which fish (or fish trimmings) have been poached, is usually made with a piece of onion, carrot, celery, a small bay leaf, parsley, and a little salt. In this case a clove of garlic can be added for a more robust taste.

Strain the fish fumet, bring it to a boil,

and cook the peas until just tender, adding a little more salt if necessary. Remove the membrane from the hard roe carefully but do not wash it. Break the egg into a bowl and beat with a fork. Add the vermicelli to the peas and fish liquid and when it is almost done, add the roe. Reduce the heat and stir in the beaten egg briskly. Serve immediately.

Buridda (Pesce in Tocchetto)
Genoese Fish Stew

$\frac{1}{4}$ c/1 oz/25 g dried mushrooms
$1\frac{1}{4}$ lb/$1\frac{1}{4}$ lb/600 g assorted very fresh fish such as conger eel, squid or cuttlefish, octopus, mackerel, and angler or frogfish
1 clove garlic
1 small carrot
1 stalk celery
2 anchovy fillets
3 Tbsp oil
3 ripe tomatoes
$1\frac{1}{2}$ tsp all-purpose (plain) flour
1 small bunch parsley
4–8 thick slices of toasted bread

The fish which gives this dish its characteristic flavor in Italy and is also used in French fish soups is the angler or frogfish, an exceedingly ugly fish of which only the tail is eaten but this is delicious and gives a gelatinous consistency.

Soak the dried mushrooms in lukewarm water for about 20 minutes. Clean and trim the fish as necessary and cut into 2 inch (5 cm) slices. Chop the garlic, carrot, and celery very finely. Mash the anchovy and reduce to a paste with the oil in a heavy pan over a low heat. Add the garlic, carrot, and celery and sauté for a few minutes, increasing the heat slightly, stirring continuously. Mix in the drained and chopped mushrooms, the peeled, seeded, and chopped tomatoes and the flour, mixed with 1 to 2 tablespoons of cold water. Simmer over a low heat, shaking the pan from side to side so that the fish does not stick to the bottom. Shortly before the fish is cooked, add the chopped parsley. Serve very hot with slices of bread fried in butter.

Rane Fritte
Fried Frogs' Legs

½ onion
1 small bunch parsley
pinch oregano
salt
freshly ground pepper
1 c/½ pt/¼ l vinegar
about ¾ lb/about ¾ lb/300–400 g frogs'
    legs, skinned
3 Tbsp/2 Tbsp/2 Tbsp all-purpose
    (plain) flour

Mix the coarsely chopped onion and parsley, the oregano, the salt and pepper and the vinegar to make a marinade. Pour over the frogs' legs and leave to marinate for about 2 hours.

Drain the frogs' legs, coat lightly with flour and fry in hot oil. Leave to drain briefly on paper towels and serve hot. The frogs' legs should be crisp on the outside but moist and tender inside.

Carciofi in Fricassea
Artichoke Fricassee

6 very young, tender artichokes
juice of 1 lemon
2 Tbsp/2 oz/50 g butter
1 clove garlic
1 small bunch parsley
salt
freshly ground pepper
2 egg yolks
¼ c/2 oz/50 g grated Parmesan cheese

Wash the artichokes and trim off the outer leaves and the stems. Slice them vertically into quarters and drop them immediately into a pan of cold water acidulated with half the lemon juice to prevent discoloration.

Melt the butter in a saucepan. Drain and dry the artichoke portions and sauté them, adding the finely chopped garlic and parsley. Moisten with approximately ⅔ cup (¼ pt/2 dl) water, season with salt and pepper, and cover tightly. Cook over a low heat, adding a little more water whenever necessary.

Meanwhile, prepare the egg mixture which will give the sauce more body and flavor: beat the egg yolks with a tablespoon of water, the grated Parmesan, the remaining lemon juice, and a pinch of salt. Remove the pan containing the artichokes from the heat, leave it for a few minutes to cool, and pour in the egg mixture, stirring continuously to prevent the eggs from curdling. The chances of this happening can be lessened by beating 1 to 2 tablespoons of the warm liquid from the artichokes into the egg mixture before adding it to the artichokes in the saucepan.

Broccoli Strascinati
Cauliflower Tossed in Anchovy Dressing

4 anchovy fillets
2 medium-sized cauliflowers
3 Tbsp oil
freshly ground pepper

At one time, broccoli strascinati was often eaten as a main dish. Today it provides an interesting accompaniment for boiled meat or poultry and is very quick and easy to prepare. The Italian word broccoli means "cauliflower" in some regions of Italy and "broccoli" as we understand it in others. This recipe could also be used with the latter.

Drain any excess oil from the anchovy fillets and pat dry with paper towels. Wash the cauliflowers and cut each one into quarters. Cook the cauliflower pieces in boiling salted water until just tender but still slightly crisp. Drain. Mash the anchovy fillets with a fork into the oil in a fairly large skillet or pan and cook over a low heat until they blend into a paste. Add the cauliflower and turn gently in the anchovy mixture until well coated. Season with pepper.

Salsa di Noci
Walnut Sauce

½ c/2 oz/50 g pine nuts
scant ½ lb/7 oz/200 g shelled walnuts
½ clove garlic
1 small bunch parsley
salt
½ c/4 oz/100 g very fresh ricotta cheese
3 Tbsp oil

Walnut sauce is a very typical dish of Liguria, and the Genoese use it on their pansoòti (ravioli) (recipe on page 72).

Toast the pine nuts in the oven until they turn a golden color. Blanch the walnuts in boiling water and remove their thin, papery inner skins. Put them in a blender with the pine nuts, the garlic, the chopped parsley and a pinch of salt and blend into a smooth paste; or pound these ingredients to a paste with a mortar and pestle. Transfer to a mixing bowl.

Mix the ricotta cheese with 3–4 tablespoons (2–3 Tbsp/2–3 Tbsp) of water and then add to the nut paste in the bowl, stirring continuously; pour in the oil gradually, mixing well so that the sauce is completely mixed.

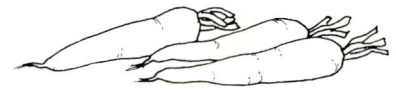

Pesto alla Genovese
Genoese Pesto

1 bunch of fresh basil (about 30 young
    leaves) picked before the basil flowers
1 Tbsp toasted pine nuts
2 cloves garlic
3 Tbsp olive oil
1 Tbsp grated Parmesan cheese
1 Tbsp grated Pecorino cheese
salt (preferably sea salt)

Whenever Parmesan cheese is included in the list of ingredients in these recipes, it cannot be stressed too strongly how important it is to buy the best Parmesan cheese available and to grate it only just before it is needed. The difference between freshly grated Parmesan and the packaged variety is so great that if one had only tasted the latter, one would wonder why it is so widely used.

Wipe the basil leaves but do not wash them. Pound them with the toasted pine nuts in a mortar (purists use a marble one), together with the garlic and sea salt, crushing all the ingredients against the sides of the mortar with the pestle as well as pounding them, so that they form a homogenous paste. Add the two types of grated cheese a little at a time (if a milder flavor is preferred, use 2 tablespoons of grated Parmesan and no Pecorino).

Transfer the paste to a bowl and add the oil a little at a time, stirring with a wooden spoon to blend thoroughly. The sauce should be creamy in texture and have an attractive bright green color. It goes with pasta extremely well (see page 73 for the classic Genoese dish Trenette al Pesto) and is an important ingredient used to enhance the flavor and appearance of soups and other dishes.

Canestrelli
"Sea Urchin" Cookies

1⅓ c/9 oz/250 g almonds
¾ c/6 oz/175 g sugar
a little orange flower water
1 Tbsp flavored sugar syrup made from
    1 c (7 oz/200 g) granulated sugar, ¾ c
    (7 fl oz/2 dl) water, and ¼ c (2 fl oz/
    60 ml) liqueur of your choice slowly
    brought to a boil and then allowed to
    boil steadily for 10 minutes
1 tsp butter
colored decorating sugar (assorted
    dragées)

Blanch and skin the almonds and put through a blender or pound well in a mortar. Place the sugar and the ground almonds in a bowl and mix in just enough orange blossom water with a wooden spoon to form a smooth, firm paste.

Grease a baking sheet with butter, shape the paste into small rings, and arrange on the baking sheet properly spaced out. It is preferable to use an aluminum baking sheet with a permanently shiny surface and dulled bottom to produce even browning. Place the baking sheet on the top shelf of the oven. After about 15 minutes, or when the cookies are a good golden-brown color, remove them from the oven, brush them with the syrup and scatter decorative sugar (assorted dragées) or crushed pralines over them.

Pandolce
Genoese Sweet Bread

2 envelopes active dry or 1 cake
    compressed yeast/1 oz/25 g fresh yeast
4 c + 2 Tbsp/1 lb/500 g all-purpose
    (plain) flour
7 Tbsp/4 oz/100 g butter
generous ½ c/4½ oz/125 g sugar
1 c/4 oz/100 g pine nuts
1 c/4 oz/100 g candied citron or other
    citrus peel
¾ c/4 oz/100 g seedless white raisins
    (sultanas)
salt

Dissolve the yeast in a little lukewarm water and then mix and work it with 1 cup (4 oz/100 g) of the sifted flour. Shape into a ball, cover with a pastry cloth and leave to rise in a warm place for at least 12 hours. After this time the dough ball will have doubled in bulk and can be worked together with the rest of the sifted flour, the butter, the sugar, the pine nuts, the coarsely chopped citron peel, the previously soaked, softened, and well drained raisins (sultanas), and a pinch of salt. Knead until the dough is smooth in consistency. Leave to rise for another 4 hours. Shape into a round cake and place on a buttered and lightly floured baking sheet. Make a crisscross incision or three incisions in the form of a triangle on top and bake in a moderate oven (375°F/190°C/mk 5) for just over an hour or until a cake tester or skewer inserted into the middle comes out clean. Leave to cool before serving.

Pasta Genovese
Génoise (Genoese Sponge)

1 c/7 oz/200 g sugar
6 eggs
grated rind of 1 lemon or 2 Tbsp liqueur
    of your choice
1⅓ c/5 oz/150 g cake flour (very fine
    flour)
6 Tbsp/2¾ oz/80 g butter, melted over hot
    water

It is particularly important not to use any utensils or equipment made of aluminum when making this cake, as aluminum colors the mixture, turning it gray, through a chemical reaction. It is also important to stir the mixture as little as possible once the butter has been added.

Place the sugar and eggs in a deep bowl or the top of a double boiler over hot (but not boiling) water. (An unlined copper bowl or a ceramic, copper-clad double boiler are preferable.) Beat with a wire whisk until the mixture is pale and lemon colored and greatly increased in volume and the consistency is light and foamy. Remove from the heat. Continue beating until the mixture is cool. At this point, add the grated lemon rind or liqueur. Gradually stir in the flour. Blending it in well but do not beat. Add the melted butter. Stir it in a teaspoon at a time and mix only until no trace of it is visible (mix as little as possible). The batter should be of a smooth and even consistency. Pour at once into a buttered and lightly floured Génoise pan or other shallow baking pan and bake in a moderate oven (350°F/180°C/mk 4) for about 30 minutes. A Génoise pan is round with sloping sides 1½–2 inches (4–5 cm) deep. The cake is done when it is a pale golden brown and springs back when pressed lightly with the fingertips. Turn out onto a cake rack.

The liqueur used to flavor this cake in the past was liquore del perfetto amore, the "liqueur of perfect love," so called because according to custom young brides used to make it at home after their weddings.

EMILIA-ROMAGNA

PIACENZA

PARMA

REGGIO
NELL'EMILIA

MODENA

FERRARA

BOLOGNA

RAVENNA

FORLÌ

Lasagne Verdi
Spinach Lasagne

scant ½ lb/7 oz/200 g spinach
2¾ c/11½ oz/325 g all-purpose (plain) flour
2 eggs
½ c + 1 Tbsp/4½ oz/120 g butter
2¼ c/18 fl oz/½ l milk
salt
freshly ground white pepper
1 pinch ground nutmeg (optional)
1 small onion
1 stalk celery
½ carrot
½ c/4 oz/100 g finely ground (minced) lean beef and veal
¼ c/2 oz/50 g fat and lean prosciutto (raw ham)
½ c/4 oz/100 g grated Parmesan cheese

Wash the spinach thoroughly, boil it in a little lightly salted water, drain very well, chop finely, and put through a food processor or push through a sieve. Mix with 2½ cups (10½ oz/300 g) flour and the eggs and work together until smooth and pliable. Roll out into a thin sheet and cut into lasagne rectangles which will fit easily into the baking or lasagne dish which will be used.

Prepare a white sauce as follows: heat 2 tablespoons (1 oz/25 g) butter in a small saucepan until it starts to foam; remove from heat. Add ¼ cup (1 oz/25 g) flour, and stir in with a wooden spoon. Return to a moderate heat and continue to stir for about 2 minutes. Remove from the heat once more and add the hot but not boiling milk, stirring briskly. Season with salt and pepper and return to heat, stirring constantly until the sauce starts to bubble. Reduce the heat and continue to cook for 10 to 15 minutes, still stirring continuously. The white sauce should have the consistency of heavy cream and a velvety texture. If it is not thick enough, add a small piece of beurre manié (a small piece of butter worked together with an equal weight of flour) and stir over the heat until the sauce thickens further. A pinch of ground nutmeg may be added at this stage (optional). Remove from the heat and cover tightly.

Chop the onion, celery, and carrot very finely and sauté in 4 tablespoons (2 oz/50 g) butter for a few minutes; then add the ground (minced) meat. Season with salt and pepper to taste and mix well. Cook slowly until the meat and vegetables are soft and tender. Moisten this mixture with a little stock or water from time to time (the mixture should be quite thick but not dry). Just before removing from the heat, stir in the very finely chopped prosciutto (raw ham).

Boil the lasagne in plenty of salted water until half cooked; drain and spread out on a pastry cloth. Butter a lasagne dish generously and cover the bottom with a layer of the lasagne; cover this with a layer of meat sauce followed by a layer of white sauce (if this has solidified while cooling, heat gently while stirring until it liquefies) and sprinkle grated Parmesan onto the layer of white sauce. Continue layering the ingredients in this order, finishing with a layer of pasta covered with a thin coat of white sauce, sprinkled with 2 to 3 tablespoons of grated Parmesan cheese. Melt the remaining butter, and drizzle over the top. Bake in a fairly hot oven (375°–400°F/190°–200°C/mk 5–6) for about 30 minutes. Serve piping hot in the lasagne dish.

Pasticcio di Maccheroni all'Uso di Romagna
Romagna Style Baked Macaroni

2¼ c/18 fl oz/½ l white sauce
2 Tbsp dried mushrooms
¾ lb/¾ lb/350 g macaroni
1 c/5 oz/150 g sweetbreads
4 Tbsp/2 oz/50 g butter
salt
freshly ground pepper
½ c/4 oz/100 g prosciutto (raw ham)
1 small black truffle (optional)
nutmeg (optional)
½ c/4 oz/100 g grated Parmesan cheese

Prepare the white sauce as directed in the previous recipe, Lasagne Verdi. Soak the dried mushrooms in hot water. Chop the sweetbreads into approximately 1 inch (2½ cm) pieces and cut the prosciutto (raw ham) into thin strips. Partially cook the macaroni in boiling salted water until half-cooked, drain, and spread out on a cloth. Heat the butter until it starts to color and add the sweetbreads; season with salt and pepper and pour in half the white sauce. Cook over a gentle heat, stirring very carefully with a wooden spoon now and again, until the sweetbreads are done (about 15 to 20 minutes). Stir in the prosciutto (raw ham) and, if used, the truffle cut into wafer-thin slivers and a pinch of nutmeg.

Butter a deep baking dish and place a layer of macaroni in the bottom, cover with a few tablespoonfuls of the sauce, and dot with butter and a little of the reserved white sauce. Continue layering the ingredients in this order, ending with a generous topping of grated Parmesan cheese dotted with small pieces of butter. Bake in a preheated oven (350°–400°F/180°–200°C/mk 4–6) for about 20 minutes. Serve piping hot directly from the baking dish.

Tagliatelle alla Romagnola

1 small bunch parsley
1 clove garlic
scant 1 lb/14 oz/400 g firm tomatoes
6 Tbsp/4 Tbsp/4 Tbsp olive oil
salt
freshly ground pepper
¾ lb/¾ lb/350 g commercial tagliatelle

Chop the parsley and garlic very finely. Blanch, skin, seed, and chop the tomatoes. Heat the olive oil in a saucepan, add the chopped parsley and garlic and tomatoes, and season with salt and pepper. Cook over a moderate heat until the sauce has reduced and thickened. Put through a food mill or sieve.

Cook the tagliatelle in a large pan of boiling, salted water. When they are al dente, drain them and turn into a deep preheated serving dish. Pour in the sauce, mix, and serve at once.

Lasagne alla Ferrarese

$\frac{3}{4}$ lb/$\frac{3}{4}$ lb/350 g commercial lasagne
scant $\frac{1}{2}$ lb/7 oz/200 g lean ground
   (minced) beef
4 Tbsp/2 oz/50 g butter
$\frac{1}{4}$ lb/4 oz/100 g prosciutto (raw ham)
$2\frac{1}{4}$ c/18 fl oz/$\frac{1}{2}$ l white sauce (see recipe
   for Lasagne Verdi, page 80)
$\frac{1}{2}$ carrot
1 small onion
1 stalk celery
$\frac{1}{3}$ c/$3\frac{1}{2}$ fl oz/1 dl dry white wine
1 lb/1 lb/500 g canned tomatoes put
   through a food mill or sieve
$\frac{1}{2}$ c/4 oz/100 g grated Parmesan cheese
salt
freshly ground pepper

Chop the onion, carrot, celery, and bacon very finely and sauté gently in 2 tablespoons (1 oz/25 g) butter, preferably in a fireproof earthenware cooking pot. Add the ground (minced) beef and sauté until just browned. Pour in the wine, increase the heat, and allow the wine to evaporate quickly. Stir in the tomatoes, reduce the heat, and season with salt and pepper. Cover and cook slowly for about 1 hour, moistening with stock or water when necessary.

Cook the lasagne in plenty of boiling salted water until half done. Drain and rinse with cold water; then spread out on a cloth. Butter a baking dish and line the bottom with a layer of lasagne, spread with meat sauce followed by a layer of white sauce, and sprinkle with grated Parmesan. Repeat this layering until all the ingredients are used, ending with a layer of lasagne covered with a thin coat of white sauce. Dot with small pieces of butter. Place in a preheated oven at about 400°F (200°C/mk 6) and bake for 30 minutes. Serve very hot directly from the lasagne dish.

Right: Lasagne Verdi (Spinach Lasagne), a classic of Bologna and Romagna generally.

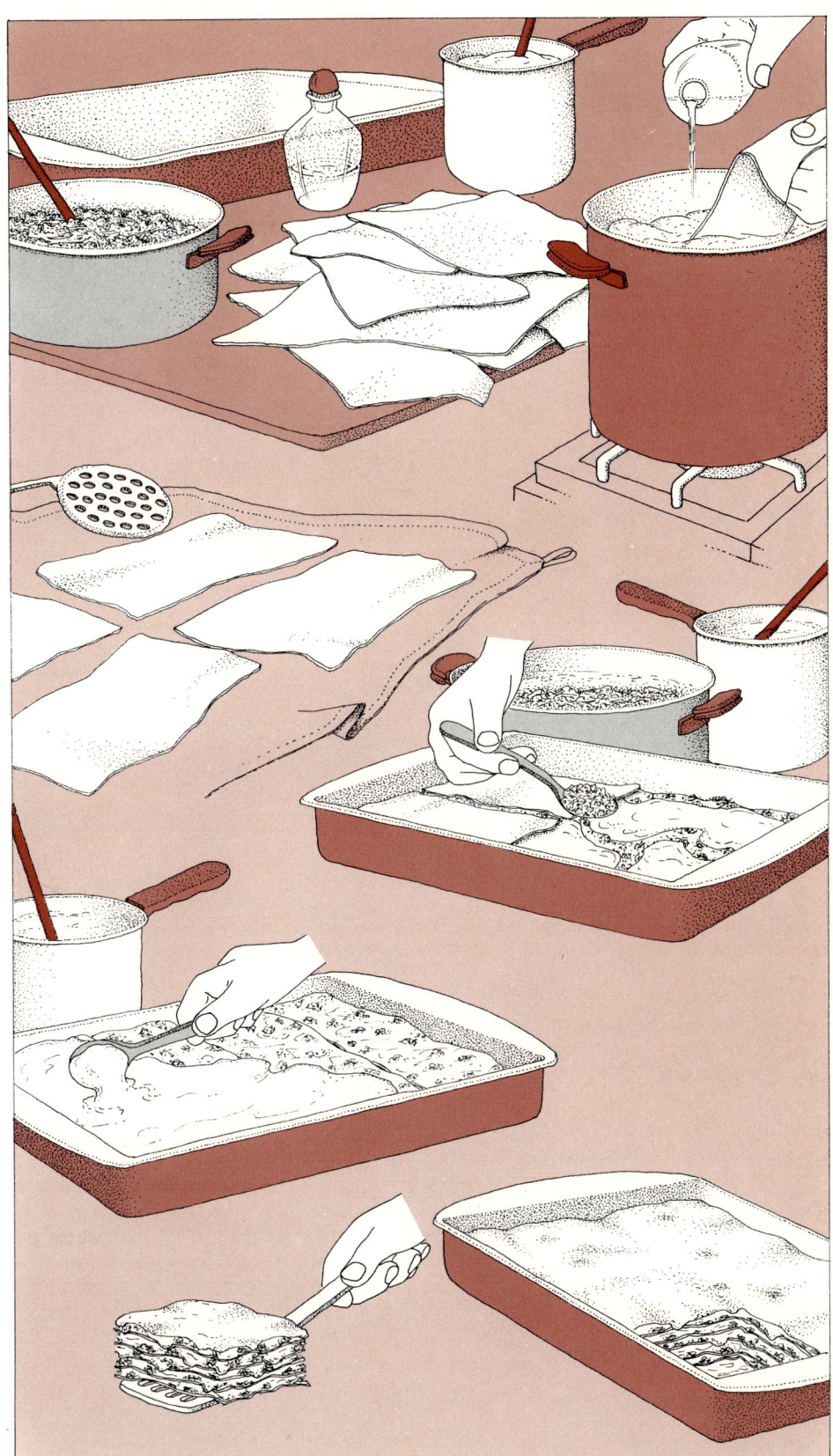

Garganelli
Pasta with Meat Sauce

2½ c/10½ oz/300 g all-purpose (plain)
　flour
3 eggs
¼ c/2 oz/50 g grated Parmesan cheese
1 medium onion
1 small carrot
1 stalk celery
¼ c/2 oz/50 g pancetta (fat bacon) or
　pork belly
3 Tbsp/scant 1½ oz/40 g butter
1 c/7 oz/200 g ground (minced) lean beef
　or veal
⅓ c/3½ fl oz/1 dl dry white wine
1¼ c/10½ oz/300 g canned tomatoes put
　through a food mill or sieve
salt
freshly ground pepper
2 chicken livers

Mix the flour, eggs, and half the grated Parmesan together and knead until the dough is smooth and elastic. Roll out into a very thin sheet and cut into 2½ inch (6 cm) squares. Curl a corner of each square (one sheet at a time, covering the rest with a damp pastry cloth until needed) around a thin wooden spoon handle. Roll up while pressing against a ridged wooden block.

Chop the onion, carrot, celery, and pancetta (bacon) finely. Heat half the butter in a saucepan and when it starts to turn color, add the chopped vegetables and the ground (minced) meat. Sauté for 4 to 5 minutes. Pour in the wine, turn up the heat, and cook until the wine has evaporated. Add the tomatoes, season, cover, and simmer over a low heat until the sauce has thickened. A few minutes before removing from the heat, add the cleaned and chopped chicken livers.

Above: Garganelli can be made by rolling squares of pasta dough over a pettine (literally, comb), the Italian tool shown here, or by rolling the dough squares over any ridged block.

Boil the *garganelli* in plenty of lightly salted water. Drain, dot with remaining butter, cover with sauce and top with remaining Parmesan.

Tagliatelle col Prosciutto
Tagliatelle with Prosciutto (Raw Ham)

2½ c/10½ oz/300 g all-purpose (plain)
　flour
3 eggs
salt
¼ lb/4 oz/100 g prosciutto (raw ham)
3 Tbsp/scant 1½ oz/40 g butter
freshly ground pepper
¼ c/2 oz/50 g grated Parmesan cheese

Mix the sifted flour with the eggs and a pinch of salt and knead the resulting dough well. Roll out into a sheet and cut into tagliatelle about ¼ inch (½ cm) wide.

While the noodles are cooking in boiling, salted water, warm the prosciutto (raw ham) in the butter over a low heat in a large pan without allowing it to fry. Drain the noodles while still very firm and turn into the pan of prosciutto (raw ham), mixing and turning over the low heat until they are thoroughly coated. Season with pepper and remove from the heat. Stir in the grated Parmesan cheese and serve at once.

Fettuccine con Prosciutto e Panna

Fettuccine with Prosciutto (Raw Ham) and Cream

2½ c/10½ oz/300 g all-purpose (plain) flour
salt
3 eggs
¾ c/7 fl oz/2 dl heavy (double) cream
¼ c/2 oz/50 g prosciutto (raw ham)
¼ c/2 oz/50 g grated Parmesan cheese
1 egg yolk
freshly ground pepper

Mix the flour, a pinch of salt, and the three whole eggs together to form a dough and work until smooth and firm. Roll out into a sheet not quite paper-thin and cut into strips about ¼ inch (½ cm) wide.

In a large mixing bowl or tureen, place the cream, the prosciutto (raw ham) cut into thin strips, half the grated Parmesan, the egg yolk and salt and pepper to taste. Stir well with a wooden spoon until thoroughly blended. Place in a warm place, away from any direct source of heat.

Cook the *fettucine* in plenty of boiling salted water until al dente, drain, and add immediately to the mixture in the bowl. Mix quickly but carefully so that all the noodles are well coated with the sauce. Serve immediately.

Strichetti

2½ c/10½ oz/300 g all-purpose (plain) flour
3 eggs
½ c/4 oz/100 g grated Parmesan cheese
nutmeg (optional)
salt
4½ c/1¾ pt/1 l homemade beef stock

Work the sifted flour, the eggs, half the grated Parmesan cheese, a pinch of nutmeg (optional), and a little salt together into a smooth, pliable egg pasta dough. Roll out into a fairly thin sheet and, using a pastry wheel, cut out into small rectangles, measuring about ¾ inch (2 cm) wide and 1½–1¾ inches long (2–4 cm). Pinch the middle of each small rectangle together between the thumb and forefinger to form a bow tie or butterfly shape. Cook the pasta in the broth until tender and serve with grated Parmesan cheese on the side.

Maccheroni ai 4 Formaggi

Macaroni with 4 Cheeses

⅓ c/2 oz/50 g Mozzarella cheese
½ c/2 oz/50 g Gruyère cheese
½ c/2 oz/50 g Fontina cheese
½ c/2 oz/50 g mild Provolone cheese
4 Tbsp/2 oz/50 g butter
1 tsp all-purpose (plain) flour
⅓ c/3½ fl oz/1 dl milk
¾ lb/¾ lb/350 g macaroni
salt
freshly ground pepper
grated Parmesan cheese

Cut all the cheese into very narrow, thin strips. Heat half the butter in a pan until it starts to foam, add the flour and cook for 30 seconds, stirring constantly and then add the milk slowly, mixing well. Bring this mixture to a boil; then reduce heat and cook for 5 minutes, stirring the whole time. Remove from the heat, add the cheese, and beat in well. Cover and leave in a warm place away from any direct source of heat.

Cook the macaroni in a large pan of boiling salted water until tender but firm. Turn into a preheated deep dish, sprinkle with freshly ground pepper and the remaining melted butter. Mix well. Return the pan of cheese sauce to the heat for a few seconds, mixing briskly and then pour it over the macaroni. Mix together and serve immediately with grated Parmesan on the side.

Gramigna con la Salsiccia

Pasta with Sausage and Tomato Sauce

1¼ lb/1¼ lb/600 g ripe fresh or canned tomatoes
½ lb/½ lb/200 g fresh Italian or other pork or pork and beef sausages
¾ lb/¾ lb/350 g gramigna or bucatini
⅓ c/2¾ oz/80 g grated Parmesan cheese

If fresh tomatoes are used, blanch them for about 30 seconds in boiling water, rinse them in cold water, and skin them. Remove the seeds and squeeze the pulp gently by hand to remove excess watery juice before chopping finely. If canned tomatoes are used, chop finely.

Wash and dry the sausages and prick their skins in a few places. Place in a heavy pan with the tomatoes and bring to a boil. Then reduce the heat, cover, and simmer very slowly for about 30 minutes. Remove from the heat, take out the sausages with cooking tongs or a slotted spoon, and skin them as soon as they are cool enough to handle. Cut them into pieces and return them to the pan to keep warm in the tomato sauce.

Cook the pasta in plenty of boiling salted water until tender but firm, drain, and turn into a heated serving dish or platter. Top with the sausage and tomato sauce. Serve immediately with grated Parmesan on the side.

Maccheroni alla Bolognese

1 small onion
1 small stalk celery
1 small carrot
¼ lb/¼ lb/100 g pancetta (fat bacon)
4 Tbsp/2 oz/50 g butter
¼ lb/¼ lb/100 g lean veal
1 tsp all-purpose (plain) flour
¾ c/7 fl oz/2 dl meat stock
salt
freshly ground pepper
nutmeg or 1 clove (optional)
⅓ c/3½ fl oz/1 dl heavy (double) cream
1 chicken liver
¾ lb/¾ lb/350 g ribbed macaroni (or
* penne rigate)*
¼ c/2 oz/50 g grated Parmesan cheese

This ragù is a classic in the repertoire of Emilian cookery. It should not be too thick but should have a creamy, velvety texture. Local expert opinion has it that the meat should not be ground (minced) but chopped very finely with a knife so that the blood from the meat can be added to the sautéing mixture in the saucepan with the meat itself, giving the sauce extra goodness.

Chop the onion, celery, carrot, and pancetta (bacon) very finely and sauté in the butter in a large, heavy pan together with the veal, mixing and turning so that the meat colors slightly but does not stick to the bottom of the pan. Add a teaspoon of flour and then pour in the stock. Add only a little salt, since the pancetta (bacon) is salty, and season to taste with pepper and either a pinch of nutmeg or a clove (optional). Simmer over a low heat for 30 minutes, stirring at frequent intervals. Shortly before the sauce is ready, add the cream and the very finely chopped chicken liver.

Boil the macaroni in plenty of salted water, drain when al dente, turn into a warmed serving dish, and cover with the meat sauce or ragù to call it by its proper name. Mix well and serve at once with grated Parmesan.

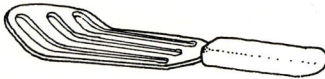

Risotto alla Parmigiana

4 Tbsp/2 oz/50 g butter
½ onion
¾ lb/¾ lb/350 g Arborio rice
4 c/1¾ pt/1 l light meat stock
⅓ c/3 oz/80 g grated Parmesan cheese
salt

For this particular risotto a special effort should be made to obtain the best Parmigiano-Reggiano cheese possible, since the dish depends on the flavor of an authentic, mature Parmesan.

Place ⅔ of the butter in a saucepan with the finely chopped onion and sauté until the onion is translucent. Add the rice and mix well with a wooden spoon for a few minutes while continuing to cook over a low heat, mixing and turning so that every grain of rice is thoroughly coated with the onion and butter. Moisten with 1 cup (8 fl oz/2.5 dl) of simmering stock, Simmer over a moderate heat. As the rice absorbs the liquid, add more stock, a cup at a time, stirring to prevent the rice from sticking to the bottom of the pan and to ensure even cooking. If the stock is used up before the rice is done, add boiling water. When the rice is tender but still has a little bite left in it, stir in the grated Parmesan and the remaining butter; the latter makes the rice glossy and helps to give the risotto a creamier texture. Add salt to taste, remove from heat, and serve at once.

Minestra di Passatelli
Cheese Pasta in Broth

scant 1 c/4 oz/100 g bread crumbs (fine
* and dry)*
salt
nutmeg
grated rind of ½ lemon
3 eggs
⅓ c/3 oz/80 g grated Parmesan cheese
2 Tbsp/1 oz/25 g butter or beef bone
* marrow*
4 c/1¾ pt/1 l meat stock

This is not only a delicious and fortifying soup but is also extremely quick and easy to prepare.

Place the bread crumbs, a pinch of salt, and a small pinch of grated nutmeg, the grated rind of half a lemon, and the eggs in a bowl. Stir together and then beat with a fork. Add the grated Parmesan cheese and the melted butter or beef marrow. Blend well together to form a firm but tender and smooth dough. If the eggs used are extra large, it may be necessary to add a little more grated Parmesan and bread crumbs to achieve the right consistency. Cover the bowl and let stand.

Bring the stock to a boil (a really good homemade stock should be used for this recipe as canned consommé or stock cubes do not have such a delicate flavor). Then, using the mesh with the largest holes, press the *passatelli* mixture through a food mill directly into the boiling broth. Gently boil the resulting short, thick, cylindrical strands in the broth for a minute or two; turn off the heat and allow to stand on the cooling burner for about 3 minutes; then serve into preheated soup plates. No extra Parmesan is served with this soup.

Lumache alla Bobbiese
Snails Bobbio Style

2 lb/2 lb/1 kg large, live snails (see the
* note in the recipe for Bovolini,*
* page 56)*
4 Tbsp/2 oz/50 g butter
¾ c/7 fl oz/2 dl olive oil
¼ c/3 Tbsp/3 Tbsp tomato paste
salt
freshly ground pepper
1 lb/1 lb/500 g leeks
1 lb/1 lb/500 g celery
2 large carrots
1 onion

The snails collected in the Bobbio region in December are much sought after for this traditional Christmas Eve dish eaten by the inhabitants of the area. The fame of these snails has spread to other regions of Italy and as far afield as New

York, where they are imported and are usually sold ready purged and sometimes canned, with their cleaned shells in a separate container.

This particular dish involves a considerable amount of preparation and should be begun two days in advance in order to allow time for the various stages in its cooking.

Purge, clean and prepare the live snails as directed in the recipe for Bovoloni on page 56. Sauté the chopped onion in the butter and oil in an earthenware or enameled pan until it has softened and is almost translucent. Do not allow it to color at all. Add the snails and pour in the tomato paste diluted with about ¾ cup (7 fl oz/2 dl) water. Bring to a boil and then reduce the heat, seasoning to taste with salt and pepper. Cover and simmer for about 2 hours, stirring frequently and moistening with hot water when necessary. At the end of this time the snails should be tender. Remove the pan from the heat and let it stand overnight in a cool place.

The following day, reheat the snails, moisten with about ¾ cup (7 fl oz/2 dl) water and add the washed, trimmed, and finely chopped vegetables. Cover and cook over a low heat, stirring frequently, for a further 2 hours, adding salt to taste and more hot water if the liquid reduces too much. The sauce should be smooth and thick.

Scaloppe di Vitello alla Bolognese
Bologna Style Veal Escalopes

1 lb/1 lb/500 g veal escalopes
3 Tbsp/2 Tbsp/2 Tbsp all-purpose
   (plain) flour
3 Tbsp/1½ oz/40 g butter
salt
freshly ground pepper
⅓ c/3½ fl oz/1 dl dry white wine
8 thin slices of prosciutto (raw ham)
8 slices of Gruyère cheese

Right: How to prepare Minestra di Passatelli (Cheese Pasta in Broth), another Emilian specialty.

Coat the escalopes with flour. Heat the butter in a frying pan and, when foaming, add the veal and sauté briskly until both sides are golden brown. Arrange the veal escalopes in a single layer in the bottom of a large, shallow preheated ovenproof dish and season lightly with salt and pepper. Return the pan in which the veal was cooked to the heat and deglaze with the dry white wine or 4 tablespoons of dry Marsala. Pour over the escalopes. Cover each slice of veal with a slice of prosciutto (raw ham) and a slice of Gruyère (if Gruyère is not available sprinkle a heaped teaspoon of grated Parmesan on top of each slice of prosciutto (raw ham)). Place in a hot oven (about 400°F/200°C/mk 6) for a few minutes until the cheese has melted Serve at once with a fresh salad.

Stracotto
Braised Beef

2 lb/2 lb/800 g boned rolled rib of beef or
    top round (topside)
2 cloves garlic
½ onion
1 stalk celery
1 small carrot
4 Tbsp/2 oz/50 g (finely diced) pork fat
4 Tbsp/2 oz/50 g butter
3 Tbsp tomato paste
1 tsp meat extract
salt
freshly ground pepper

Make several incisions in the beef roast and insert fine slivers of garlic. Sauté the finely chopped vegetables in the diced pork fat and the butter in a large pot. Place the meat in the cooking pot and brown well on all sides, turning frequently. Dilute the tomato paste and meat extract in 2¼ cups (18 fl oz/½ liter) hot water and add to the meat. Add enough more hot water to come at least half way up the sides of the meat. Cover with a tight-fitting lid and braise over a very low heat, turning the meat from time to time, until the beef is very tender. Add a little hot water when necessary. Halfway through cooking, season with

salt and pepper. The meat should simmer slowly but steadily for at least 4 hours to achieve the best results: succulent and tender braised beef surrounded by a smooth, full-flavored sauce.

When the meat is done, carve into thick slices and cover with the sauce.

Zampone di Modena
Stuffed Pig's Foot (Trotter)

1 zampone from Modena (the skin of a
    pig's foot (trotter) stuffed with the
    same mixture as that used for
    cotechino, the lightly salted pork
    salami or sausage which is a specialty
    of the whole of Emilia-Romagna but
    particularly of Modena).

Soak the zampone in cold water for 12 hours or overnight. Remove from the water, loosen the strings which are tied round it and make two incisions with a sharp knife in the form of a cross and puncture the skin. Wrap fairly tightly in a piece of cheesecloth (muslin) and tie up with string. Take a tall, narrow cooking pot which can take the whole zampone hanging down vertically from a skewer into the simmering water without actually touching the bottom of the pot. Cover and bring to a boil. Reduce the heat immediately and simmer very slowly for 5 to 6 hours, topping up with boiling water from time to time as the cooking liquid evaporates.

Arista di Maiale al Forno
Pork Loin Braised in Milk

1½ lb/1¼ lb/700 g boned, rolled and
    securely tied pork loin
⅓ c/3½ fl oz/1 dl oil
1 sprig fresh rosemary or a pinch of dried
    rosemary
2 garlic cloves
1 c/8 fl oz/¼ l milk
1 Tbsp vinegar
salt
freshly ground pepper

The piece of pork loin should have a little fat left on it. This small amount of fat will dissolve in the milk to help form the nutty-brown sauce, which is so delicious, will help keep the pork juicy and tender.

Make a marinade in a mixing bowl with the vinegar, rosemary, crushed garlic cloves, a little salt, and a generous pinch of freshly ground pepper. Place the pork loin in the marinade and marinate for 24 hours, turning frequently.

Heat the oil in a heavy pot which will just accommodate the pork comfortably. Remove the pork from the marinade and brown evenly on all sides in the oil; then add the strained marinade and the milk. Cover very tightly and simmer very gently for about 1 hour, turning several times. Add a very little hot water if too much liquid has evaporated, but the juices and cooking liquid in this recipe should, in fact, coagulate into small, nut-brown clusters and be fairly thick or at least have a certain amount of body. If the sauce is too pale, uncover the pan, raise the heat to high and cook fairly fast until it darkens.

Pork loin is a tender and lean cut and cooked in this way makes a tasty and not too heavy dish.

Rognone in Umido
Calf Kidneys with Garlic and Parsley

2 calf kidneys
salt
3 Tbsp/1 oz/2 Tbsp all-purpose (plain)
    flour
2 Tbsp/1 oz/25 g butter
2–3 Tbsp oil
2 cloves garlic
1 bunch parsley
freshly ground pepper

Opposite: A steaming tureen of Canèderli (Tyrolean Dumplings) in broth and another way of serving this Trent specialty— on its own.

Overleaf: Baccalà alla Vicentina (Stockfish Vicenza Style) and Cape Sante (Scallops Sautéed in Garlic) are two dishes typical of the Veneto.

Remove the hard suet (white core) from the kidneys and carefully peel off the delicate membrane which covers them. Cut them into thin slices and sprinkle with a teaspoon of fine salt. Rub the salt into the slices of kidney so that it clings to them. Let stand for 10 minutes; then place in a colander and rinse well in fresh water. Pat dry with paper towels. Then flour the kidney slices lightly and evenly, keeping them separated. Heat the butter in a frying pan or saucepan. (Do not use an enameled pan. An earthenware or non-stick coated pan is better as is an untinned copper sautéing pan.) When the butter begins to foam, add the kidney slices. Stir gently and continuously while cooking the kidneys over a low heat until the coating of flour is crisp and brown. Pour in just enough water to make a small quantity of light, creamy sauce. Pour on the oil and season with salt and pepper. Chop the garlic and parsley very finely and sprinkle into the pan. Simmer very gently for about 10 minutes, stirring now and again, but do not allow the sauce to boil. Do not overcook. Kidneys harden and become unpleasantly tough if they are cooked for too long. During this last period of cooking, the sauce should reduce until it is about the same consistency as white sauce. The kidneys should be served immediately, preferably with polenta.

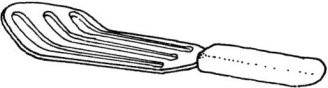

Arrosto Farcito
Stuffed Braised Veal

1 lb/1 lb/500 g spinach
3 eggs
¼ c/2 oz/50 g grated Parmesan cheese
¼ c/2 oz/50 g Mortadella sausage
salt
½ c/4 oz/100 g butter
¼ c/3 Tbsp/3 Tbsp oil
1¾ lb/1¾ lb/800 g boned, loin, shoulder, or breast of veal (unrolled)
¼ lb/¼ lb/100 g pancetta (fat bacon)
¾ c/7 fl oz/2 dl milk
freshly ground pepper

Trim and wash the spinach very well in several changes of water. Cook in the water that remains on the leaves after washing. Drain and squeeze out as much liquid as possible. Chop very finely and place in a mixing bowl. Add the eggs, grated Parmesan, and finely chopped Mortadella sausage. Mix well and add salt to taste. Heat about 2 teaspoons of butter and a tablespoon of oil in a large frying pan, or large, oval sautéing pan and when the butter foams, add the spinach and egg mixture, spreading it out evenly to form an omelet. When this is set on the underside, turn carefully or place under the broiler (grill) at a low heat to cook the other side. Spread the meat out on a board, cover with slices of pancetta (bacon), leaving a margin all round the edges of the meat. Place the omelet on top of the pancetta (bacon), again being careful to leave a margin of about ½ inch (1 cm) of uncovered meat. Roll up carefully and sew up the ends of the roll.

Heat the rest of the butter and 2 tablespoons of oil in a large, heavy cooking pot or saucepan and brown the meat roll well over a low heat, turning every few minutes. Add the milk and an equal quantity of water, cover tightly, and barely simmer until the meat is very tender—this will take about 1½ to 2 hours. Turn the meat occasionally during cooking.

Cotolette di Vitello alla Bolognese con Tartufo
Escalopes of Veal Bologna Style with Truffle

2 large, juicy lemons
salt
freshly ground pepper
8 thin veal escalopes
2 eggs
4 Tbsp/2 oz/50 g butter
bread crumbs
1 truffle
3 Tbsp/2 Tbsp/2 Tbsp grated Parmesan cheese
½ c/4 fl oz/generous 1 dl stock

Make a simple marinade for the veal by combining the juice of 1 lemon with salt and pepper. Place the veal in a shallow dish, pour over the marinade, and leave to marinate for about 1 hour, turning several times.

Beat the eggs lightly with a fork in a separate dish and place the marinated escalopes in the beaten egg for a short time. Heat the butter in a frying pan wide enough to take all the escalopes laid flat, so that they can all cook at the same time. Drain excess beaten egg from the escalopes, and dredge with bread crumbs. When the butter is hot and has started to foam, add the veal (the escalopes should sizzle gently as they are placed in the butter). Fry briskly until the first side is golden brown, turn, and brown the other side. The escalopes should be quite crisp on both sides. Arrange slivers of truffle on top of the escalopes and sprinkle with freshly grated Parmesan. Pour 3 ladlefuls of light stock (made with a small bouillon cube, dissolved in hot water, if necessary) carefully into the pan between the slices, cover, and simmer very slowly. When the juices and stock have reduced and thickened, transfer the escalopes to a heated serving platter, add the juice of the second lemon to the liquid in the pan, and cook over a high heat for 1 minute; then pour over the veal.

Cotechino in Fagotto
Pork Sausage Wrapped in Ham and Veal

1 cotechino sausage weighing ¾–1 lb/ ¾–1 lb/300–400 g (see instructions)
1¾–1 lb/¾–1 lb/400 g slice of veal cut from the top round (topside)
3 slices prosciutto (raw ham)
1 stalk celery
1 small carrot
½ onion
4 Tbsp/2 oz/50 g butter
¾ c/7 fl oz/2 dl dry red wine
1 tsp meat extract or bouillon (stock) cube

Cotechino is a large, mildly spiced fresh pork sausage about 3 inches (7 cm) in diameter and 8 to 9 inches (20–23 cm) long. Try to get the best as the quality varies.

Remove the string from the sausage but do not puncture the skin. Place in a pan large enough for the sausage to lie flat, cover with cold water, bring to a boil and then simmer until the sausage is half cooked (about 1¼ hours). Remove from water, skin, and allow to cool.

Pound the slice of veal until it is thin and evenly flattened. Spread the prosciutto (raw ham) over the veal and in the center place the skinned cotechino sausage. Roll the sausage up in the meat carefully and tie up each end with string, rather like a salami. Chop the celery, carrot, and onion coarsely and sauté in the butter in a large, heavy pan. Place the meat-and-sausage roll in the pan with the sautéed vegetables and brown on all sides. Pour in the wine, turn up the heat and cook until the wine has evaporated. Add the stock, turn down the heat, cover tightly, and simmer for about 1 hour, adding water if necessary. Take the meat from the cooking liquid, place on a heated platter, remove the string and carve into thick slices. Keep the slices warm without allowing them to dry out. Reduce the sauce over a fairly high heat until it has some body. Pour it over the sliced meat and serve.

Pollo alla Bolognese
Chicken Bologna Style

1 2½ lb/2½ lb/1.2 kg chicken
1 slice of prosciutto (raw ham)
2 cloves garlic
1 sprig fresh rosemary or a pinch of dried rosemary
4 Tbsp/2 oz/50 g butter
3 Tbsp oil
2 large ripe tomatoes (skinned and seeded) or
  ¼ c/3 Tbsp/3 Tbsp tomato paste diluted in 1 c/8½ fl oz/2.5 dl boiling water
salt
freshly ground pepper
1 lb/1 lb/500 g potatoes

Bone the chicken (see instructions for Pollo Ripieno, page 190). Sauté the prosciutto (raw ham), the chopped garlic, and the rosemary in the butter and oil using a large frying pan. If fresh rosemary is used, wrap it in cheesecloth (muslin) to prevent the leaves being shed into the sauce. After a few minutes add the chicken pieces, stirring and turning frequently, until they are golden brown. Add the tomatoes or tomato paste. Season with salt and pepper to taste. Cover and simmer very gently, adding a little water from time to time if the sauce reduces too much. When the chicken is done, remove the pieces from the pan and set aside. Add enough water to the cooking liquid to cook the potatoes which have previously been peeled and diced. When the potatoes are tender, return the chicken pieces to the pan and cook until thoroughly heated through, stirring the mixture gently over a moderate heat. Serve.

Cotolette alla Bolognese
Veal Escalopes Bolognese

4 veal escalopes cut from the top round (topside) weighing 5–6 oz/5–6 oz/ 150 g each
salt
1 rounded Tbsp all-purpose (plain) flour
1 egg
bread crumbs
4 Tbsp/2 oz/50 g butter
4 slices prosciutto (raw ham)
4 slices of table Parmesan
⅔ c/¼ pt/1.5 dl tomato sauce (see instructions)
3 Tbsp/2 Tbsp/2 Tbsp dry white wine or dry Marsala wine

Flatten the escalopes evenly until they are quite thin. Season with a little salt and dredge lightly with flour, shaking off any excess. Dip them into the lightly beaten egg and then coat well with bread crumbs. Heat the butter in a frying pan until it starts to foam and then add the veal. Sauté golden brown.

Transfer to a large, shallow oven-proof dish. Cover each escalope with a slice of prosciutto (raw ham) and a slice of cheese and pour in the tomato sauce and the wine. Bake in a hot oven (about 400°F/200°C/mk 6) for approximately 10 to 15 minutes.

For the tomato sauce, finely chop 1 onion, 1 carrot, 1 stalk celery, and sauté in oil or butter until soft. Add 2 pounds (2 lb/1 kg) of fresh or canned tomatoes (follow directions for Gramigna con la Salsiccia on page 83). Season, and add 2 tablespoons of chopped parsley. Cover and simmer until the tomatoes have turned almost to a purée. Put the sauce through a food mill or sieve. Makes approximately 3 cups (1½ pt/900 ml).

For stuffed veal escalopes prepare 8 smaller escalopes as directed above; lay each slice flat, cover with a thin slice of prosciutto (raw ham), then with a slice of cheese, leaving a margin for sealing all round. Top with another escalope and press the two escalopes tightly together. Dredge lightly with the flour, dip carefully in the beaten egg, and cover with the bread crumbs. Sauté the stuffed veal until browned, transfer to a shallow baking dish and pour in a mixture of 4 tablespoons (3 Tbsp/3 Tbsp) light (single) cream and ⅔ cup (¼ pt/1.5 dl) tomato sauce. Season with salt and pepper and place in a very slow oven for 20 minutes.

Anguilla Marinata
Marinated Eel

2 medium-sized eels, together weighing about 2 lb/2 lb/1 kg
6½ c/2 pt 12 fl oz/1½ l vinegar
1 sprig fresh sage or a pinch of dried sage
1 clove garlic
several bay leaves
3–4 Tbsp/2–3 Tbsp/2–3 Tbsp oil
salt
freshly ground pepper
rind of 2 oranges or lemons

Usually eel is sold prepared and ready for cooking. If the eels have not been cleaned, follow the instructions on page 53, in the recipe for Risotto di Bisato. The eels should be cut into pieces about 2 inches (5 cm) long for this recipe.

Pour the vinegar into a saucepan (do not use aluminum); add the sage, orange rind, crushed clove of garlic, and a little salt and pepper; and simmer for about 30 minutes.

Put the pieces of eel on skewers, alternating them with pieces of bay leaf. Heat the oil in a large frying pan and when very hot, fry the kebabs, turning frequently. When evenly cooked, place the skewered eels in a dish and season with salt and freshly ground pepper. When the marinade is ready, pour it through a strainer directly onto the skewered eels. Cover the dish and let it stand for at least two or three days.

Anguilla di Comacchio
Comacchio Braised Eel

2 medium-sized eels, together weighing about 2 lb/2 lb/1 kg
2 medium onions
1 clove garlic
3 Tbsp/2 Tbsp/2 Tbsp oil
⅓ c/3½ fl oz/1 dl vinegar
2 large ripe (or canned) tomatoes
salt
freshly ground pepper

Clean the eels as directed on page 53 in the recipe for Risotto di Bisato but then cut into 4 inch (10 cm) pieces. Sauté the very finely chopped onion and garlic in the oil, using a wide, non-metallic pan. Pour in the vinegar and cook until it has evaporated. Add the tomatoes, which have been put through a food mill or sieve, and season with salt and pepper. Cover the pan and simmer for about 10 minutes. Place the pieces of eel in the pan in a single layer, cover tightly, and simmer for 30 to 40 minutes. Avoid stirring, as this will break up the delicate flesh of the eel; instead, shake the pan gently or give it a couple of sharp jerks at intervals during cooking so that the eel will not stick to the bottom of the pan.

This dish takes its name from the famous source of the best eels in Italy, Comacchio, situated at the mouth of the Po river on the Adriatic coast, where they are farmed on a very large scale.

Baccalà alla Bolognese
Salt Cod Bologna Style

⅓ c/3½ fl oz/1 dl oil
1¼ lb/1¼ lb/600 g soaked, drained salt cod (see the recipe for Baccalà alla Vicentina on page 58 and prepare the salt cod in the same way as the stockfish)
2 garlic cloves
1 bunch parsley
freshly ground pepper
salt
juice of 1 lemon
4 Tbsp/2 oz/50 g butter

Oil the inside of a heavy pan. Cut the salt cod into fairly large pieces and place them in the pan in a single layer. Chop the garlic and parsley finely and sprinkle over the fish. Season with pepper and a very little salt and pour the remainder of the oil evenly over the fish, dotting the top with small pieces of butter. Sauté briskly, turning the pieces of fish very carefully so that they do not flake or break up. When the fish is done, sprinkle with the lemon juice and serve immediately, directly from the pan.

Coniglio in Umido alla Reggiana
Reggio Emilia Rabbit Casserole

1 fresh rabbit or frozen young rabbit weighing about 2½ lb/2½ lb/1.2 kg
1 clove garlic
1 onion
1 stalk celery
¼ c/2 oz/50 g pancetta (fat bacon)
4 Tbsp/2 oz/50 g butter
⅓ c/3½ fl oz/1 dl dry white wine
2 Tbsp tomato paste
salt
freshly ground pepper
1 small bunch parsley

The method for preparing this dish varies only slightly throughout Italy. The subtle differences from region to region consist mainly in omitting certain ingredients or substituting others, or simply in the proportions of one ingredient to the others. The method given here is that of Reggio Emilia.

If fresh rabbit is used, (do not use wild rabbit for this recipe) soak the skinned, paunched, and cut-up rabbit in plenty of cold water for 12 hours or more (refrigerate if necessary while soaking). Rinse in several changes of cold water and pat dry. Chop the garlic, onion, celery, and pancetta (bacon). Heat the butter (preferably in an earthenware fireproof cooking pot or in a heavy lidded, cast-iron skillet, add the chopped pancetta (bacon) and vegetables, and fry for a few minutes while stirring. Then add the pieces of rabbit. Cook these, turning frequently, until they are lightly browned on all sides. Turn up the heat, pour in the wine, and cook while stirring until the wine has evaporated. Dilute the tomato paste with ⅓ cup (3½ fl oz/1 dl) hot water, add to the rabbit, and season with salt and pepper. Cover and simmer over a low heat until the rabbit is very tender (about 1½ to 2 hours), turning and basting the pieces from time to time. Moisten with a little hot water as the cooking liquid reduces but allow the juices to acquire a little more body towards the end of the cooking. Just before the rabbit is done, add the very finely chopped parsley. Serve the portions with some of the cooking juices spooned over them.

In Italy, the wines most likely to be drunk with this Emilian casserole would be Sangiovese from the Forlì region or Lambrusco from Modena (Villa di Sorbara).

Lenticchie in Umido
Boiled Lentils

1½ c/10½ oz/300 g lentils (preferably the brown variety)
¼ c/2 oz/50 g chopped pancetta (fat bacon)
1 small onion
salt

Soak the dried lentils overnight in lukewarm water. Drain well before using.

Sauté the chopped onion and pancetta (bacon) together gently, mixing and turning frequently, until the onion turns a pale golden color. Add the drained lentils, season with salt and pour in enough fresh water to cover. Simmer with the lid on for about 1 hour or until the lentils are tender and have absorbed nearly all the cooking liquid (if the liquid reduces too quickly, add a little boiling water).

Lentils prepared in this way make up a classic regional dish with boiled cotechino sausage or zampone (pig's foot (trotter) stuffed with cotechino sausage meat). Freshly-made polenta is an ideal accompaniment and rounds off the flavor perfectly.

Cardi alla Parmigiana
Cardoons Parma Style

1 small cardoon
6 Tbsp/3 oz/80 g butter
⅓ c/3 oz/80 g grated Parmesan cheese
juice of 1 lemon
salt

Wash and trim the cardoon, discarding any tough, outer stalks and removing the celery-like strings from the tender stalks (only the hearts and inner stalks of this edible member of the thistle family are used). Cut them into pieces about 4 inches (10 cm) long and drop immediately into water acidulated with the lemon juice to prevent their discoloring. Boil the pieces of cardoon in lightly salted water for about 3 hours; then drain.

Grease a baking dish liberally with butter, place a layer of cardoon in the bottom of the dish and sprinkle with melted butter and a little grated Parmesan cheese. Continue to layer the cardoon, ending with melted butter and grated Parmesan. Place the dish in a

Right: Soft and fluffy Patate Duchessa (Duchesse Potatoes).

preheated oven at about 350°F (180°C/ mk 4) and bake for 20 to 30 minutes. Serve very hot in the baking dish.

Cooked in this way, cardoons go very well with *bollito misto* (mixed boiled meats) or with boiled pickled tongue.

Patate Duchessa
Duchesse Potatoes

1¾ lb/1¼ lb/800 g baking potatoes
1 whole egg
2 egg yolks
⅓ c/3 oz/80 g butter
salt

Wash and peel the potatoes. Dice large, rinse once more under running water, and then boil in plenty of lightly salted water until tender. When done, remove with a slotted spoon and drain well. To ensure that no excess moisture remains, which would prevent them from holding their shape when creamed and piped, spread them out in a baking dish and place in a preheated oven for a few minutes. Put the potatoes through a ricer or push through a sieve into a saucepan while still very hot. Allow them to cool very slightly, then beat the egg yolks in as quickly and vigorously as possible to ensure that they do not set before they are properly incorporated. Add the butter and return the pan to a low heat for a couple of minutes, mixing constantly with a wooden spoon. Pack the Duchesse potato mixture into a pastry bag (forcing bag) and, using a large, fluted nozzle, pipe it in rings onto a lightly oiled baking sheet as shown in the illustration on the opposite page. As the pastry bag (forcing bag) empties, fill it up again with more mixture. Lightly brush the potato rings with beaten egg and bake in a hot oven (about 400°F/ 200°C/mk 6) for 20 minutes, until the fluted edges are golden brown. Serve very hot with roasts or with broiled (grilled) meats.

These Duchesse potatoes can be further embellished by placing finely diced Fontina cheese on the rim of the potato rings once they have been trans-

ferred to a hot serving platter. The cheese will melt and run into the centers of the rings.

Tortino di Zucchine
Zucchini (Courgette) Pie

1¾ lb/1¾ lb/800 g zucchini (courgettes)
¼ c/3 Tbsp/3 Tbsp oil
½ Tbsp butter
1 clove garlic
1 bunch parsley
salt
freshly ground pepper
1 recipe white sauce (see recipe for Lasagne Verdi, page 80)

Wash the zucchini (courgettes) and cut into thin slices. Heat the oil and butter in a skillet and sauté the sliced zucchini (courgettes) with the very finely chopped garlic and parsley over a moderate heat, stirring and turning continuously so that the zucchini (courgettes) cook but do not color. Season with salt and pepper and arrange in a baking dish; top with the white sauce and bake in a preheated oven (about 400°F/200°C/mk 6) for a few minutes.

Spinaci di Magro
Lenten Spinach

---

1 lb/1 lb/500 g spinach
1 clove garlic
1 small bunch parsley
6 Tbsp/4 Tbsp/4 Tbsp oil
salt
freshly ground pepper
1 pinch of sugar

Trim and clean the spinach, washing it very thoroughly in several changes of water. Cook it until just tender with only the water that is left clinging to the leaves after washing. Drain and squeeze or press out excess water. Do not chop. Transfer the spinach to a pan in which the very finely chopped garlic and parsley have been gently and lightly

sautéed in the oil. Season to taste with a little salt and pepper and add a pinch of sugar to counteract any lingering bitterness in the spinach. Warm over a low heat for a few minutes, mixing and turning carefully, so that all the spinach leaves are coated with the herb and garlic flavored oil.

In Romagna it used to be the custom to give a subtle added sweetness to this dish by adding some large plumped and seeded raisins to the spinach at the same time as the sugar.

Fritto alla Garisenda
Sandwich Fritters

---

1 truffle
¼ lb/4 oz/100 g table Parmesan cheese or Gruyère
1 loaf of stale bread
½ c/4 oz/100 g prosciutto (raw ham) (sliced very thin)
1 c/8 fl oz/¼ l milk
2–3 eggs
bread crumbs
½ c/4 oz/100 g butter

Cut the truffle and cheese into wafer-thin slices. Trim the crusts off the stale bread and cut into slices. Placing two slices together, one on top of the other, carefully cut into small squares measuring about 1½–2 inches (4–5 cm) square and keep the matching pairs together. For a more decorative effect, the bread can be cut into diamonds, triangles, or any other shape.

Place a sliver of prosciutto (raw ham) on the bottom slice and trim the edges to match the outline of the bread. Arrange a single layer of truffle slices on top, making sure it does not overlap the edges of the bread. Lastly, do the same with the cheese and top with the other half of the bread to form the sandwich. Press firmly together so that the layers adhere to one another.

When all the sandwiches are made, pour the cold milk into a bowl. Beat the eggs in a shallow dish and have the bread crumbs standing ready in another plate. Holding the sandwiches firmly together, dip them one by one first in the milk and then in the egg; then press on the bread crumbs to coat. This procedure should ensure that the sandwiches do not fall apart when fried and that they will turn a crisp light brown on the outside.

When all the sandwiches have been dipped and coated, heat the butter in a wide skillet until it starts to foam. Place the sandwiches carefully in the pan and fry until the first side is crisp and golden brown; then turn and cook the other side. Serve immediately.

These little fried sandwiches can be eaten as a snack or light meal in themselves or they can be served as part of a mixed fry.

Cavolfiore alla Romagnola
Romagna Style Cauliflower

1 medium-sized cauliflower
1 clove garlic
1 small bunch parsley
6 Tbsp/4 Tbsp/4 Tbsp oil
salt
freshly ground pepper
6 Tbsp/4 Tbsp/4 Tbsp tomato paste
¼ c/3 Tbsp/3 Tbsp grated Parmesan cheese

Trim and wash the cauliflower, and divide it into florets. Sauté the very finely chopped garlic and parsley in the oil, add the cauliflower, and season with salt and pepper. Mix and turn gently so that the cauliflower pieces become well-coated with the oil. Dilute the tomato paste in about ¾ cup (7 fl oz/2 dl) of hot water and pour over the cauliflower. Cover the pan and simmer over a low heat, stirring from time to time and adding a little hot water if the liquid reduces too much. When the cauliflower is tender, but still firm, and some sauce is left in the pan, remove it from the heat, sprinkle with grated Parmesan, and serve at once.

Cooked in this way, cauliflower makes an interesting accompaniment to boiled cotechino sausage or other boiled meats.

Tortino di Patate
Potato Pie

2 lb/2 lb/800 g waxy potatoes, such as Idaho or large new potatoes
salt
4 Tbsp/2 oz/50 g butter
6–7 oz/6–7 oz/190 g sliced, processed cheese, such as Giglio "Gigliette" or Kraft
freshly ground pepper
¾ c/7 fl oz/2 dl milk

Wash the potatoes, boil in salted water until fairly tender, and then skin. When they are cool, cut them into slices. Butter a pie pan or fairly deep baking dish and cover the bottom with a layer of potato slices. Place a layer of cheese slices on top, sprinkle with a little pepper, and dot with small pieces of butter. Repeat this process until all the ingredients have been used up, ending up with a layer of potato slices dotted with a little butter. Pour the milk over the pie. Bake in a preheated oven at about 400°F (200°C/mk 6) for 15 minutes, until the top of the pie is lightly browned.

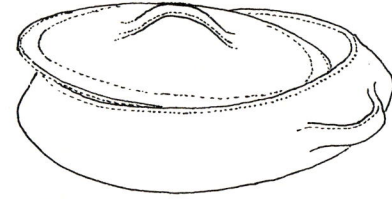

Ragù alla Bolognese
Bolognese Meat Sauce

1 medium onion
1 small carrot
1 stalk celery
¼ c/2 oz/50 g pancetta (fat bacon)
4 Tbsp/2 oz/50 g butter
½ lb/½ lb/200 g mixed finely ground (minced) meat (pork, veal, and beef)
½ c/3½ fl oz/1 dl good dry red wine
¼ c/3 Tbsp/3 Tbsp tomato paste
1 tsp meat extract
freshly ground pepper
salt
1 c/8 fl oz/¼ l milk

Chop the onion, carrot, celery, and pancetta (bacon) finely. Melt the butter. When it starts to foam, add the vegetables and pancetta (bacon) and the ground (minced) meat. Crumble the meat with a fork and, when it just starts to turn pale brown on all sides, pour in the red wine, turn up the heat, and stir until the wine has evaporated. Mix in the tomato paste and the meat extract both diluted with a little hot water and season with pepper and salt. Cover the pan tightly and simmer very gently until the sauce starts to thicken. Then add the milk, mix well, replace the lid, and simmer until all the milk has been absorbed.

This is one of the oldest recipes for Ragù alla Bolognese, but there are many variants, all of which tend to remain true to the Bolognese tradition of full-bodied flavors. Chicken livers are sometimes added with the ground (minced) meats, or a few dried mushrooms, soaked and drained of excess moisture, may be chopped and added with the vegetables and pancetta (bacon). Small strips of prosciutto (raw ham) can also be added at that point; or, best of all, all three can be used together.

Ragù can be made the day before it is needed and kept, covered, in a cool place overnight, provided it is not stored in an aluminum pan.

Pane Bolognese
Bolognese Fruit and Nut Bread

1 rounded Tbsp pine nuts
1 rounded Tbsp candied peel (preferably citron peel)
1 rounded Tbsp raisins
2 c/9 oz/250 g cake flour (very fine flour)
1½ tsp baking powder
scant 1 c/3½ oz/100 g confectioners' (icing) sugar
1 pinch salt
⅓ c/3½ fl oz/1 dl milk
6 Tbsp/3 oz/80 g butter
a few drops of vanilla extract (essence)
1 egg
1 egg yolk

Chop the pine nuts coarsely and cut the candied peel into thin strips. Soak the raisins in hot water for 20 minutes and then remove seeds if necessary. Sift the flour carefully with the baking powder, sugar, and salt so that it falls into a mound on the pastry board or working surface. Make a well in the center.

Warm the milk and the butter very gently over hot water until the butter has melted. Stir in the vanilla. Place the whole egg and extra yolk in the well and pour in the milk and butter mixture. Mix gradually into the flour to form a mixture which is firm enough to handle easily. Work in the pine nuts, candied peel, and the well-drained raisins. Knead well for a few minutes.

Divide the dough in half and shape each half into an oval (or other loaf shape) about $\frac{3}{4}$–$1\frac{1}{4}$ inches (2–3 cm) thick. Brush lightly with the egg yolk and place in a preheated oven at 400°F (200°C/mk 6). Bake for 20 to 30 minutes, when the sweet bread should be golden brown. Avoid opening the oven door until it is necessary to test whether the loaves are done.

Torta di Riso
Rice Pudding

$\frac{1}{4}$ c/2 oz/50 g sweet almonds
$\frac{1}{3}$ c/2 oz/50 g mixed peel, preferably orange and citron, chopped
$4\frac{1}{2}$ c/1$\frac{3}{4}$ pt/1 l milk
salt
scant 1 cup/6$\frac{1}{4}$ oz/180 g rice, preferably round-grain sweet (pudding) rice
$\frac{3}{4}$ c/5 oz/150 g sugar
2 eggs
grated rind of 1 lemon
$\frac{1}{4}$ c/1 oz/25 g pine nuts
a few drops vanilla extract (essence)
2–3 Tbsp fine fresh bread crumbs

Blanch the almonds for 2 to 3 minutes in boiling water. Skin and chop finely. Bring the milk to the boiling point, add a pinch of salt, then stir in the rice and $\frac{1}{3}$ of the sugar. Continue to cook over a moderate heat, stirring frequently, until the rice is done; then remove from heat and leave to cool.

Beat the egg yolks in a bowl with the rest of the sugar and, when they are thick and creamy, stir in the rice, the grated lemon rind, almonds, chopped candied peel, pine nuts, and vanilla extract (essence). Mix thoroughly.

Beat the egg whites until they are stiff and fold in the rice mixture gently.

Butter a tubed cake pan (ring mold) and sprinkle with bread crumbs. Turn the mixture into the pan (mold) and bake in a preheated oven at about 325°F (160°C/mk 3) for 1 hour or until a cake tester comes out clean.

This pudding is best eaten the day after baking.

Lat Brülè
Caramel Custard

1 qt/1$\frac{3}{4}$ pt/1 l fresh, whole (full-cream) milk
2 whole eggs
4 egg yolks
1$\frac{1}{4}$ c/10 oz/300 g sugar
a few drops of vanilla extract (essence)

Pour the milk into a large, heavy pan and allow to cook just below the boiling point until it has reduced by more than half. Pour into a bowl and allow to cool. Place the two whole eggs and the 4 egg yolks together with $\frac{1}{2}$ cup (6 oz/180 g) sugar in a separate bowl and beat until the mixture turns to a foamy, velvety cream. Add vanilla extract (essence) to taste and then blend this mixture into the cooled milk.

Sprinkle the remaining sugar into an unlined copper (pudding) mold with 3 tablespoons of water and heat carefully, turning and tipping the mold so that the caramelized sugar coats the inside.

Pour the milk and egg mixture into the caramel-coated mold and cook in a pan of water in a 300°F (150°C/mk 2) oven. The water in the pan should not come more than $\frac{2}{3}$ of the way up the sides of the mold. Bake for 1 hour or longer— the caramel custard is done when the center only shakes very slightly when moved gently. Lift the mold out of the pan of water, allow to cool to room temperature, and then chill in the refrigerator for a few hours. Before turning out, run a sharp knife around the edges to loosen, place a serving platter over the mold and invert the mold onto the serving dish with a quick, sharp jerk. The caramel will have partly permeated the set custard, but some will still be free to trickle down the sides of the custard, making the pudding look most attractive.

Cassatella
Chocolate Almond Freezer Cake

$\frac{1}{2}$ c/2 oz/50 g Amaretti (little almond macaroons)
$\frac{1}{2}$ c/2 oz/50 g plain butter cookies (rich tea biscuits)
4 oz/4 oz/100 g unsweetened (bitter cooking) chocolate
1 Tbsp anise-flavored liqueur such as Sassolino or Sambuca, or Amaretto di Saronno if an anise flavor is not liked
2 eggs (separated)
$\frac{1}{2}$ c/4 oz/100 g sugar
7 Tbsp/4 oz/100 g butter
$\frac{3}{4}$ c/2 oz/50 g ladyfingers (Boudoir biscuits)

Crush the macaroons and cookies (biscuits) and grate the chocolate. Place in a bowl and sprinkle with the liqueur. In a separate bowl beat the two eggs with the sugar and, when pale and frothy, add the softened and kneaded butter. Mix well. Beat the egg whites and, when they are firm but not dry, fold into the egg yolk and sugar mixture. Lastly fold in the cooky, macaroon and chocolate mixture. Cut the ladyfingers (Boudoir biscuits) in half and line the bottom and sides of a lightly oiled springform (spring-release) pan. Turn the mixture into the pan, level with a spatula and freeze for 2 hours. To serve, release onto a serving dish. This dessert keeps well in the freezer and can be made several days in advance.

Tortellini, like other similar stuffed pastas, merit a few words of their own. To be sure, they originated in Emilia, but they have become the gastronomic heritage of many other regions; and from Italy they have been exported to the entire world. Next to pizza and spaghetti, come tortellini, perhaps the third standard bearer of Italian cuisine. Here are three recipes, but we could list a hundred others. In fact, tortellini, having become part of the public domain, can easily be adapted to the personality and the imagination of the cook.

Tortellini Verdi Gratinati
Spinach Tortellini au Gratin

1 onion
¼ lb/4 oz/100 g lean ground (minced)
   beef
¼ c/3 Tbsp/3 Tbsp olive oil
scant 1 lb/14 oz/400 g ripe (or canned)
   tomatoes
salt
freshly ground pepper
½ c/4 oz/100 g ricotta cheese
½ c/4 oz/100 g grated Parmesan cheese
nutmeg
scant ½ lb/7 oz/200 g spinach
2½ c/10½ oz/300 g all-purpose (plain)
   flour
2 eggs
4 Tbsp/2 oz/50 g butter
1 very fresh Mozzarella cheese

Sauté the chopped onion and ground (minced) beef in the oil and add the puréed tomatoes. Season and simmer uncovered, until reduced.

Prepare the filling for the tortellini by blending the ricotta, half the grated Parmesan, nutmeg, and a little salt.

Wash the spinach well, boil in a very little lightly salted water, drain well, and chop finely. Work the sifted flour, eggs, spinach and a little salt (optional) together to form a pasta dough (see instructions on page 11, Pasta Ripiena). Cook the tortellini in a large pan of boiling salted water until they are al dente. Drain and transfer to a baking dish, sprinkle with melted butter and the remainder of the grated Parmesan cheese, and mix well. Cut the Mozzarella cheese into thin slices and arrange a layer of these on top of the tortellini. Top with the meat-and-tomato sauce. Bake in a moderate oven (350°F/180°C/mk 4) for about 15 minutes.

Cappelletti all'Uso di Romagna
Cappelletti Romagna Style

2 chicken breasts
7 Tbsp/4 oz/100 g butter
salt
freshly ground pepper
¼ lb/4 oz/100 g very fresh ricotta
   cheese
nutmeg
4 eggs
2½ c/10½ oz/300 g all-purpose (plain)
   flour

Sauté the chicken in 3 tablespoons (1½ oz/40 g) of butter for a few minutes on each side, season with salt and pepper, moisten with a few tablespoons of hot water, and finish cooking. Drain the chicken breasts and chop very finely, mixing the meat with the ricotta in a bowl and adding the nutmeg, 1 egg, and a little more salt if needed. Blend thoroughly. Leave to stand.

Make the egg pasta dough by working the flour, the three remaining eggs (and a little salt if desired) together and kneading until it is soft and pliable. Roll out into a thin sheet. Cut out circles of dough approximately 2 inches (5 cm) in diameter and follow instructions for making tortellini and cappelletti on page 11. To prevent the dough drying out, roll up the sheet of pasta in a pastry cloth, leaving only a strip exposed at any one time. Cook in plenty of boiling, salted water. When the cappelletti are tender, drain, sprinkle with melted butter and grated Parmesan, mix, and serve immediately.

Cappelletti are often topped with a meat sauce (see page 94 for Ragù alla Bolognese) as a change from the butter and Parmesan dressing.

Anolini alla Parmigiana

1 small carrot
1 stalk celery
1 clove garlic
1 medium onion
7 Tbsp/4 oz/100 g butter
1 Tbsp olive oil
2¼ c/10½ oz/300 g ground (minced) beef
⅓ c/3½ fl oz/1 dl dry red wine
salt
freshly ground pepper
1 Tbsp tomato paste
1 c/4 oz/5 Tbsp dried or lightly toasted
   bread crumbs
½ c/4 oz/100 g grated Parmesan cheese
4 eggs
2½ c/10½ oz/300 g all-purpose (plain)
   flour

Chop the carrot, celery, garlic, and onion very finely and sauté gently in half the butter and the oil. Add the beef and brown, mixing well. Pour in the wine and cook until it has evaporated. Reduce heat, season, and add the tomato paste diluted in a little hot water. Cover tightly and simmer until the meat is done. Place the bread crumbs and slightly less than half the grated Parmesan in a bowl and add enough of the meat sauce and 1 egg to make a fairly firm filling.

Prepare pasta dough as directed on page 11. When the pasta has been rolled out into a thin sheet, cut into rounds about 1½ inches (4 cm) in diameter. Place a little of the filling in the center of half the rounds, cover with the remaining rounds, and press gently but firmly all around the edges to seal tightly. Cook the anolini in plenty of boiling salted water until tender, drain, top with remaining butter, the meat sauce and Parmesan.

TUSCANY

CARRARA
MASSA
PISTOIA
LUCCA
FLORENCE
PISA
LEGHORN
AREZZO
SIENA
GROSSETO

Crostini di Fegatini
Chicken Liver Canapes

2–3 fresh sage leaves or a pinch of dried
   sage
¼ c/1½ oz/40 g chopped prosciutto (raw
   ham) (more fat than lean)
½ onion
1 Tbsp oil
¾ c/5 oz/150 g chicken livers
salt
freshly ground pepper
1 Tbsp butter
½ lemon
8 slices stale bread
grated Parmesan cheese

Wash the sage leaves and pat dry. Chop the prosciutto (raw ham) and half an onion coarsely and sauté gently in the oil with the sage. When the onion is translucent but not browned, add the washed, trimmed, and chopped chicken livers. Cook briskly, stirring constantly and moisten with 2–3 tablespoons water. Season with a little salt and pepper. Discard the sage leaves and push the cooked chicken liver mixture through a sieve into a mixing bowl. Stir in the butter and a few drops of lemon juice with a wooden spoon. When the ingredients are blended into a smooth paste, spread each slice of bread with it, sprinkle with a little grated Parmesan cheese and place in a very hot oven for a few minutes. These crisp little snacks are ideal as appetizers and are at their best when very hot.

Crescentine

2½ c/10½ oz/300 g all-purpose (plain)
   flour
1 Tbsp butter, lard, or pounded pork fat
½ cake compressed/½ oz/15 g fresh yeast
⅓ c/3½ fl oz/1 dl stock
oil and lard
salt

Sift the flour and salt onto the pastry board, make a well in the center, and gradually mix in the stock, in which the butter or other shortening (fat) has been melted. Add the stock slowly, so the amount can be adjusted according to the absorbency of the flour. The dough should be quite soft and elastic, but workable. Roll out into a thick sheet, fold over twice to form four layers, roll out again as before and repeat the folding and rolling operation 5 or 6 times, ending by rolling out to a sheet between ¼ and ½ inch (½–1 cm) thick. Cut the sheet of dough into strips about 1 inch (2½ cm) wide with a fluted pastry cutter or knife, and then divide the strip into rectangular sections about 3 inches (7–8 cm) long. Heat plenty of oil and lard in a deep fryer until it reaches the boiling point and fry the rectangles a few at a time. They will puff up in a few seconds, small bubbles forming over their surfaces, and turn golden brown. Remove quickly but gently with a slotted spoon; if the bubbles on the surface of the puffs burst, they will fill with oil. Drain on paper towels. Sprinkle with a little salt and serve at once on a warm platter as an appetizer, or sprinkle with sugar for a sweet snack or dessert.

Pasta alla Cacciatora
Hunter's Pasta with Wild Duck

2 wild ducks weighing in total 1 lb/1 lb/
   500 g
1 small carrot
1 stalk celery
1 bunch parsley
salt
¾ lb/¾ lb/350 g commercial short pasta,
   such as nocciole, penne, etc.
4 Tbsp/2 oz/50 g butter
¼ c/2 oz/50 g grated Parmesan cheese

In the original Italian recipe the teal, a marsh bird which frequents the Maremma, is used. The teal is a duck about the size of a large pigeon and is at its best before Christmas.
   Pluck and singe the ducks. Draw and clean them, reserving the livers but discarding the heads, necks, and feet. Wash them well. Place them in a large, heavy cooking pot with water to cover, adding the livers, carrot, celery, parsley, and a little salt. Poach until tender and well done. Remove from cooking liquid, take the flesh from the carcasses, and chop the meat and livers. Boil the pasta until tender but still firm in the duck stock. Drain and dress with melted butter, adding the chopped meat and plenty of grated Parmesan cheese. Mix well and eat at once.
   This is a very digestible dish, since wild duck is much less fatty than domestic duck and has a delicate, pleasing flavor.

Testaroli al Pesto
Pancake Strips with Pesto

2½ c/10½ oz/300 g all-purpose (plain)
   flour
salt
1 small bunch fresh basil
1 clove garlic
¼ c/2 oz/50 g Pecorino cheese
6 Tbsp/4 Tbsp/4 Tbsp olive oil
¼ c/2 oz/50 g Parmesan cheese

Mix the flour, a little salt, and enough water to make a thin batter, which forms a ribbon as it falls from the spoon. This batter used to be cooked in earthenware pots or testi from which the dish got its name. These earthenware cooking vessels were covered with flat or concave lids on which red hot coals and glowing embers were spread, and the batter took only 4 to 5 minutes to cook in the heat which they generated. Nowadays the batter is cooked into thin pancakes like crêpes in a cast-iron skillet or frying pan about 10–12 inches (25–30 cm) wide; see illustration of method (opposite). The pancakes can be prepared in advance and set aside.
   Prepare the dressing by pounding the basil leaves, garlic clove, and Pecorino cheese in a mortar until they blend into a paste. Then add the olive oil gradually, stirring constantly.
   Bring plenty of water to a boil in a large saucepan, add the testaroli, and

immediately turn off the heat. Leave the testaroli in the hot water for 4 to 5 minutes to heat up. Lift them out of the water carefully with a large slotted spoon, drain, cut into strips, and sprinkle with the basil sauce. Serve in a very hot serving dish with grated Parmesan cheese on the side.

Lasagne al Basilico
Lasagne with Basil Sauce

$\frac{1}{3}$ c/2$\frac{3}{4}$ oz/80 g Pecorino Sardo cheese
1 large bunch fresh basil
10 whole walnuts
3 Tbsp/2 Tbsp/30 g olive oil
$\frac{3}{4}$ lb/$\frac{3}{4}$ lb/350 g commercial lasagne
salt

This is a delicious dish with a robust flavor, which takes virtually no time to prepare.

Pound the cheese, the basil, and the nuts together in a mortar (or use a blender) until they are reduced to a paste; then add the oil a little at a time.

Cook the lasagne in plenty of boiling salted water (always add the salt to the water before the pasta goes in, never after). Drain when al dente, add the basil sauce, mix well, and serve immediately.

Testaroli al Pesto (Pancake Strips with Pesto), a characteristic Tuscan dish which hails from Lunigiana.

Pappardelle sulla Lepre
Noodles with Hare

¾ lb/¾ lb/350 g all-purpose (plain) flour
3 eggs
1 egg yolk
salt
1 Tbsp/scant 1 oz/20 g chopped pancetta
*   (fat bacon)*
½ onion
1 stalk celery
½ carrot
1 small sprig parsley
3 Tbsp/1½ oz/40 g butter
4 leg portions (quarters) of hare
2 hare's kidneys
stock
1 Tbsp tomato paste
pepper

Reserve a generous tablespoon of the flour. Work the rest into a soft, elastic dough with the 3 eggs, the egg yolk, and a pinch of salt. Roll out into a sheet about twice as thick as for normal fettucine (ribbon noodles)—about ⅛ inch (3 mm). Leave to dry for a little while until the sheet starts to look slightly wrinkled and leathery. Cut into strips ¾ inch (2 cm) wide for pappardelle.

Chop the pancetta (bacon), onion, celery, carrot, and parsley and sauté with the butter in a skillet or cooking pot. Dredge the pieces of hare and kidneys with flour and add them to the vegetables and pancetta (bacon). Brown the meat on all sides and then add some hot stock with the tomato paste diluted in it. Remove the kidneys, chop them finely, and return them to the pan. Season with salt and pepper, cover, and simmer until the hare is very tender, moistening whenever necessary with a little stock. Remove the pieces of hare and keep them warm.

Cook the noodles in plenty of boiling salted water, drain well, and put in a fairly deep heated bowl. Pour the sauce from the meat over them, mix well, serve on individual heated plates, placing a piece of hare on top of each portion. (Homemade noodles should only take a few minutes to cook.)

Pappardelle all'Aretina
Duck Arezzo Style

scant 1 lb/14 oz/400 g fresh pappardelle
*   (see previous recipe)*
1 duckling
⅓ c/2 oz/50 g prosciutto (raw ham)
1 medium onion
1 stalk celery
1 small carrot
2 Tbsp/1 oz/25 g butter
salt
pepper
1 Tbsp tomato paste
stock

Follow the directions for making pappardelle given in the previous recipe, Pappardelle sulla Lepre. The only difference in this recipe is that the wide ribbon noodles should really be cut out with a fluted pastry wheel, so that the pappardelle will be scalloped.

Make sure the duck is properly prepared, cleaned, and washed; reserve the liver. Chop the prosciutto (raw ham), onion, celery, and carrot. Heat the butter in a deep skillet or heavy saucepan and brown the duck and the liver all over. Add the chopped prosciutto (raw ham) and vegetables, season with salt and pepper, cover, and cook over a moderate heat, adding some of the stock in which the tomato paste has been diluted, a little at a time, whenever the duck and vegetables need moistening (a light bouillon cube dissolved in boiling water, can be used if necessary). Just before the duck is done, remove the liver from the pan, mash it to a paste with a fork, and then return it to the cooking juices, mixing well.

Cook the noodles in a large pan of boiling salted water, drain when al dente, and pour the sauce from the duck over them. They should be served immediately, as a first course. The duck can follow as the main dish accompanied by a fresh salad.

Spaghetti con Sugo di Seppie
Spaghetti with Cuttlefish Sauce

2 cuttlefish or squid, weighing together
*   about ¾ lb/¾ lb/ 300–400 g*
1 small bunch parsley
1 clove garlic
⅓ c/2 oz/50 g bread crumbs
6 Tbsp/4 Tbsp/4 Tbsp olive oil
salt
pepper
¼ c/3 Tbsp/3 Tbsp tomato paste
¾ lb/¾ lb/350 g spaghetti

Prepare the cuttlefish or squid as directed in the recipe for Seppie alla Veneziana on page 58.

Chop the parsley, garlic, and the four tentacles of the fish finely, add the bread crumbs, moisten with a tablespoon of oil, and season with salt and pepper. Stuff the cuttlefish or squid with this mixture, sewing up the openings. Chop the onion and fry it in the remaining oil until golden, add the stuffed fish, season with a little salt, and sauté on all sides. Add a little hot water with the tomato paste diluted in it, cover, and simmer for about 3 hours, until the cuttlefish or squid are tender. Add a little more hot water from time to time as needed.

Cook the spaghetti in boiling, salted water, drain, and pour the sauce from the fish over it. The stuffed fish can be eaten with the spaghetti and sauce or later as the main dish.

Riso e Fagioli alla Fiorentina
Florentine Rice and Bean Soup

1½ lb/1½ lb/700 g fresh white navy
*   (haricot) beans or*
1 lb/1 lb/500 g dried white navy
*   (haricot) beans*
salt
4 Tbsp/2 oz/50 g pork fat
⅓ c/3¼ fl oz/1 dl oil
1 bunch parsley
1 medium onion
1 small carrot
1 stalk celery

2 cloves garlic
1 small piece of red chili pepper
scant 1 lb/14 oz/400 g ripe tomatoes
1 c/7 oz/200 g rice

Shell the beans (if dried beans are used, soak them overnight) and boil in about 2 quarts (3½ pt/2 liters) of water. Season with salt when the beans are nearly done (otherwise the skins become tough).

Pound the fat well or chop finely with a heated knife. Heat the fat in a saucepan with the oil and add the finely chopped parsley, onion, carrot, celery, and garlic. Sauté gently for a few minutes, then add the finely chopped piece of chili pepper and the skinned, seeded, and roughly chopped tomatoes. Mix well and simmer for 15 to 20 minutes with the lid on, then add to the cooked beans (the tomato sauce can be strained (sieved) if a smoother consistency is preferred). Add a little more salt, if needed and simmer for 5 minutes. Rinse the rice in cold water in a strainer (sieve), add to the beans and tomato sauce and cook until just tender.

Some people prefer to leave the rice out of this soup and serve it with croûtons instead.

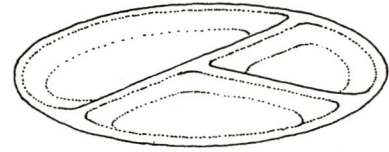

Risotto coi Carciofi
Risotto with Artichokes

6 very young tender artichokes
juice of 1 lemon
1 small bunch parsley
¼ c/2 oz/50 g prosciutto (raw ham)
1 Tbsp butter
1 qt/1¾ pt/1 l homemade beef stock (skimmed of fat) or good quality canned beef consommé diluted with a little hot water
1¼ c/10½ oz/300 g Arborio rice
salt
freshly ground pepper
6 Tbsp/4 Tbsp/4 Tbsp grated Parmesan cheese

Remove and discard the tougher, outer leaves of the artichokes and trim the points off all the easily accessible remaining leaves with a pair of scissors. Cut the artichokes vertically into slices and immediately plunge them into cold water acidulated with the juice of a lemon to keep them from discoloring. Heat the stock. Chop the prosciutto (raw ham) finely and sauté lightly with the butter in a fairly deep cooking pot. Place the artichokes in this pan and pour in about ⅓ cup (3½ fl oz/1 dl) stock. Cover and cook over a gentle heat for about 10 minutes, by which time the liquid will have reduced to almost nothing. Stir in the rice and mix well with a wooden spoon so that each grain is moistened and flavored by the remaining artichoke cooking liquid. Add more stock and continue as for any risotto, moistening and stirring until the rice is tender but still firm. Season with a little salt, if needed, and some freshly ground pepper. Just before the rice is done, add the very finely chopped parsley, turn off the heat, and mix in the grated Parmesan, taking care not to crush the rice. Serve immediately.

Risotto Nero alla Fiorentina
Florentine "Black" Rice

1 lb/1 lb/500 g cuttlefish or squid
1 onion
2 cloves garlic
⅓ c/3½ fl oz/1 dl oil
⅓ c/3½ fl oz/1 dl dry white wine
¼ c/3 Tbsp/3 Tbsp tomato paste
salt
1¼ c/½ lb/250 g Arborio rice

Prepare the fish carefully as instructed on page 58 in the recipe for Seppie alla Veneziana. Reserve the ink sacs, wash the fish, and cut into small pieces. Meanwhile chop the onion and the garlic cloves very finely and fry them very gently in the oil until the onion has begun to color slightly, stir in the cuttlefish or squid, and cook for a few minutes. Turn up the heat, pour in the wine, and allow to evaporate. Add the

tomato paste diluted with ¾ cup (7 fl oz/2 dl) hot water and then add a little salt. Cover and simmer for 20 minutes, stirring from time to time. Keep a separate pan of water boiling from this point onwards. Add the rice to the fish and sauce in the cooking pot and stir with a wooden spoon so that the rice is impregnated with the flavor of the fish and sauce. Cook until the rice is al dente, adding a ladleful of the boiling water whenever necessary. Just before serving the rice, stir in the reserved ink. This gives this dish its distinctive appearance.

Ribollita

1 onion
slices of stale bread from large coarse-textured loaf
6 Tbsp/4 Tbsp/4 Tbsp grated Parmesan cheese
leftover Zuppa di Fagioli (see recipe on page 102)
olive oil

Ribollita (literally, "reboiled") is reheated leftover bean soup, which is just as delicious as when first made, especially when "recycled" in this way.

Slice the onion into very thin rings. Cover the bottom of a baking dish with ½-inch (1 cm) slices of stale bread (remove the crusts if you prefer). Sprinkle with a couple of tablespoons of grated Parmesan cheese, pour in the leftover bean soup, and spread the onion rings over the surface, topping with the remaining grated Parmesan. Place in a preheated moderate oven (350°F/180°C/mk 4) for about 20 minutes when the onion rings should be golden brown. Take the baking dish to the table, pour a very thin film of the best olive oil onto the surface of the soup, and then serve into individual bowls.

Minestra di Ceci
Chick Pea Soup

1 c/7 oz/200 g dried chick peas
½ c/2 oz/50 g all-purpose (plain) flour
salt
6 Tbsp/4 Tbsp/4 Tbsp oil
1 sprig fresh rosemary or a pinch of dried
*   rosemary*
1 clove garlic
1 large ripe tomato (put through a food
*   mill) or 2 tbsp tomato paste diluted in*
*   ⅓ c/3½ fl oz/1 dl hot water*
freshly ground pepper
2–3 Tbsp Parmesan cheese (optional)

Soak the chick peas in lukewarm water for at least 24 hours; then drain and boil them in about 1½ quarts (2¾ pt/1½ liters) lightly salted water. When they are tender, remove about half of them with a slotted spoon and push them through a strainer (sieve) back into the pan.

Make *strisce* (wide ribbon noodles) by combining the flour and a pinch of salt (optional) with just enough cold water to make a workable dough. Roll out, let dry a little, and cut into strips like broad tagliatelle.

Heat the oil in a small saucepan and gently sauté the rosemary (tie it up to keep the tough leaves out of the soup) and the garlic. As soon as the garlic begins to color, add the tomato or tomato paste. Simmer for 5 to 10 minutes, remove the rosemary and the garlic, and add the sauce to the chick peas. Add salt, if needed, and some freshly ground pepper. Finally, add the noodles and cook for a few minutes until tender.

This is a very flavorful soup, and in Tuscany it is eaten with no further embellishment. Elsewhere, two or three tablespoons of grated Parmesan are added just before serving.

Pappa col Pomodoro
Tomato Soup

½ lb/½ lb/225 g stale coarse bread
1½ lb/1½ lb/700 g ripe (or canned)
*   tomatoes*
4 cloves garlic
1 sprig parsley (preferably the flat-
*   leafed Italian variety)*
2 small fresh basil leaves
1 qt/1¾ pt/1 l homemade stock
olive oil
salt
freshly ground pepper

Slice the bread thickly, remove the crusts and bake in the oven until crisp and lightly browned. Wash the tomatoes, cut them in half, and scoop out the seeds. Place them in a saucepan with the garlic, parsley, and basil and simmer. If canned tomatoes are used, put them through a food mill or sieve. Add the stock, the toasted slices of bread, and the oil. Season to taste with salt and plenty of pepper and simmer over a low heat until the soup is thick.

Zuppa di Fagioli
Bean Soup

½ lb/½ lb/225 g dried cannellini or
*   white navy (haricot) beans*
1 onion
1 clove garlic
1 small bunch parsley
1 stalk celery
3–4 fresh basil leaves
⅓ c/3½ fl oz/1 dl olive oil
2–4 leaves each of green and black
*   cabbage (if the latter is unavailable,*
*   substitute red cabbage)*
¼ c/3 Tbsp/3 Tbsp tomato paste
salt
pepper
½ lb/½ lb/225 g stale bread (preferably
*   whole-wheat (wholemeal))*
grated Parmesan cheese (optional)

Soak the beans overnight in lukewarm water. Boil them in 2½ quarts (4½ pt/

2½ liters) lightly salted water, preferably in an earthenware cooking pot. Chop the onion, garlic, parsley, celery, and basil finely and place in a heavy saucepan with the oil. Sauté them until soft and, just before they start to color, pour in about 1 cup of the cooking liquid from the beans. Cut the cabbage leaves into strips, and add to the chopped vegetables. Season with salt and plenty of pepper. Dilute the tomato paste in a little of the cooking liquid from the beans and add to the vegetables. Cover and cook for at least one hour over a moderate heat, moistening frequently with a little more of the bean liquid.

Remove the vegetables from the heat and proceed as follows: Remove at least half the beans from the cooking pot and push through a strainer (sieve) into the saucepan containing the chopped vegetables and cabbage. Remove the rest of the beans (which have been left whole) from their cooking liquid with a slotted spoon and transfer to the cooking pot. Add just enough of the remaining cooking liquid to give the soup the desired consistency. Slice the bread about ½ inch (1 cm) thick and place in the oven for a few minutes to toast lightly. Place the bread slices in the bottom of a warmed soup tureen, pour the soup onto them, and, if desired, sprinkle with some grated Parmesan. Cover and let stand for 15 minutes before serving.

Acquacotta
Tuscan Mushroom Soup

generous ¾ lb/14 oz/400 g fresh cèpes
*   (see note under the recipe for Funghi*
*   Trifolati on page 27)*
8 slices stale bread (crusts removed)
2 cloves garlic
6 Tbsp/4 Tbsp/4 Tbsp oil
scant ½ lb/7 oz/200 g ripe (or canned)
*   tomatoes*
1 bouillon cube
salt
freshly ground pepper
3 eggs
¼ c/2 oz/50 g grated Parmesan cheese

This famous dish, a meal in itself, pays tribute to the Italian ability to conjure up a delicious dish out of next to nothing. Significantly, Acquacotta literally means "cooked water," and the ingredients and method of preparation may vary considerably.

Clean and trim the mushrooms, wash them well, and cut them into fairly thick strips. Place the slices of bread in the oven to brown lightly. Then place two slices in the bottom of each earthenware bowl or soup plate. Sauté the mushrooms with the finely chopped garlic in the oil for 10 minutes in a deep, covered skillet. Peel the tomatoes (blanch them first for easy peeling), remove the seeds, and chop them. If canned tomatoes are used, put them through a food mill or sieve. Add them to the mushrooms. Add ½–1 bouillon cube (preferably chicken or other light flavor) and a little salt and pepper. Pour in about 1 quart (1¾ pt/ 1 liter) boiling water, stir well, and continue cooking for at least 30 to 40 minutes.

Break the eggs into a soup tureen, add the grated Parmesan, and beat lightly with a fork or whisk. Then add the boiling stock, a ladleful at a time, stirring continuously. Pour 2 ladlefuls of soup onto the slices of toasted bread in each individual bowl.

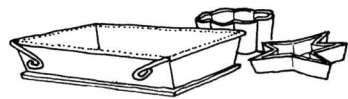

Cacciucco alla Livornese
Leghorn Fish Stew

about 2 lb/2 lb/1 kg assorted fish (see instructions)
1 onion
1 small piece of red chili pepper
5 cloves garlic
1 carrot
1 stalk celery
1 bunch parsley
1 lb/1 lb/500 g ripe (or canned) tomatoes
¾ c/7 fl oz/2 dl oil
salt
¾ c/7 fl oz/2 dl dry white wine
8 slices of stale French or Italian bread

Like French bouillabaisse, this substantial fish soup is meant to be eaten as a main course. The variety of fish used depends on availability (locals say at least as many varieties as there are c's in Cacciucco). Use such fish as: conger eel, moray eel, small octopus, red mullet, squid, mussels (scrubbed, with beards removed), cod fillets, John Dory, sole, porgy (gilt-head bream), crawfish (crayfish), whiting, hake, and a few shrimp (prawns).

Wash the selected fish as necessary; leave the small fish whole and cut the larger fish or pieces into 2-inch (5 cm) slices. Use the heads and bones to make a fumet with 2 cups (1¼ pt/½ liter) lightly salted water, half the onion, chili, 2 cloves garlic, the carrot, celery and a few leaves of parsley. Boil for 30 minutes, strain and reserve.

Put the tomatoes through a food mill or sieve. Using half the oil, sauté the remaining half onion, 2 cloves of garlic, and a few leaves of parsley, all finely chopped, in a large, heavy pan. When the onion starts to color, add the tomatoes and a little salt. Cook until somewhat reduced. Pour in the wine and turn up the heat to allow the wine to evaporate. Push this mixture through a strainer (sieve) and return it to the pan, add the prepared fish (add the firm fish, which will not disintegrate so easily, first and the more delicate fish at intervals during cooking), and return the pan to the heat. Cover and simmer gently for about 20 minutes, add a little fumet when necessary. Stir only very gently when adding the more delicate fish, some of which need be added only about 5 minutes before the end of the cooking time. The liquid should have a certain amount of body. Turn off the heat and add the rest of the parsley, very finely chopped. Brown the slices of bread in the oven and rub them with a cut clove of garlic. Place them in the soup bowls allowing two per person. Place an assortment of fish on the bread and ladle some of the broth over it.

Pan Molle del Ghiottone
Gourmet Open Sandwiches

2 c/¾ pt/4 dl dry white wine
1 bay leaf
1 sprig fresh rosemary or ¼ tsp dried rosemary
2 cloves
black peppercorns
salt
12 slices, stale, coarse bread
3 cloves garlic
gherkins
1 small jar Italian mushrooms in oil (drained)
1 small bunch parsley
3–4 small fresh basil leaves
1 onion
20 pitted (stoned) black olives
12 anchovy fillets
freshly ground pepper
olive oil for dressing
¼ c/3 Tbsp/3 Tbsp best wine vinegar
6 hard-boiled eggs
1 cucumber

To prepare the marinade use a non-metallic bowl, preferably earthenware or ceramic. Mix the white wine with ½ cup (4 fl oz/125 ml) water, the crumbled bay leaf, rosemary, cloves, a few black peppercorns, and a pinch of salt. Let it stand for 24 hours, then strain. Rub the slices of bread with garlic and immerse them briefly in the marinade. Chop the gherkins, mushrooms, parsley, basil, onion, eight black olives, and the anchovy fillets roughly. Place the dipped bread slices on a serving platter, top with the chopped vegetable and anchovy mixture, season with a very little salt and some freshly ground pepper, and dress with plenty of the best quality olive oil mixed with the vinegar. Place half a hard-boiled egg and a black olive on top of each portion. Garnish with thin slices of fresh cucumber.

Pane al Ramerino
Rosemary Buns

1 Tbsp seedless white raisins (sultanas)
¼ c/2 fl oz/60 ml oil
*1 sprig of fresh rosemary or a pinch of
    dried rosemary*
*scant ¾ lb/11 oz/300 g ready-to-use
    bread dough*

These tasty buns can be eaten as a snack or with meals instead of ordinary bread rolls.

Soak the raisins (sultanas) in lukewarm water. Pour the oil into a small saucepan, add the rosemary leaves, and sauté gently for 5 to 10 minutes. Strain the oil immediately (do not allow the rosemary leaves to turn color or darken). Place the dough ball on a pastry board, make a hollow in it, and pour the flavored oil into it. Work the dough until it has absorbed the oil. Squeeze the white raisins (sultanas) free of excess moisture and work into the dough. Oil your hands lightly and divide the dough into small, plump oval (or round) buns. Make a crisscross incision in the top of each bun and place on a lightly floured baking sheet. Cover with a pastry cloth and leave to stand in a warm, draft-free area for 30 minutes. Bake in a hot oven (400°F/200°C/mk 6) for 15 to 20 minutes.

Rognone alla Fiorentina
Sautéed Calf Kidneys

2 fresh calf kidneys
3 Tbsp/1¼ oz/40 g butter
salt
freshly ground pepper
1 small bunch parsley
bread crumbs
1 lemon

Skin the kidneys; slit them in two and remove the suet (the hard white core). Wash them well and pat dry. Heat the butter in a small frying pan until it starts to foam, add the kidneys and brown them lightly on both sides. Remove them from the heat; season with salt, pepper, and the chopped parsley; and let them stand in a cool place (do not refrigerate) turning now and again for about 2 hours. The fat and seasoning will congeal and form a coating around the kidneys. Transfer the kidney halves one by one into a plate of fine bread crumbs and cover well, pressing gently to make the crumbs adhere. Reheat the pan in which the kidneys were cooked and return the kidneys to it; or better still, cook the kidneys on a griddle. Brown them lightly on both sides. Never overcook kidneys, or they will harden and become tough. Serve at once, garnished with lemon wedges.

Bistecca alla Fiorentina
Steak Florentine

*2–4 prime T-bone steaks cut at least 1
    inch (2 cm) thick*
sea salt
freshly ground pepper
olive oil (optional)
1 lemon

Florentine steak at its best is superb, its success depends upon the meat not being more than 2 years old and upon the method of cooking. Do not pound the steaks or season them in any way. Broil (grill) the steaks over a charcoal or wood fire. Only this way of cooking them will give them an authentic taste. Once one side is done (do not overcook), turn and season the cooked side with sea salt and freshly ground pepper. Turn once more so that any excess salt will melt away and remove the steaks from the broiler (grill) or barbecue when they are browned and seared on both sides but still juicy and underdone (according to taste) inside. Transfer to a serving platter and top (if desired) with a very little of the best quality olive oil. Garnish with lemon wedges.

A Tuscan gourmet would consider any condiment other than the salt, pepper, lemon juice and the juices from the meat itself as sacrilege. The steaks should be eaten right away, accompanied by a fresh tossed salad.

Pollo alla Diavola
Broiled (Grilled) Chicken

*1 young broiling (grilling) chicken
    weighing about 2½ lb/2½ lb/1.2 kg*
⅓ c/3½ fl oz/1 dl oil
salt
freshly ground pepper
1 lemon

In Italy a pullet or cockerel about 7 to 8 months old would be used for this recipe.

Split the dressed chicken in half down the backbone (or have your butcher do this for you) and open out (the two halves should still be attached by the breast bone). Flatten as much as possible without splintering the bones. If your broiler (grill) cannot accommodate the whole flattened out bird, separate the two halves down the breast bone. Mix the oil, salt, and plenty of freshly ground pepper in a bowl and sprinkle all over the chicken on both sides. Place the chicken on the rack of a broiler (grill) about 5 inches (12–13 cm) beneath a medium flame or a moderate electric setting.

Cook for about 10 minutes basting occasionally, until one side has cooked and browned lightly. Turn, baste with more of the oil, and cook for another 10 minutes until the other side is done. Turn once more when the two sides are cooked to ensure that the fleshy side is crisp and golden brown on the outside. Transfer to a heated oval serving dish and garnish with wedges of lemon.

The chicken must be served very hot and goes well with a fresh salad.

*Opposite: Two Ligurian specialities— Torta
Pasqualina (Genoese Easter Pie) and Trenette al
Pesto (Trenette with Pesto).*

*Overleaf: Zampone di Modena (Stuffed Pig's Foot
(Trotters) and Tortellini in Brodo (Stuffed Pasta
in Broth), two dishes from Emilia-Romagna.*

Faraona al Cartoccio
Guinea Hen (Fowl) en Papillote

1 guinea hen (fowl) weighing about
2½ lb/2½ lb/1.2 kg
1 Tbsp butter
1 Tbsp oil
1 sprig fresh sage
1 clove garlic
salt
freshly ground pepper
¼ lb/¼ lb/100 kg unrolled pancetta (fat
bacon) thinly sliced
pig's caul (see method)

If the guinea hen (fowl) is not prepared, pluck, singe, trim, and draw it, reserving the liver, lungs and heart. Wash the bird well and pat dry. Melt the butter in a saucepan and sauté the giblets with a few sage leaves and the garlic clove (crushed with the blade of a knife) for a few minutes, stirring with a fork. Season with salt and pepper. Remove from the heat and discard the garlic and sage leaves. Lift out the giblets, chop them finely, and return them to the cooking juices in the pan. Mix and then use as stuffing for the guinea hen.

Sprinkle the bird with salt (preferably coarse sea salt) and then lard it with the pancetta (bacon) and wrap the pig's caul round it. (This is sold ready cleansed and prepared by the butcher, and is the membrane enclosing the foetus. Do not be put off by this; the fine webbing of fat provides a marvelous method of basting and protection from excess heat when roasting many kinds of meat.) If no pig's caul is obtainable, mix a small rich cream cheese with the stuffing; this helps to keep poultry and game birds moist while cooking. Place the bird on a large piece of foil or greaseproof paper; bring two edges of the paper together over the bird, pleat and fold to seal; fold the foil or paper on both sides so the bird is completely encased, leaving some air space. Prick a few holes in the top of the casing to allow a little steam to escape. This method is internationally known as cooking *en papillote*, and it leaves the food juicy and tender. Cook in a preheated oven at 350°F (180°C/mk 4)

for about 1 hour. Transfer the bird, still in its paper or foil case onto the table and open the casing just before serving. Accompany it with roast potatoes and a fresh salad.

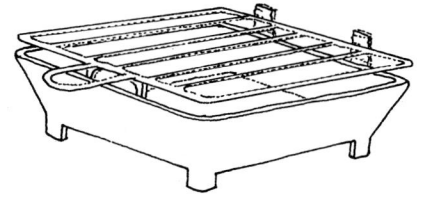

Arista alla Fiorentina
Florentine Roast Pork

salt
freshly ground pepper
grated rind of 1 lemon
2 cloves garlic
1 sprig of fresh rosemary or a pinch of
dried rosemary
2–2½ lb/2–2½ lb/1 kg loin of pork

Mix together in a bowl a little salt, a generous pinch of pepper, the grated lemon rind, the very finely chopped garlic, and the rosemary leaves. Make small slits in the pork with a very sharply pointed knife and insert the mixture in these slits. Cook the loin on a spit at a moderate setting, basting it frequently with its own fat and juices. Alternatively, place the loin in a roasting pan and cook in a moderate oven (about 325°F/170°C/mk 3) allowing about 35 minutes per pound. Turn frequently. If spit roasting, the roast is done when the juices run clear with no trace of pink.

Take the meat out of the oven and keep warm. Potatoes, carrots, cabbage or little turnips complement the roast excellently. When serving, carve the meat in slices about ½ inch (1 cm) thick.

Pork roasted in this way is also delicious cold and keeps well in the refrigerator for several days.

Trippa e Zampa alla Fiorentina
Florentine Tripe and Calf's Foot

1 lb/1 lb/500 g dressed tripe
salt
1 onion
2 stalks celery
2 small carrots
1 bunch parsley
1 calf's foot
1 clove garlic
2–3 fresh basil leaves or a pinch of dried
basil
1 sprig fresh rosemary or a pinch of dried
rosemary
⅓ c/3½ fl oz/1 dl oil
4 Tbsp/2 oz/50 g butter
½ lb/½ lb/225 g firm ripe tomatoes
freshly ground pepper
3 Tbsp/2 Tbsp/2 Tbsp grated Parmesan
cheese

If the tripe is not sold ready dressed, refer to the preparation recommended on page 32 in the recipe for Bûsêca. Cut the tripe into pieces about 2–2½ inches (5–6 cm) square and place in a large pan of salted water with half the onion, a stalk of celery, and one carrot, all coarsely chopped; add a few leaves of parsley.

Wash the calf's foot and place in another large pan of salted water. Cover both pans and cook over a moderate heat for about 2 hours until the tripe is tender and the meat comes away easily from the calf's foot. Dressed tripe will need considerably less cooking: 30 to 45 minutes of gentle simmering should suffice. Drain the tripe and cut it into thin strips. Remove the flesh from the calf's foot and dice. Chop the remaining onion, carrot, celery, garlic, two or three fresh basil leaves, parsley, and a few rosemary leaves very finely. Heat the oil and butter in a wide pan, add the chopped vegetables and herbs, allow to soften over a low heat; then add the tripe, calf's foot meat, and the skinned, seeded and roughly chopped tomatoes. Salt lightly and add plenty of pepper. Cover and simmer very gently for up to 2 hours moistening with the strained tripe cooking liquid or hot water when necessary. When ready, remove from the heat, add the grated Parmesan cheese, mix gently and, serve at once.

Anguilla coi Piselli
Eel with Peas

$1\frac{1}{4}$ lb/$1\frac{1}{4}$ lb/600 g eel
$\frac{3}{4}$ lb/$\frac{3}{4}$ lb/350 g shelled peas
1 clove garlic
1 small onion or shallot
1 small bunch parsley
$\frac{1}{3}$ c/$3\frac{1}{2}$ fl oz/1 dl oil
$\frac{1}{3}$ c/$3\frac{1}{2}$ fl oz/1 dl dry white wine
1 ripe (chopped, put through a food mill, or sieved) tomato (or canned)
salt
freshly ground pepper

If the eel is not already prepared, clean and skin it (see the recipe for Risotto di Bisato on page 53) and cut it into 2-inch (5 cm) lengths. Sauté the chopped onion together with the garlic clove, which has been crushed with the flat of a knife blade but left whole. When the garlic starts to color, discard it, and add the eel. Fry the eel gently, turning carefully to avoid breaking up the flesh. Turn up the heat, pour in the wine, and allow it to evaporate. Add the tomato and the peas and season with salt and a generous pinch of pepper. Cover the saucepan and simmer gently until cooked (about 10 to 15 minutes), stirring very delicately now and then and adding a little hot water if needed.

Triglie alla Livornese
Leghorn Red Mullet

1 stalk celery
3 cloves garlic
1 bunch parsley
$\frac{1}{3}$ c/$3\frac{1}{2}$ fl oz/1 dl oil
$1\frac{1}{2}$ lb/$1\frac{1}{2}$ lb/600 g ripe (or canned) tomatoes
salt
freshly ground pepper
8 medium or 4 large red mullet

Chop the celery, garlic, and parsley together, reserving a few sprigs of parsley. Heat the chopped mixture for a few minutes in the oil in a wide, deep skillet and when it has started to soften, add the skinned, seeded and chopped tomatoes (put them through a food mill or sieve if canned). Season and simmer for 15 minutes, then push through a strainer (sieve) and return the sauce to the pan. Place the mullet in the pan in a single layer and cook over a moderate heat. If the mullet are small, there is no need to turn them, larger fish, however, will need turning to cook evenly. This should be done with care, using a fork and a spatula, so that they remain intact. Just before the mullet are ready, sprinkle them with plenty of very finely chopped parsley, and serve immediately, straight from the cooking dish. A fresh salad can be served with them or better still Fagioli all'Uccelletto, the recipe for which is given on page 110.

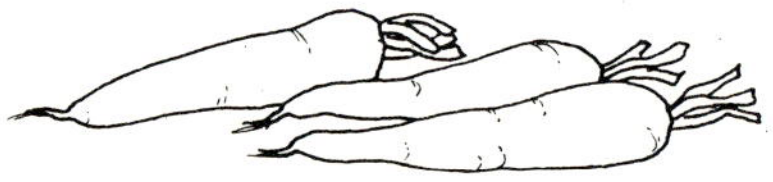

Trote Affogate all'Aretina
Trout Arezzo Style

4 small trout each weighing about $\frac{1}{2}$ lb/ $\frac{1}{2}$ lb/225 g
2 cloves garlic
1 large bunch parsley
$\frac{3}{4}$ c/7 fl oz/2 dl oil
$\frac{3}{4}$ c/7 fl oz/2 dl dry white wine
3 Tbsp/2 Tbsp/2 Tbsp all-purpose (plain) flour
salt
freshly ground pepper

Gut and clean the trout, cut off their fins and tails, and wash well. Pat dry, and roll in the flour. Choose a frying pan wide enough to hold all the trout lying flat in one layer, and sauté the very finely chopped garlic and parsley in the oil, stirring with a wooden spoon, until the garlic begins to color. Place the trout in the pan, season with salt and pepper, and fry gently, turning once, until both sides are lightly browned. Pour in the wine and allow to reduce slowly without increasing the heat. When the fish are cooked (about 20 minutes after they are placed in the pan), transfer them to a heated serving platter and sprinkle with the pan juices. Serve at once.

Folaghe alla Puccini
Coot or Scoter Puccini

2 coots or scoters or 2 wild duck (teal, widgeon) (see instructions)
4 anchovy fillets
wine vinegar for marinating
1 onion
1 carrot
1 stalk celery
1 bunch parsley
4–5 fresh basil leaves
1 bay leaf
$\frac{1}{3}$ c/$3\frac{1}{2}$ fl oz/1 dl oil
1 Tbsp butter
salt
freshly ground pepper
$\frac{1}{3}$ c/$3\frac{1}{2}$ fl oz/1 dl dry white wine
$\frac{1}{4}$ c/3 Tbsp/3 Tbsp tomato paste

Wild duck or fresh-water fowl can be blanched for a few minutes in boiling salted water to rid them of a slightly fishy look. If plucking and dressing the wild birds, remove the two oil sacs near the tail. *Folaghe* abounded in the days before the marshy Maremma region of Tuscany was drained, and are still found in the remaining watery patches.

Rinse the anchovies to get rid of excess salt; then chop them. Prepare the duck, quarter it, and marinate it in the vinegar in a non-metallic bowl for a couple of hours. Remove it from the marinade, wash thoroughly and dry. Chop the vegetables and herbs finely, mix with the anchovies, and sauté in the oil and butter for a few minutes. Add the quartered duck or wild fowl, season with salt and pepper and brown the portions lightly all over. Pour in the wine and allow to reduce, then add the

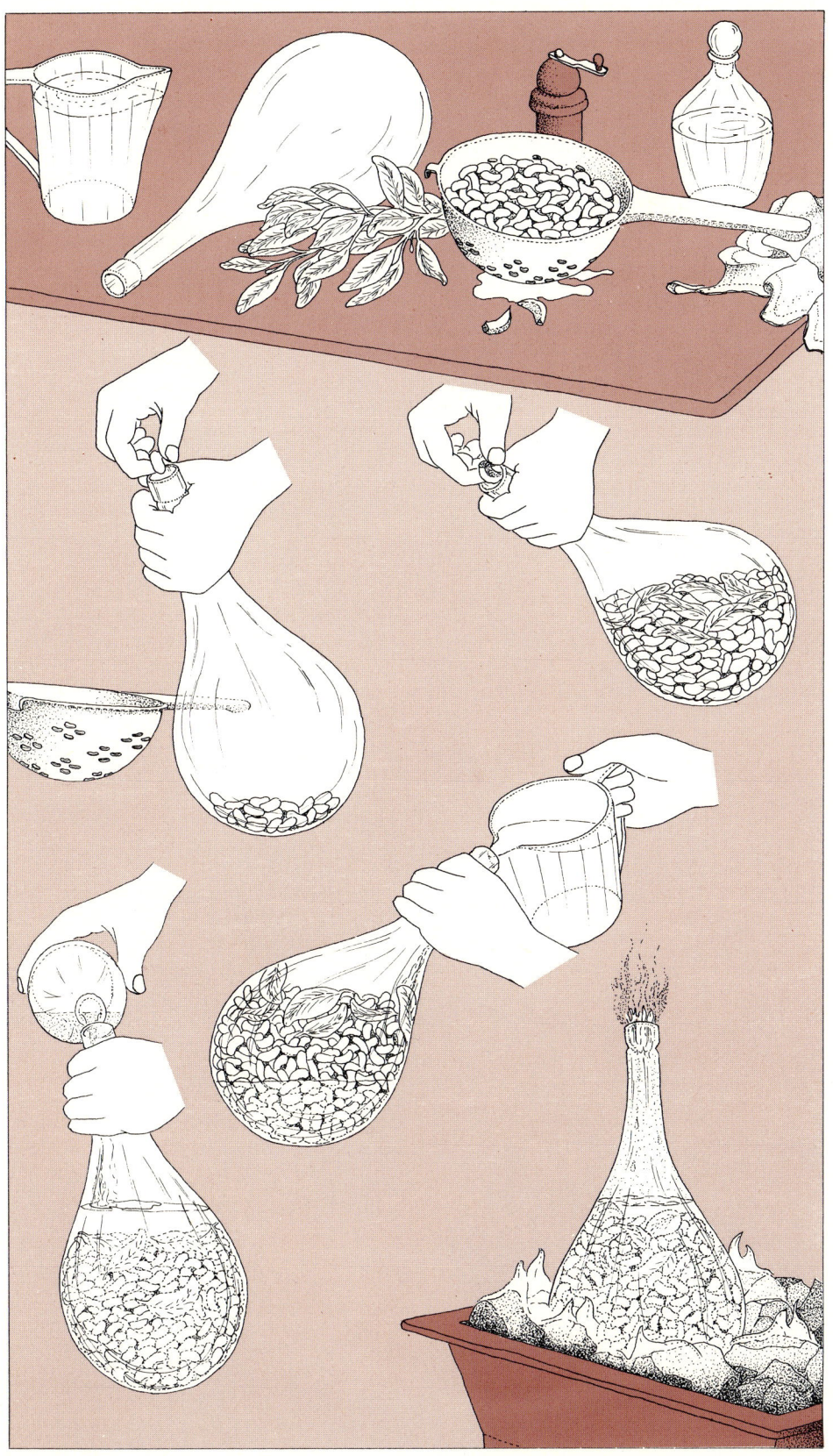

tomato paste diluted with about 1 cup (8 fl oz/¼ liter) hot water, stir gently, cover the cooking pot, and simmer for about 30 minutes. Remove the duck from the pan, pour the sauce through a strainer (sieve), return the meat and sauce to the pan, and serve hot with thick slices of bread, lightly browned in the oven.

Tortino di Carciofi
Baked Artichoke Omelet

4 very tender young artichokes
1 lemon
a few Tbsp all-purpose (plain) flour
⅓ c/3½ fl oz/1 dl oil
salt
4 eggs
freshly ground pepper
scant ¼ c/2–3 Tbsp/2–3 Tbsp milk

Remove the tough outer leaves of the artichokes, trim the tips off the remaining leaves with a pair of scissors, and cut the artichokes vertically into slices. Plunge the slices immediately into plenty of water acidulated with the juice of a lemon to prevent discoloration. When all four artichokes have been prepared, remove them from the water, dry them, and coat them, with flour. Heat half the oil in a wide frying pan and fry the artichoke halves over a low heat, turning frequently until they are cooked through. Moisten with a little hot water when they dry out too much. After about 15 minutes, remove them from the heat and add a little salt. Transfer the artichoke slices to a baking dish, arranging them in one layer, and sprinkle with the remaining oil. Beat the eggs with a little salt, a generous pinch of pepper, and the milk and pour this mixture over the artichokes. Bake in a preheated oven at 350°F (180°C/mk 4) for about 20 minutes. Serve the artichokes directly from the baking dish while still piping hot.

Left: White navy (haricot) beans or cannellini beans can be cooked in a wine flask over a charcoal fire.

Fagioli in Fiasco
Beans Cooked in a Wine Bottle

¾ lb/¾ lb/350 g shelled fresh white navy
(haricot) beans or cannellini beans
(equivalent to just over 2 lb/2 lb/1
kg unshelled beans) or
½ lb/½ lb/225 g dried beans (soaked
overnight)
⅓ c/3½ fl oz/1 dl olive oil
2 cloves garlic
5–6 fresh sage leaves
salt
freshly ground pepper

Wash the shelled beans and drop them
into a wine bottle such as the kind
Chianti comes in (be sure to remove the
straw). Pour in the oil, add the crushed
garlic cloves, the sage leaves, a little
freshly ground pepper, and generous 1
pint (1½ pt/½ liter) water. Cork the bottle
with a wad of cheesecloth (muslin)
pushed into the top of the neck, leaving
it just loose enough for the steam to
escape slowly. Place the wine bottle on
smoldering charcoal embers or in a slow
oven (taking care to give it some means
of safe support) and cook for 3 hours.
Empty into a warm earthenware dish
and add salt to taste (if the salt were
added earlier it would toughen the thin
inner skins of the beans), and a little
more pepper if desired.

These beans can be eaten on their own
or as a side vegetable. They are equally
good hot or cold.

Funghi Trippati
Mushrooms Cooked like Tripe

1 lb/1 lb/500 g large fresh field
mushrooms or imported fresh Regal
Agaric (Amanita caesaria)
mushrooms
2 Tbsp/1 oz/25 g butter
2 cloves garlic
1 Tbsp oil
3 Tbsp grated Parmesan cheese
salt
freshly ground pepper

Unfortunately the *funghi ovuli* which are
used for this dish in Italy are rarely
available and, when they are, command
a high price. They look far more highly-
colored and suspect than some of the
poisonous varieties of mushroom but
are delicious.

Wash and trim the mushrooms, pat
dry, and cut into strips. Slightly crush
the garlic cloves and sauté in the butter
and oil until they begin to color. Discard
the garlic and add the mushrooms,
cooking for a few minutes while stirring
with a wooden spoon. Season with salt,
pepper and lastly, just before they are
done, the grated Parmesan. They will
need only 10 to 15 minutes' cooking in
all.

Fagioli all'Uccelletto
Beans Uccelletto

¾ lb/¾ lb/350 g fresh white navy
(haricot) beans or black-eyed beans
(2 lb/2 lb/1 kg before shelling) or
½ lb/½ lb/225 g dried beans (soaked
overnight)
1 sprig sage
6 Tbsp oil
salt
freshly ground pepper
3 Tbsp tomato paste or 2 ripe tomatoes
(seeded and chopped)

Boil the beans in lightly salted water and
then drain. Wash and dry the sage leaves
and sauté them in the oil in a large pan.
Add the cooked beans and a little salt
and pepper. Mix well over a low heat
allowing the beans to absorb some of the
oil; then stir in the tomatoes or the
tomato paste diluted in ½ cup (4 fl oz/1.2
dl) water. Cook over a low heat until the
beans have absorbed the liquid. Remove
from the heat and serve with boiled
meats or poultry. These beans are also
tasty on their own.

Fagiolini all'Aretina
Arezzo Style Green Beans

1 lb/1 lb/500 g green beans (French
beans) (see instructions)
2 cloves garlic
¼ c/3 Tbsp/3 Tbsp oil
3 ripe (or canned) tomatoes
salt
freshly ground pepper

The original Italian recipe calls for a
particular variety of very long, thin
bean. These sometimes have a purple
tinge and melt in the mouth when young
and tender but become stringy if picked
when they are older or not cooked soon
after picking. If the beans are very fresh,
add less water when cooking.

Cut the ends off the beans, wash them,
and cut each bean in thirds. Warm the
finely chopped garlic cloves in the oil
and then add the beans and the chopped
or sieved tomatoes. Season with a little
salt and a generous pinch of pepper, stir
well, and pour in enough cold water to
cover the beans. Simmer, tightly
covered, until the beans are tender. By
this time, the sauce should have reduced
considerably and should be fairly thick.
If necessary, reduce the liquid by cooking briskly without the lid on, stirring
continuously but carefully, so that the
beans do not break up.

These beans go well with boiled
dishes; but they are also full-flavored
enough to eat as part of a vegetarian
meal or as a light supper dish instead of
meat.

Salsa al Dragoncello
Tarragon Sauce

1 small fresh loaf of white bread (crusts
removed)
2 cloves garlic
1 small bunch fresh tarragon
⅓ c/3½ fl oz/1 dl red wine vinegar
oil
salt

This sauce is excellent with boiled meat and poultry of all kinds; it keeps well for several days.

Crumble the white bread into a small mixing bowl and add the vinegar. Wash and pick over the leaves from the tarragon; then chop them finely with the garlic. Squeeze the bread crumb mixture by handfuls to get rid of excess vinegar. Push the soaked bread crumbs through a strainer (sieve) together with the chopped tarragon and garlic (or combine in a blender). Transfer to a bowl. Using a wooden spoon, stir continuously while adding the oil a very little at a time. Add salt to taste and beat until the sauce is very smooth and creamy.

Castagnaccio alla Toscana
Tuscan Chestnut Cake

1 small sprig of fresh rosemary or
    a pinch of dried
3 Tbsp/2 Tbsp/2 Tbsp seedless white
    raisins (sultanas)
scant 1 lb/14 oz/400 g chestnut flour
6 Tbsp/4 Tbsp/4 Tbsp oil
$\frac{1}{2}$ c/3 Tbsp/3 Tbsp sugar
salt
2$\frac{1}{4}$ c/18 fl oz/$\frac{1}{2}$ l cold milk
2$\frac{1}{4}$ c/18 fl oz/$\frac{1}{2}$ l cold water
2–3 Tbsp fine bread crumbs
3 Tbsp/2 Tbsp/2 Tbsp pine nuts

Chop the rosemary leaves very finely. Soak the white raisins (sultanas) in lukewarm water for about 20 minutes, squeeze out excess water, and dry on paper towels. Place the chestnut flour in a mixing bowl, add 6 tablespoons (4 Tbsp/4 Tbsp) oil, the sugar, and a pinch of salt. Work all these ingredients together throughly and then add the milk and water, stirring continuously. The batter should be thin and free from lumps. Butter a cake pan 9 inches (22–24 cm) in diameter, sprinkle with the bread crumbs, tipping out excess, and pour in the cake batter. Sprinkle the white raisins (sultanas), pine nuts, and rosemary leaves evenly over the surface of the batter and drizzle with a very little oil. Bake in a medium to hot oven (350°F–400°F/180°C–200°C/mk 4–6) for about 1 hour or until a cake tester comes out clean. The cake should be crisp and crusty on the outside and soft and moist inside. It is good warm or cold.

Cenci
Tuscan Fried Pastries

2$\frac{1}{4}$ c/9 oz/250 g cake flour (very fine
    flour)
3 Tbsp/1 oz/25 g sugar
salt
rind of $\frac{1}{2}$ lemon
2 eggs
2 Tbsp/1 oz/25 g butter
1 Tbsp brandy (optional)
1–2 Tbsp white wine
oil (or lard) for frying
confectioners' (icing) sugar

Sift the flour, sugar, and a pinch of salt onto a working surface or pastry board. Add the grated lemon rind and shape into a mound with a well in the center. Place the eggs in the well, together with the kneaded and softened (not melted) butter and a tablespoon of wine. This mixture should be given prolonged and thorough kneading and must be quite firm. If it is too stiff, moisten with a tablespoon of wine or brandy; if too soft, add a little flour. Shape into a ball, lightly dredge with flour, wrap in a pastry cloth, and leave to stand for about 1 hour.

Roll the dough out into a fairly thin sheet and cut out rectangles measuring 3 × 4$\frac{1}{2}$ inches (8 × 12 cm) with a fluted pastry wheel. Then make four parallel lengthwise cuts in each rectangle, stopping short of the edge at each end. Heat the oil or lard (or a mixture of both) in a deep, heavy pan until it is boiling. Fry one pastry at a time, having, so far as is possible, intertwined the strips and pulled some slightly, so the pastries will curl into strange shapes as they puff up in the hot oil. "Cenci" means "rags and tatters" which is descriptive of their appearance. Remove the pastries with a slotted spoon when they are puffed and golden and drain on paper towels, then transfer to a wide dish and dredge with plenty of confectioners' (icing) sugar. Cenci are very good eaten hot or cold; they go well with a smooth sweet wine such as Vin Santo.

Brigidini
Aniseed Wafers

1 egg
$\frac{1}{4}$ c/2 oz/50 g granulated sugar
1$\frac{3}{4}$ c/7 oz/200 g cake flour (very fine
    flour)
salt
1 tsp aniseed
3 Tbsp/scant $\frac{1}{2}$ oz/40 g butter
a few Tbsp milk
a few drops vanilla extract (essence)
1 tsp baking powder

Break the egg into a bowl, add the sugar, sifted flour, salt, aniseed, and softened butter and mix, adding a little milk and vanilla extract (essence) to obtain a firm dough. Add the baking powder and stir well. Working quickly, since the rising agent in the baking powder starts to work on contact with moisture, break off small pieces and roll into little balls no bigger than walnuts between the palms of your hands. Flatten the balls into small, thin rounds and cook one at a time in the special hand-held waffle iron (stiaccia) used to cook these wafers over a gas burner or other direct source of heat. Alternatively flatten the wafers very thin with a rolling pin and cook them on a griddle or in a heavy (cast iron) frying pan until both sides are crisp and golden.

UMBRIA

PERUGIA

TERNI

Spaghetti col Tartufo Nero
Truffled Spaghetti

1 black truffle about the size of an egg
4 anchovy fillets
6 Tbsp/4 Tbsp/4 Tbsp olive oil
1 small bunch parsley
¾ lb/¾ lb/350 g spaghetti
salt

Rub the truffle with a brush or coarse cloth to clean; do not wash it. Cut it into wafer-thin slices. Chop the anchovies very finely and place them in a small bowl. Add the oil drop by drop and work with a fork until the anchovies and oil blend into a smooth thin paste. Add the truffle slivers and the finely chopped parsley.

Boil the spaghetti in a large pan of salted water and drain when al dente. Turn into a warmed serving dish and mix with the truffle sauce. Such an exquisite taste obviously needs no additions, so no grated Parmesan is added.

Tagliolini alla Francescana

scant ¾ lb/scant ¾ lb/320 g tagliolini
(⅛-inch-wide (3 mm) fresh ribbon noodles)
4 Tbsp/2 oz/50 g butter
1 lb/1 lb/500 g ripe (or canned) tomatoes (seeded and chopped or put through a food mill or sieve)
¼ c/2 oz/50 g grated Parmesan cheese
1 medium onion
1 small carrot
1 stalk celery
1 small bunch parsley
1 sprig of fresh thyme or a pinch of dried thyme
salt

Chop the onion, carrot, and celery very finely and sauté gently with the butter in a wide pan for 5 to 6 minutes. When the vegetables have started to soften but have not colored, add the tomatoes, the chopped parsley, and the thyme. Increase the heat to moderate, cover,

and cook and reduce for 15 minutes.

Meanwhile, boil the tagliolini in plenty of salted water until tender but firm. Drain (not too thoroughly) and mix well with the sauce in a warmed deep serving dish. Sprinkle with half the grated Parmesan, mix once more, and serve with the remaining Parmesan cheese on the side.

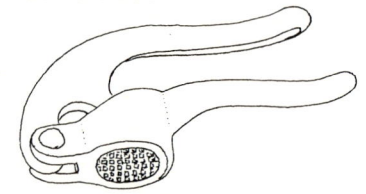

Minestra di Farro
Pearl Barley Soup

1 ham bone with a few scraps of meat on it (ideally bone from prosciutto (raw ham))
1 small carrot
1 stalk celery
½ onion
3 ripe tomatoes (peeled and seeded) or ½ lb/½ lb/225 g canned tomatoes (put through a food mill or sieve)
salt
scant ½ lb/7 oz/200 g pearl barley
¼ c/2 oz/50 g mixture of grated Parmesan and Pecorino cheese

Boil the ham bone in water for approximately 15 minutes to get rid of excess salt. Drain and pour in just over 6 cups (2¾ pt/1½ liters) of fresh cold water. Chop the carrot, celery, and onion into small pieces and add to the water, followed by the tomatoes. Cook briskly for approximately 15 minutes, remove the ham bone, strain the liquid and return to the rinsed pan. Add a very little salt if any is needed and bring to a boil.

Slowly add the pearl barley by handfuls into the boiling broth, stirring constantly with a wooden spoon. Reduce the heat to low and cook for a further 30 minutes. Just before removing from the heat, add any scraps of meat which can be trimmed from the ham bone. Take the pan from the heat, add the Parmesan and Pecorino, mix well once more and serve at once.

Minestra alla Perugina
Beef and Vegetable Soup Perugia Style

1 carrot
1 leek
1 stalk celery
1 egg white
scant ¼ c/1¾ oz/50 g oil
½ lb/½ lb/225 g ground (minced) lean beef
1 qt/1¾ pt/1 l homemade beef stock or good quality canned beef consommé (diluted)
salt
¼ c/2 oz/50 g grated Parmesan cheese

Roughly chop the carrot, leek, and celery and sauté gently for a few minutes in the oil over a low heat. Place the egg white, ground (minced) beef, stock, and an equal quantity of cold water in a large cooking pot and heat to the boiling point. Add the vegetables, stir very thoroughly, and allow to boil gently until the liquid has reduced to half its original volume and is clear (the egg white will help clarify the soup). Season with salt to taste. Pour the soup into a warmed soup tureen, sprinkle with the grated Parmesan, and serve at once.

Cipollata
Thick Onion Soup

2 lb/2 lb/1 kg large onions
6 Tbsp/4 Tbsp/4 Tbsp oil
4 Tbsp/2 oz/50 g pork fat
4–5 small, fresh basil leaves
salt
freshly ground pepper
1 lb/1 lb/500 g ripe (or canned) tomatoes
2 eggs
¼ c/2 oz/50 g grated Parmesan cheese

This onion soup should be thick and will be even more appetizing if served with thick slices of lightly toasted coarse Italian bread.

Start the preparation of this dish at least 12 hours in advance by slicing the onions very finely and soaking them in a large bowl of cold water overnight. The next day heat the oil in a heavy pan with the pounded pork fat for a few minutes; then add the drained onion slices and the roughly chopped basil leaves. Season with salt and a little pepper. Cover the pan and sauté the onions over a low heat until they are tender and translucent but do not allow them to color. Put the tomatoes through a food mill or sieve. Add them to the onions along with a generous quart (1¾ pt/ 1 liter) of water. Stir thoroughly, replace the lid, and simmer over a low heat for 1 hour or longer to reduce the liquid considerably and give it body. Just before removing the soup from the heat, break the eggs into a bowl, add the grated Parmesan cheese, and beat well. Remove the onion soup from the heat and pour in the egg and cheese mixture while stirring briskly.

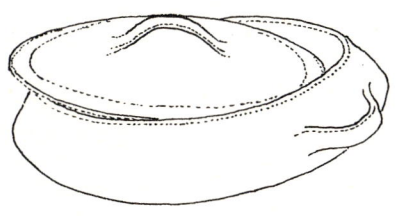

Fettine di Maiale in Salsina
Pork in Piquant Sauce

1 lb/1 lb/500 g tender, lean pork
¼ c/3 Tbsp/3 Tbsp oil
⅓ c/3½ fl oz/1 dl dry red wine
juice of ½ lemon
salt
freshly ground pepper
1 Tbsp capers (pickled or salted)

Slice the pork fairly thinly. Heat the oil gently in a pan and sauté the pork slices until they are light brown on both sides. Pour in the wine, the lemon juice, a little salt and pepper to taste, and then the capers (washed and drained if salted and roughly chopped if large). Cover tightly and simmer over a low heat until the sauce thickens. Serve while still very hot.

Cardi alla Perugina
Cardoons Perugia Style

1 cardoon weighing about 1¾ lb/1¾ lb/ 800 g
juice of 1 lemon
salt
flour for coating
2 eggs
bread crumbs for coating
oil for frying
1 Tbsp butter
1 small onion
¼ lb/¼ lb/100 g ground (minced) lean beef
⅓ c/3½ fl oz/1 dl dry white wine
1½ lb/1½ lb/700 g ripe (or canned) tomatoes
1 Tbsp dried Italian mushrooms (soaked in warm water)
freshly ground pepper
½ c/4 oz/100 g grated Parmesan cheese
scant ½ lb/7 oz/200 g Fontina cheese

Soak the mushrooms in lukewarm water to soften. Wash and trim the cardoon, discarding the tough outer leaves and removing any strings from the more tender leaves. Cut into 2-inch (5 cm) lengths and drop into cold water acidulated with the lemon juice to prevent discoloration.

Bring a large pan of water to a boil, add salt, and boil the pieces of cardoon until they begin to get tender. Drain them well and coat them with flour. Beat the eggs and dip the floured portions of cardoon in the egg; then cover with bread crumbs. Heat plenty of oil to the boiling point in a skillet or fairly deep frying pan and fry the breaded cardoons a few at a time until they are golden brown. Drain on paper towels.

Heat the butter together with 3 tablespoons (2 Tbsp/2 Tbsp) oil in a heavy pan and sauté the finely chopped onion until soft and almost translucent. Add the ground (minced) beef and brown, mixing well. Pour in the wine and turn up the heat so that the wine will evaporate. Add the peeled, seeded, and chopped tomatoes (if canned tomatoes are used, put them through a food mill or sieve) and the mushrooms, drained

and chopped into very small pieces. Add salt and pepper to taste, stir well, and cover tightly. Simmer over a moderate heat for at least 30 minutes. The sauce should become smooth and fairly thick. Butter a baking dish, place a layer of the cardoons in the bottom, cover with several spoonfuls of the meat and tomato sauce, sprinkle with some grated cheese, and top with thinly sliced Fontina cheese. Repeat the layering until all the ingredients have been used, ending with a generous layer of sliced Fontina completely covering the surface of the dish. Place in a preheated hot oven (400°F/200°C/mk 6) and bake for 15 minutes. Serve in the baking dish while the cardoons are very hot.

Uccelletti dell'Umbria
Small Game Birds Braised Umbria Style

8–12 woodcock, snipe, or small quail
⅓ c/3½ fl oz/1 dl oil
1 Tbsp butter
1 clove garlic
1 sprig fresh sage or a pinch of dried sage
¾ c/4 oz/100 g green olives
1 lemon
⅓ c/3½ fl oz/1 dl dry white wine
salt
freshly ground pepper

In Umbria songbirds such as thrushes and larks are trapped or shot and eaten but in countries where these species are protected, woodcock, snipe, or quail can be substituted. Pluck, singe, draw, and wash the birds thoroughly, patting dry with paper towels. (Snipe are often cooked plucked but undrawn). Heat the oil and butter in a lidded skillet. Add a crushed clove of garlic (flatten it with the blade of a knife), and, when the garlic starts to color, discard it and sauté the birds with the sage, the pitted (stoned) and halved olives, and half a lemon cut into thin rounds. Cover the skillet and cook over a fairly high heat for a few minutes. Then pour in the wine, add salt, and simmer with the lid on for about 30 minutes, moistening with a little hot water when necessary. Add only a very little water at a time, so that the birds cook gently. When the birds are done, remove and discard the sage and the lemon slices. Add the juice of the remaining ½ lemon, season with salt and pepper to taste, and serve.

Piccioni allo Spiedo
Spit-Roasted Pigeons

2 young, plump pigeons or other small
  birds, such as quail, partridge, or rock
  Cornish game hens
¼ c/3 Tbsp/3 Tbsp oil
salt
1 Tbsp vinegar
¾ c/7 fl oz/2 dl dry red wine
1 Tbsp pitted (stoned) black olives
4–5 small, fresh sage leaves or ¼ tsp dried
  sage
1 lemon

If the pigeons are not bought already prepared, pluck, singe, draw, and wash them well. Mount them on the spit skewer and broil (grill) them very gently, basting them with oil and sprinkling them with a little salt. Pour the vinegar and wine into the pan which catches the juices from the spit while the meat is cooking. Add the chopped olives, the sage, and the peeled lemon, sliced into rounds (remove all the white part, or pith). This mixture is used to baste the pigeons frequently during cooking and will gradually combine with the juices which drip into it from the pigeons. When the pigeons are done (they need slow but thorough cooking if they are to be moist and tender), remove them from the spit and keep them warm, covered with foil.

If the giblets have been reserved, or the birds have not been drawn, remove the innards and chop the liver, heart and lungs very finely and stir into the juices in the drip tray with a wooden spoon. Cut the pigeons in half (with poultry shears, if possible), place on a warmed serving platter, cover with the sauce from the pan, and eat without delay.

The pigeons can be placed on pieces of toasted bread before the sauce is poured over them, or thickly cut toast can be served as an accompaniment.

Trota della Nera
Nera Trout

1 trout weighing about 2 lb/2 lb/1 kg
¼ c/3 Tbsp/3 Tbsp bread crumbs
1 bunch parsley
salt
freshly ground pepper
oil
1 lemon

Gut the trout and trim the tail and fins. Wash it thoroughly and dry it well with paper towels.

Place the bread crumbs in a bowl with the finely chopped parsley, a good pinch of salt, and some pepper and mix well. Stuff the trout with this mixture, reserving about 1 tablespoonful. Heat some oil in a skillet or frying pan, preferably cast iron, place the fish in the pan, sprinkle with the remaining bread crumb and parsley mixture, and cook slowly. When the trout is cooked through, transfer carefully to a heated serving dish and drizzle a little oil over it. Garnish with lemon wedges or slices and serve at once.

Bocconcini di Baccalà
Salt Cod Fritters

1¾ lb/1¾ lb/800 g salt cod
1 egg
¼ c/3 Tbsp/3 Tbsp all-purpose (plain)
  flour
salt
milk
oil for frying
1 lemon

Prepare the salt cod by pounding it and soaking it for 12 to 24 hours in several changes of fresh water. Remove the skin and any bones and cut into small pieces.

Make a coating batter by mixing the egg, flour, a generous pinch of salt, and enough milk to achieve the correct consistency. Heat plenty of oil in a deep skillet (or deep fryer) until very hot. Dip the pieces of cod one by one in the batter and fry them until they are crisp and golden brown. Drain and place on paper towels to get rid of excess oil. Transfer the cod to a heated serving dish, garnish with lemon wedges and serve.

Anguilla in Umido
Braised Eel in Tomato Sauce

1 eel weighing about 1¾ lb/1¾ lb/800 g
1 onion
2 cloves garlic
⅓ c/3½ fl oz/1 dl oil
⅓ c/3½ fl oz/1 dl dry white wine
½ lb/½ lb/225 g very ripe (or canned)
  tomatoes (put through a food mill or
  sieve)
1 bunch parsley
salt
freshly ground pepper

If the eel is not bought already prepared, clean, skin, and wash it well. Cut it into 2-inch (5 cm) lengths. (See instructions on page 53, in the recipe for Risotto di Bisato for the correct and easiest way to prepare eel.) Chop the onion and garlic finely and fry gently in the oil until the onion starts to color. Lay the pieces of eel in the pan and sauté briskly. Pour in the wine and allow it to evaporate. Add the tomatoes and chopped parsley. Season with salt and pepper, cover the pan, and cook slowly for about 20 minutes, stirring frequently but gently to prevent the eel from sticking to the bottom of the pan. Add a little hot water if the liquid reduces too quickly. The sauce should be fairly thick and the portions of eel should remain intact.

Salsina per Arrosti e Cacciagione
Sauce for Roast Meats and Game

¼ c/2 oz/50 g prosciutto (raw ham)
2 chicken livers
2 cloves garlic
2 c/¾ pt/4 dl dry white wine
3 fresh sage leaves or a pinch of dried
    sage
1 sprig of rosemary or ¼ tsp dried
    rosemary
a few juniper berries
½ lemon
⅓ c/3½ fl oz/1 dl oil
¾ c/7 fl oz/2 dl red wine vinegar
salt
freshly ground pepper

Chop the prosciutto (raw ham), the chicken livers, and the garlic and place in a non-aluminum pan (i.e., cast-iron, earthenware, or enameled) together with the white wine, sage, rosemary, juniper berries, peeled lemon cut into rounds, the oil, and the vinegar. Add salt and pepper and simmer over a gentle heat, stirring frequently until the sauce is reduced to half its original volume and has acquired some body.

Pinocchiate
Pine Nut Candies

generous 1 c/5 oz/150 g pine nuts
¾ lb/¾ lb/350 g granulated sugar
grated rind of ½ lemon

These candies are eaten at Christmas and date back to the fifteenth century.
   Toast the pine nuts in the oven for a few minutes so that they become dry and crunchy but do not allow them to color. Place the sugar in a heavy saucepan with ½ cup (4 fl oz/125 ml) of water and bring slowly to a boil. Boil until a small quantity of syrup forms threads when

Right: Pinocchiate (Pine Nut Candies) from Umbria can be flavored with lemon or chocolate.

dropped into cold water, then remove from the heat and add the pine nuts and the grated lemon rind, stirring constantly. Turn out immediately onto a dampened marble slab or working surface and level out an equal thickness. Working quickly before the mixture cools and sets hard, cut into squares, diamonds or other shapes as desired. When cold these are placed in colored wrappers.

A chocolate flavor can be substituted for the lemon flavor; simply replace the grated lemon rind with 1 tablespoon grated bitter chocolate.

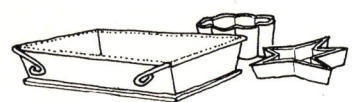

hot and fry the dough balls a few at a time, removing them with a slotted spoon when they are done. Drain them on paper towels.

Blanch the almonds for 2 minutes to make them easier to skin, then skin them and cut them into thin slivers. Heat the honey in a heavy saucepan until it turns a light russet brown, remove it from the heat, and add the little fried dough balls. Mix well, then add the almonds and the chopped candied fruit. Oil a tube pan (ring mold) and place the mixture in it, smoothing the surface. Refrigerate for several hours and then turn out onto a dish and sprinkle with the cube sugar, crumbled with a rolling-pin between two sheets of paper. This will produce a coarser, more decorative sugar than ordinary granulated sugar.

Cicerchiata
Umbrian Honey Cake

3 eggs
oil for frying
3 Tbsp/2 Tbsp/2 Tbsp sweet liqueur
   (such as Cointreau, Grand Marnier,
   or Orange Curaçao)
¼ c/2 oz/50 g granulated sugar
grated rind of ½ lemon
scant 1 c/¼ lb/100 g all-purpose (plain)
   flour
½ c/2 oz/50 g shelled almonds
1 c/¾ lb/350 g honey
½ c/2 oz/50 g candied fruit
cube sugar

Beat the eggs in a bowl with a tablespoon of oil, the liqueur, the granulated sugar, and the grated lemon rind. Add the sifted flour and stir well. Transfer to a pastry board or other working surface, and work well to form a soft, pliable dough which can be handled easily. Roll out into long cylinders about the diameter of a pencil and cut into ¼-inch (½ cm) lengths. Roll these pieces between the palms of the hands into little balls. Heat plenty of oil in a deep skillet until very

THE MARCHES

PESARO

ANCONA

MACERATA

ASCOLI PICENO

Vincisgrassi
Layered Lasagne

2½ c/10½ oz/300 g all-purpose (plain)
    flour
scant 1 c/5 oz/150 g semolina
3 eggs
½ c/4 oz/120 g butter
3 Tbsp/2 Tbsp/2 Tbsp Marsala or Vin
    Santo
salt
¼ lb/4 oz/100 g sweetbreads
¼ lb/4 oz/100 g calf brains
4 Tbsp/2 oz/50 g pork fat or lard
½ onion
1 small carrot
½ lb/½ lb/225 g chicken giblets
⅓ c/3½ fl oz/1 dl dry white wine
1 Tbsp tomato paste
⅓ c/3½ fl oz/1 dl homemade stock or
    bouillon cube dissolved in hot water
freshly ground black and white pepper
1½ c/12 fl oz/4 dl milk
nutmeg
⅓ c/3 oz/80 g grated Parmesan cheese

Mix 2 cups (9 oz/250 g) of the all-purpose (plain) flour with the semolina, the eggs, 1½ tablespoons (1 Tbsp/15 g) butter, the Marsala or Vin Santo, and a level teaspoon of salt. Knead well until smooth and pliable. Roll out into a thin sheet, cut into strips 4 inches (10 cm) wide with a fluted pastry cutter, and cut the strips to the correct length to fit the baking dish to be used.

Blanch the sweetbreads and brains in boiling water for a few minutes and remove any membrane. Pound the pork fat or chop it very finely. Chop the onion and carrot finely and sauté with the fat in 4 tablespoons (2 oz/50 g) of the butter for a few minutes until the onion is translucent. Then add the chopped chicken giblets, reserving the liver. Add the dry white wine and turn up the heat to allow the wine to evaporate completely. Pour in the tomato paste diluted with the hot stock or an equal amount of hot water. Season with salt and freshly ground pepper, cover, and simmer for about 1 hour, stirring at intervals and adding a couple of tablespoons of milk when the liquid has reduced. About 20 minutes before the hour is up, add the sweetbreads, the brains and the liver, all diced small.

Boil the noodles in plenty of salted water until half-cooked, rinse with cold water, drain, and lay out on a pastry cloth to dry.

Make a white sauce in a small saucepan with 2 tablespoons (1 oz/25 g) of butter, ¼ cup (1 oz/25 g) of flour, and 1¼ cups (10 fl oz/3 dl) of milk. Melt the butter until it starts to foam, then add the flour and cook until the roux turns a very light golden brown. Remove from heat, add the hot (not boiling) milk, stirring briskly, and return the mixture to the heat, stirring continuously, so that the sauce will not lump or stick. Once the sauce has come to a boil, reduce the heat, season with salt, freshly ground white pepper, and a pinch of grated nutmeg and cook gently for 15 to 20 minutes, stirring frequently. The white sauce should be used at once. If it has to be made in advance it should be covered until needed and then gently reheated to regain its smooth, creamy consistency.

Grease a baking dish generously with butter, place a layer of lasagne in the bottom, cover with a few spoonfuls of white sauce, sprinkle with grated Parmesan, and then top with an even covering of the meat sauce; place another layer of noodles on top and continue in this fashion until all the ingredients have been used, ending with a topping of white sauce. Let the dish stand in a cool place for a few hours; then bake it in a preheated oven at about 350°F (180°C/mk 4) for about 30 minutes or until the top is well browned. Drizzle a little melted butter over the surface and serve while still very hot.

Vincisgrassi is a famous specialty of the province of Macerata and other ingredients can be used to vary the taste. One suggestion is to use ground (minced) veal together with 2 to 3 tablespoons of dried Italian mushrooms soaked in hot water instead of the brains and sweetbreads.

Maccheroni alla Pesarese
Macaroni Pesaro Style

1 small onion
¼ lb/¼ lb/100 g lean veal
¼ lb/¼ lb/100 g butter
¾ c/7 fl oz/2 dl light stock
salt
freshly ground pepper
½ c/4 oz/100 g chicken livers
1 black truffle
⅓ lb/5 oz/150 g cooked ham
¾ c/7 fl oz/2 dl heavy (double) cream
scant ¾ lb/10½ oz/300 g large macaroni
    for stuffing (for example, cannelloni)
½ c/4 oz/100 g grated Parmesan cheese

Chop the onion and the veal very finely. Heat 2½ tablespoons (just over 1 oz/40 g) of the butter in a heavy saucepan and sauté the onion and veal gently, stirring continuously, for 2 to 3 minutes. Pour in the stock (if homemade stock is unavailable, dissolve a ¼ teaspoon of meat extract in the same amount of boiling water). Season with salt and pepper, cover, and simmer for about 30 minutes, stirring now and again.

Wash and trim the chicken livers. Scrub the truffle, chop it finely, and put it in the blender together with the chopped ham. Blend to form a smooth, thick paste. Mix in a little salt and pepper with a wooden spoon and stir in about ⅔ of the cream, mixing thoroughly. This should make a smooth stuffing mixture.

Boil the pasta in a large pan of salted water until it is half done; rinse with cold water, drain, and place on a cloth to dry.

Butter a baking dish. Fill a pastry (forcing) bag with some of this mixture and, using a wide nozzle, stuff each of the macaroni. Arrange them in a neat layer in the baking dish, cover with a few spoonfuls of veal sauce, and sprinkle with some grated Parmesan. Continue with another layer of stuffed macaroni, cover these with the remaining veal sauce, and sprinkle with more grated Parmesan. Pour over the rest of the cream, dot with small pieces of the remaining butter and place the baking dish in a preheated oven at about 400°F

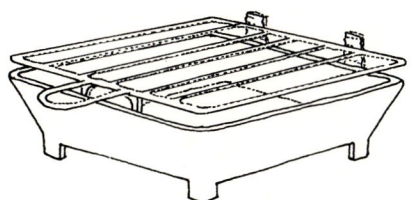

How to trim, scale, gut, and clean a fish.

(200°C/mk 6) to cook for at least 15 to 20 minutes, until golden brown. Serve immediately.

Brodetto alla Porto Recanati
Saffron Fish Soup

*generous 2 lb/2 lb/1 kg mixed seafood
   and fish (scampi, crawfish (crayfish)
   lobster, shrimp (prawns), baby squid,
   mussels, sole, sea bass, halibut or
   winter flounder, brill)*
1 onion
2 cloves garlic
¾ c/7 fl oz/2 dl oil
*1 qt/1¾ pt/1 l fumet or fish stock (see
   Cacciucco alla Livornese on page 103
   for instructions)*
salt
freshly ground pepper
½ tsp saffron
1 small bunch parsley

Clean and wash the fish and shellfish as necessary. Chop the onion and garlic finely and cut the larger fish into pieces. Sauté the chopped onion and garlic in the oil in a large pan for a few minutes, stirring continuously and then add the fish, beginning with the squid which should cook for 30 minutes before adding the white fish, and lastly the shellfish. Pour in the fish stock. After 15 minutes, season with salt and pepper and add the saffron mixed with a cup of hot fish stock. Cook gently until all the fish are tender (about 15 minutes) and add the very finely chopped parsley. Serve hot with toasted bread, if desired.

Tagliolini alla Marinara

*2¼ c/10½ oz/300 g all-purpose (plain)
   flour*
3 eggs
1 tsp grated lemon rind
*1 small sole weighing about ½ lb/½ lb/
   225 g*
½ lb/½ lb/225 g cod or hake fillets
2 small whiting
salt
6 Tbsp/4 Tbsp/4 Tbsp olive oil
1 clove garlic
1 small bunch parsley
1 Tbsp tomato paste
freshly ground pepper

Mix the flour, eggs, and a teaspoon of grated lemon rind together and work into a firm dough. Roll out into a very thin sheet and leave to dry out on the working surface until the surface becomes slightly leathery (15 to 30 minutes); then roll up and cut into thin noodles. (See page 12 for illustration.) Tagliolini are very narrow thin tagliatelle. Care must be taken not to overcook them since they take only a few minutes when fresh.

Make a fish fumet as directed in Cacciucco alla Livornese on page 103; (clean and gut the fish but do not remove the heads). Place the fish in the fumet in a fish steamer (kettle) with a little salt. Poach for 15 minutes and then remove the fish carefully and set aside. Heat the olive oil in a large, heavy cooking pot, add the finely chopped garlic, half the parsley, also finely chopped, and the fish stock (strain it through a fine strainer (sieve) and remove the heads from the fish, squeezing them to extract their juices). Stir in the tomato paste. Season with salt and pepper and simmer until the stock has reduced considerably and acquired a certain body.

Cook the noodles in plenty of boiling salted water, drain while still very firm, and add to the fish stock, cooking while stirring continuously until they are al dente. Serve very hot with a sprinkling of the remaining finely chopped parsley. (Do not chop parsley too long before it is used, as it loses its flavor quite quickly.) No grated Parmesan is served with this dish.

Fillet and skin the poached fish and dress them with oil, salt, freshly ground pepper, and some chopped parsley. They can then be served, garnished with lemon wedges, as a main course with boiled new potatoes.

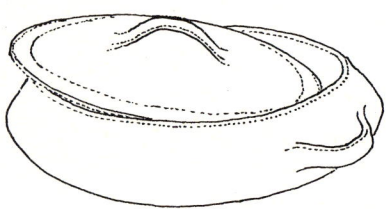

Agnolotti alla Marchigiana

$2\frac{1}{2}$ c/$10\frac{1}{2}$ oz/300 g all-purpose (plain) flour
3 eggs
salt
$\frac{1}{2}$ lb/$\frac{1}{2}$ lb/225 g ground (minced) lean beef
$\frac{1}{4}$ lb/$\frac{1}{4}$ lb/100 g butter
scant 1 lb/14 oz/400 g spinach
1 slice of Mortadella $\frac{1}{4}$ inch ($\frac{1}{2}$ cm) thick
freshly ground pepper
1 lb/1 lb/500 g ripe fresh (or canned) tomatoes
$\frac{1}{4}$ c/2 oz/50 g grated Parmesan cheese

Follow the instructions for making stuffed pasta given on page 11, using the flour, eggs, a pinch of salt and the following filling: Sauté the ground (minced) beef in 2 tablespoons (1 oz/25 g) butter with a pinch of salt and then transfer to a bowl. Wash the spinach thoroughly, trim, and boil in a little salted water for a few minutes. Drain well, chop finely, and mix with 2 tablespoons (1 oz/25 g) melted butter in a saucepan, warming over a low heat while stirring for 2 or 3 minutes, then add to the beef. Chop the Mortadella into tiny pieces and mix into the other ingredients in the bowl. Add a little salt, if needed, and some pepper and mix.

Place the remaining butter in a saucepan with the chopped or sieved tomatoes and a pinch of salt and simmer until the sauce has reduced.

Boil the agnolotti in a large pan of salted water, drain when tender but firm, transfer to a heated dish, and cover with the tomato sauce and a little Parmesan cheese. Serve the rest of the cheese separately.

Maccheroncelli alla Campofilone

$2\frac{1}{2}$ c/$10\frac{1}{2}$ oz/300 g all-purpose (plain) flour
3 eggs
$\frac{1}{4}$ lb/$\frac{1}{4}$ lb/100 g butter
scant $\frac{1}{2}$ lb/scant $\frac{1}{2}$ lb/150 g lean veal cut in chunks
scant $\frac{1}{2}$ lb/scant $\frac{1}{2}$ lb/150 g loin of pork cut in chunks
$\frac{1}{4}$ lb/$\frac{1}{4}$ lb/100 g chicken liver or giblets
1 lb/1 lb/500 g canned tomatoes (put through a food mill or sieve)
grated Pecorino cheese
salt
freshly ground pepper

This appetizing dish is a great favorite and standby in the region. Its success depends upon the quality and balanced use of the ingredients. The flavor of the tomatoes should never drown that of the meat juices and chicken livers.

Mix the flour and eggs and work together to form a smooth, pliable dough; roll out into a very thin sheet and leave to dry out for a little while before rolling up and cutting into very thin noodles (almost as thin as the spaghetti known as capelli d'angelo, angel's hair). A fruit knife or Chinese cleaver will do this most efficiently.

Sauté the veal and pork gently in the butter until lightly browned on all sides. Add the tomatoes, season with salt and pepper, and simmer slowly for about 1½ hours. Add a little stock or water if the liquid reduces too much during cooking. Shortly before the cooking time is up, add the cleaned, trimmed and finely chopped chicken livers to the meat and sauce. Cook the maccheroncelli for a minute at most in plenty of boiling, salted water, drain, transfer to a heated serving dish, and add the sauce from the

Opposite: Bistecca alla Fiorentina (Steak Florentine) and homemade, full-flavored Pappa col Pomodoro (Tomato Soup)—both from Tuscany.

Overleaf: Two dishes from Latium—Bucatini all' Amatriciana and Carciofi alla Giudìa (Fried Artichokes Jewish Style).

meat. Sprinkle with grated Pecorino (or Parmesan if a milder taste is preferred) and serve.

Serve the veal and pork as a main dish with a fresh salad.

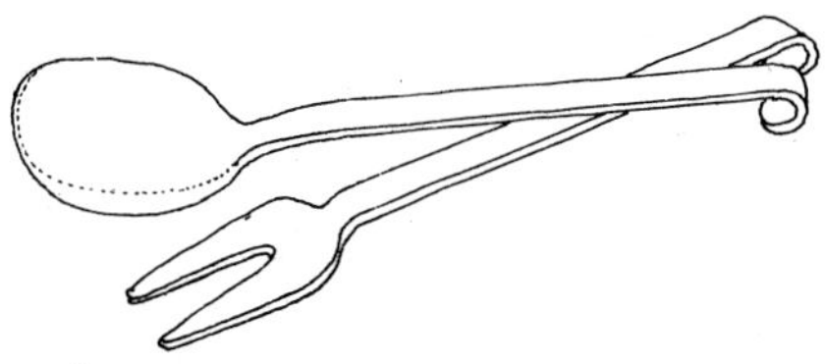

Gnocchi al Sugo di Papera

Gnocchi with Duck Sauce

1¾ lb/1¾ lb/800 g potatoes
2 eggs
salt
2 c/9 oz/250 g all-purpose (plain) flour
1 medium onion
1 small bunch parsley
6 Tbsp/4 Tbsp/4 Tbsp olive oil
1 duck (boned and cut into fairly small pieces)
⅓ c/3½ fl oz/1 dl dry white wine
1½ c/10½ oz/300 g canned tomatoes (put through a food mill or sieve)
freshly ground pepper
¼ c/2 oz/50 g grated Parmesan cheese

Prepare the gnocchi as directed in the instructions given on page 54 for Gnocchi alla Pastissada. You will use the potatoes, the eggs, a pinch of salt, and the flour.

Chop the onion and parsley finely and sauté in the olive oil until the onion is translucent. Dredge the pieces of duck with flour and lightly brown in the oil, parsley and onion mixture. Turn up the heat, pour in the wine, and allow it to evaporate. Add the tomatoes, season with salt and pepper, and bring to a boil. Turn down the heat, cover, and simmer, stirring frequently to prevent burning.

Boil the gnocchi (in batches if necessary) in plenty of boiling salted water, removing them with a slotted spoon as they rise to the surface. Drain well and place in heated individual dishes, topping each portion with 3 or 4 tablespoons of the duck sauce and just a few of the smaller pieces of duck meat. Serve with grated Parmesan cheese. The remaining pieces of duck, served with vegetables in season, can form the main course.

Insalata di Riso e Frutti di Mare

Seafood and Rice Salad

1 carrot
1 stalk celery
½ onion
1 clove garlic
salt
½ lb/½ lb/225 g shrimp (prawns)
4 crawfish (crayfish) or *½ lb scampi (Dublin Bay prawns)*
½ c/10½ oz/300 g Arborio rice
1 lemon
⅓ c/3½ fl oz/1 dl oil
1 small bunch parsley
freshly ground pepper

Chop the carrot, celery, onion, and garlic coarsely and place in a large pan of salted water. Bring to a boil. Add the shrimp (prawns) and crawfish (crayfish), well washed in running water, or scampi (Dublin Bay prawns) and boil gently for about 10 minutes. Strain the cooking liquid into a cooking pot and reserve. Shell the shrimp (prawns) and chop into pieces, keeping the crawfish (crayfish) or scampi (Dublin Bay prawns) whole. Set aside.

Bring 1 quart (1¾ pt/1 liter) of the strained cooking liquid to a boil and pour in the rice. Cook until al dente and turn into a deep, warmed serving dish. Sprinkle with the juice of half a lemon, the oil, and plenty of freshly ground pepper. Add the shrimp (prawns) and mix well without crushing the rice. Place the rice in four individual plates, garnishing each portion with a lemon slice and a crawfish (crayfish) or scampi (Dublin Bay prawn) and chopped parsley.

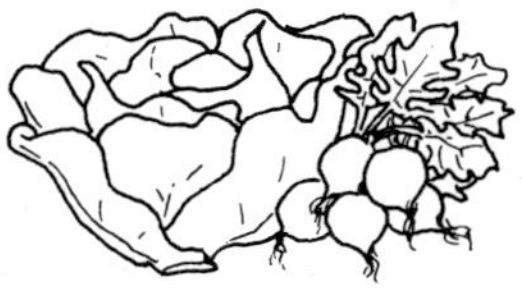

Pizza al Formaggio

Cheese Pizza

⅓ c/3 oz/80 g Parmesan cheese
scant ¼ lb/3 oz/80 g Gruyère cheese
scant ¼ lb/3 oz/80 g Provolone cheese
1½ Tbsp/1 oz/25 g Pecorino cheese (optional)
1 cake compressed/1 oz/25 g fresh yeast
3 c/¾ lb/350 g all-purpose (plain) flour
salt
olive oil
2 eggs

This dish is traditionally eaten at Easter time as a first course with salami and hard-boiled eggs. See the illustration on page 127 for its preparation.

Grate ¼ cup (2 oz/50 g) of the Parmesan cheese, 1½ tablespoons (1 oz/25 g) of the Gruyère, and 1½ tablespoons (1 oz/25 g) of the Provolone. Dice the remaining cheese small.

Dissolve the yeast in a little lukewarm water and allow it to stand until it foams. Sift ⅓ of the flour onto the pastry board and mix in the yeast. Work very thoroughly into a soft, smooth dough, shape into a ball, place in a lightly floured bowl, make a crisscross incision with a sharp knife on the top, and cover with a cloth. Leave the dough to rise and at least double in bulk in a warm, draft-free place.

Meanwhile sift the remaining flour onto the pastry board, add a pinch of salt and a tablespoon of best quality olive oil, and then gradually mix in enough lukewarm water (adding it a little at a time) to make a firm but very pliable dough. Beat the eggs in a shallow dish, add the grated cheeses and the diced cheeses, and gradually work into this latter dough. Lastly, incorporate the raised dough ball and knead the whole very thoroughly for some time. You should have a soft, smooth dough. Place this dough in a well-oiled, high-sided, narrow cake pan and allow it to rise again in a warm place. Place an inverted colander over the pan and cover with a damp cloth to prevent the top from drying and hardening. The ideal temperature for this is approximately 80°F (30°C). This can be reached by setting the pan in a larger container of warm (*not* hot) water. The dough will take at least 2 to 3 hours to rise sufficiently. When the dough has risen considerably and is light and spongy, place in a preheated oven at 350°F–400°F (180°C–200°C/mk 4–6) and bake for 30 minutes. As soon as the cake pan is removed from the oven, invert it over a serving dish and turn the pizza out.

Coniglio Farcito

Stuffed Rabbit

1 young rabbit weighing about 3 lb/3 lb/ 1.5 kg
¼ c/2 oz/50 g grated Parmesan cheese
1⅔ c/½ lb/225 g bread crumbs
grated rind of ½ lemon
2 cloves garlic
1 small bunch parsley
4 Tbsp/2 oz/50 g pork fat
several Tbsp oil
2 eggs
nutmeg
cinnamon
salt
freshly ground pepper
vinegar

Skin and dress the rabbit, withdrawing the innards through an incision made in the anal region rather than the usual slit down the belly. Wash well and reserve the heart and liver. Place the rabbit in a mixture of equal parts of vinegar and water in a large earthenware bowl, and soak for 12 hours. Dry thoroughly with paper towels and stuff with the following mixture: Pound the pork fat and heat it in a small pan. Add the very finely chopped heart and liver with a pinch of salt and sauté for a few minutes. Place the bread crumbs in a mixing bowl with the grated Parmesan, the very finely chopped garlic and parsley, the cooked heart and liver, the grated rind of half a lemon, 1–1½ tablespoons (1 Tbsp/ 1 Tbsp) of oil, a pinch of cinnamon, a small pinch of freshly ground nutmeg and a little pepper. Stir well and then bind with the eggs. Adjust the seasoning to taste. Work the mixture so that it is well mixed. Then stuff the rabbit with it, sewing up the opening with kitchen string and a large needle. Brush all over with oil and place on a rack in a baking or roasting pan and cook in a medium oven (350°F180°C/mk 4) for about 1 hour. Turn the rabbit frequently, basting it with its own juices. Cut into quarters and top each portion with stuffing. It should be served very hot.

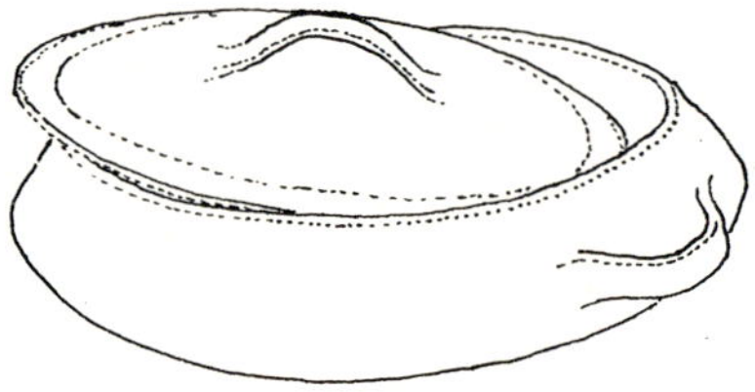

Mùscioli alla Pescatora

Fishermen's Mussels

2–2¼ lb/2–2¼ lb/1 kg fresh mussels
¾ c/7 fl oz/2 dl olive oil
juice of 1 lemon
1 small bunch parsley
salt
freshly ground pepper

The success of this dish depends on the quality and freshness of the ingredients. Scrub the mussels thoroughly, removing all traces of beard. Soak them in a large bowl of cold water for 1 to 2 hours, discarding any mussels which remain open when removed from the water (they may be dead and unsafe to eat). Open the mussels carefully, using a small sharp knife and remove any sand or other debris. Leave the mussels attached to the half shells and place them in a heavy skillet or frying pan. Sprinkle with oil, lemon juice, finely chopped parsley, salt, and pepper. Cook over a moderate heat for 7 to 8 minutes. Serve the mussels on individual plates, moistening each portion with some of the cooking liquid.

Pollo in Potacchio

Braised Chicken

1 young chicken weighing about 2¼ lb/ 2¼ lb/1 kg
⅓ c/3½ fl oz/1 dl oil
1 onion
2 cloves garlic
1 sprig fresh rosemary or ¼ tsp dried
⅓ c/3½ fl oz/1 dl dry, white wine
scant ¾ lb/scant ¾ lb/300 g very ripe (or canned) tomatoes
salt
freshly ground pepper or a piece of dried red chili pepper

If the chicken is not bought already dressed, pluck, singe, and draw it; wash and dry it well; and cut it into fairly small portions. Heat the oil in a large skillet and sauté the onion, cut into fine rings, the crushed garlic cloves, and the finely chopped rosemary leaves, together with the chicken pieces. When the garlic cloves start to color, discard them and continue frying the chicken, turning frequently. Pour in the wine, turn up the heat and allow the wine to evaporate. Add the peeled, seeded, and chopped tomatoes, seasoning with a little salt and a generous pinch of pepper (or a little crumbled dried chili pepper). Stir well, cover, and simmer over a low heat for about 40 minutes, adding a little hot water if necessary. Place the chicken portions on a preheated serving platter, cover with the sauce, and serve.

Quaglie in Teglia (con Piselli)

Casserole of Quail with Peas

4–8 (depending on size) quail
¾ lb/¾ lb/300 g–400 g shelled peas
2 Tbsp/1 oz/25 g butter
¼ lb/¼ lb/100 g fat prosciutto (raw ham)
salt
freshly ground pepper
⅓ c/3½ fl oz/1 dl dry white wine
¾ lb/¾ lb/350 g ripe, fresh tomatoes

Quail are usually sold already cleaned and prepared (plucked, singed, drawn, and with the wing tips, feet, and head removed).

Wash the birds and pat dry with paper towels. Place the peas, one third of the diced prosciutto (raw ham) and enough cold water to cover in a fireproof dish. Heat to the boiling point and, when the peas are nearly done, add salt and pepper. (If the salt is added earlier, the peas will be tough.)

Place the rest of the diced prosciutto (raw ham) in a wide, fairly deep, lidded skillet, sauté for a few minutes, and then add the quail, turning frequently so that they brown evenly. Pour in the wine and allow it to evaporate over a brisk heat. Add the peeled, seeded, and chopped tomatoes, stir, and cover the skillet. Simmer over a moderate heat, stirring from time to time until the quail are tender.

When the quail are done and the sauce has reduced and thickened, add the peas, turn up the heat, stir gently, and cook for a few minutes. Arrange the quail in a circle on a heated serving dish and pour the sauce and peas into the center. Serve at once.

Triglie al Prosciutto
Mullet with Prosciutto (Raw Ham)

4 red mullet weighing about $\frac{1}{2}$ lb/$\frac{1}{2}$ lb/
   225 g each
1 sprig of fresh sage
4 slices prosciutto (raw ham)
a little all-purpose (plain) flour
oil
$\frac{3}{4}$ c/7 fl oz/2 dl dry, white wine
salt
freshly ground pepper

Cut the heads off the fish, make a slit down the belly, and remove the backbone and the bones attached to it. Make sure the fish remains as intact as possible. Wash well and pat dry. Place a

Right: Making Pizza al Formaggio (Cheese Pizza), a specialty of the Marches.

couple of sage leaves and a slice of prosciutto (raw ham) inside each fish. Roll the fish in the flour. Heat enough oil for frying in a skillet and, when very hot, fry the mullet on both sides. Remove the fish from the heat and transfer to a heated platter. Discard the oil for frying, wipe the inside of the skillet with paper towels, and return the fish to the skillet, adding the wine, a few sage leaves and a little salt and pepper. Reduce the liquid almost completely over a low heat and serve the mullet very hot.

Stoccafisso in Potacchio
Braised Stockfish

1¼–1½ lb/1¼–1½ lb/600–700 g best
    quality stockfish (Ragno)
1 onion
2 cloves garlic
1 small bunch parsley
1 sprig of fresh rosemary or ¼ tsp dried
    rosemary
¾ c/7 fl oz/2 dl oil
6 anchovy fillets
scant 1 lb/14 oz/400 g very ripe tomatoes
1 red chili pepper (dried)
⅓ c/3½ fl oz/1 dl dry white wine
salt
freshly ground pepper

Pound the stockfish with a wooden mallet; then soak it in plenty of cold water for up to 1 week. The water should be changed 3 or 4 times a day. When the fish is thoroughly softened, drain well, pat dry, and cut into fairly evenly-sized pieces. Chop the onion, garlic, parsley, and rosemary very finely. Sauté the chopped mixture in the oil in an earthen-ware cooking pot or enameled cast-iron pan. Add the anchovy fillets, the skinned, seeded, and chopped tomatoes, the crumbled chili pepper, and finally the pieces of fish. Cover the pan and simmer the fish over a moderate heat until done, adding the white wine when the sauce starts to reduce. Moisten with hot water when necessary. The fish will take about 1 hour to cook. Season with a little salt and pepper and serve.

Zucchine alla Marchigiana
Zucchini (Courgettes) Marches Style

½ onion
4 Tbsp/2 oz/50 g butter
scant 1 lb/14 oz/400 g ripe (or canned)
    tomatoes (chopped or put through a
    food mill or sieve)
salt
½ lb/½ lb/225 g ground (minced) lean
    veal
1½ Tbsp/1 Tbsp/1 Tbsp grated Parmesan
    cheese
1 small bunch parsley
freshly ground pepper
8 medium zucchini (courgettes)
oil

Sauté the finely sliced onion in half the butter, using a fairly large pan. When the onion is translucent, add the tomatoes. Add a little salt and simmer until the sauce thickens. Keep warm.

Heat the rest of the butter in a small pan until it starts to foam, add the ground (minced) veal, and sauté gently. Transfer to a mixing bowl and allow to cool. Blend the grated Parmesan and the chopped parsley with the veal, adding a pinch of salt and a little pepper.

Trim the ends off each zucchini (courgette) and remove the flesh carefully with a small scoop—you should form hollow but firm cylinders. Stuff each with the meat filling. Fry the stuffed zucchini (courgettes) in hot oil in a skillet, and, when they are tender, place them in the warm tomato sauce. Place over a moderate heat and turn the zucchini (courgettes) so they absorb the sauce evenly. Serve without delay.

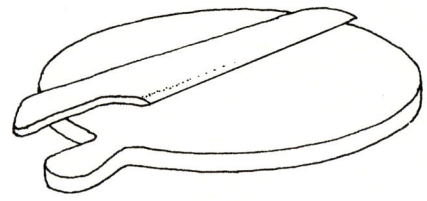

Olive Farcite
Stuffed Olives

40 large green olives preserved in brine
2 Tbsp/1 oz/25 g butter
½ lb/½ lb/225 g mixed ground (minced)
    meat: veal, pork, Mortadella,
    prosciutto (raw ham)
salt
freshly ground pepper
nutmeg
⅓ c/3½ fl oz/1 dl dry white wine
2 eggs
¼ c/1½ oz/40 g grated Parmesan cheese
a little all-purpose (plain) flour
oil

The most suitable olives for this dish are the large fleshy Piceno olives which are relatively easy to stuff.

Drain the olives and pat dry with paper towels. Heat the butter in a pan, add the ground (minced) meats, and sauté for a few minutes, stirring continuously. Season with a little salt, a pinch of pepper, and a hint of freshly grated nutmeg. Pour in the wine, turn up the heat, and cook until the wine has evaporated. When there is virtually no liquid left, reduce the heat and add one whole egg which has been beaten with the grated Parmesan cheese. Mix until well blended, set aside, and allow to cool.

Pit (stone) the olives neatly, using an olive or cherry pitting tool (cherry stoner). Stuff the pitted (stoned) olives with the filling. Beat the remaining egg in a shallow dish and dip the olives in the beaten egg and then coat them with flour. Fry in plenty of very hot oil for 2 to 3 minutes. Drain and serve.

LATIUM

VITERBO •

• RIETI

• ROME

• FROSINONE

• LATINA

Crostini Gustosi alla Romana
Baked Cheese and Anchovy Toast

8 slices coarse white bread
8 anchovy fillets
4 slices Mozzarella cheese
4 Tbsp/2 oz/50 g butter

Chop the anchovies. Heat the butter in a small saucepan until it is just starting to melt. Remove from the heat immediately, add the anchovies, and work them into a thin paste with the butter. Spread the slices of bread with this mixture and cover with a slice of mozzarella (the cheese should not overlap the edges of the bread). Place in a preheated hot oven (450°F/230°C/mk 8) for a few minutes until the Mozzarella starts to melt.

Pandorato

1 square loaf of bread weighing
    approximately 1 lb/1 lb/400 g
½–¾ lb/½–¾ lb/300 g Mozzarella
¼ lb/¼ lb/100 g sliced prosciutto (raw
    ham)
milk
all-purpose (plain) flour
2 eggs
salt
oil

Remove all the crust from the bread and cut into ¾–1-inch-thick (2 cm) slices. Then slice these thick slices in half, leaving them attached at the bottom so that you have a series of "hinged" sandwiches.

Trim the sliced Mozzarella and prosciutto (raw ham) to fit inside the sandwiches and place a slice of each in each sandwich. Press the edges firmly together and dip quickly in the milk to moisten rather than soak them. Dredge them with flour and arrange them in a deep serving dish. Break the eggs into a bowl, beat well, adding a pinch of salt and pour over the prepared sandwiches. Let them stand for 2 hours.

Shortly before the sandwiches are to be served, heat plenty of oil in a wide skillet until it is very hot and fry the sandwiches a few at a time until golden brown on both sides. Remove them from the frying pan with a slotted spatula (fish slice), drain on paper towels, and keep them warm on a heated serving plate. As soon as all the sandwiches are ready, cover with paper towels or a napkin and serve. Eat while fresh and hot either as a first course or a snack.

Pasta e Broccoli
Macaroni and Broccoli with Tomato Sauce

1 lb/1 lb/500 g broccoli or cauliflower
4 anchovy fillets
1 small onion
1 clove garlic
1 small bunch parsley
¼ c/3 Tbsp/3 Tbsp olive oil
1 piece of red chili pepper
⅓ c/3½ fl oz/1 dl dry white wine
1–1¼ c/½–¾ lb/300 g canned tomatoes
    (put through a food mill or sieve)
salt
2–3 c/¾–1¼ pt/½–¾ l homemade stock (or
    1–2 bouillon cubes dissolved in the
    same amount of boiling water
⅔ lb/10½ oz/300 g commercial short pasta,
    such as macaroni, nocciole, penne, etc.
grated Parmesan cheese (optional)
¼ c/2 oz/50 g prosciutto (raw ham)
    (optional)

Prepare the broccoli or cauliflower by dividing into florets or spears and wash well. Cut the anchovy fillets into small pieces and finely chop the onion, garlic, and parsley. Heat the oil in a saucepan and add the chopped vegetables, the crumbled or chopped chili pepper, and the anchovies. Sauté gently, add the wine and the tomatoes, season with salt, and simmer for about 15 minutes. Add the broccoli or cauliflower and cook gently for 5 to 6 minutes. Pour in 1–2 cups boiling stock and add the pasta. Cook until the pasta is tender but firm, adding a little more stock if necessary.

Transfer to a heated serving dish and serve without delay. Grated Parmesan may be served on the side.

A simple variation of this dish is to add prosciutto (raw ham), thinly sliced, just before transferring the pasta and broccoli to the serving dish.

Frittata di Spaghetti

¾ lb/¾ lb/350 g spaghetti
salt
3 Tbsp/1½ oz/40 g butter
⅓ c/3 oz/80 g grated Parmesan cheese
2 eggs
freshly ground pepper
1 small bunch parsley
3–4 Tbsp/2–3 Tbsp/2–3 Tbsp olive oil

This is a very economical dish and quick to prepare, since leftover spaghetti with butter or tomato sauce can be used. If there is no leftover spaghetti, cook the quantity given above in plenty of boiling salted water until al dente. Then drain and mix with the melted butter and half of the grated Parmesan cheese. Allow to cool, stirring from time to time with a fork so that the spaghetti does not stick together.

To prepare the frittata, add the eggs to the spaghetti, together with the rest of the Parmesan cheese, some freshly ground pepper and the finely chopped parsley. Mix gently but thoroughly. Heat most of the oil in a large cast-iron skillet. Add the spaghetti-and-egg mixture, distributing it evenly to look like an omelet. Cook over a moderate heat—the secret lies in browning the frittata evenly—shaking the pan with a circular motion so that the frittata does not stick. When the frittata is browned on one side, turn upside down onto a large plate, add a little oil to the pan and slide the frittata back into the pan. When it is browned on the other side, remove it from the heat and allow it to cool a little before serving, since it is more tasty when eaten warm.

Gnocchi alla Romana

2¼ c/18 fl oz/½ l milk
1½ c/5 oz/150 g semolina
2 egg yolks
½ c/4 oz/100 g butter
⅓ c/3 oz/80 g grated Parmesan cheese

Reserve 3 tablespoons of the milk. Bring the rest to just below the boiling point in a saucepan, pour in the semolina slowly as shown in the illustration at right, mixing continuously with a wooden spoon and making sure that the semolina does not stick to the bottom of the pan. Stop adding semolina every so often and stir vigorously before adding more. The semolina should be fairly liquid during this first phase. Cook for 15 to 20 minutes and remove from the heat. Break the egg yolks into a bowl and mix in the reserved milk. Add half the butter to the cooked semolina mixture and stir in well so that it melts completely. Add the egg yolks and milk to the semolina, stirring briskly to keep the eggs from setting before they are incorporated. Rinse a large shallow dish with water and pour the semolina mixture into it, so that it forms an even layer about ½ inch (1 cm) thick. Cool for at least 2 hours. Turn upside down on to a pastry board and cut out circles of the mixture 1½ inches (4 cm) in diameter with an inverted wine glass or pastry cutter. Oil a baking dish and arrange the circles carefully, overlapping them slightly, as shown in the illustration right. If there are too many semolina gnocchi to form just one layer, sprinkle the first layer with melted butter and grated Parmesan and put more circles on top. Cover the top layer with melted butter and grated Parmesan and bake in a medium oven (350°F/180°C/mk 4) until the gnocchi are lightly browned on the surface. Sprinkle with cheese and serve right away.

Right: Gnocchi alla Romana— semolina dumplings are a great Roman specialty.

Penne all' Arrabbiata
Macaroni with Spicy Tomato Sauce

1 medium onion
1 clove garlic
¼ lb/¼ lb/100 g sliced (streaky) bacon
1 lb/1 lb/500 g very ripe fresh tomatoes
    or
    2 c/14 oz/400 g canned tomatoes
¾ lb/¾ lb/350 g penne rigate (see illustration number 20 on page 18)
1 tsp butter
1 red chili pepper
¼ c/2 oz/50 g grated Pecorino Romano cheese

Chop the onion and garlic very finely. Cut the bacon into very thin strips. If fresh tomatoes are used, blanch and skin them, remove the seeds, and chop, or cut them into strips. If canned tomatoes are used, put them through a food mill or sieve. While the pasta is cooking in plenty of boiling salted water, sauté the chopped onion and garlic and the strips of bacon in the butter in a large skillet until they are lightly browned. Add the tomatoes and the chili pepper and simmer over a moderate heat for a little while. Remove the chili pepper at this point unless a spicier dish is desired.

Drain nearly all the water from the pasta when it is half cooked. Transfer the pasta into the skillet containing the sauce and add 1–2 tablespoons of grated Pecorino cheese. Stir slowly but continuously while cooking until the pasta is done. If the sauce reduces too quickly, add a few tablespoons of the water in which the pasta was cooked. Transfer into heated individual plates or bowls and serve with a side dish of the remaining grated Pecorino cheese. (Parmesan can be used instead of Pecorino to give a milder but equally delicious taste.)

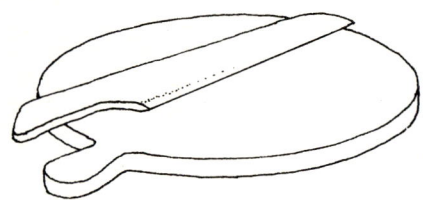

Spaghetti Cacio e Pepe
Spaghetti with Cheese and Pepper

¾ lb/¾ lb/350 g spaghetti
freshly ground pepper
⅓ c/3 oz/80 g grated Pecorino Romano cheese

This dish is unexpectedly mild in taste and is said to have originated among the shepherds of Latium and Abruzzi many centuries ago.

Plunge the spaghetti into a large pan of boiling salted water. When it is tender but still firm, drain it, reserving some of the cooking water, and turn it into a deep, warmed dish. Season with coarsely ground pepper, sprinkle with grated Pecorino cheese, and moisten with a few tablespoons of the reserved cooking water (just enough to melt the cheese and make it creamy). Mix well and serve immediately.

Rigatoni con la Pagliata
Macaroni and Tripe in Tomato Sauce

1¼ lb/1¼ lb/600 g beef (ox) or calf's tripe (precooked)
1 medium onion
1 small stalk celery
1 clove garlic
1 small bunch parsley
¼ c/2 oz/50 g sliced (streaky) bacon
6 Tbsp/4 Tbsp/4 Tbsp olive oil
⅓ c/3½ fl oz/1 dl dry white wine
2 c/14 oz/400 g canned tomatoes (put through a food mill or sieve)
salt
freshly ground pepper
nutmeg (optional)
½ lb/½ lb/225 g rigatoni (large, ribbed macaroni)
¼ c/2 oz/50 g grated Pecorino Romano cheese

Tripe is usually sold blanched and cooked. The difference between beef (ox) and calf's tripe is minimal, however, calf's tripe is the more tender whereas beef (ox) tripe has more flavor.

Remove any excess fat from the tripe with a small knife. Cut into pieces 7–10 inches (20–25 cm) long, and then sew the ends together with kitchen string or thread in order to form rings.

Chop the onion, celery, garlic, parsley, and the bacon very finely. Pour the oil into an earthenware cooking pot or a heavy pan, add the chopped vegetables and bacon, and sauté gently until the onion is translucent. Place the tripe rings in the pan and fry evenly. Pour in the white wine and cook until it has completely evaporated, then add the tomatoes. Season with salt and freshly ground pepper, and, if desired, a hint of ground nutmeg. Cover and simmer very slowly for about 3 hours, stirring from time to time. Add a little hot water if the sauce thickens too much during cooking.

Cook the pasta in a large pan of boiling salted water; drain when al dente. Transfer to a deep preheated serving dish, adding the sauce from the tripe and the grated Pecorino cheese. Mix well, top with the tripe rings (remove the thread or string), and serve.

Spaghetti alla Carbonara

¼ lb/¼ lb/100 g pancetta (fat bacon)
1 Tbsp olive oil or butter
¾ lb/¾ lb/350 g spaghetti
4 egg yolks
3 Tbsp/2 Tbsp/2 Tbsp light (single) cream or half and half (half cream)
¼ c/2 oz/50 g grated Parmesan cheese
freshly ground pepper

Cut the pancetta (bacon) into thin strips. Heat the oil or butter in a large pan with the pancetta (bacon) and cook over a moderate heat until the fat is translucent. Remove from the heat and keep warm. While the spaghetti is cooking in plenty of boiling salted water, beat the egg yolks in a bowl with a whisk until they are thick and creamy. Then add the cream, half the grated Parmesan cheese and a generous amount of freshly ground black pepper. Drain the spaghetti while it still has plenty of bite left. Return the pan containing the pancetta (bacon) to the heat and stir in the spaghetti, mixing well. Remove from the heat and immediately pour in the egg and cream mixture, stirring quickly. Serve immediately on heated individual plates. The heat retained in the spaghetti lightly cooks the egg and cream mixture forming a delicious coating sauce. Hand around the remaining grated Parmesan cheese.

For a more pronounced flavor, smoked pancetta (bacon) can be used, and 1–2 tablespoons of Pecorino can be added to the Parmesan.

Bucatini all'Amatriciana

$\frac{3}{4}$ lb/$\frac{3}{4}$ lb/350 g bucatini (see drawing number 5 on page 17)
$\frac{1}{2}$ c/4 oz/100 g diced sliced (streaky) bacon
1$\frac{1}{2}$ Tbsp/1 Tbsp/1 Tbsp olive oil
1 Tbsp finely chopped onion
3 large slightly underripe firm tomatoes
$\frac{1}{2}$ red chili pepper (crumbled)
$\frac{1}{4}$ c/2 oz/50 g grated Pecorino cheese
salt

Blanch and skin the tomatoes, remove the seeds, and slice. Sauté the bacon in the oil over a low heat. When the fat turns transparent, remove with a slotted spoon and set aside. Fry the onion and chili pepper in the remaining oil and, when the onion is golden brown, add the sliced tomatoes, drained of excess juice. Add a little salt, stir, and simmer for about 10 minutes. Remove from the heat and add the sautéed bacon.

Cook the bucatini in plenty of boiling salted water, drain when al dente, turn into a serving dish, and add the sauce and the Pecorino cheese. Mix and serve very hot.

Bucatini all'Amatriciana should not swim in the tomato sauce but just be lightly coated with it, and the sautéed diced bacon should be crisp, as if just cooked.

Fettuccine alla Trasteverina

2$\frac{1}{2}$ c/10$\frac{1}{2}$ oz/300 g all-purpose (plain) flour
3 eggs
$\frac{1}{4}$ c/3 Tbsp/3 Tbsp olive oil
salt
$\frac{1}{2}$ onion
1 clove garlic
3 Tbsp/1$\frac{1}{2}$ oz/40 g butter
2 c/14 oz/400 g ripe (or canned) tomatoes
2 lb/2 lb/1 kg clams in their shells
$\frac{1}{2}$ lb/$\frac{1}{2}$ lb/225 g shrimp (prawns) (peeled)
freshly ground pepper
1 small bunch parsley

Mix the flour with the eggs, a teaspoon of olive oil, and a pinch of salt and work until the dough is soft and smooth. Roll out a sheet about $\frac{1}{8}$ inch (3 mm) thick, roll up and cut into fettuccine (ribbon noodles) $\frac{1}{2}$ inch (1 cm) wide.

Chop the onion and garlic and sauté in the remaining oil and the butter for a few minutes. Add the peeled, seeded tomatoes cut into strips (if canned tomatoes are used, put them through a food mill or sieve). If the clams are still in their shells, cook them in a saucepan with $\frac{1}{3}$ cup (3$\frac{1}{2}$ fl oz/1 dl) water. As they open, remove them from the pan with a slotted spoon and then remove clams from their shells (discard any clams which do not open). Reserve the cooking liquid. Rinse the shrimp (prawns) and chop; add to the tomato sauce and simmer over a moderate heat, strain the cooking liquid from the clams through a very fine strainer (sieve) or cheesecloth (muslin) and add it to the shrimp (prawn) and tomato sauce, turn up the heat slightly, season with salt and pepper, and reduce the sauce until it thickens. Before removing from the heat, add the clams.

Cook the noodles in a large pan of boiling salted water until they are firm but tender. Drain, turn into a deep heated dish, and add the sauce. Sprinkle with a tablespoon of finely chopped parsley, mix thoroughly, and serve immediately.

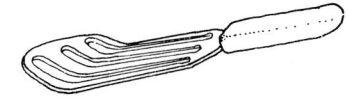

Fettuccine al Triplo Burro Maestose (all'Alfredo)

Fettuccine Alfredo

2$\frac{1}{2}$ c/10$\frac{1}{2}$ oz/300 g all-purpose (plain) flour
3 eggs
salt
$\frac{1}{2}$ c/4 oz/100 g grated Parmesan cheese
generous $\frac{1}{2}$ c/generous 4 oz/120 g butter

Make an egg pasta dough with the flour, eggs, and a pinch of salt. Knead until it is smooth and pliable, incorporating plenty of air bubbles. Cover it with a pastry cloth and leave it to rest for a little while. Then roll it out into a fairly thin sheet and let it dry for 15 to 20 minutes before cutting into $\frac{1}{4}$–$\frac{1}{2}$-inch-wide (1 cm) strips. Cook the noodles in plenty of boiling salted water and drain when al dente, leaving a little water in the pan, since it is vital that the noodles do not stick to each other. Turn into a preheated dish or bowl. Sprinkle with the Parmesan cheese, mixing rapidly so the noodles do not have time to get cold, and add the butter a little at a time. (The noodles are "double buttered" or "triple buttered" according to how much butter is used; the quantity should always be generous.) Serve onto warmed individual plates. This simple dish is absolutely delicious so long as good butter and the best quality Parmesan cheese are used.

Always add the cheese first, then the butter; never the other way round. Serve as hot as possible.

Fettuccine alla Papalina
Fettuccine with Egg and Cheese Sauce

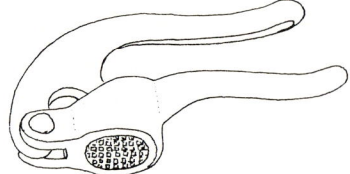

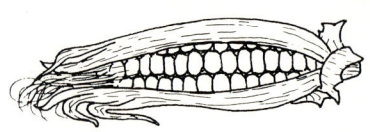

2½ c/10½ oz/300 g all-purpose (plain)
*   flour*
5 eggs
1 Tbsp olive oil
salt
scant ¼ lb/3 oz/80 g lean prosciutto (raw
*   ham)*
½ onion
4 Tbsp/2 oz/50 g butter
⅓ c/3 oz/80 g grated Parmesan cheese
⅓ c/3½ fl oz/1 dl light (single) cream
freshly ground pepper

Mix an egg pasta dough with the flour,
three whole eggs, 1 tablespoon of olive
oil, and a pinch of salt. Knead well until
the dough is soft and smooth (if plenty
of tiny air bubbles are visible when the
dough is cut, it has been worked
sufficiently). Roll out into a fairly thin
sheet on a pastry board or working
surface, and cut into strips about ¼–½
inch (1 cm) wide.

   While the pasta is cooking in plenty of
boiling salted water, very gently sauté
the prosciutto (raw ham) (cut into thin

strips) and the finely chopped onion
with 1 tablespoon (½ oz/15 g) of butter
in a small pan. When the noodles are
almost done, heat the rest of the butter
in a large pan and, when it starts to
foam, add the remaining two eggs,
beaten with 3 tablespoons (2 Tbsp/
2 Tbsp) of Parmesan cheese and the
cream. Stir, and, when the egg mixture
has just started to thicken, add the
drained noodles, sautéed prosciutto
(raw ham) and onions, and some freshly
ground pepper. Mix quickly, and remove from the heat immediately. Transfer into individual plates, sprinkle with
grated Parmesan cheese, and then enjoy
this delicate and flavorsome dish while it
is still very hot.

N.B. Great care must be taken to add the
noodles to the egg and cream mixture at
just the right time. The less experienced
cook might find it easier to mix the eggs,
cream, and butter together and heat
them in a double boiler and add the
noodles to the mixture.

Below: Uccellini di Campagna (Country Style
Veal Birds).

Stracciatella alla Romana
Roman "Ragged Egg" Broth

1 qt/1¾ pt/1 l good homemade light meat
*   stock*
4 eggs
6 Tbsp/4 Tbsp/4 Tbsp grated Parmesan
*   cheese*
salt
freshly ground pepper (optional)
nutmeg (optional)

Place the eggs in a bowl, with the grated
Parmesan cheese and a pinch of salt and
beat well with a fork. Bring the stock to
a boil in a large saucepan and add the
egg-mixture beating it into the stock
quickly with a wire whisk. Allow the
soup to simmer for a few minutes and
serve. If desired, a generous portion of
freshly ground pepper or a hint of
freshly grated nutmeg can be added to
the beaten egg mixture.

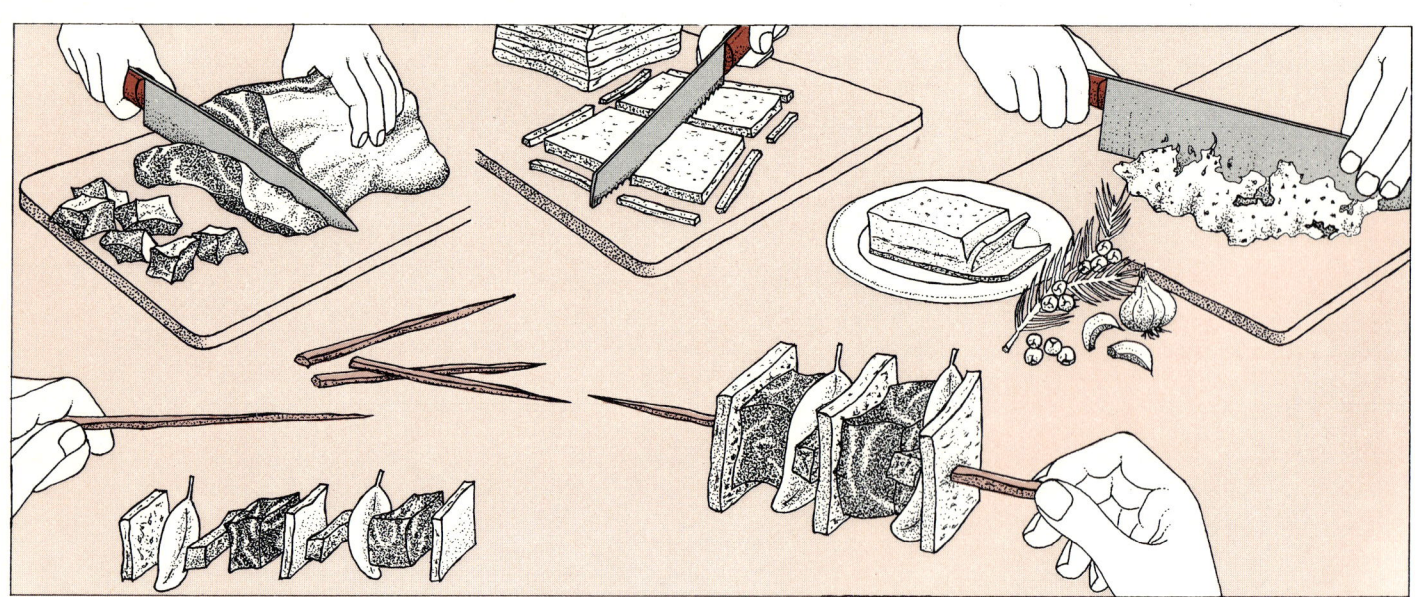

Minestra di Fave
Fresh Bean and Tomato Soup

*2 lb/2 lb/1 kg unshelled large Fordhook
    lima beans, butter beans, or broad
    beans*
1 onion
1 c/2 oz/50 g pork fat
*3 large ripe (or canned) tomatoes (put
    through a food mill or sieve) or*
2–3 Tbsp tomato paste
salt
freshly ground pepper
scant ½ lb/7 oz/200 g Arborio rice

Shell the beans, chop the onion finely, and pound the pork fat. Cook the onion and pork fat for a few minutes in a large cooking pot. Add the beans and, immediately afterwards, the tomatoes or the tomato paste dissolved in 1 scant cup 7 fl oz/2 dl) of boiling water. Simmer for about 15 minutes, then add 1 quart (1¾ pt/1 liter) of water. Season with salt and pepper and, when the soup has returned to a boil, pour in the rice and cook until tender. Grated Parmesan is not usually served with this soup.

A scant ½ cup (2 oz/50 g) of flour can be mixed together with a little cold water and added instead of the rice to thicken the soup. Slices of toast or croûtons can also be served with this dish. Again, no Parmesan cheese is served.

Bruschetta
Garlic Bread

8 slices coarse, white bread
2 cloves garlic
salt
freshly ground pepper
olive oil

In Roman dialect this snack is called *cappone*—"capon." Originally it consisted of a round loaf cut in half, broiled (grilled) over the embers of a fire, and then dressed with oil and garlic and sometimes a little pepper. Italian coarse white bread has always had consid-

erable nutritional value and the poor had to be content with this substitute for meat as a main meal. It was sardonically called "capon" since only the rich could afford the genuine article.

Simply bake the thickly sliced bread in the oven until crisp and golden brown, rub with a cut clove of garlic and sprinkle with salt, pepper, and olive oil.

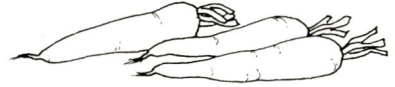

Pizza Romana
Roman Pizza

Basic pizza dough:
1 cake compressed/1 oz/25 g fresh yeast
3¾ c/1 lb/450 g all-purpose (plain) flour
salt

Sauce:
*6 Tbsp/4 Tbsp/4 Tbsp canned tomatoes
    (put through a food mill or sieve)*
⅓ c/2 oz/50 g diced Mozzarella cheese
a pinch of dried oregano
4 anchovy fillets
olive oil
salt

Dissolve the yeast in a little lukewarm water. When it begins to foam, work it into ¾ cup (4 oz/100 g) of the flour, adding more lukewarm water as necessary to form a soft dough which can be handled quite easily. Leave in a floured bowl covered by a cloth for 30 minutes to double in volume.

Sift the remaining flour and salt together to form a mound on the pastry board, make a well in the center, place risen dough ball in this, and work in the remaining flour well. Knead vigorously until the dough is smooth and elastic. Shape into a large ball, put in a floured bowl in a warm draft-free place and leave it to rise for 2 hours, or until has doubled in bulk. It is now ready to be used for the pizzas.

Punch down the risen dough and shape into a large flat disk about ½ inch (1 cm) thick. Top this circle of dough with the tomatoes, diced Mozzarella, oregano, and chopped anchovy fillets, drizzle with a little oil, sprinkle with salt

and bake in a preheated oven (375°F/190°C/mk 5) for up to 30 minutes.

Calzone alla Ricotta
Ricotta Calzone

1 hard-boiled egg
*4 Tbsp/2 oz/50 g Mortadella or cooked
    ham (chopped)*
1 c/½ lb/225 g ricotta cheese
2 fresh basil leaves
*1 recipe pizza dough (see previous recipe
    for Pizza Romana)*

Chop the hard-boiled egg and mix well with the chopped Mortadella or ham, the ricotta and the finely chopped basil leaves. Divide the dough into 4 portions, roll out and shape into circles ½ inch (1 cm) thick. Place an equal amount of filling on each circle, stopping well short of the edges, fold each circle over to form a half-moon and press the edges together firmly to seal the contents. Bake until brown (about 30 minutes) in a 375°C (190°C/mk 5) oven.

Uccellini di Campagna
Country Style Veal Birds

*16–20 thick squares of coarse white
    bread measuring 1½ inches (4 cm)
    square*
*1 lb/1 lb/500 g lean veal (cut into 2-inch
    (5-cm) cubes)*
¼ lb/¼ lb/100 g pork fat
a few fresh sage leaves
salt
freshly ground pepper

Pound the fat and spread carefully on both sides of the squares of bread. Thread the bread onto metal skewers alternating with the cubes of veal and fresh sage leaves. Place these in an ovenproof earthenware dish or non-stick roasting pan, and cook in a hot oven (400°F/200°C/mk 6). Baste with the pan juices and, when done, serve still on the skewers.

This dish is open to many variations. You may, for example, add pieces of salsiccia (small firm sausages) or small pieces of pancetta (bacon). This recipe is this region's equivalent of the Venetian dish *oseléti scapai*.

Fave col Guanciale
Braised Beans with Bacon

*5¼ lb/5¼ lb/2.5 kg fresh unshelled lima
    beans, butter beans or broad beans or
    1¼–2 lb/1¼–2 lb/550–900 g fresh (or
    frozen) shelled beans
2 Tbsp/1 oz/25 g pork fat
¾ c/5 oz/150 g diced bacon
1 shallot
¾ c/7 fl oz/2 dl stock made with a
    bouillon cube
salt
freshly ground pepper*

Choose young, tender beans and remove them from their pods. Sauté the fat and diced bacon in a large heavy pot; add the beans, the shallot, and the stock; and season with salt and pepper. Cook over a low heat, stirring frequently. If the liquid reduces too much, add a little hot water. Do not add more stock, since this would make the liquid too strongly flavored.

Saltimbocca alla Romana

*8 thin escalopes cut from the top round
    (topside) of veal; total weight: 1 lb/
    1 lb/500 g
8 slices prosciutto (raw ham)
8 fresh sage leaves or ¼–½ tsp dried sage
4 Tbsp/2 oz/50 g butter
salt
freshly ground pepper
1 c/7 fl oz/2 dl dry white wine*

Place the veal escalopes between sheets of wax paper and flatten them with the flat side of a meat cleaver or the bottom of a skillet. Lay a slice of prosciutto (raw ham) and a sage leaf (or a pinch of dried sage) on each escalope, and then secure with wooden cocktail sticks. If dried sage is used, roll the escalopes to prevent the sage spilling out.

Heat the butter in a frying pan and, when it is foaming, add the veal and brown quickly for about 2 minutes on each side. Reduce the heat slightly, season with salt and pepper, and add a little wine. Allow the wine to evaporate fairly quickly (do not overcook the veal). Transfer to a hot serving platter, remove cocktail sticks, and keep warm.

Deglaze the pan with the remaining wine, scraping the sides and bottom of the pan with a wooden spoon. Reduce the sauce by ¼ and pour over the veal. A few spoonfuls of water can be used to deglaze the pan if you prefer.

Abbacchio alla Romana
Leg of Lamb Roman Style

*2–2¼ lb/2–2¼ lb/1 kg leg of lamb (as
    young as possible)
2 lamb's kidneys
3 cloves garlic
¼ c/2 fl oz/60 ml olive oil
1 sprig of rosemary or ¼ tsp dried
    rosemary
4 anchovy fillets
6 Tbsp/4 Tbsp/4 Tbsp white wine vinegar
salt
freshly ground pepper*

In Italy suckling lamb, *abbacchio*, would be used for this dish. Buy the youngest and the most tender lamb available.

Cut the meat from the leg and the kidneys into 1½ inch (4 cm) cubes. Sauté two whole but crushed garlic cloves in the oil until they start to turn brown; then discard them. Brown the meat lightly in the butter and continue to cook, turning frequently. Meanwhile pound the remaining garlic clove (or put it through a garlic press). Then pound it together with the rosemary leaves and the anchovy fillets. Transfer the resulting paste to a small bowl and add the white wine vinegar. Stir well to blend. When the pieces of lamb are cooked, add the vinegar and herb mixture and mix well, cooking over a high flame, season. Transfer the pieces of lamb to a heated serving platter, sprinkle with the juices, and serve immediately.

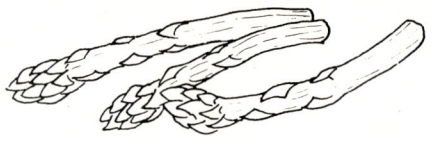

Coda alla Vaccinara
Oxtail Braised with Wine and Vegetables

*2 lb/2 lb/1 kg oxtail, skinned and jointed
4 Tbsp/2 oz/50 g pork fat
2 Tbsp/1 oz/25 g butter, oil, or lard
1 onion
1 carrot
1 clove garlic
1 small bunch parsley
2 stalks celery
¾ c/7 fl oz/2 dl dry white wine
3 Tbsp/2 Tbsp/2 Tbsp tomato paste
salt
freshly ground pepper*

Wash the oxtail well and soak it in cold water for a couple of hours. Chop the onion, garlic, carrot, and parsley very finely and sauté in a cooking pot (preferably earthenware) with the pounded pork fat and the butter until the vegetables have softened. Add the pieces of oxtail and brown well on all sides, turning frequently. Season with salt and pepper and pour in the wine a little at a time. When the wine has reduced by half, add the tomato paste diluted with about 2½ cups (1 pt/½ liter) hot water. Stir well, cover and simmer very slowly for three to four hours. When the oxtail is fairly tender but not quite done (the meat will fall away from the bones when it is completely done), add the celery, cut into very small pieces, and cook for another 30 minutes. Place the pieces of oxtail in a heated serving dish, pour on the sauce, and serve piping hot.

Originally, a few pieces of beef (ox) cheek were added to the stew and braised along with the oxtail.

Garofolato di Manzo
Braised Beef with Cloves

1½–1¾ lb/1½–1¾ lb/700–800 g beef, top
   round (top side)
2 cloves garlic
4 Tbsp/2 oz/50 g pork fat (diced)
about 6–12 cloves
4 Tbsp/2 oz/50 g oil
1 Tbsp butter
¾ c/7 fl oz/2 dl dry red wine
4 large ripe tomatoes (chopped) or
   1 lb/1 lb/500 g canned tomatoes put
   through a food mill or sieve
freshly ground pepper
salt

With a small, sharp knife make several
incisions in the beef and insert small
pieces of garlic, pork fat and a clove (if

too strong a taste is not desired, do not
insert cloves in all the incisions). Heat
the oil and butter gently in a cooking
pot, add the beef, and brown lightly on
all sides, turning frequently. Pour in the
wine, turn up the heat, and allow the
wine to evaporate. Add the tomatoes
and season with salt and pepper. Cover
and simmer for about 1 hour, turning
the meat and stirring from time to time.
When the beef is tender, take it from the
pan and carve it into thick (½–¾-inch/1-
cm) slices.

In Italy nearly all the cooking liquid
or sauce would be used for the pasta
course. The pasta would be cooked al
dente and then added to the hot sauce
and stirred over a moderate heat for a
couple of minutes. The sauce can, of
course, be poured over the sliced beef,
which is served as the main course.

In Ciociaria this recipe is also used for
leg of lamb or ox.

*Above: How to trim, season, and stuff young,
tender artichokes for Carciofi alla Romana
(Artichokes Roman Style).*

Carciofi alla Romana
Artichokes Roman Style

8 young, tender artichokes
1 lemon
10–12 leaves of fresh mint or 1 tsp dried
   mint
1 clove garlic
¾ c/2 oz/50 g fresh bread crumbs
salt
freshly ground pepper
¾ c/7 fl oz/2 dl olive oil

Remove the tougher, outer leaves of the
artichokes. Cut across the top of each as

shown in the illustration above and trim and pare the stalk to within 1½–2 inches (4–5 cm) of the base. Taking each artichoke, turn it slowly round, gently open out the leaves, and cut off the hard tips. As you proceed, rub the cut surfaces of the artichokes with slices of lemon to prevent discoloration. Chop the mint and garlic very finely and mix with the bread crumbs, salt and pepper, and a little olive oil to make a stuffing which should be pushed well down in between the leaves of the artichokes. Place the artichokes, stalks upward, snugly next to each other in an earthenware Dutch oven or casserole. Pour in a little water, cover with a sheet of oiled waxed (greaseproof) paper and then place the lid on top of this. Bake in a hot oven (400°F/200°C/mk 6) for about 1 hour. Remove the artichokes from the baking dish and arrange attractively in a heated serving dish to be eaten as a vegetable with the main course or serve them cold as an appetizer.

N.B. If older artichokes are used, the hairy choke must be removed before stuffing; otherwise the choke can be removed before or after cooking. Open out the leaves, removing a few of the inner ones to reveal the choke which is then scooped out with a teaspoon.

Carciofi alla Giudìa
Fried Artichokes Jewish Style

8 very small, young and tender
artichokes
juice of 1 lemon
¾ c/7 fl oz/2 dl olive oil
salt
freshly ground pepper

This dish is still very popular in Roman cuisine, having been celebrated over 100 years ago by Giuseppe Gioachino Belli (1791–1863), a poet who wrote in Roman dialect.

This dish can only be really successfully prepared with the very young artichokes so beloved of the Romans. If older artichokes are used, remove the choke, as indicated above.

Proceed as above but trim the stalks to within 1–1½ inches (3–4 cm) of the artichoke base, and finally immerse in cold water acidulated with the juice of a lemon to prevent discoloration. When the artichokes are ready, they should be shaped like lemons with one blunt end and the remaining stalk at the other.

Place the oil in a tall, narrow cooking pot (preferably earthenware and certainly with a non-metallic lining) and, when hot, place the artichokes, stem downwards, in the oil (cook in two batches if the pot is very small), sprinkle with salt and pepper, cover, and cook slowly for about 10 minutes, then carefully turn the artichokes over, sprinkle with a little more salt and cook for another 10 minutes. Just before the artichokes are done, sprinkle them with water, turn up the heat a little, and cook with the lid off until the water has evaporated. Remove the artichokes from the oil, drain on paper towels, and serve quickly on a heated serving platter.

Carciofi coi Piselli
Artichokes with Peas

4 young, tender artichokes
juice of 1 lemon
1¾ c/10½ oz/300 g small, tender peas
*   (fresh or frozen)*
1 onion
¼ c/2 oz/50 g prosciutto (raw ham)
1 Tbsp shortening (lard or margarine)
3 Tbsp/2 Tbsp/2 Tbsp olive oil
salt
freshly ground pepper

Prepare the artichokes as above, finally plunging in acidulated water. Place the peas in plenty of cold water. Chop the onion and the prosciutto (raw ham) finely and sauté in the shortening (lard) and oil in a heavy pan. Cut the artichokes in half vertically (if older artichokes are used, remove the choke at this stage) and place in the pan, cover, and cook over a moderate heat for about 15 minutes. Add a little salt (remember that the prosciutto (raw

ham) is salty), some pepper, the peas, and a little water. Moisten with a little more water from time to time as needed and cook until the peas and artichokes are tender.

Frittata di Carciofi
Artichoke Frittata

4 fairly large but tender artichokes
5 eggs
⅓ c/3½ fl oz/1 dl olive oil
stock (preferably light, homemade
*   stock)*
juice of 1 lemon
salt
freshly ground pepper

Prepare the artichokes as above, but cut off all the stalk and before immersing in cold water acidulated with the juice of a lemon, cut in half vertically and slice thinly (if older artichokes are used, remove choke at this stage). Heat half the oil in a frying pan, add the artichokes, and fry, pouring in a little hot stock from time to time. When they are browned on both sides remove them from the pan and drain them on paper towels.

Break the eggs into a bowl, season with salt and pepper, and beat thoroughly. Add the fried artichokes. Stir well and then pour into a large skillet containing the rest of the oil, heated until very hot. Smooth the top surface of the frittata while the bottom sets and browns lightly, then turn carefully and brown the other side. Serve at once if the frittata is to be eaten hot or allow it to cool—it is almost equally delicious eaten cold.

Other frittatas, made with spinach, onion, zucchini, asparagus, etc. can also be made by this method. A thicker omelet, called a *tortino* is found in other regions of Italy.

Frittata alla Menta
Fresh Mint Frittata

1 Tbsp all-purpose (plain) flour
⅓ c/3½ fl oz/1 dl milk
6 very fresh eggs (separated)
1 small bunch of fresh, young mint
butter for frying
salt

Place the flour in a dry cup and add the milk a little at a time, stirring to form a smooth, lump-free mixture. Beat the egg whites in a bowl until stiff but not dry, then fold in the lightly beaten egg yolks, and then the flour and milk. Season and mix well. Select the youngest, most tender mint leaves, chop them finely, and add them immediately to the egg mixture. Melt a little butter in a non-stick skillet or omelet pan and fry the mixture in four equal portions, adding a very little more butter between frittatas. The frittatas should be very thin, so tilt the pan to allow unset egg to spill over the edges and cook. Turn with a spatula. This type of frittata is often eaten cold as a first course. Special covered (reversible) frying pans, which facilitate turning frittatas are to be found in Italian hardware stores.

Fondi di Carciofo Trifolati
Artichoke Hearts Sautéed with Garlic and Parsley

8 artichoke hearts
2 cloves garlic
1 bunch parsley (finely chopped)
⅓ c/3½ fl oz/1 dl olive oil
juice of 1 lemon
3 Tbsp/2 Tbsp/2 Tbsp all-purpose (plain) flour
stock (optional)
salt
freshly ground pepper

Buy already prepared fresh artichoke hearts if possible. They should be fairly large but tender. To keep their color, soak them in cold water mixed with the lemon juice until just before cooking. Sauté the crushed garlic cloves in the oil until they begin to color and then discard the garlic. Dredge the artichoke hearts lightly with flour and arrange in one layer in the pan or skillet. Fry gently in the oil, adding a little water or stock. Cover the pan and cook slowly. Add a little salt just before the hearts are done (if added sooner it will discolor them). When they are tender, transfer them to an oval serving dish, sprinkle with their cooking juices, and decorate with plenty of finely chopped parsley.

Cipolle al Forno
Baked Onions

4 firm, medium onions
⅓ c/3½ fl oz/1 dl olive oil
3 Tbsp/2 Tbsp/2 Tbsp vinegar
salt
freshly ground pepper

Remove the dry papery outer skin from the onions and blanch them in boiling water for a few minutes so they will remain a good color during baking. Plunge them into cold water, drain and then bake in a hot oven (400°F/200°C/mk 6) for about 1 hour. Allow the onions to cool, remove the outermost skin, and then slice. Arrange the slices in a deep serving dish, dress with oil, salt, pepper, and a little good wine vinegar, and serve as a first course or as an accompanying vegetable with mixed boiled meats.

Pomodori Farciti
Stuffed Tomatoes

8 large firm tomatoes
½ onion
3 Tbsp/2 Tbsp/2 Tbsp fine bread crumbs
4 anchovy fillets
¼ c/1½ oz/40 g finely diced cooked ham
2 hard-boiled eggs
oil
salt

Wash and dry the tomatoes and skin them carefully. Placing them in a bowl, covering them with boiling water for 10 seconds, and immediately plunging them in cold water will make the skins far easier to remove without softening the pulp. Slice off the top of each tomato and remove the seeds with a small spoon, sprinkle with a little salt, and place the tomatoes upside down in a colander so that their juices can drain off.

Sauté the chopped onion in some oil; then add the bread crumbs and stir well. Remove from the heat. Chop the anchovy fillets (if salted anchovies are used, remove the bones, and rub the fillets with lemon slices to remove excess salt before chopping). Hard-boil the eggs and push through a strainer (sieve). Add the anchovies, eggs, and diced cooked ham to the bread crumb mixture and mix well. Fill the tomato cavities with this stuffing and serve cold on a bed of fresh, crisp lettuce leaves. This dish is very good as a summer appetizer or as part of a cold meal.

Peperoni Ripieni
Stuffed Peppers

1 c/3 oz/90 g fresh bread crumbs
milk
⅔ can/4 oz/100 g canned tuna fish
10 black olives
salt
freshly ground pepper
oil
4 large, firm yellow or green sweet peppers

Moisten the bread crumbs with a little lukewarm milk and leave to stand in a bowl. Flake the tuna, chop the olives very finely, and place together in a bowl, add the bread crumbs (squeezed to drain off the milk), and season with salt and pepper. Mix well with a wooden spoon, then pour in 6 tablespoons (4 Tbsp/4 Tbsp) oil, a little at a time while stirring to blend thoroughly.

Cut the peppers in half vertically; remove the seeds and membrane; and fill with the olive, tuna, and bread crumb mixture. Place in a large baking dish containing a little oil and bake in a moderate oven (325°F/170°C/mk 3) for 3 to 4 hours. These peppers are equally good eaten hot or cold.

This dish is improved if fresh *ventresca* (belly), or middle cut tuna (the tenderest part of the fish) is used instead of canned fish. Using a blender to mix the filling will speed up preparation and make the mixture smoother.

Broccoletti Strascinati
Turnip Tops with Garlic

1¾ lb/1¾ lb/800 g fresh young turnip tops
⅓ c/3½ fl oz/1 dl olive oil
2 cloves garlic
salt
freshly ground pepper
¼ bouillon cube, preferably light
    stock, dissolved in hot water

Turnip tops are a much underrated and little known vegetable nowadays. The Romans, however, still appreciate them. Pick out and discard the older, tougher leaves of the turnip tops. Wash and dry the remaining leaves. Heat the oil in a large pan together with the garlic cloves, crushed with the flat of a knife blade. When the garlic begins to color, discard. Add the turnip tops to the oil, season with salt and pepper, cover, and cook over a very gentle heat for about 30 minutes, moistening with a little stock.

Maritozzi
Lenten Buns

⅓ c/2 oz/50 g seedless white raisins
    (sultanas)
½ c/2 oz/50 g candied orange peel
scant ¾ lb/10½ oz/300 g kneaded and
    proofed bread dough (see page 15)
3 Tbsp/2 Tbsp/2 Tbsp olive oil
3 Tbsp/2 Tbsp/2 Tbsp granulated sugar
salt
½ c/2 oz/50 g pine nuts

These buns, as their name suggests, are eaten during Lent, accompanied by white wine.

Soak the raisins (sultanas) in lukewarm water for 20 minutes and finely dice the candied orange peel. Place the prepared bread dough on a pastry board and work in the oil, sugar and a pinch of salt. Knead very well until the dough is smooth and pliable. Add the drained raisins (sultanas), squeezed of excess water, the pine nuts, and the diced orange peel, and knead. Shape into small oval buns and arrange, well spaced out, on an oiled cookie (baking) sheet. Cover with a cloth and leave to rise in a warm place away from drafts, for 4 to 5 hours. Then bake in a preheated oven at about 400°F (200°C/mk 6) for approximately 15 minutes. The buns should be well browned.

Crostata di Visciole
Cherry Tart Roman Style

2½ c/10½ oz/300 g cake flour (very fine
    flour)
1¼ c/5 oz/150 g confectioners' (icing)
    sugar
salt
5 Tbsp/3 oz/80 g butter
5 Tbsp/2½ oz/70 g shortening (lard)
2 whole eggs
juice of 1 lemon
milk
scant 1 lb/14 oz/400 g Morello or sour
    cherry jam
1 egg yolk

Visciola is a variety of cherry which is cultivated in Latium. It is much larger and sweeter than normal cherries and is therefore excellent for jams and jellies.

Mix the sifted flour with the sugar and a pinch of salt. Then add the softened (not melted) butter and lard, two whole eggs and the lemon juice. Work the dough as little as possible—just enough to incorporate the ingredients properly and make a smooth, elastic dough. Add a little milk if the dough is too firm. Place the dough in a bowl, cover with a cloth, and leave it to rest for an hour in the refrigerator. Roll out the pastry into a fairly thick sheet and line the bottom and sides of a flan tin with a removable base about 11 inches (28 cm) in diameter, which has been buttered and lightly dredged with flour. Spread the cherry jam thickly over the pastry and level off the surface with a spatula. Roll out the rest of the pastry and cut into strips ½ inch (1 cm) wide with a fluted pastry wheel. Arrange the strips in a lattice over the jam. Beat the egg yolk and, using a pastry brush, glaze the lattice. Bake in a preheated oven at 350°F/180°C/mk 4 for about ¾ hour. The tart is done when the pastry is golden brown. Remove from the oven, allow to cool, and then remove from the tin and serve. This tart is better eaten the day after it is made.

Opposite: Pizza Margherita, Torta di Ricotta (Italian Cheese Cake), and Sfogliatelle, all specialties from Campania.

Overleaf: A pan of young, tender broccoli and a plate of orecchiette, both typical of Apulian cuisine.

ABRUZZI AND MOLISE

Maccheroni alla Chitarra
"Guitar" Macaroni

2½ c/10½ oz/300 g fine durum wheat flour
4 eggs
salt
¼ c/2 oz/50 g pancetta (fat bacon)
4 Tbsp/2 oz/50 g butter
4 large ripe tomatoes
¼ c/2 oz/50 g grated Pecorino Romano
   cheese
freshly ground pepper

This type of pasta is a specialty of the
Abruzzi region and really should be
made with a special utensil, the *chitarra*
(guitar), illustrated left. This is a rectangular
frame strung with taut steel wires
about ⅛ inch (3 mm) apart, which is used
to cut the pasta.

Mix an egg pasta dough (see page 11)
with the flour, eggs, and a pinch of salt
and work thoroughly until the dough is
soft, smooth, and pliable. Roll out into a
sheet of the same thickness as the spaces
between the wires of the *chitarra*.

Cut the sheet of pasta into rectangles
the size of the *chitarra* and cut them one
by one with the aid of a rolling pin as
shown in the illustration. The same
result can be obtained painstakingly
with a sharp knife in the absence of the
special cutting tool. The aim is to
produce square spaghetti. This pasta
will not cut neatly unless it has been
thoroughly kneaded beforehand.

Cook in a large pan of boiling salted
water until al dente and drain thoroughly.
Serve with a good simple sauce.

This is one of the most delicious types
of homemade pasta and the following
sauce goes very well with it: Cut the
pancetta (bacon) into thin strips and
sauté in the butter. Skin (see instructions
for Pomodori Farciti on page 139) and
seed the tomatoes and chop them. Add
to the pancetta (bacon) and simmer
until the sauce has reduced a little.
Sprinkle with the grated Pecorino cheese
and a little freshly ground pepper.

Left: Making Maccheroni alla Chitarra
("Guitar" Macaroni).

Lasagna all'Abruzzese

6 eggs
1 Mozzarella cheese
5 Tbsp/2½ oz/70 g butter
1¼ c/10½ oz/300 g finely chopped lean
 veal
6 Tbsp/4 Tbsp/4 Tbsp dry white wine
scant 1 lb/14 oz/400 g canned tomatoes
 (put through a food mill or sieve)
1 Tbsp tomato paste
½ c/4 oz/100 g grated Parmesan cheese
salt
freshly ground pepper
2¼ c/10½ oz/300 g all-purpose (plain)
 flour

Hard-boil and chop 2 of the eggs. Dice the Mozzarella. Heat just over half the butter in a heavy saucepan, and when it starts to form, add the veal and brown lightly, mixing well. Pour in the wine and cook until it has evaporated. Add the tomatoes and the tomato paste and bring to a boil.

In a mixing bowl place ¼ cup (2 oz/ 50 g) of grated Parmesan and 1 egg and season with salt and pepper. Mix well. Turn the heat under the tomato sauce to low and add the cheese and egg mixture a teaspoon at a time. Stir the sauce over a gentle heat. Make an egg pasta dough (see page 11) with the flour, 3 eggs, and a pinch of salt. Work until smooth and elastic and then roll out into a thin sheet. Cut into pieces which will fit the bottom of a narrow baking dish. One piece should be cut larger to line the bottom and sides of the dish. Half-cook these lasagne in a large pan of boiling salted water, drain, and carefully lay out on a cloth. Butter the baking dish generously, line the bottom and sides with the largest lasagna sheet, and sprinkle with a few tablespoons of the sauce; scatter some of the diced Mozzarella and the chopped hard-boiled eggs evenly over the surface and then follow this with a sprinkling of grated Parmesan cheese. Continue to layer the ingredients in this order, ending with a sheet of pasta covered with a little melted butter. Bake in a preheated oven at about 400°F

(200°C/mk 6) for approximately 15 minutes.

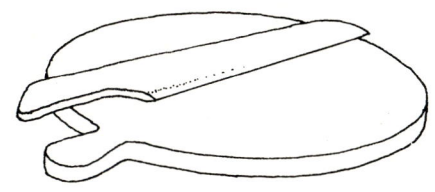

Zuppa di Lenticchie
Lentil Soup

scant ½ lb/scant ½ lb/200 g dried lentils
 (preferably brown)
mixed herbs (bay leaf, basil, marjoram,
 thyme, and rosemary)
4 Tbsp/2 oz/50 g pork fat
3 Tbsp/2 Tbsp/2 Tbsp oil
15 roasted chestnuts
1 Tbsp tomato paste
salt
freshly ground pepper
8 slices of coarse white bread

This dish is also widely known as Lenticchie alla Montanara (Lentils Mountain Style).

Soak the lentils in lukewarm water for 24 hours. The next day boil them in lightly salted water with a bay leaf. While the lentils are cooking, prepare the sauce by sautéing the finely diced pork fat in the oil together with the chopped chestnuts and some leaves of basil, marjoram, thyme, and rosemary. When the pieces of pork fat are translucent, add the tomato paste diluted in about ½ cup (4 fl oz/125 ml) of hot water, season to taste with salt and pepper, and pour the resulting sauce into the pan containing the lentils. Remove the bay leaf. Simmer for a few minutes longer, stirring well; there should be about 1 quart (1¾ pt/1 liter) of liquid left with the lentils. Ladle the soup into heated bowls, each containing 2 thick slices of bread.

Ravioli all'Abruzzese

5 eggs
2 tsp granulated sugar
a pinch of cinnamon
¾ lb/¾ lb/350 g fresh ricotta cheese
3 c/¾ lb/350 g all-purpose (plain) flour
salt
4 Tbsp/2 oz/50 g butter
¾ c/5 oz/150 g ground (minced) meat
1 small onion
1 clove garlic
1 clove
freshly ground pepper
6 Tbsp/4 Tbsp/4 Tbsp dry white wine
6 Tbsp/4 Tbsp/4 Tbsp tomato paste
¼ c/2 oz/50 g grated Parmesan or
 Pecorino cheese

Beat one of the eggs well; add the sugar, cinnamon, and ricotta; and blend to form a smooth filling for the ravioli.

Make an egg pasta dough by working 3 eggs with the flour and a pinch of salt. Knead well until the dough is smooth and pliable and then roll out into a thin sheet. Beat the remaining egg and a little water together and brush over the pasta sheet. Distribute the filling in small evenly spaced heaps on half the pasta sheet (see page 11 and the illustration on page 15). Cover with the other half of the pasta and press the two sheets firmly together between the heaps of filling with your fingers. Cut out into filled squares, and let them dry for 15 to 30 minutes.

Heat the butter in a pan until it starts to color. Then add the ground (minced) meat, the chopped onion, the very finely chopped garlic, and the clove. Season with salt and pepper and sauté for a few minutes, stirring constantly. Pour in the wine, turn up the heat, and cook until it has evaporated. Remove the garlic and add the tomato paste diluted in a little warm water. Cover and simmer over a low heat until the sauce has reduced and thickened.

Cook the ravioli in plenty of boiling salted water, remove carefully from the pan with a slotted spoon, and place in individual heated plates. Pour on the sauce and serve at once with Parmesan cheese on the side. Those who like a stronger taste may use mature Pecorino cheese instead of the Parmesan.

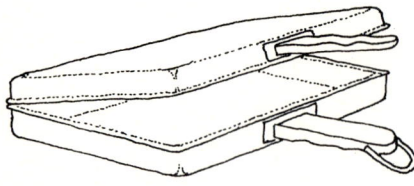

Zuppa Santè
Chicken Soup with Meatballs

½ lb/½ lb/225 g ground (minced) lean
   veal
⅓ c/3 oz/80 g Caciocavallo cheese
about ½ c/2 oz/50 g chicken giblets
4 Tbsp/2 oz/50 g butter
1 egg
5½ c/2¼ pt/1¼ l chicken stock (preferably
   homemade)
3 Tbsp/2 Tbsp/2 Tbsp grated Pecorino
   cheese
all-purpose (plain) flour
8 slices stale bread
salt
freshly ground pepper

Place the ground (minced) meat in a bowl with the egg and the Pecorino cheese (use Parmesan if a milder taste is preferred). Season with salt and pepper and mix well. Flour the hands lightly and roll the mixture between the palms of the hand into small balls about the size of hazelnuts. Roll these in flour and sauté in hot butter.

Brown the slices of bread in the oven. Skim any fat from the top of the chicken stock and bring it to a boil in a saucepan with the finely chopped chicken giblets. Reduce the heat and simmer.

Place two of the crisp, pieces of toast together with ¼ of the finely diced Caciocavallo cheese in each of 4 heated soup plates. Distribute the veal balls among the soup plates. Ladle some chicken stock and chopped giblets into each plate and serve at once, so that the soup can be eaten while the bread is still slightly crunchy.

Brodosini (Brudisigli)
Pasta and Bacon Broth

scant 2 c/7 oz/200 g all-purpose (plain)
   flour
2 eggs
5½ c/2¼ pt/1¼ l good homemade meat
   stock
¼ c/2 oz/50 g bacon (finely chopped)

Folk wisdom in the Abruzzi would have it that this soup is particularly good for nursing mothers.

Following the instructions for Maccheroni alla Chitarra on page 144. Heat the stock in a large saucepan and while it is coming to a boil, sauté the very finely chopped bacon in a small pan. Add the "guitar" macaroni to the boiling stock and immediately afterwards the sautéed bacon. Cook the macaroni until al dente and serve at once.

Some recipes for this soup omit the meat stock. The bacon is simply added to the macaroni which is cooked in boiling salted water.

Brodetto di Pesce
Fish Soup

2 lb/2 lb/1 kg assorted fish and seafood
   (whiting, red mullet, small sole, dabs,
   turbot, scampi, small squid, mussels,
   etc.)
1 onion
12 small sweet red peppers (the long,
   thin variety)
1 small piece red chili pepper
¾ c/7 fl oz/2 dl oil
⅓ c/3½ fl oz/1 dl red wine vinegar
2 large, very ripe tomatoes (peeled,
   seeded, and finely chopped)
salt
freshly ground pepper

This soup is a great speciality of the cuisine of Pescara and the Vasto and Ortona areas. The small sweet red peppers used in this dish are known locally by the name of fufulloni.

Clean, trim, and wash the fish as

necessary, and plunge into several changes of cold water (very important for the mussels). Remove the beards from the mussels and heat the shells in a cast-iron skillet until all have opened (any which do not open should be discarded). Let them cool and then remove the mussels from their shells and place in a bowl. Chop the onion coarsely and sauté with whole small sweet peppers and the piece of chili pepper in the oil. Remove the sweet peppers and pound them very well, preferably using a pestle and mortar. Discard the chili pepper. Return the pounded sweet peppers to the pan and pour in the vinegar and the tomatoes. Once the liquid has come to a gentle boil, add the fish cut into pieces and season to taste with salt and pepper. Add the mussels last. Cover and cook briskly for about 20 minutes. Like other fish soups and stews, this soup should be served extremely hot with slices of coarse homemade bread.

Triglie al Cartoccio
Mullet en Papillote

4 large red mullet
4 cloves garlic
1 bay leaf
oil
salt

Gut and trim the mullet; then wash and dry them. If the mullet are very fresh, leave the livers inside them when gutting; since mullet liver has no gall it is not bitter. Place each mullet on a sheet of oiled waxed (greaseproof) paper or foil and season inside and out with a finely chopped clove of garlic, a piece of bay leaf, a little oil, and salt. Bring the two edges of the paper together over the fish, and fold over twice. Then fold the ends so that no juices escape. Leave plenty of room around the fish. Oil the outside of the papillotes and place them in a buttered baking dish. Cook in a preheated oven at 400°F (200°C/mk 6) until the bags are inflated. The fish will take 15 to 20 minutes to cook. Transfer

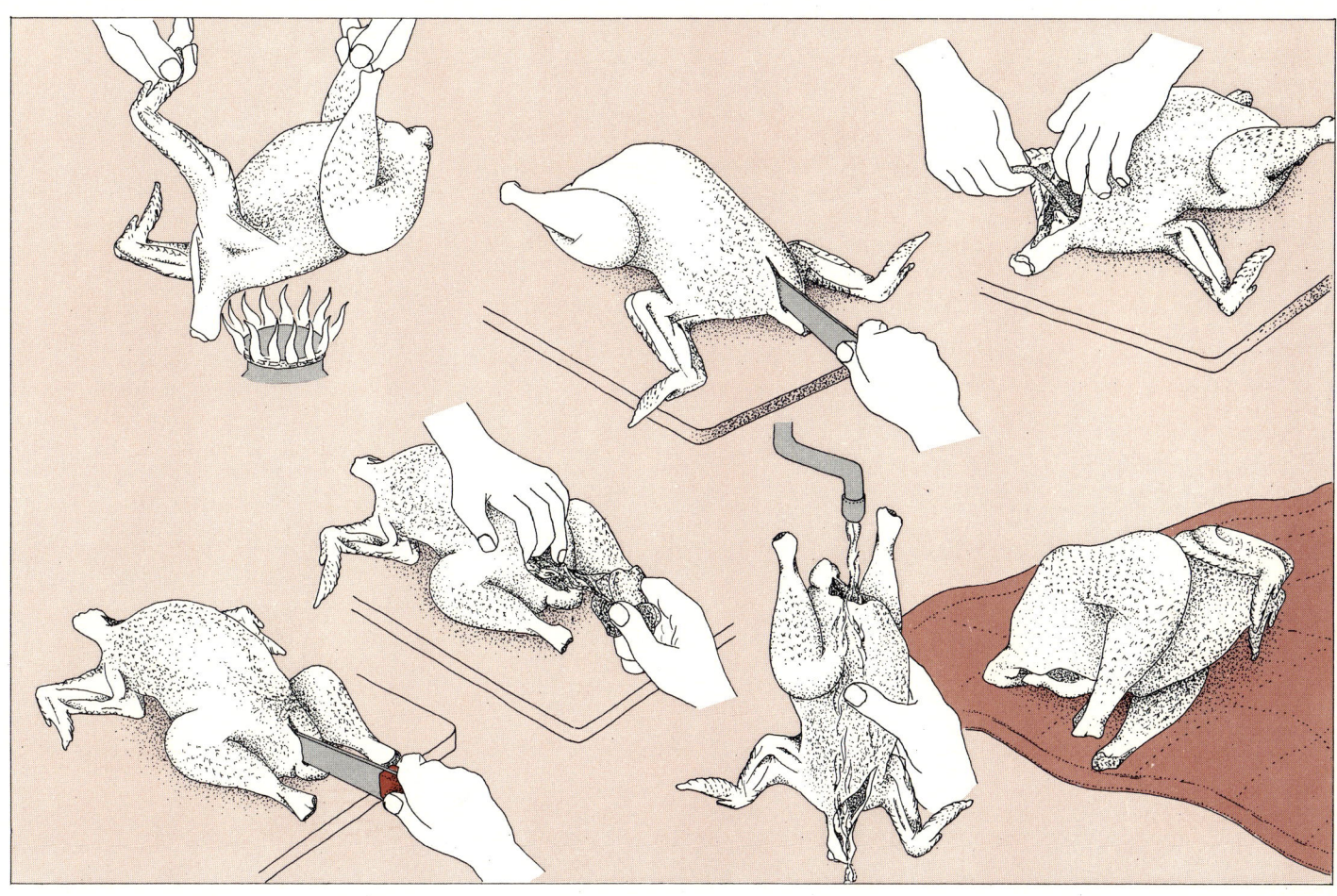

the papillotes to individual hot plates and let each person open his own.

Agnello con Salsina all'Uovo e Limone
Lamb with Egg and Lemon Sauce

1¾ lb/1¾ lb/800 g leg of lamb (boned)
⅓ c/3½ fl oz/1 dl oil
⅓ c/3½ fl oz/1 dl dry white wine
1 clove garlic
2 egg yolks
1 lemon
salt
freshly ground pepper

This is a favorite dish of the Abruzzi region and is traditionally eaten at Easter.

Cut the lamb into large cubes which are then sautéed in the oil with the crushed garlic clove and, when the garlic turns a dark brown, discard it. Turn the lamb frequently to ensure even browning. Pour in the wine and reduce over a fairly high heat for a few minutes. Season with salt and pepper, cover, and simmer over a low heat, moistening with a little hot water every now and then. When the lamb is really tender, take it out of the pan and keep it warm on a serving platter while finishing the sauce: Take the pan in which the lamb has cooked off the heat. Beat the egg yolks well with the lemon juice and add them to the juices in the pan. Beating constantly with a whisk, cook over a very low heat until the egg yolks increase in volume and are light and foamy, rather like Zabaglione. Pour over the lamb and serve.

Above: Singeing and cleaning a chicken.

Pollo all'Abruzzese
Chicken Braised with Tomatoes and Peppers

1 young chicken weighing about 3 lb/
   3 lb/1½ kg
⅓ c/3½ fl oz/1 dl oil
1 onion
¾ lb/¾ lb/300 g ripe tomatoes
salt
freshly ground pepper
2 green or yellow peppers

Prepare the chicken as shown in the illustration above and cut into pieces.
   Place the oil, the onion cut into thin slices, and the chicken pieces in a pan

and fry gently until the chicken is well browned on all sides. Add the blanched, peeled, seeded, and chopped tomatoes; season with pepper and salt; and then cover and simmer over a low heat for at least 30 minutes, stirring occasionally.

Place the peppers under the broiler (grill) for a few minutes, turning frequently, to loosen their outer skins. Plunge into cold water and peel. Remove any seeds and membrane and cut the peppers into thin strips. When the chicken has cooked for 30 minutes, add the peppers and simmer for 15 minutes more before serving.

Scamorze ai Ferri
Barbecued Cheese

4 Scamorza cheeses
salt
freshly ground pepper

Scamorza is a drawn curd cheese, originally made from buffalo milk, though today cow's milk is used. It is a little like Mozzarella.

Cut the cheeses in half, season with salt and pepper, and place under the broiler (grill) until the surface turns golden brown and the cheese softens and releases its delicate flavor. Eat very hot, since the cheese hardens as it cools. The cheese should really be cooked by the heat of charcoal or wood embers and a barbecue would be ideal.

'Ndocca 'Ndocca
Marinated Braised Pork

1¾ lb/1¾ lb/800 g assorted pork cuts,
    such as pig's feet (trotters), rind,
    head, spare ribs,
⅓ c/3½ fl oz/1 dl vinegar
1 bay leaf
1 clove garlic
1 sprig of rosemary or ¼ tsp dried
    rosemary
1 piece of red chili pepper
salt
freshly ground pepper

This dish is a specialty of the Teramano area and is delicious hot or cold. Its strange dialect name stems from the local expression for "cut into large pieces."

Scrub the pig's feet (trotters) in several changes of water. Chop up the head and rind and together with the other pork cuts marinate overnight in cold water mixed with the vinegar and the crumbled bay leaf. The following day, drain the meat and place it in a large cooking pot (preferably earthenware) with plenty of water and the garlic, rosemary, and chili pepper. Add salt and pepper and simmer, covered for about 4 hours.

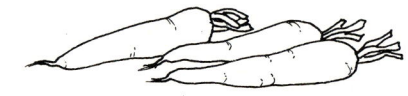

Timballo di Melanzane
Eggplant (Aubergine) Casserole

3 large, long eggplants (aubergines)
salt
all-purpose (plain) flour
oil for frying
½ lb/½ lb/225 g Scamorza or Mozzarella
    cheese
¼ lb/¼ lb/100 g prosciutto (raw ham)
4 Tbsp/2 oz/50 g butter

Slice the eggplants (aubergines) thinly, sprinkle with salt, and place them in a colander with a plate and a weight on top for 1 hour, so that their bitter juices drain off. Pat dry, coat lightly with flour, and fry them in plenty of hot oil. Drain on paper towels.

Slice the cheese and cut the prosciutto (raw ham) in thin strips. Line the bottom of a buttered baking dish with a layer of eggplant (aubergine) slices, then add some prosciutto (raw ham) and dot with butter, and cover with a layer of cheese slices. Repeat until all the ingredients are used up, ending with a layer of eggplants (aubergines). Drizzle a little melted butter on top. Place in a moderate oven (about 325°C/170°C/mk 3) for about 30 minutes or until the top is well browned.

Frittata di Cipolle
Onion Frittata

4 large onions
salt
freshly ground pepper
oil
oregano

Slice the onions into fine rings, place in a dish and sprinkle with salt and pepper. Heat 2–3 tablespoons of oil in a skillet and sauté gently until the onions soften and become translucent. Stir frequently and add a few tablespoons of water from time to time. When the onions are cooked set them aside to cool.

Beat the eggs with the oregano and salt and pepper in a bowl and stir in the onions. Heat a little oil in a skillet or large omelet pan until it is very hot, then pour in the frittata batter and cook until firm and golden brown on both sides.

Like most Italian frittatas, this is equally good hot or at room temperature. The onions can be replaced by other vegetables, such as artichokes, spinach, zucchini (courgettes), etc.

Piselli col Guanciale
Peas with Bacon

2 lb/2 lb/1 kg young, tender peas in their
    pods or 1 lb/1 lb/500 g shelled fresh or
    frozen peas
2 onions
¼ c/4 oz/100 g chopped bacon
6 Tbsp/4 Tbsp/4 Tbsp oil
salt
freshly ground pepper

If fresh peas are used shell and wash them. Chop the onions and bacon finely and sauté in the oil for a few minutes. Add the peas, season with salt and pepper, and pour in about 1¼ cups (½ pt/4 dl) of water. Cover and simmer until the peas are tender, stirring occasionally. Serve as soon as the peas are done and the cooking liquid has reduced.

CAMPANIA

Mozzarella all'Origano
Mozzarella Cheese with Oregano

2 very fresh Mozzarella cheeses
 (preferably buffalo milk Mozzarella)
2 large ripe tomatoes
salt
freshly ground pepper
oregano
⅓ c/3½ fl oz/1 dl oil

The Mozzarella cheese must be absolutely fresh and dripping with its own buttermilk for this dish. Slice the cheese and tomatoes evenly and arrange alternately on a round serving platter. Sprinkle with salt (preferably sea salt) and pepper and a generous pinch of oregano and pour over a little best quality olive oil.

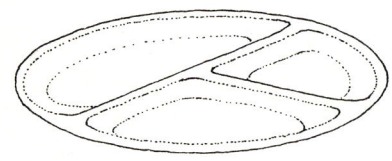

Crostini alla Napoletana
Baked Neapolitan Open Sandwiches

8 anchovy fillets
4 ripe tomatoes
2 Mozzarella cheeses
8 slices of bread from a sandwich loaf
6 Tbsp/3 oz/80 g fresh butter (preferably
 unsalted)
salt
freshly ground pepper
oregano
oil

Drain the anchovy fillets and cut them in half lengthwise. Wash, dry, and slice the tomatoes. Cut the Mozzarella cheese into 8 equal slices (leave the rounded ends for use at some other time). Spread the slices of bread evenly with butter, top with a slice of Mozzarella (it should not overlap the edges of the bread), two half fillets of anchovy, and a few slices of tomato. Season with salt, pepper, and oregano to taste. Oil a cookie sheet or

baking tray, place the prepared open sandwiches neatly on it, and bake at about 350°F (180°C/mk 4) for 10 minutes at most. These sandwiches should be eaten very hot as an appetizer or quick snack.

Spaghetti al Pomodoro e Basilico
Spaghetti with Tomato and Basil Sauce

1¼ lb/1¼ lb/600 g firm ripe tomatoes
6 Tbsp/4 Tbsp/4 Tbsp olive oil
1 small bunch fresh basil
salt
freshly ground pepper
¾ lb/¾ lb/350 g spaghetti or vermicelli
¼ c/2 oz/50 g grated Pecorino cheese

This sauce is simple and delicious.

Blanch the tomatoes for 10 seconds, skin, remove seeds, and cut into strips. Drain off excess juice. If canned tomatoes have to be used, remove the whole tomatoes from the liquid and put them through a food mill or sieve. Heat the oil gently and, when it is just warm, add the tomatoes and the basil. Season with salt and pepper, cover, and simmer over a moderate heat for about 30 minutes, stirring from time to time so the sauce does not stick. Remove and discard the fresh basil leaves when the sauce is ready.

Cook the spaghetti in a large pan of boiling salted water until al dente, drain, and mix with the tomato sauce. Serve the grated Pecorino (or Parmesan) cheese separately.

Spaghetti Aglio e Olio
Spaghetti with Garlic and Oil

¾ lb/¾ lb/350 g spaghetti
4 cloves garlic
6 Tbsp/4 Tbsp/4 Tbsp best quality olive
 oil
1 small bunch parsley
salt
freshly ground pepper

While the spaghetti is cooking in plenty of boiling salted water, sauté the garlic cloves, crushed with the blade of a large knife, in the oil until they are brown. Then remove and discard them. Keep the pan containing the flavored oil hot. Chop the parsley very finely. Drain the spaghetti when al dente then quickly dress with freshly ground pepper, the very hot oil, and the chopped parsley. Mix and serve very hot.

For those who like a little stronger, peppery taste, a small piece of chili pepper may be sautéed and removed with the garlic.

Spaghetti alle Vongole
Spaghetti with Clams and Tomato Sauce

1¼ lb/1¼ lb/600 g clams (in their shells)
 or
 about ½ c/4 oz/100 g canned clams in
 their own juice
4 large ripe tomatoes or
 2 c/14 oz/400 g canned tomatoes
2 cloves garlic
1 small bunch parsley
¼ c/3 Tbsp/3 Tbsp olive oil
salt
freshly ground pepper
¾ lb/¾ lb/350 g spaghetti

Wash the clams well if they are still in their shells, place in a pan containing ¼ inch (5 mm) of water, and steam, removing the clams as they open; discard those which do not open at all or only a little. Reserve the cooking liquid. When the clams have cooled slightly, remove them from their shells. Strain the cooking liquid (after allowing it to stand so that any sand falls to the bottom) through a piece of cloth placed in a fine sieve.

Blanch the tomatoes for 10 seconds, peel and put through a food mill or sieve. Chop the garlic and half the parsley finely and place in a pan with the oil and the strained clam liquid, add a little salt, and boil until the liquid has reduced to a few tablespoonfuls. Stir in the tomatoes and continue to cook briskly until the sauce thickens. Add freshly ground pepper and the clams and reduce the heat (the clams should only be heated, not boiled).

Boil the spaghetti in plenty of salted water, drain, and transfer to a heated serving dish, add the clam sauce, and sprinkle with the rest of the parsley, which should be chopped at the last minute so it retains its full flavor. No cheese is served with this dish.

A lighter even more digestible dish is achieved if the unheated oil is added to the cooked and drained spaghetti rather than cooked in the sauce.

Spaghetti alla Pizzaiola
Spaghetti with Caper and Tomato Sauce

1 clove garlic
scant 1 lb/14 oz/400 g very ripe tomatoes
 or
½ lb/½ lb/225 g canned tomatoes
6 Tbsp/4 Tbsp/4 Tbsp olive oil
salt
freshly ground pepper
1 Tbsp capers
¾ lb/¾ lb/350 g spaghetti
a pinch of oregano
1 small bunch parsley
grated Pecorino cheese (optional)

Chop the clove of garlic very finely (garlic is more easily digested if the central sprout is removed). Blanch and skin the fresh tomatoes, remove the seeds, and cut into thin slices. If canned tomatoes are used, put them through a food mill or sieve. Simmer the oil, garlic, and tomatoes; season with salt and pepper; and cook quickly until the sauce thickens. Add the capers and then remove from the heat.

Cook the spaghetti in a large pan of boiling salted water; drain when al dente. Turn into a heated serving dish and top with the sauce, sprinkling with a generous pinch of oregano and freshly chopped parsley. For best results, serve piping hot.

This dish may be accompanied by a side dish of Pecorino cheese.

Spaghetti con le Cozze
Spaghetti with Mussels

1¾ lb/1¼ lb/800 g small mussels (in their shells)
¾ lb/¾ lb/350 g spaghetti (or vermicelli)
6 Tbsp/4 Tbsp/4 Tbsp olive oil
2 cloves garlic
2 Tbsp chopped parsley
salt
freshly ground pepper
grated rind of 1 lemon
a pinch of oregano (optional)

Scrub the mussels thoroughly, removing any beard; wash well; place in a large skillet with just enough water to cover the bottom of the pan; and steam. Remove the mussels as they open. Discard any which do not open fully. Detach the mussels from their shells and rinse in warm water to get rid of all traces of sand. Do not throw away the cooking liquid. Let it stand so that the sand will settle; then strain it into a small bowl.

While the spaghetti cooks in a large pan of boiling salted water, heat the oil in a pan with the very finely chopped garlic, a tablespoon of chopped parsley, and the strained cooking liquid (pour this in slowly so that any last remaining trace of sand will remain in the bottom of the bowl). Reduce slightly over a high heat, add the mussels, and cook. Just before removing the pan from the heat, season with salt, pepper, and a teaspoon of grated lemon rind.

Drain the spaghetti while still firm, place in a deep, heated serving dish, pour on the sauce and mussels, and sprinkle with the remaining chopped parsley. Mix well and serve without grated cheese. A pinch of oregano can be added with the parsley, just before serving.

Sartù
Neapolitan Rice Timbale

¼ c/¼ lb/100 g ground (minced) lean veal
fine bread crumbs made from fresh bread
oil for frying
⅓ c/4 Tbsp/4 Tbsp grated Parmesan cheese
2 eggs
1 clove garlic
1 small bunch parsley
salt
freshly ground pepper
¼ lb/¼ lb/100 g fresh mushrooms or
 1 Tbsp/1 oz/25 g dried Italian mushrooms
2 small firm sausages weighing about
 ¼ lb/¼ lb/100 g each
butter
¾ c/5 oz/150 g chicken giblets
2 oz/2 oz/50 g prosciutto (raw ham)
½ lb/½ lb/225 g young tender shelled peas
4 ripe tomatoes
1 c/5 oz/150 g very fresh Mozzarella cheese
1¼ c/½ lb/225 g Arborio rice

Place the ground (minced) veal, 1 tablespoon of bread crumbs, half the grated Parmesan, an egg, and the finely chopped garlic and parsley in a mixing bowl. Season with salt and pepper and mix thoroughly with a wooden spoon until well blended. Shape into little rissoles about the size of cherries, roll in bread crumbs and fry in boiling oil until well browned. Drain and keep warm.

Wash and dry the mushrooms, salt them lightly, and sauté them gently in the same oil for about 10 minutes (if dried mushrooms are used, soak them in lukewarm water for 15 minutes before cooking). Remove from the oil and set aside in a bowl.

Slice the sausages into fairly thin rounds and fry for a few minutes in a frying pan; then take them out of the pan and reserve them. Melt about 1 tablespoon of butter in the same skillet and sauté the coarsley chopped chicken giblets for 10 minutes, adding a little salt.

Cut the prosciutto (raw ham) into thin strips and sauté in a tablespoon of butter in a fairly large saucepan, add the peas and a little water, and season with pepper and salt. When the peas are tender and the liquid has reduced, remove the pan from the heat. Put the tomatoes through a food mill or sieve into another saucepan, add a little salt, and about 1 tablespoon butter and cook uncovered over a moderate heat until they thicken. Finally, slice the Mozzarella cheese thinly.

Boil the rice in salted water until more or less al dente (this should not take longer than 10 minutes). Drain and turn into a large bowl and gently mix in the tomato sauce together with the remaining egg and the rest of the Parmesan. When the rice is almost cold, reserve a small quantity and turn the rest into a large buttered 2-quart ($3\frac{1}{4}$ pt/2 liter) timbale coated with fine bread crumbs. Press gently down into the mold and up against the sides forming a hollow in the center, into which will go all the prepared ingredients: the rissoles, mushrooms, little sausage slices, chicken giblets, Mozzarella, and peas. Cover this with the reserved rice, sprinkle the surface with fine bread crumbs and dot with small pieces of butter. Cook in a preheated oven at 325°F–350°F (170°C–180°C/mk 3–4) for about 45 minutes, by which time the top should be well browned. Remove from the oven and allow the mold to stand and settle for 10 minutes; then run a sharp knife round the inside of the sides of the mold before inverting onto a serving platter.

This is a very popular Christmas dish. Its name is said to derive from the 17th-century French word *surtout*, a large decorative container for food, usually in gold or silver, which was placed in the middle of the table and held such delicacies as these timbales or molds. Guests at banquets could help themselves to the various molds at will. The word is little used in French but survives in this form in Italian. This dish is found in Tuscany and other more northern regions of Italy but varies from place to place: the rice is sometimes dressed simply with butter and cheese, the center filled with sliced hard-boiled eggs and so on. When well executed, this dish is excellent.

Spaghetti alla Carrettiera
Spaghetti with Tuna and Tomato Sauce

$\frac{1}{4}$ c/2 oz/50 g bacon
$\frac{1}{4}$ c/2 oz/50 g canned tuna fish
$\frac{1}{2}$ lb/$\frac{1}{2}$ lb/225 g fresh cèpes or
  1 Tbsp dried cèpes (preferably Italian)
1 clove garlic
$\frac{1}{4}$ c/3 Tbsp/3 Tbsp olive oil
salt
freshly ground pepper
$\frac{1}{2}$ tsp meat extract (dissolved in a little hot water)
$\frac{3}{4}$ lb/$\frac{3}{4}$ lb/350 g spaghetti
$\frac{1}{4}$ c/2 oz/50 g grated Parmesan cheese

Cut the bacon into thin strips, flake the tuna fish, and slice the mushrooms (if dried mushrooms are used, soak in lukewarm water for 15 minutes). Sauté the finely chopped garlic clove and bacon in the olive oil until the bacon fat turns translucent, add the mushrooms, season with salt and pepper, and simmer for about 10 minutes, adding the dissolved meat extract half way through cooking. Add the flaked tuna, stirring over a low heat for 1 to 2 minutes.

Cook the spaghetti in plenty of boiling, salted water, drain when al dente and turn into a heated serving dish. Pour on the sauce, mix, and serve. Serve the grated Parmesan cheese separately.

Spaghetti alla Marinara
Spaghetti in Spicy Tomato Sauce

6 Tbsp/4 Tbsp/4 Tbsp olive oil
20 black olives
1 Tbsp capers
1 clove garlic
1 lb/1 lb/500 g firm, ripe (or canned) tomatoes
3 small fresh basil leaves
$\frac{3}{4}$ lb/$\frac{3}{4}$ lb/350 g spaghetti
1 small piece chili pepper (optional)

The sauce for this dish should be prepared in advance. Place the oil and

the pitted (stoned) and chopped olives in an earthenware or enameled cooking pot together with the very finely chopped capers and garlic, the blanched, skinned, seeded, and chopped tomatoes (if canned tomatoes have to be used put them through a food mill or sieve) and the basil leaves. Leave aside for $\frac{1}{2}$ hour so the flavors can mingle, then cook quickly until the mixture becomes a dark, thick, creamy sauce. Remove and discard the basil leaves.

Pour the sauce over the spaghetti, which has been boiled until al dente in plenty of boiling salted water and then drained. Mix quickly and serve without cheese.

For a spicier sauce, a small piece of chili pepper can be added with the capers and garlic and removed from the sauce just before serving.

Penne alla Vesuviana

$\frac{3}{4}$ lb/$\frac{3}{4}$ lb/350 g penne rigate (see illustration number 20 on page 18)
4 large ripe tomatoes or
  1 lb/1 lb/500 g canned tomatoes
12 black olives
1 Mozzarella cheese made from buffalo milk, if possible
1 clove garlic
1 small bunch fresh basil
salt
6 Tbsp/4 Tbsp/4 Tbsp olive oil
freshly ground pepper
2 Tbsp capers (drained)
a pinch of oregano

While the pasta is boiling in plenty of boiling salted water, put the tomatoes through a food mill or sieve, pit (stone) the olives and cut them in half, dice the Mozzarella cheese, and crush the garlic clove with the blade of a large knife. Place the tomatoes, garlic, and several basil leaves in a saucepan, add salt, and reduce the sauce over a high heat until it thickens. Remove the garlic clove and keep the sauce warm.

Boil the pasta in plenty of water. Drain when tender but firm, transfer to a bowl or deep serving dish, stir in the oil and a little freshly ground pepper, and mix quickly. Add the capers, olives, and Mozzarella, and then the tomato sauce. Sprinkle with oregano and serve without delay. For contrast, garnish with a small bunch of fresh basil. No cheese is served with this dish.

Vermicelli alle Alici Salse
Vermicelli with Anchovy Sauce

¾ lb/¾ lb/350 g vermicelli
1 clove garlic
6 Tbsp/4 Tbsp/4 Tbsp olive oil
8 anchovy fillets
freshly ground pepper (optional)

Prepare the sauce while the vermicelli is cooking in plenty of boiling salted water. Sauté the crushed garlic in the oil until it colors, then discard it. Add the chopped anchovies to the oil and work into a thin paste using a fork. Drain the vermicelli when al dente, turn into the pan containing the oil, and mix and turn gently over a moderate heat for a couple of minutes. Add a little freshly ground pepper, if desired, and serve at once.

Maccheroni alla Napoletana di Artusi
Pellegrino Artusi's Neapolitan Macaroni

1 small onion
1 small bunch basil
4 Tbsp/2 oz/50 g butter
2 c/14 oz/400 g very ripe (or canned) tomatoes
salt
freshly ground pepper
¾ lb/¾ lb/350 g macaroni
¼ c/2 oz/50 g grated Parmesan or Pecorino cheese

Chop the onion finely with the basil leaves, and sauté slowly in 2 tablespoons (1 oz/25 g) of butter for a few minutes. Add the skinned, seeded, and coarsely chopped tomatoes (put canned tomatoes, if used, through a food mill or sieve), season with salt and freshly ground pepper, and simmer until the sauce has reduced to the desired consistency.

Boil the macaroni in a large pan of salted water. Drain when tender but firm, place in a serving dish, and dot with small pieces of the remaining butter. Stir in the sauce and sprinkle with grated Parmesan cheese (Pecorino can be used instead to give a stronger taste), mix well, and serve very hot.

Strangulaprièvete
Gnocchi in Tomato and Basil Sauce

1 lb/1 lb/500 g baking potatoes
2 c/9 oz/250 g all-purpose (plain) flour
salt
2½ c/1 lb/500 g canned tomatoes (put through a food mill or sieve) or 4 very large ripe tomatoes (peeled, seeded, and chopped)
6 Tbsp/2 fl oz/60 ml olive oil
freshly ground pepper
a few fresh basil leaves
⅓ c/3 oz/80 g grated Parmesan cheese

These Neapolitan potato gnocchi differ from their counterparts from Lucania *strangulaprevete* or *strangulapreti*, which are of far more ancient origin and, although of roughly the same shape, are made from a simple dough of white flour and boiling water. The Italian name means "priest stranglers."

Boil the potatoes, peel them as quickly as possible and while they are still hot put them through a potato ricer or sieve allowing them to fall onto a pastry board. Work the flour in very gradually together with a teaspoon of salt (use a little more flour if the dough is too soft or sticky to handle easily). Knead well until smooth and pliable. Roll into cylinders ½ inch (1 cm) thick, cut these into short lengths, and form gnocchi as directed on page 54 (illustration, page 55). Leave the strangulaprièvete on a lightly floured pastry cloth for about 15 minutes to dry out. Space them out neatly so they do not stick to each other.

Prepare the sauce: place the tomatoes and the oil in a saucepan, season with salt and pepper, and add a few leaves of basil. Simmer over a low heat until the sauce has reduced; in the meantime, boil the gnocchi in a large pan of boiling salted water, removing them with a slotted spoon as they rise to the surface. Place them in individual heated dishes. Top each portion with a few tablespoons of sauce and serve with a side dish of grated Parmesan.

Fusilli alla Napoletana

1 medium onion
1 stalk celery
1 small carrot
1 clove garlic
¼ c/2 oz/50 g pancetta (fat bacon)
1 c/5 oz/150 g Mozzarella cheese
¼ c/3 Tbsp olive oil
⅓ c/3½ fl oz/1 dl dry white wine
4 very ripe (or canned) tomatoes
1 Tbsp tomato paste
freshly ground pepper
salt
¾ lb/¾ lb/350 g fusilli (see illustration number 8 on page 17)
¼ c/2 oz/50 g grated Pecorino cheese
a pinch of oregano

Chop the onion, celery, carrot, and garlic very finely, and cut the pancetta (bacon) into thin strips. Dice the Mozzarella and set aside. Sauté the chopped vegetables and pancetta (bacon) in the oil in a large skillet and, when the vegetables have softened, pour in the wine, turn up the heat and allow the wine to evaporate quickly. Add the skinned, seeded, and chopped tomatoes (put through a food mill or sieve, if canned) and the tomato paste; season with pepper and salt; turn down the heat; and stir occasionally while slowly reducing the sauce.

Cook the fusilli in plenty of boiling salted water. Drain when they are still al dente, reserving some of the cooking liquid, and stir them into the tomato sauce, to which a tablespoon of grated Pecorino cheese has been added. If the sauce is too thick, add a little of the cooking liquid drained from the pasta. Cook until the fusilli are tender, remove from the heat, and turn into a heated serving dish. Scatter the diced Mozzarella over the top, sprinkle with a pinch of oregano, and serve immediately. Serve the rest of the Pecorino separately.

Very fresh ricotta can be substituted for the Mozzarella, though of course the ricotta would be crumbled rather than diced.

Pizza Quattro Stagioni
Four Seasons Pizza

1 recipe pizza dough (see the recipe for
Pizza Romana, page 135).
4 canned tomatoes
⅓ c/2 oz/50 g Mozzarella (sliced)
½ c/2 oz/50 g button mushrooms cooked
in a little butter for 15 minutes
¼ c/2 oz/50 g cooked ham
2–3 small canned or bottled artichokes
7–8 black olives
olive oil
salt

Shape the proofed and flattened dough into a large disk the size of your pizza pan. Spread the roughly chopped tomatoes and the Mozzarella evenly over the disk. Then distribute the ingredients so that each covers ¼ of the dough. Drizzle with oil, add salt to taste, and bake for approximately 20 minutes in a preheated oven at 350°F–400°F (180°C–200°C/mk 4–6).

Pizza Margherita

1 recipe pizza dough (see the recipe for
Pizza Romana, page 135).
6 Tbsp/4 Tbsp/4 Tbsp canned tomatoes
(put through a food mill or sieve)
⅓ c/2 oz/50 g diced Mozzarella cheese
3 fresh basil leaves or
a pinch of dried oregano
olive oil
salt

Roll or shape the dough into a large disk. Top with the above ingredients in the order in which they are listed. Bake for about 20 minutes in a preheated oven at 350°F–400°F (180°C–200°C/mk 4–6).

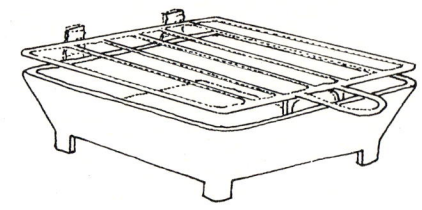

Pollo alla Diavola
Broiled (Grilled) Marinated Chicken

1 young chicken weighing about 3 lb/
3 lb/1.2 kg
¾ c/7 fl oz/2 dl dry white wine
1 sprig of fresh sage or ¼ tsp dried sage
a little oil
salt
freshly ground pepper

If the chicken is not already dressed, pluck and draw it, remove the neck, wing tips and feet, and singe. Wash well and cut in half. Pour the wine into a large earthenware or enameled dish, add the finely chopped sage leaves, and place the chicken halves in this marinade. Marinate for several hours, turning frequently. Take out the chicken, pat it dry with paper towels, brush it all over with oil, and then broil (grill) it slowly, turning every now and then, basting frequently with small quantities of oil or with its own juices. When the chicken is almost done, sprinkle it with salt and pepper. The chicken can also be cooked in a frying pan large enough to contain both halves lying flat. Sauté gently and moisten with some of the wine marinade when necessary. If the chicken is very young, it will only take about 20 minutes to cook.

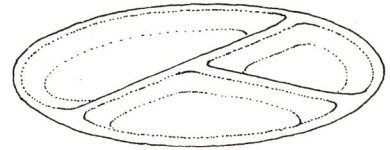

Bistecchine alla Napoli
Steak Neapolitan

1¼–1½ lb/1¼–1½ lb/600 g prime beef (filet
mignon, châteaubriand, contrefilet, or
4 steaks cut from the rib end of
the short loin)
½ c/2 oz/50 g fresh mushrooms
½ c/4 oz/100 g prosciutto (raw ham)
1 small bunch parsley
oil
salt
freshly ground pepper
juice of ½ lemon

If the beef is still in one piece, cut into 4 steaks of about the same weight and size. Wash the mushrooms and slice finely. Chop the prosciutto (raw ham) and the parsley. Oil a very large baking dish in which all the steaks will lie flat with 1 tablespoon oil, sprinkle the bottom with the chopped prosciutto (raw ham), then scatter the mushrooms, and season with a very little salt and some pepper. Sprinkle the chopped parsley over these two layers and drizzle a little oil over them. Place the steaks on this prepared bed, brush the tops very lightly with oil, and cook in a hot oven (400°F/200°C/mk 6) for 15 to 20 minutes (depending on how rare you want them to be); then turn the steaks carefully, sprinkle them with the juice of half a lemon and a little salt. Cook for 5 minutes more and serve straight from the baking dish, topping each portion with the vegetables, prosciutto (raw ham), and cooking juices.

Calamari Ripieni
Stuffed Squid

8 medium-sized squid
1 large bunch parsley
2 cloves garlic
1 sprig of rosemary or ¼ tsp dried
salt
freshly ground pepper
6 Tbsp/4 Tbsp/4 Tbsp olive oil
1 egg

¾ c/7 fl oz/2 dl dry white wine
2 tomatoes
1 lemon

Clean and trim the squid, removing the hard mouth parts, the quill or bone inside and the ink sac. Wash in cold running water until the squid are very white and all the yellowish deposits have disappeared. Cut the heads and tentacles off the squid (see illustration right), and chop them very finely with the parsley, garlic and rosemary. Season and add 3 tablespoons (2 Tbsp/2 Tbsp) oil, and the egg and mix thoroughly. Stuff the squid with this mixture and sew the opening with string or secure it with cocktail sticks. Place the squid in a large lidded skillet containing the remaining heated oil. Sauté, turning carefully and then pour in the wine and, when it has reduced a little, cover the pan and cook slowly. (The squid can now be baked in the oven, at 375°F/190°C/mk 5 if desired.) When the flesh of the squid is tender (45 minutes or longer) and the liquid has almost reduced to nothing, transfer to a heated serving dish, garnish with slices of raw tomato and lemon wedges, and serve.

Manzo alla Pizzaiola
Beef in Wine and Tomato Sauce

1½ lb/1½ lb/700 g prime lean, tender beef
2 cloves garlic
⅓ c/3½ fl oz/1 dl oil
1 lb/1 lb/500 g very ripe tomatoes
salt
freshly ground pepper
a pinch of oregano
⅓ c/3½ fl oz/1 dl dry white wine

This delicious beef dish owes its wonderful flavor, in part, to the use of oregano, the fragrant herb which is so popular in the Naples region.
 Carve the beef into very thin slices, using a very sharp knife (tie the meat

Right: The various steps involved in preparing Calamari Ripieni (Stuffed Squid).

neatly with string to make this easier). Sauté the finely chopped garlic in the oil in a large pan. When the garlic starts to color, add the slices of beef and sear on both sides. Then take the slices out of the pan, drain them, and keep them warm.

Stir the skinned, seeded, and very coarsely chopped tomatoes into the juices in the pan, season with salt and pepper and a generous pinch of oregano to taste. Pour in the wine and cook fast until it has evaporated. Keep the heat fairly high so the sauce will reduce and acquire body quickly. Stir gently so that the pieces of tomato do not disintegrate. Return the beef to the sauce in the pan and heat for 2 minutes at most. Serve immediately.

Agnello al Forno con Patate e Cipolle
Roast Lamb with Potatoes and Onions

2½–2¾ lb/2½–2¾ lb/1.2 kg young, tender lamb, preferably leg
⅓ c/3½ fl oz/1 dl oil
2 Tbsp/1 oz/25 g butter
1 clove garlic
1 sprig of fresh rosemary or ¼ tsp dried rosemary
1¾ lb/1¾ lb/800 g small new potatoes or larger, waxy potatoes, cut in pieces
6 shallots or
    2 large onions cut in pieces
salt
freshly ground pepper

Wash and dry the meat. Heat the oil and butter in a very large, heavy pan with the very fine chopped garlic and rosemary leaves. When the mixture begins to sizzle, place the leg of lamb in the pan and brown lightly on all sides. Add the peeled potatoes and shallots and then roast in a preheated hot oven (400°F–425°F/200°C–220°C/mk 6–7) for 20 minutes per pound, turning frequently and basting with a little oil if necessary. Serve very hot.

Cervella alla Napoletana
Brains Neapolitan

1 lb/1 lb/500 g lamb's or calf's brains
bread crumbs
oil
salt
freshly ground pepper
1 tsp capers
¼ c/2 oz/50 g black olives

Soak the brains for several hours in several changes of water and remove as much of covering membrane as possible without tearing the delicate flesh. Or, to prepare them more quickly, blanch them in not-quite-boiling acidulated water, then remove them with a slotted spoon, and rinse them in cold water. Lightly oil a baking dish and place the brains in a single layer covering the bottom, season with salt and pepper, and distribute the rinsed capers and the pitted (stoned) and halved olives evenly on top. Sprinkle a light but even layer of bread crumbs over the surface and moisten with a little olive oil. Bake in a preheated oven at 350°F (180°C/mk 4) for about 20 minutes. Serve straight from the baking dish.

Cozze al Forno
Baked Mussels

48 very fresh mussels (if very large, allow only 10 per person)
1 Tbsp vinegar
7 Tbsp/5 Tbsp/5 Tbsp olive oil
juice of 2 lemons
1 small bunch parsley
2 cloves garlic
bread crumbs

Scrub the mussels well with a stiff brush, removing all traces of beard. Discard any damaged mussels or any which do not close tightly when tapped sharply (these are probably already dead and unsafe to eat). Open the mussels with a very strong, small knife or a special oyster shucking knife and throw away

the empty half of the shell. Steam the mussels open side upwards in a large covered skillet in just enough water to barely cover the bottom of the pan. Cook them in batches if necessary. A few minutes over a high heat is enough. Strain the liquid through a cloth placed in a fine strainer (sieve) and mix with the vinegar, 6 tablespoons (4 Tbsp/4 Tbsp) of oil, the lemon juice, and the chopped parsley. Place each mussel in a large, shallow baking dish, sprinkle with the dressing, and drizzle with the remaining oil into which the pressed garlic has been mixed. Top each mussel with some bread crumbs and bake in a hot oven (400°F–425°F/200°C–220°C/mk 6–7) for about 15 minutes. Serve the mussels piping hot straight from the baking dish.

Polipetti Affogati
Braised Octopus

6 young small octopus weighing about 2 lb/2 lb/1 kg
⅓ c/3½ fl oz/1 dl oil
2 cloves garlic
1 large bunch parsley
3 very ripe tomatoes
1 small piece red chili pepper
salt

Octopus are usually sold already prepared: they must be skinned and the insides, eyes, and mouth (or beak) removed as well as the ink sac. Pound them well with a meat mallet to tenderize them and wash them in running water. Place the octopus in the oil in an earthenware or heavy enameled cooking pot; add the skinned, seeded, and chopped tomatoes; the chili pepper; the very finely chopped garlic and parsley; and a little salt. Cover the pot with foil and fold tightly, or tie with string. Place the lid on top to prevent any steam escaping. The octopus must simmer for at least two hours over a low heat. Jerk the pot sharply from time to time to keep the contents from sticking to the bottom of the pot and burning. Serve the octopus directly from the cooking pot when they are tender.

Polpo alla Luciana
Octopus Luciana

2 or more small octopus weighing a
    total of 1¾–2 lb/1¾–2 lb/800 g
    (approx)
½ c/3½ fl oz/1 dl olive oil
3 large, ripe tomatoes
1 small piece red chili pepper
1 bunch parsley
2 cloves garlic
salt

Italians usually choose the *Octopus vulgaris* with its twin rows of suckers along the tentacles for this dish rather than the curled octopus which has only one row of tentacles or the other, smaller varieties found in the sea around Italy which make inferior eating. The octopus must be cleaned by removing the beak, eyes and interior organs; it should also be well beaten to tenderize it and skinned— most fish dealers will have done this before selling these molluscs. The ink is not used in this recipe.

Wash the octopus thoroughly and place in a lidded enameled cast-iron pan or a fireproof earthenware dish together with the oil, the peeled, seeded and chopped tomatoes, chili pepper and the very finely chopped parsley and garlic. Season with a little salt (preferably sea salt). Cover the pan with waxed (grease-proof) paper or kitchen foil, tie securely with string and cover with the lid so that no moisture will escape during the long, slow cooking (at least 2 hours). Shake the pan from time to time to prevent the octopus sticking and burning and keep the heat very gentle. Carry the pan to the table, then unseal, and carve portions of the tender octopus for each person or, if preferred, transfer the octopus to a carving board and cut into small pieces before returning to the pot and serving.

Baccalà alla Napoletana
Salt Cod Naples Style

1¾ lb/1¾ lb/800 g presoaked salt cod
all-purpose (plain) flour
oil
4 large peppers: 2 green, 2 yellow or red
2 onions
1 lb/1 lb/500 g very ripe tomatoes
salt
oregano
1 bunch parsley
1 small piece red chili pepper

Skin, bone and cut the fish into pieces about 2 inches (5 cm) square. Coat the fish lightly with flour and fry in plenty of very hot oil (375°F/190°C) until it is browned on both sides. Remove with a slotted spatula (fish slice) and drain on paper towels.

Place the peppers in a hot oven for a few minutes. Plunge into cold water, peel, cut away the stalk, split open, remove seeds and membrane, and cut into thin strips. Heat ⅓ cup (3½ fl oz/1 dl) oil in a pan and sauté the sliced onion gently, add the peeled, seeded, and chopped tomatoes and season with salt and a generous pinch of oregano. When the sauce thickens, add the strips of pepper, the chopped parsley, and the chili pepper and cook over a moderate heat until the pepper strips are tender. Add the fried pieces of salt cod and allow them to heat gently and absorb the sauce for 10 minutes. This dish is not only delicious when hot, but can also be eaten cold the following day.

Pomodori Gratinati
Baked Tomatoes

4 large ripe firm tomatoes
salt
1 clove garlic
1 bunch parsley
1 tsp capers
4 Tbsp/3 Tbsp/3 Tbsp bread crumbs
oregano
oil

Cut the tomatoes in half horizontally, remove the seeds, sprinkle with salt, and leave them upside down on a slightly tilted plate or in a colander to drain. Pat dry with paper towels. Chop the garlic, parsley, and capers and mix with 3 tablespoons (2 Tbsp/2 Tbsp) of bread crumbs, a little salt, and a generous pinch of oregano. Fill the tomatoes with this mixture, and place the tomatoes carefully in an oiled baking dish, sprinkle with a little oil and the rest of the bread crumbs, and bake in a preheated oven at 350°F (180°C/mk 4) for approximately 30 minutes. Serve very hot.

Mozzarella in Carrozza
Fried Mozzarella Sandwiches

8 slices of bread from a sandwich loaf
1 large, very fresh Mozzarella cheese
¾ c/7 fl oz/2 dl milk
all-purpose (plain) flour
2 eggs
salt
olive oil

Cut the crusts off the bread. Slice the Mozzarella thinly and cover half the bread slices with the cheese, taking care they do not overlap the edges. Trim the Mozzarella slices so that they form even layers; if they overlap each other, the sandwiches will tend to fall apart. Top each open sandwich with another slice of bread, pressing the sandwiches firmly together.

Pour the milk into a bowl and have the flour ready in a plate. Holding the sandwiches firmly together, dunk the edges in the milk and then dip in the flour. This will form a seal which will prevent the Mozzarella from oozing out during cooking. Place the sandwiches in a concave platter large enough to accommodate them, and pour over the eggs previously beaten with a pinch of salt. Soak for 10 minutes. Turn very carefully and soak for a further 10 minutes. Heat some oil in a large frying pan until very hot. Then place the Mozzarella sandwiches carefully in the pan and fry until golden brown on both sides. Remove from the oil, drain on paper towels, and serve hot.

Melanzane Trifolate a Fungitelli
Eggplant (Aubergine), Tomato and Caper Sauce

1 lb/1 lb/500 g eggplants (aubergines)
⅓ c/3½ fl oz/1 dl oil
salt
2 very ripe tomatoes (put through a food mill or sieve)
1 Tbsp capers in brine
1 clove garlic
1 small bunch parsley

This sauce is excellent cold with boiled meats, or steaks.

Wash the eggplants (aubergines), dice small, sprinkle with salt and place them in a colander with a plate and a weight on top to drain. Leave for 1 hour, rinse thoroughly, turn onto paper towels, and dry.

Heat the oil in a pan and fry the eggplants (aubergines). Add a little salt, the tomatoes, and the well-drained capers. Stir continuously while the sauce reduces and thickens. Just before removing from the heat, add the finely chopped garlic and parsley.

Scarola 'Mbuttunata
Stuffed Escaroles (Scaroles)

⅓ c/2 oz/50 g seedless white raisins (sultanas)
4 large escaroles (scaroles)
4 anchovy fillets
scant ¼ lb/scant ¼ lb/100 g small, black olives
1 Tbsp capers
½ c/2 oz/50 g pine nuts
oil
2 cloves garlic

Soften the raisins (sultanas) by soaking them in lukewarm water for 15 minutes; then squeeze and dry them. Rinse the escaroles (scaroles). Blanch them in boiling salted water for 2 to 3 minutes (to remove any bitter taste) and drain well. Ease the leaves apart slightly in the center to facilitate stuffing.

Finely chop the anchovies, the pitted (stoned) olives, and the capers. Place them in a bowl and add the pine nuts and raisins (sultanas). Stir in 2–3 tablespoons oil and mix well. Insert the mixture in the center of each escarole (scarole) and close the leaves again to enclose the stuffing. Sauté the slightly crushed garlic cloves in a little oil in a skillet until they color and then discard them. Place the stuffed escaroles (scaroles) in the pan, cover, and cook for about 10 minutes, turning them gently once or twice.

The escaroles (scaroles) can also be sprinkled with bread crumbs and baked in a moderate oven (325°F/170°C/mk 3) for 15 minutes. In this case, chop the garlic finely and stir it into the stuffing.

Peperoni Ripieni con Pasta
Peppers Stuffed with Pasta

4 large peppers (red and yellow)
½ c/3 oz/80 g small pasta (avemarie, nocciole, conchigliette, etc. See illustrations 26–41 on page 18)
4 anchovy fillets
1 Tbsp capers
10 small black olives
fresh parsley
oil
oregano
salt
freshly ground pepper

Boil the pasta in salted water, drain, and leave to cool (leftover pasta is ideal for this dish. Chop it if it is too large or long).

Place the peppers in a hot oven for a few minutes to loosen the skins, then peel them. Cut off the very top of each pepper, removing the stalk, seeds and membrane, keeping the peppers as intact as possible. Place the pasta, the pitted (stoned) and chopped olives, the capers, the chopped anchovies, and the finely chopped garlic and parsley together in a bowl; add a generous pinch of oregano and a little freshly ground pepper. Mix well and then stir in 1–2 tablespoons of oil. Stuff the peppers with this mixture and place them upright in an oiled baking dish and bake in a moderate oven (325°F–350°F/170°C–180°C/mk 3–4) for 30 to 40 minutes.

Torta Glassata
Sponge Cake with Fondant Frosting

For the cake:
¾ c + 1 Tbsp/4 oz/100 g all-purpose (plain) flour
½ c + 2 Tbsp/2¾ oz/80 g potato flour
6 eggs (separated)
1½ c/7 oz/200 g sifted confectioners' (icing) sugar
a few drops of vanilla extract (essence)
1 tsp baking powder
butter

Fondant frosting:
1 c/7 oz/200 g granulated sugar
1 Tbsp/scant 1 Tbsp/20 g white corn syrup or a pinch of cream of tartar
⅔ c/5⅓ fl oz/1.6 dl warm water
1 tsp orange flower water or 2 tsp orange (or other flavored) liqueur (slightly warmed)

Sift the all-purpose (plain) flour with the potato flour 3 times and place in a bowl. (If no potato flour is available substitute ⅓ cup (1½ oz/40 g) each arrowroot and all-purpose (plain) flour, sifted together.) Place the egg yolks in a bowl and beat them very well with the sugar, vanilla, and baking powder. In a separate bowl beat the egg whites until they form soft peaks. Fold the egg yolk and

Opposite: Pasta con le Sarde (Macaroni with Sardines and Tomato Sauce). The dish on the right contains a selection of exquisite Sicilian pastries and candies.

Overleaf: Carta da Musica (top left), Lasagne allo Spezzatino d'Agnello (Lamb Lasagne) (top right), Malloreddus (bottom left), and Culingiones (bottom right), all typical of Sardinian cooking.

sugar mixture into the beaten whites and then slowly pour this mixture into the bowl containing the sifted flour, stirring constantly but gently with a wooden spoon. The mixture should be creamy. Do not overmix at any time or the cake will not be soft and light. Turn the batter into a lightly buttered round 10-inch (25 cm) cake pan and place in a preheated oven at 375°F (190°C/mk 5) for about 35 minutes or until a cake tester comes out clean. Remove from the oven and leave to cool.

Fondant:

Mix all ingredients except the flavoring together and stir for at least 10 minutes, or place the ingredients in a blender and whirl at high speed for 2 minutes. This must be done before cooking. If the syrup is stirred once it is on the hob, the sugar will crystallize and the fondant will be impossible to make. When the sugar is dissolved, place the syrup in a small, heavy saucepan (untinned copper is ideal) over a moderate heat and bring it to a boil. When it comes to a boil, cover the pan to allow the steam to wash down any sugar crystals clinging to the sides. Remove the lid after 2 minutes and continue cooking until the syrup reaches the soft ball stage (238°F/113°C on a candy thermometer). At that temperature the syrup will form a soft ball when dropped into very cold water. The ball will flatten when removed from the water. Pour it out immediately onto a lightly oiled marble slab or working surface until it is cool to the touch and does not stick to the fingers. Take a spatula and knead the paste over onto itself until it turns opaque white (about 3 minutes). Gather the ball into your hands and knead it until white and creamy (the heat of the hands is essential here). Ideally, the fondant should now be shaped into a roll or ball, placed in a jar with a screw top and stored in the refrigerator for two days before using.

When you are ready to use the fondant, place it in a small, heavy enamel saucepan on an asbestos mat over medium heat (do not overheat or the gloss will be lost) and add one or two drops boiling milk or boiling water. Remove it from the hob, stir until lukewarm, and, if it is still too thick, add a few drops more of hot liquid. Stir in the flavoring and, if desired, a drop of food coloring and pour evenly over the cake, spreading it over the top and sides.

The fondant icing can be decorated with candied fruit or small marzipan candies.

Tarallucci
Fried Rings

2 eggs
1 Tbsp sugar
1 tsp liqueur such as Chartreuse, Grand
Marnier etc.
a few drops vanilla extract (essence)
a pinch of cinnamon
all-purpose (plain) flour
oil

Mix the eggs, sugar, liqueur, vanilla, and cinnamon in a bowl and add as much sifted flour as needed to make a mixture the consistency of bread dough. Knead thoroughly on a pastry board. Then wrap the dough in a pastry cloth and leave it to rest for 30 minutes. Break off evenly-sized pieces from the dough and roll by hand into cylinders. Then join the two ends to form a ring. When the rings are all ready, heat some oil in a pan (375°F/190°C) and fry them; when the rings are half-cooked, take them out of the pan and make diagonal incisions all over the surface with a sharp knife. Return them to the hot oil and finish cooking them. When ready they should be a deep golden-brown. Drain on paper towels.

These cookies are mouth-watering, hot or cold.

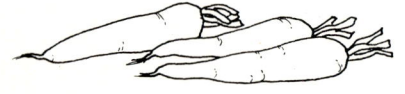

Zeppole
Neapolitan Doughnuts

This recipe will serve 6
¾ c/5 oz/150 g granulated sugar
salt
1 bay leaf
1¾ c/7 oz/200 g all-purpose (plain) flour
¼ c/1 oz/25 g semolina
⅓ c/3½ fl oz/1 dl Marsala wine
4 egg yolks
3 Tbsp/2 Tbsp/2 Tbsp oil
plenty of oil or lard for frying
1–2 Tbsp vanilla sugar (see instructions)

Pour 1 pint (18 fl oz/½ liter) of water into a saucepan, add the sugar, salt and bay leaf. Bring to a boil, remove from the heat, and add the flour and semolina (mixed together), stirring briskly the whole time. Once the flour has blended smoothly with the water, return to the heat and mix continuously for 20 minutes. Discard the bay leaf, leave the batter to cool until lukewarm, and then add the Marsala and the egg yolks. The mixture must be satin smooth and firm with no lumps at all. Turn out onto an oiled marble or formica slab, break off portions of dough, roll them into cylinders and join the ends to form rings. Drop the rings into the hot oil or fat in a deep fryer, just before it reaches the boiling point. Prick the rings with a sharp knife as they cook so that little bubbles of mixture bulge out on their surface. Remove with a slotted spoon when crisp and golden. Drain on paper towels and dust with vanilla sugar. This can be made at home by simply storing a vanilla bean (pod) in an airtight jar of granulated or confectioners' (icing) sugar. After a few days the sugar will have taken up the aroma and taste of the vanilla.

Torta di Ricotta
Italian Cheese Cake

2½ c/10½ oz/300 g all-purpose (plain) flour
1¼ c/9 oz/250 g sugar
3 eggs
2–3 Tbsp orange-flavored liqueur (Grand Marnier, Cointreau) or rum
1 tsp baking powder
a pinch of salt
⅔ c/5 oz/150 g butter
1 lb/1 lb/500 g ricotta cheese
3 Tbsp/2 Tbsp/2 Tbsp sweetened powdered chocolate (drinking chocolate)
1 c/5 oz/150 g almonds

Sift the flour onto a pastry board and mix in half the sugar. Gradually add the eggs, liqueur, a pinch of salt and the melted butter, reserving a small amount to butter the cake pan. Mix until smooth. Mix the ricotta cheese vigorously with the remaining sugar until a smooth creamy consistency is obtained. Add the chocolate and finely chopped almonds.

Divide the mixture and roll out into three circles, two the same size as the cake pan and the third slightly larger. Line the base and sides of the buttered pan with the larger circle and cover evenly with half the ricotta filling. Cover with the smaller circle of dough, followed by the remaining ricotta filling and finally the third circle of dough, which should be pressed to the edge of the pan. Cook in a preheated oven (350°F/180°C/mk 4) for 45 minutes or until a cake tester inserted into the center comes out clean. This cake may be eaten warm or cold, sprinkled with confectioners' (icing) sugar and decorated with candied fruit.

BASILICATA

POTENZA

MATERA

Lasagne coi Fagioli
Lasagne with Beans

⅓ c/14 oz/400 g bread (strong) flour or
*   all purpose (plain) flour*
salt
1 lb/1 lb/500 g fresh white beans or
*   scant ½ lb/scant ½ lb/210 g dried beans*
*   (soaked overnight)*
4 Tbsp/2 oz/50 g pork fat or lard
2 cloves garlic
freshly ground pepper
1 small bunch parsley

Sift the flour with a generous pinch of salt into a heap on a pastry board, make a well in the center, mix in enough water to make a firm dough, and knead very thoroughly for up to 30 minutes until the dough is smooth and even in texture. Roll out into a thin sheet and cut into large lasagne. Boil the beans in plenty of salted water. Chop the pork fat very finely or melt the shortening (lard) and sauté together with the crushed garlic cloves until the garlic colors. Discard the garlic.

Meanwhile, boil the lasagne in a large pan of boiling salted water, drain, transfer to a heated dish, and pour the garlic-flavored fat over it. Stir well. Add the strained beans and sprinkle with plenty of pepper and very finely chopped parsley. Mix again and serve at once without any grated cheese.

Minestra alla Potentina
Tomato and Pasta Potenza Style

⅓ c/14 oz/400 g bread (strong) flour or
*   all-purpose (plain) flour*
salt
1 lb/1 lb/500 g very ripe (or canned)
*   tomatoes*
4 Tbsp/2 oz/50 g pork fat or lard
2 Tbsp oil
freshly ground pepper
¼ c/3 Tbsp/3 Tbsp grated Pecorino
*   cheese*

Follow the instructions for making the pasta dough given in the previous recipe, but after cutting the pasta sheet into large lasagne, roughly cut them into *maltagliati*—ragged triangular pieces.

Place the skinned, seeded, and chopped tomatoes in a saucepan with the pounded pork fat or lard, the oil, and salt and pepper and simmer, uncovered, stirring from time to time with a wooden spoon until the sauce reduces.

Cook the pasta in boiling salted water. Drain and place in a deep heated serving dish or bowl and stir in the sauce and grated Pecorino cheese (for a milder taste, Parmesan can be substituted for some of the stronger cheese).

Grano al Sugo
Boiled Wheat with Pork and Tomato Sauce

¾ lb/¾ lb/350 g wheat grains
4 Tbsp/2 oz/50 g pancetta (fat bacon)
4 Tbsp/2 oz/50 g pork fat
2 cloves garlic
½ c/4 oz/100 g chopped lean pork
⅓ c/3½ fl oz/1 dl dry white wine
1 red chili pepper
2 c/14 oz/400 g very ripe tomatoes
salt
6 Tbsp/4 Tbsp/4 Tbsp grated Pecorino
*   cheese*

Soak the wheat in plenty of cold water for at least 12 hours.

Chop the pancetta (bacon), pork fat, and garlic and sauté lightly. Add the chopped pork and cook for a few minutes more, mixing well with a wooden spoon. Pour in the wine and allow it to evaporate. Add the chopped or crumbled chili pepper, the peeled, seeded, and chopped tomatoes, and salt to taste. Mix well and cover. Simmer for about 2 hours, stirring frequently and adding a little boiling water if the sauce gets too thick.

Drain the wheat. Place it in a saucepan, cover with cold water, add a little salt, and bring to a boil. Cook until tender. Drain the wheat, turn it into a heated serving dish, and top with the sauce and the Pecorino cheese. Serve at once.

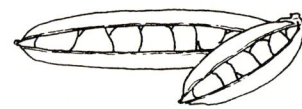

Pollo alla Lucana
Chicken Lucania Style

1 young chicken weighing about 2¾ lb/
*   2¾ lb/1.2 kg*
4 Tbsp/2 oz/50 g pork fat or lard
4 chicken livers
salt
freshly ground pepper
a sprig of fresh rosemary or ¼ tsp dried
*   rosemary*
2 eggs
3 Tbsp/2 Tbsp/2 Tbsp grated Pecorino
*   cheese*

If the chicken is not already dressed, pluck, draw, and wash it, removing the feet, neck, and wing tips. Pat it dry. Chop the pork fat (heat the knife blade over a flame to make this easier) and heat it in a small pan. When it is sizzling, add the chicken livers and season with salt and pepper. Stir while sautéing for a few minutes, then remove the chicken livers and chop them finely. Beat the eggs with the grated Pecorino cheese in a bowl; then add the chicken livers and blend thoroughly. Sprinkle the inside of the chicken with a little pepper and salt, then stuff with the prepared stuffing, insert the rosemary, sew up the opening with raffia or string and truss the chicken neatly so it will keep its shape while cooking. Sprinkle a little pepper and salt over the outside of the bird, brush with the pork fat in which the chicken livers were fried, and place in a roasting pan in a moderate oven (about 300°F/150°C/mk 2), and cook for approximately 1 hour. Turn and baste the chicken frequently with its own juices and fat. Once the chicken is done, remove the trussing and sewing string, place the bird on a heated serving platter, and pour the cooking juices over it. Carve at the table and serve with a fresh mixed salad.

Agnello ai Funghi Cardoncelli
Baked Lamb with Mushrooms

1 lb/1 lb/500 g oyster mushrooms or
*   chanterelles*
2 lb/2 lb/1 kg leg of very young lamb or
*   kid*
2 garlic cloves
salt
freshly ground pepper or a piece of red
*   chili pepper*
⅓ c/3½ fl oz/1 dl oil

Kid is not eaten very often in the United States and Britain but it is tender and tasty, not unlike lamb.

Wash the mushrooms and pat dry. Cut 1½-inch (3 cm) cubes from the leg of lamb or kid, and place in a heavy baking dish or roasting pan. Add the mushrooms, the finely chopped garlic, a good pinch of salt, and plenty of pepper (a crumbled piece of chili pepper is even better). Drizzle the oil over the ingredients and bake in a moderate oven (300°F/150°C/mk 2) for about 1 hour, turning the meat frequently and basting it with its own juices. Carve at the table and serve straight from the roasting pan.

Testina di Agnello al Forno
Baked Lambs' Heads

2 very young lambs' or kids' heads
3 Tbsp/2 Tbsp/2 Tbsp grated Pecorino
*   cheese*
3 Tbsp/2 Tbsp/2 Tbsp bread crumbs
1 bunch parsley
salt
oregano
olive oil
1 lemon

Have the butcher cut the heads in half with a cleaver. Check that any fragments of bone are washed away as well as any traces of wool, hair, etc. Do not remove the brains and tongues—these are the most delicious parts. Drain dry. Mix the grated Pecorino with the bread crumbs and the finely chopped parsley in a bowl and add salt and oregano to taste. Place the heads, cut side upwards, in a baking dish, sprinkle each half with the bread crumb mixture and then moisten with oil. Bake at 300°F–325°F (150°C–170°C/mk 2–3) for about 1 hour.

Beccacce in Salmì
Braised Woodcock

2 plump. well-hung woodcock
salt
4 thin slices of prosciutto (raw ham)
⅓ c/3½ fl oz/1 dl oil
⅓ c/3½ fl oz/1 dl dry white wine
⅓ c/3½ fl oz/1 dl dry Marsala wine
1 tsp capers
4 anchovy fillets
8 slices toasted bread

The woodcock should be aged by hanging in a cool, dry place for 3 to 4 days before being plucked and drawn. Reserve the livers, stomachs, hearts, and lungs. Sprinkle a little salt inside each bird and wrap each with two slices of prosciutto (raw ham). Heat half the oil in a heavy pan and brown the woodcock on all sides over a low heat. Moisten with 3 tablespoons (2 Tbsp/2 Tbsp) of white wine and the same quantity of Marsala, cover the pan tightly, and simmer slowly until the woodcock are done. Moisten occasionally with a little hot water if necessary. Meanwhile chop the capers, anchovies, and the reserved entrails together finely and sauté in the remaining oil in a small pan, adding salt, the rest of the white wine and Marsala. Cook for 10 minutes, stirring frequently. Spread on the toast and serve with the woodcock.

Sugna Piccante
Chili Suet

fresh suet
chili pepper
salt

Pound the fresh suet with salt and a chopped chili pepper (use more or less of the latter, according to taste) until thoroughly blended and smooth. The result can be used as a spread on bread or as a condiment to lend extra flavor to soups and other dishes (see the following recipe). It will keep well for some time in an airtight glass jar.

Cavolfiore Piccante
Spicy Cauliflower

1 onion
12 black olives
1 large cauliflower
Sugna Piccante (see preceding recipe)

Slice the onion finely and pit (stone) the olives. Wash and trim the cauliflower, keeping only the white part. Make a crisscross incision with a knife in the base of the main stalk and stand upright in a narrow earthenware or enameled cooking pot. Spread the chili suet mixture carefully but liberally over the head and surround with the sliced onion and olives. Pour a little salted water into the pot, cover and steam over a low heat. (See the illustration overleaf.)

Melanzane al Forno
Baked Eggplants (Aubergines)

4 large, long eggplants (aubergines)
salt
oil
12 anchovy fillets
¼ c/4 oz/100 g black olives
2 cloves garlic
1 bunch parsley
2 Tbsp/2 oz/50 g capers
1 c/3 oz/90 g soft bread crumbs from
*   stale bread*
oregano

Wash the eggplants (aubergines), cut them in half lengthwise, and make deep incisions in the flesh of each half, cutting to within ¼ inch (½ cm) of the skin.

Sprinkle a generous amount of salt on the incisions and place the eggplants (aubergines) cut side down in a colander with a weight on top of them. Leave them to drain for 1 hour. Rinse and pat dry. Remove the pulp from each half, to within ¼ inch (½ cm) of the skin, dice, and sauté in hot oil until crisp and brown; then drain on paper towels and sprinkle with a little salt. Chop the anchovies finely.

Pit (stone) the olives and chop with the garlic and parsley. Place the chopped anchovies, olives, garlic, and parsley in a bowl with the diced eggplants (aubergines), capers, bread crumbs, and a pinch of oregano and mix thoroughly. Place the eggplant (aubergine) shells in a baking dish in a single layer, and fill with the prepared mixture. Peel and seed the tomatoes and slice them into thin strips. Top the stuffed shells with these strips, sprinkle them with a pinch of salt, and slowly drizzle oil over them, allowing it to soak in. Bake for 1 hour at 300°F–325°F (150°C–170°C/mk 2–3).

Mandorlata di Peperoni
Sweet and Sour Peppers with Almonds

3 Tbsp/2 Tbsp/2 Tbsp seedless white
  raisins (sultanas)
12 sweet almonds
4 large, firm, fleshy peppers
⅓ c/3½ fl oz/1 dl oil
1 Tbsp vinegar
4 very ripe tomatoes
salt

Soften the raisins (sultanas) by soaking in lukewarm water for 15 minutes. Blanch and skin the almonds and cut into slivers. Wash and dry the peppers, remove the seeds and any membrane, and cut into thin strips. Heat the oil in a non-metallic pan and sauté the pepper strips gently until tender. Then add the vinegar, raisins (sultanas), almonds, and skinned, seeded, tomatoes, and salt. Cover and simmer gently for 30 minutes.

Left: Preparing Cavolfiore Piccante (Spicy Cauliflower).

APULIA

FOGGIA

BARI

BRINDISI

TARANTO

LECCE

Orecchiette al Sugo d'Agnello
Orecchiette with Lamb and Rosemary

scant 1 c/4 oz/100 g all-purpose (plain) flour
2¼ c/9 oz/250 g durum wheat flour
2–2¼ lb/2–2¼ lb/1 kg lamb, cut from the leg into small cubes
7 Tbsp/4 oz/100 g butter
3 Tbsp/2 Tbsp/2 Tbsp olive oil
1 sprig of fresh rosemary or a pinch of dried rosemary
salt
freshly ground pepper
¼ c/2 oz/50 g grated Parmesan cheese

Mix the two flours together with enough water to make a fairly firm dough. Knead it well until it is smooth and pliable. Roll out into long sausage shapes about ½ inch (1 cm) thick. (See the illustration opposite.) Cut into small disks ⅛ inch (3–4 mm) thick; then press quite firmly with a small palette knife or your thumb so that they curl into the typical orecchiette (little ears) shape. Spread the orecchiette out on a pastry cloth and leave them to dry for at least 24 hours.

Rinse and dry the lamb. Place the butter, oil, and pieces of lamb with the rosemary in a heavy cooking pot. Cover and cook over a low heat, stirring from time to time, until the lamb is well browned on all sides. Season with salt and pepper and simmer (adding a little water at intervals) until the lamb is done. Remove the rosemary and discard.

Boil the pasta in plenty of salted water, drain when al dente and turn into a deep, heated serving dish, moistening with the juices from the lamb which should be a dark, rich color and have a certain amount of body. Mix well and serve with grated Parmesan cheese on the side. The lamb itself makes a good main dish and goes well with a fresh salad.

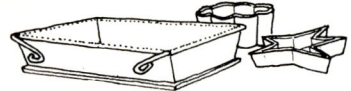

Orecchiette col Pomodoro e la Ricotta
Orecchiette with Cheese and Tomato Sauce

¾ lb/¾ lb/350 g orecchiette (see previous recipe)
1½ c/10½ oz/300 g very ripe (or canned) tomatoes
salt
1 c/5 oz/150 g fresh ricotta cheese
freshly ground pepper

Prepare the orecchiette a day in advance, as directed above, and, while they are boiling in a large pan of salted water, put the tomatoes through a food mill or sieve into a small saucepan, add a little salt, and reduce over a fairly high heat until creamy. Remove from the heat. Cream the ricotta with a fork until it is smooth and blend it into the tomato sauce. When the pasta is tender but firm, drain it, and transfer it to a deep dish. Sprinkle generously with freshly ground pepper, stir in the sauce, and serve.

Orecchiette con le Cime di Rapa Strascicate
Orecchiette with Turnip Tops

¾ lb/¾ lb/350 g orecchiette
scant 1 lb/scant 1 lb/400 g turnip tops
6 Tbsp/4 Tbsp/4 Tbsp olive oil
a piece of red chili pepper
1 clove garlic

Make the orecchiette as directed in the recipe for Orecchiette al Sugo d'Agnello above (or buy them from an Italian or specialty store).

Wash and trim the turnip tops, then boil them in plenty of salted water until they are tender but still bright green and slightly crisp. Drain them well, reserving the cooking liquid. Boil the pasta in the reserved turnip top cooking liquid (adding more water if necessary) until they are tender but firm. While they are cooking heat the oil gently in a pan with the chili pepper and the finely chopped garlic; add the turnip tops and salt sparingly. Stir so that the leaves are evenly coated with oil and remove the chili pepper when the vegetables are peppery enough. Drain the pasta and add it to the turnip tops, mix well, and then serve while still very hot. No grated cheese is served with this dish.

Orecchiette col Ragù
Orecchiette with Meat Sauce

1 medium onion
1 stalk celery
4–5 fresh basil leaves
6 Tbsp/4 Tbsp/4 Tbsp olive oil
1¼ c/10½ oz/300 g ground (minced) lean beef
1¼ c/10½ oz/300 g canned tomatoes
salt
freshly ground pepper
¾ lb/¾ lb/350 g orecchiette
¼ c/2 oz/50 g grated Parmesan cheese

The recipe for fresh orecchiette can be found above in the recipe for Orecchiette al Sugo d'Agnello.

Chop the onion, celery, and basil finely and sauté in the oil over a moderate heat. Add the meat, turn up the heat a little, and brown the beef lightly, stirring frequently. Put the tomatoes through a food mill or sieve into the saucepan, season with salt and pepper, stir, and cover, simmering gently until the sauce has thickened. Boil the orecchiette in a large quantity of salted water until they are al dente, drain, and place in a heated bowl. Mix in the sauce and grated Parmesan. This easy and economical but delicious dish should be served very hot.

Spaghetti alla Tarantina

generous ½ lb/generous ½ lb/300 g clams
scant ½ lb/7 oz/200 g mussels
scant ½ lb/7 oz/200 g shrimp (prawns)
1 clove garlic
6 Tbsp/4 Tbsp/4 Tbsp olive oil
generous ¼ lb/generous ¼ lb/150 g eel
*   (chopped)*
salt
freshly ground pepper
generous 1 c/8 oz/225 g very ripe (or
*   canned) tomatoes*
1 bunch parsley
¾ lb/¾ lb/350 g spaghetti

Wash the clams and mussels well and scrub off the beards. Steam them open in a large covered skillet or saucepan with a little water, removing them as they open. Discard any which do not open properly. Remove them from their shells and wash well in lukewarm water to get rid of all traces of sand. Keep the juice from the shells and the cooking liquid from the pan and let it stand to allow the sand to settle; then strain through a piece of cheesecloth (muslin) in a very fine strainer (sieve) and set it aside in a cup.

Shell the shrimp (prawns). Sauté the finely chopped garlic in the oil until it starts to color, add the prepared seafood and the chopped eel. Season with salt and pepper and add the peeled, seeded tomatoes cut into strips (if canned tomatoes are used put them through a food mill or sieve). Simmer over a moderate heat, adding the liquid from the clams and mussels. Just before removing from the heat, add the finely chopped parsley.

Boil the spaghetti in plenty of salted water until it is al dente. Drain, transfer to a heated serving dish, and top with the seafood sauce.

Bottled clams can be used as long as they are not preserved in a highly-flavored liquid. In this case, reduce the quantities somewhat. In Italy each portion is topped with a delicately

Right: Making orecchiette, a delicious pasta, which is immensely popular in Apulia.

flavored mollusc resembling a mussel, called a date mussel. A large scampi or one of the larger shrimp (prawns) left in its shell can be substituted.

Spaghetti alla Sangiovanniello
Spaghetti San Giovanni

1 lb/1 lb/500 g very ripe (or canned)
   tomatoes
6 anchovy fillets
6 Tbsp/4 Tbsp/4 Tbsp olive oil
1 clove garlic
2–3 basil leaves
a piece of red chili pepper
¾ lb/¾ lb/350 g spaghetti
1 small bunch parsley

Blanch, skin, and seed the tomatoes, and roughly tear into pieces by hand. (If canned tomatoes are used, put through a food mill or sieve.) Chop the anchovies finely and heat gently in the oil in a large saucepan, working the anchovies into a thin paste with a fork. Add the tomatoes, the finely chopped garlic and basil, and the piece of chili pepper. Simmer over a moderate heat until the sauce has reduced somewhat (it should not be too thick). Remove the chili pepper when the sauce is spicy enough for your individual taste.

Bring a large pan of salted water to a boil, add the spaghetti and cook until half done. Drain and add to the sauce. Turn up the heat and cook until the spaghetti is tender, stirring continuously. Dilute the sauce a little with hot water. It must not be too dense, or the spaghetti will not cook properly. Shortly before removing from the heat, add the coarsely chopped parsley. Serve very hot. No grated cheese is necessary.

For extra flavor, add a tablespoon of chopped capers and about 12 pitted (stoned) black olives at the same time as the parsley.

Spaghetti con Capperi e Olive Nere
Spaghetti with Capers and Black Olives

scant ¾ lb/10½ oz/300 g spaghetti
1 Tbsp capers
20 large, black pitted (stoned) olives
1 red chili pepper
1 Tbsp tomato paste
6 Tbsp/4 Tbsp/4 Tbsp olive oil (if the
   sauce is prepared in advance)

Cook the spaghetti in plenty of boiling salted water. Meanwhile place the drained and chopped capers in a bowl and add the quartered olives and the chili pepper (remove the seeds but keep the pepper whole). Stir in the tomato paste thoroughly. When the spaghetti is tender but still firm, drain and add the tomato mixture mixing thoroughly for 2 to 3 minutes. Remove the chili pepper, which by this time should have imparted a spicy flavor to the hot spaghetti. No grated cheese is served with this dish.

The dressing can be prepared several days in advance, since it keeps well in the refrigerator. Cover the surface with a very thin film of olive oil to keep it from drying out.

Timpano di Maccheroni con le Melanzane
Eggplant (Aubergine) and Macaroni Timbale

6 or 7 eggplants (aubergines)
salt
1¼ c/10½ oz/300 g ground (minced) lean
   beef
1 egg
1 Tbsp all-purpose (plain) flour
7 Tbsp/4 oz/100 g butter
1 onion
⅓ c/3½ fl oz/1 dl dry red wine
5 large ripe (or canned) tomatoes
freshly ground pepper
¼ c/3 Tbsp/3 Tbsp olive oil
scant ¾ lb/10½ oz/300 g macaroni
¼ c/2 oz/50 g grated Parmesan cheese

Slice the eggplants (aubergines) lengthwise, sprinkle with salt, and place in a colander with a plate and weight on top. Leave to drain for 1 hour.

Place half the meat in a bowl, add a little salt, and the egg and blend well with a wooden spoon. Divide into eight equal portions and shape into rissoles, coat these with flour, and sauté them in 1½ tablespoons (scant 1 oz/20 g) butter until they are well browned. Remove from the pan and drain on paper towels.

Heat 4 tablespoons (2 oz/50 g) butter in a pan and fry the chopped onions and the remainder of the ground (minced) meat. Pour in the wine and allow to evaporate. Reduce the heat, add the tomatoes, season with salt and pepper, and simmer until the sauce has reduced and thickened. Heat the oil in a skillet or frying pan until very hot and add the eggplants (aubergines) (pat dry with paper towels before frying). Fry until crisp and golden and drain on paper towels.

Cook the macaroni in plenty of boiling salted water, drain, and turn onto a wide serving platter and allow to cool. Grease a fairly deep baking dish with a little butter and line the bottom and sides with the fried eggplants (aubergines), reserving enough slices to form another layer. Place half the macaroni in the lined dish, cover with some of the sauce and arrange the rissoles neatly on top, sprinkling with some grated Parmesan. Cover with the rest of the macaroni and the sauce and a layer of grated Parmesan. Finish with a layer of eggplants (aubergines) and bake in a preheated moderate (350°F/180°C/ mk 4) oven for about 15 minutes.

Spaghetti con le Seppie
Spaghetti with Cuttlefish

scant 1 lb/14 oz/400 g cuttlefish or squid
1 small onion
1 stalk celery
1 clove garlic
1 small piece carrot
6 Tbsp/4 Tbsp/4 Tbsp olive oil
⅓ c/3½ fl oz/1 dl dry white wine
freshly ground pepper
salt
2 c/17 fl oz/½ l light stock
1 small bunch parsley
¾ lb/¾ lb/350 g spaghetti

Prepare the cuttlefish as directed for Seppie alla Veneziana on page 57, discarding the ink sac, cutting the tentacles into small pieces and the bodies into thin strips. Chop the onion, celery, garlic, and carrot very finely and sauté in the oil until soft. Add the prepared cuttlefish and fry gently until tender. Pour in the wine and cook without a lid until the wine has completely evaporated. Season with pepper and salt and simmer over a moderate heat until the cuttlefish are done. Add a little hot stock whenever necessary. Add the chopped parsley just before removing the pan from the heat.

Boil the spaghetti in plenty of salted water, drain when al dente, turn into a heated bowl and mix with the sauce.

A variation on this recipe is to omit the wine and stock and use 2 cups (14 oz/400 g) ripe or canned tomatoes put through a food mill or sieve.

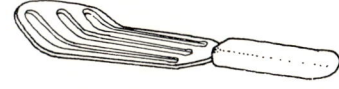

Spaghetti coi Broccoli
Spaghetti with Broccoli and Anchovies

8 anchovy fillets
1¾ lb/1¾ lb/800 g broccoli
¾ lb/¾ lb/350 g spaghetti
6 Tbsp/4 Tbsp/4 Tbsp olive oil
1 clove garlic
1 red chili pepper (optional)

Chop the anchovies finely. Wash the broccoli and divide into spears, each with its share of the fleshy stalk. Boil until tender but still fairly crisp in plenty of salted water. Drain well, reserving the liquid. Keep the broccoli warm. Cook the spaghetti in the reserved liquid, topped up with boiling water if necessary. While the spaghetti is cooking, heat the olive oil with the finely chopped garlic and the chopped anchovies, working the latter into the oil with a fork so that they dissolve and form a thin paste. When the spaghetti is cooked al dente, drain and turn into a deep, heated serving dish, mix in the flavored oil, and add the broccoli spears. Stir very gently so as not to break up the broccoli and serve at once, without grated cheese.

A very finely chopped chili pepper can be added to the oil to give the dish a spicy taste.

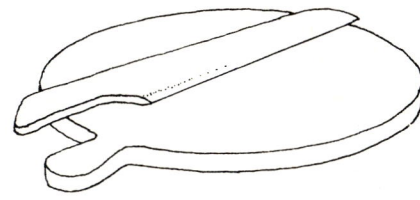

Cialdedda

4 large slices of stale white or
    whole-wheat (wholemeal) bread
olive oil
3 ripe firm tomatoes
salt
freshly ground pepper
oregano

Place the slices of bread on a large flat dish or platter, sprinkle with olive oil, and let stand for about 30 minutes. Then turn the slices over, cover with the thinly sliced tomatoes and season with salt, pepper and oregano. This is a deliciously simple and healthy summer snack, especially if the bread is homemade or made from whole-wheat (wholemeal) flour.

Pizza Pugliese

1 recipe pizza dough (see the recipe for
    Pizza Romana on page 135)
1 onion
1½ Tbsp/1 oz/25 g grated Pecorino
    cheese
3 Tbsp/2 Tbsp/2 Tbsp canned tomatoes
    (put through a food mill or sieve)
3 Tbsp/2 Tbsp/2 Tbsp olive oil
salt

When mixing the dough incorporate 1 tablespoon oil. When the dough has risen and been punched down as usual, roll out and shape into a large disk. Garnish this with the very finely chopped onion, the grated Pecorino cheese, and the tomatoes. Drizzle with the remaining oil, sprinkle with a little salt, and bake in a hot oven for 20 to 30 minutes.

Involtini alla Barese
Stuffed Beef Rolls Bari Style

4 thin slices of sirloin cut about ¼-inch
    thick, weighing in total about 1¼ lb/
    1¼ lb/600 g
salt
freshly ground pepper
scant ¼ lb/3 oz/80 g pork fat
2 oz/2 oz/50 g Pecorino cheese (in one
    piece)
3 cloves garlic
1 bunch parsley
6 Tbsp/4 Tbsp/4 Tbsp oil
1 lb/1 lb/500 g ripe tomatoes

Flatten the slices of beef until they are of an even thickness with the flat side of a meat cleaver and season with salt and pepper. Cut the pork fat and the Pecorino cheese into thin matchstick strips. Chop the parsley and garlic coarsely and spread evenly on the flattened steaks, stopping ¼ inch (½ cm) short of the edges; spread the pounded pork fat and the Pecorino on top; and roll up, tying securely with string or fastening with wooden cocktail sticks.

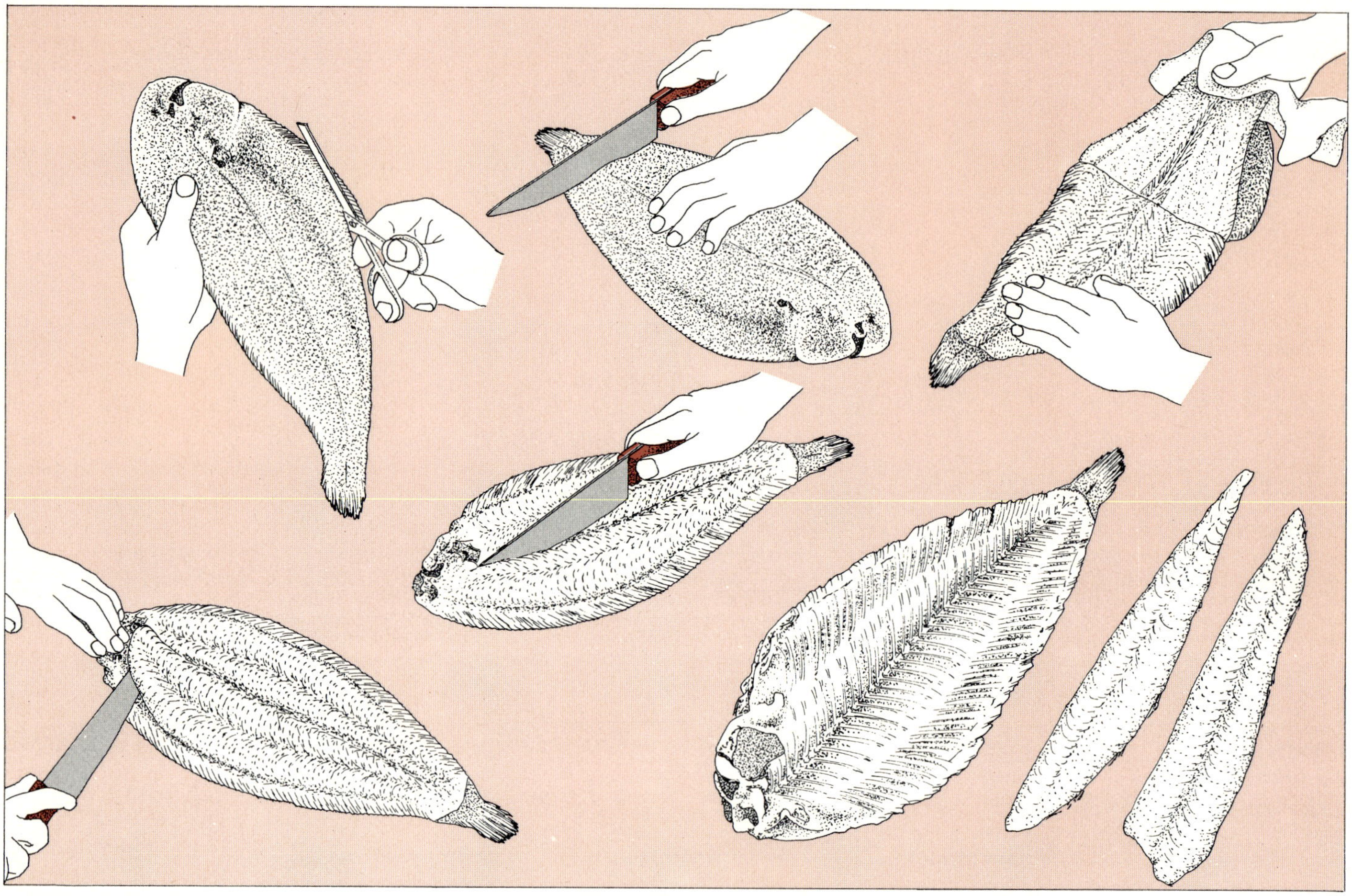

Above: How to skin and fillet flat fish.

Sauté the rolls in the oil for a few minutes, turning frequently. Add the skinned, seeded, and chopped tomatoes and a little salt; then cover and simmer gently for about 20 to 30 minutes, allowing the sauce to thicken. When the meat is cooked, take the rolls out of the pan, remove the string or cocktail sticks, arrange on a serving platter, and coat with the sauce.

The original Italian recipe uses horsemeat and, therefore, needs more garlic and Pecorino to balance the stronger flavor of the meat.

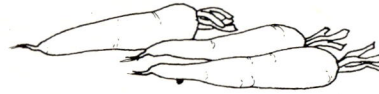

Filetti di Sogliola
Fillets of Sole with Black Olives

4 small sole or flounder
1 small bunch parsley
¼ c/2 oz/50 g black olives
a pinch of oregano
olive oil
freshly ground pepper
salt

Fillet the sole as shown above. Trim off all the lateral fins with a pair of scissors, then remove the skin from both sides of the fish by loosening a little of it near the tail with a very sharp knife and then, holding the tail firmly with a dry cloth to prevent its slipping, pull off the skin in one quick motion. Using the same sharp knife, carefully remove the fillets from the backbone: loosen the flesh carefully all round the outside edge, with the point of the knife, then cut down the center of the fish, against the spine, cut off the head and ease the fillets off the bone, working from the spine outwards, towards the outer edges.

Rinse the fillets and pat dry, arrange on a sheet of kitchen foil, sprinkle with finely chopped parsley and olives and a pinch of oregano. Moisten with some olive oil, season with pepper and salt, seal the foil and bake in the oven at about 400°F (200°C/mk 6) for 15 to 20 minutes. Remove the fillets from the oven, transfer them very carefully to an oiled baking dish, and sprinkle the juices from the foil over them. Return the fish to a very hot oven (475°F/240°C/mk 9) for 5 minutes. The excess moisture will partly be absorbed by the fish, giving them more flavor, and will partly evaporate. This recipe suits other varieties of flat fish.

Polpettine ai Capperi
Beef and Caper Rissoles with Wine

1¼ c/10½ oz/300 g finely chopped lean
    beef
1 Tbsp capers
⅓ c/3½ fl oz/1 dl white wine
⅓ c/3½ fl oz/1 dl oil
a pinch of marjoram
1 Tbsp butter
3 Tbsp/2 Tbsp/2 Tbsp fresh bread
    crumbs
1 Tbsp all-purpose (plain) flour
a little milk
salt

Soak the bread crumbs in milk briefly and then squeeze out the excess milk. Place the very finely chopped beef (use a half-moon cutter to chop) in a bowl together with the bread crumbs and butter; season with marjoram and salt. Blend very well into a homogeneous mixture and shape into walnut-sized balls. Incorporate 2 or 3 capers into each rissole. Coat with flour. Heat the oil in a large heavy pan and sauté the rissoles (choose a pan large enough to accommodate them all), turning frequently so that they cook evenly. Pour in the wine and cook for a few minutes more. Transfer the rissoles to a hot serving platter, deglaze the pan with a few spoonfuls of hot water, and spoon over the meat. Serve immediately.

Caldariello
Lamb Hot Pot

1 clove garlic
1 small bunch parsley
a little wild fennel (trimmed of feathery
    leaves and any tough outer stalks) or
    a pinch of dried fennel
1 onion
⅓ c/3½ fl oz/1 dl oil
2 c/¾ pt/4 dl milk (sheep's milk if
    possible)
1¾ lb/1¾ lb/800 g leg of lamb (boned)
salt
freshly ground pepper

This dish takes its name from the small, pot-bellied, typically Apulian cauldron or kettle in which it is traditionally cooked in the inland part of Apulia.

Chop the garlic, parsley, and fennel and slice the onion in thin rings. Place with the unheated oil in a heavy saucepan or fireproof Dutch oven, add the milk, and heat. Add the lamb, cut into large cubes, season with salt and pepper and cook with the lid on over a very low heat. Stir from time to time so that the lamb does not stick to the bottom of the pan and burn. Simmer until the lamb is tender (the cooking time will vary according to the age and quality of the lamb—it will take from 40 minutes to over 1 hour) by which time you should have wonderfully moist meat.

Alici Arraganate
Fresh Anchovy Pie

1 lb/1 lb/500 g fresh anchovies
2 cloves garlic
1 bunch parsley
1 c/3 oz/90 g bread crumbs from stale
    bread
milk
3 Tbsp/2 Tbsp/2 Tbsp toasted bread
    crumbs
olive oil
freshly ground pepper
salt

Trim the anchovies, removing their fins, tails and heads. Slit open their bellies and remove the guts and backbone. Wash and pat dry. Chop the garlic and parsley very finely. Soak the untoasted bread crumbs in milk for a few minutes; then squeeze to drain. Oil a baking dish lightly and cover the bottom with a layer of anchovies. Sprinkle with some of the chopped garlic and parsley and some of the dampened bread crumbs, season with pepper and salt, and moisten with a little olive oil. Repeat this layering process, topping with the toasted bread crumbs. Sprinkle with a little oil and bake in a preheated oven at 350°F (180°C/mk 4) until the top is well browned (about 30 minutes).

Polipetti Arrabbiati
"Baby" Octopus in Chili Sauce

1¾ lb/1¾ lb/800 g polipetti (see
    instructions below)
⅓ c/3½ fl oz/1 dl oil
a piece of red chili pepper
6 anchovy fillets
1 clove garlic
4 ripe tomatoes
freshly ground pepper
salt
1 small bunch parsley

Polipetti are a very small variety of mollusc; if unavailable small octopus, squid or cuttlefish may be substituted. If octopus are used see recipe Polipetti Affogati on page 156; if squid or cuttlefish are used see recipe below. Once cleaned, drain and place in an earthenware cooking pot, cover, and cook over a low heat with no added moisture or fat for 5 minutes. Stir in the oil, chili pepper, chopped anchovies, finely chopped garlic, and the skinned, seeded, and chopped tomatoes. Season with pepper and a little salt, replace the lid and simmer for at least 30 minutes, stirring now and then and adding a little water from time to time if necessary. Just before removing from the heat, sprinkle with finely chopped parsley. Serve extremely hot.

Seppie Ripiene
Stuffed Cuttlefish

4 medium-sized cuttlefish or squid
2 cloves garlic
1 small bunch parsley
3 Tbsp/2 Tbsp/2 Tbsp bread crumbs
salt
freshly ground pepper
oil
¾ c/7 fl oz/2 dl dry white wine

Clean the cuttlefish meticulously, rubbing off the outer skin and removing the eyes, mouth, bone or quill, and ink sac. Wash well in plenty of fresh water and cut off the tentacles; keep the body sac intact. Chop the tentacles very finely with the garlic and parsley, place in a bowl, and add the bread crumbs, season with salt and pepper and then stir in 3 tablespoons (2 Tbsp/2 Tbsp) oil. Mix thoroughly; stuff the cuttlefish ⅔ full to allow room for the stuffing to swell. Place the cuttlefish side by side in a single layer in the bottom of a skillet in which 6 tablespoons (4 Tbsp/4 Tbsp) of oil have been heated and fry the cuttlefish, turning frequently. Season with pepper and salt and add a little more oil and the white wine. Cover and cook over a very low heat until tender and then serve without delay.

Orata alla Pugliese
Apulian Porgy (Gilt-head Bream)

1 large porgy (gilt-head bream)
  weighing 1¾ lb/1¾ lb/800 g
1 bunch parsley
2 cloves garlic
¾ c/7 fl oz/2 dl oil
4 medium potatoes
1 Tbsp butter
salt
freshly ground pepper
3 Tbsp/2 Tbsp/2 Tbsp grated Pecorino
  cheese

Remove the scales from the porgy (bream), trim off the fins and the tail, gut, wash well, and pat dry. Chop the parsley and garlic, place in a bowl and stir the oil in thoroughly. Peel the potatoes and slice them into ½-inch (1 cm) slices. Butter a baking dish; cover the bottom with half the parsley, garlic, and oil mixture; arrange a layer of potato slices (use about half) on top; and sprinkle with a little salt, freshly ground pepper, and 1 tablespoon grated Pecorino. Place the porgy (bream) on top, sprinkle with the remaining Pecorino, cover with the rest of the potato slices, sprinkle with a little more salt, and distribute the rest of the parsley, garlic, and oil mixture over the potatoes. Bake in a preheated oven at 350°F (180°C/mk 4) for 45 minutes.

Pomodori Farciti
Stuffed Tomatoes

8 ripe firm tomatoes
1 bunch parsley
1 clove garlic
4 Tbsp/3 Tbsp/3 Tbsp bread crumbs
3 Tbsp/2 Tbsp/2 Tbsp grated Parmesan
  cheese
2 egg yolks
salt
freshly ground pepper
a little milk
⅓ c/3½ fl oz/1 dl oil

Wash and dry the tomatoes. Cut them in half horizontally, scoop out the pulp, taking care not to pierce the outer flesh and skin.

Chop the parsley and garlic and mix in a bowl with the bread crumbs, Parmesan, egg yolks, and salt and pepper. Add enough milk to make a moist yet firm stuffing and fill the tomatoes. Place the tomatoes in a large, shallow oiled baking dish, pour a trickle of oil over them and bake in a preheated oven at 350°F (180°C/mk 4) for 30 minutes. The tomatoes may be eaten hot or cold.

Carciofi Fritti
Fried Artichokes

8 fleshy tender artichokes
juice of 1 lemon
a little all-purpose (plain) flour
2 eggs
oil
salt

Try to buy very young, tender artichokes, since they should not have developed a choke. If this is not possible, use artichoke hearts.

Wash the artichokes well, snip off the pointed tips of the leaves, discard the tougher outer leaves, and slice the artichokes vertically in half. Cut each half into thin vertical slices, dropping the slices immediately into cold water acidulated with the juice of a lemon to prevent discoloration. Remove the slices from the water, dry, coat with flour, then with beaten egg, and fry in very hot oil in a large frying pan. Remove the slices with a slotted spatula (fish slice) when they are golden brown, drain on paper towels, sprinkle with salt, and serve at once.

Melanzane Ripiene
Stuffed Eggplants (Aubergines)

4 small round eggplants (aubergines)
salt
1 clove garlic
⅓ c/3½ fl oz/1 dl oil
1¼ lb/1¼ lb/600 g ripe tomatoes
freshly ground pepper
½ tsp granulated sugar
1 small bunch parsley
a few fresh basil leaves
3 Tbsp/2 Tbsp/2 Tbsp bread crumbs

Wash the eggplants (aubergines), slice off a cap at the stalk and scoop out the flesh from this end to within about ¼ inch (½ cm) of the skin. Reserve the caps, having removed the stalks and prickly calyces. Sprinkle the inside of each hollow eggplant (aubergine) with salt and leave it upside down for 1 hour so the bitter juice will drain away. Dice the flesh, salt, and drain in a colander with a weight on top. Sauté the garlic in half the oil until it starts to color; then discard it. Add half the skinned, seeded, and chopped tomatoes, season with a little salt and pepper and the sugar, and then stir in the diced flesh (previously dried on paper towels) and the chopped parsley and basil. Reduce the sauce over a fairly high heat for about 15 minutes until it thickens. Then add the bread crumbs.

Wash the eggplant (aubergine) shells, dry and fill with the prepared mixture. Fit the eggplants (aubergines) neatly into a deep, fireproof baking dish, top with their caps, and pour on the rest of the tomatoes, put through a food mill or sieve. Sprinkle with a little salt and some pepper, pour about ½ cup (5 fl oz/1.5 dl) water into the bottom of the dish, and drizzle a little olive oil over the eggplants (aubergines). Cover and cook over a low heat, moving them gently now and again to prevent their sticking. The eggplants (aubergines) will shrink during cooking, so it is important to fit them tightly into the dish to begin with, so they will not topple over during cooking. They are very good eaten hot or cold.

Melanzane alla Campagnola
Eggplants (Aubergines) Country Style

4 eggplants (aubergines)
salt
2 cloves garlic
1 small bunch parsley
a few leaves of fresh mint
3–4 fresh basil leaves
freshly gound pepper
⅓ c/3½ fl oz/1 dl olive oil

Wash the eggplants (aubergines), cut them into rounds about ½-inch (1 cm) thick, sprinkle them with salt, and leave them in a colander with a small plate and weight on top for 1 hour to drain. Then wash and dry them well. Arrange the slices carefully on the broiler (grill) rack and cook, turning once, until they are golden brown on both sides.

Chop the garlic, parsley, mint, and basil and mix them together. Arrange the slices of eggplant (aubergine) on a serving platter, sprinkle them with the chopped garlic and herb mixture, season with salt and pepper, and then cover with a very thin film of the best quality olive oil. Let the eggplants (aubergines) stand for 7 to 8 hours before serving.

Cime di Rapa Stufate
Braised Turnip Tops

3¼ lb/3¼ lb/1½ kg turnip tops
2 onions
salt
freshly ground pepper
⅓ c/3½ fl oz/1 dl oil

Trim the turnip tops, discarding the stalks and tougher, older leaves. Wash well. Pour about ¾ cup (7 fl oz/2 dl) of water into a saucepan, add the turnip tops, the onion sliced in thin rings, and a little salt and pepper. Cover and cook gently for 10 minutes, stirring now and then. Remove the lid, sprinkle the oil over the turnip tops, and turn up the heat. When the turnip tops are almost done, mix well and allow the remaining liquid to evaporate. Prepared in this way turnip tops are particularly suited to boiled, roasted, and broiled (grilled) meats.

Pinoccate
Orange Flavored Pine Nut Candies

1 c/4 oz/100 g pine nuts
1 c/7 oz/200 g granulated sugar
¼ c/1 oz/25 g candied orange peel (finely diced)
rice paper

Dry out the pine nuts by placing in a preheated oven at 325°F (170°C/mk 3) for a few minutes. Do not let them brown. Place ¾ of the sugar in a small saucepan (heavy untinned copper is best) with 2–4 tablespoons of water and cook over a fairly low heat, stirring until the sugar is dissolved. As soon as the water has evaporated and the soft crack stage (270°F/290°C) is reached—when a little is dropped into cold water, the syrup separates into threads which are hard but not brittle—remove the pan from the heat and stir vigorously with a wooden spoon until the mixture turns opaque (this means that the sugar has re-crystallized). Add the dried-out pine nuts and then the finely diced candied orange peel. Mix well and drop small heaps of the mixture onto the rice paper which can be trimmed neatly once the candy mixture has cooled and set. These candies will keep for a long time provided they are not exposed to any moisture. Keep them in a tightly sealed jar or tin.

These candies are also a Christmas specialty of Perugia.

Ciambella Pugliese
Apulian Sweet Bread Ring

generous ¼ lb/5 oz/125 g bread dough (see p. 15)
generous ¼ lb/5 oz/125 g baking potatoes
¾ c/5 oz/150 g granulated sugar
3 Tbsp/2 oz/50 g shortening (lard)
5 eggs
1 Tbsp butter
all-purpose (plain) flour

Peel and boil the potatoes and put them through the ricer while still very hot, allowing them to fall in a mound on a pastry board or other working surface. Into this mix the sugar, reserving 1 tablespoon (½ oz/15 g), the bread dough and the shortening (lard). Knead well, adding just enough flour to keep the dough workable but soft. When the dough is smooth and even, shape into a ball, dredge lightly with flour and leave in a bowl covered with a cloth for 24 hours to rise. The following day shape the dough into a ring and place in a tube cake pan or savarin mold which has been lightly buttered and dusted with flour. Let the dough rise in a warm draft-free place for 2 hours. Then bake in a preheated oven at 325°F (170°C/mk 3) for 1 hour. When the sweet bread is golden brown, remove from oven and sprinkle immediately with the reserved sugar. Turn out when cool.

CALABRIA

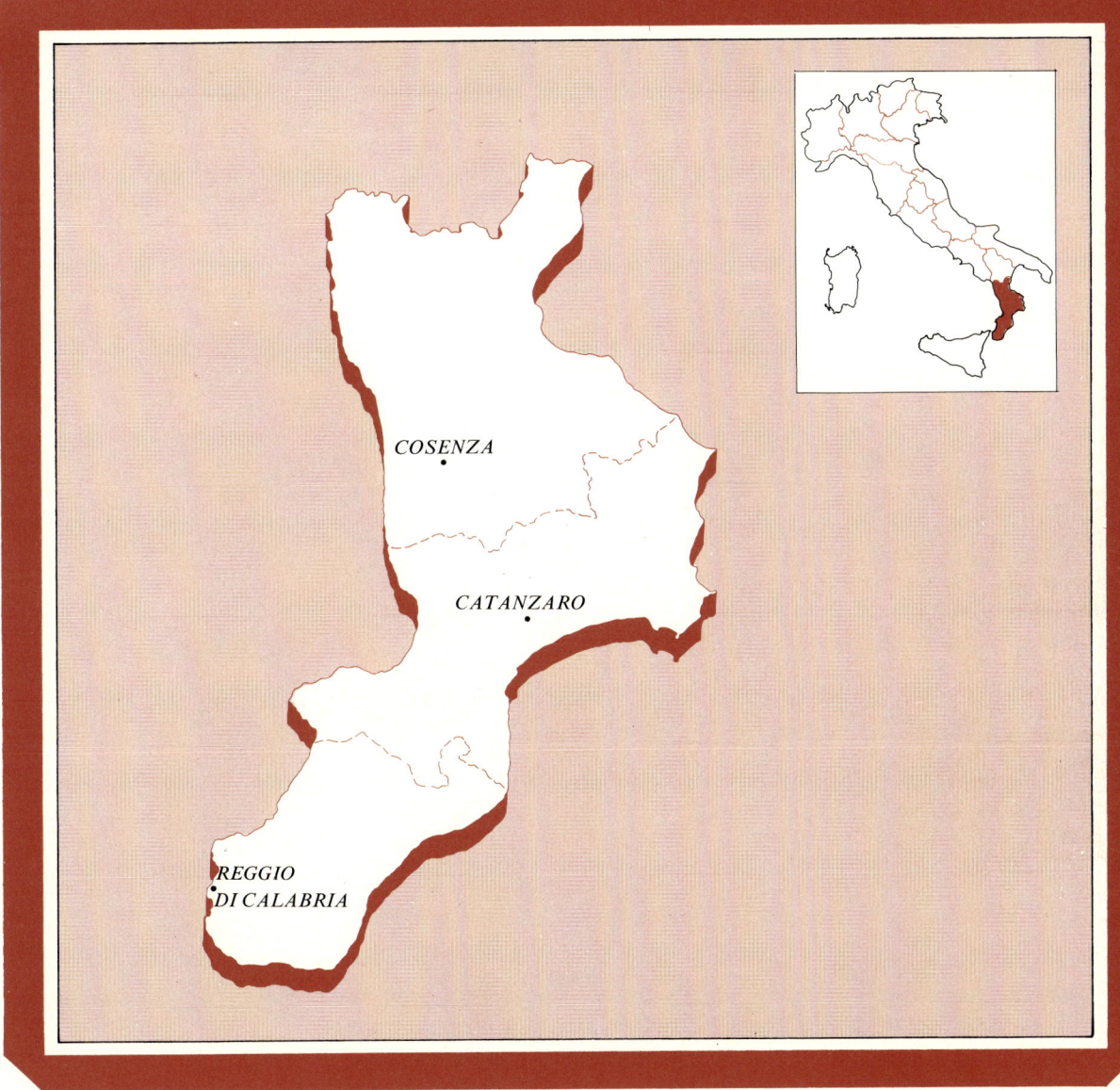

COSENZA

CATANZARO

REGGIO
DI CALABRIA

Aringhe alla Calabrese
Herrings Calabria Style

2 cloves garlic
1 small bunch parsley
1 piece of red chili pepper
1½ lb/1½ lb/700 g fresh herrings
⅓ c/3½ fl oz/1 dl oil
salt
a few spoonfuls of dry white wine
8 or more slices of toast

Chop the garlic, parsley and chili pepper. Gut, trim, wash and fillet the herrings. Pour the oil into a pan, add the chopped mixture, cover with the fish fillets, sprinkle with salt and simmer over a low heat with the lid on for about 1 hour, stirring frequently so the fish does not stick to the pan and burn. Add a few spoonfuls of dry white wine or water to keep the fish moist. When the fish has disintegrated into a thick creamy mixture, spread on the pieces of hot toast and serve at once. Very good as an appetizer or nourishing snack.

Spaghetti con Polpi e Totani
Spaghetti with Octopus and Squid

scant ½ lb/7 oz/200 g squid
scant ¾ lb/10½ oz/300 g octopus
1 medium onion
2 cloves garlic
6 Tbsp/4 Tbsp/4 Tbsp olive oil
2 c/14 oz/400 g canned tomatoes (put
    through a food mill or sieve)
salt
¾ lb/¾ lb/350 g spaghetti
freshly ground pepper

The original Italian dish is made with "flying" squid, so called because it can propel itself out of the water and glide through the air; however ordinary squid is an acceptable alternative.

Clean the squid (see instructions for Seppie alla Veneziana on page 57) and cut it into rings. Pound the octopus (see instructions for Polpo alla Luciana on page 157) and cut into pieces. Finely chop the onion and garlic and place in a heavy pan with the oil, squid, and octopus. Sauté over a gentle heat. Stir in the tomatoes, season with salt, add about ⅓ cup (3–4 fl oz/1 dl) hot water, if necessary, and simmer until thick.

Boil the spaghetti until tender but firm in plenty of salted water. Drain and turn into a heated tureen or deep serving dish and top with the sauce and a little freshly ground pepper.

Lasagna Imbottita
Layered Surprise Lasagna Pie

2½ c/10½ oz/300 g durum wheat flour
salt
1 lb/1 lb/500 g loin fillet of pork
¼ c/2 oz/50 g grated Pecorino cheese
3 eggs
freshly ground pepper
olive oil
¼ lb/¼ lb/100 g Mozzarella cheese
1 small onion or shallot
scant ½ lb/7 oz/200 g fresh (shelled) or
    frozen peas
1 Tbsp/scant 1 oz/20 g dried imported
    Italian mushrooms (soaked in warm
    water)
1 stalk celery
1 small carrot

Make an egg pasta dough with the flour, a pinch of salt, and a little warm water (see page 11). Roll out into a thin single sheet, and cut into very wide strips.

Cut four thin escalopes from the fillet of pork and set aside. Chop the remainder. Place 2 tablespoons (1 oz/25 g) grated Pecorino cheese in a bowl with a whole egg, the chopped pork, salt, and pepper. Blend together with a wooden spoon, shape into rissoles the size of walnuts, and fry in very hot oil. Hard-boil 2 eggs, shell them, and cut them into rings. Dice the Mozzarella cheese. Sear the pork escalopes in oil, sealing both sides. Chop the onion, celery and carrot very finely, and sauté gently in 3 tablespoons (2 Tbsp/2 Tbsp) oil in a saucepan, with the presoaked chopped mushrooms. Add the peas and a little water and then cover the pan and cook until tender.

Boil the lasagne in plenty of salted water until tender but firm and then drain carefully. Carefully spread the lasagne out on a cloth to dry out a little and then line an oiled baking dish with some of them. Cover the lasagne with a few rounds of hard-boiled egg, some diced Mozzarella, and a few rissoles, then sprinkle with some sauce and a little grated Pecorino. Cover with another layer of lasagne, repeat the layer of eggs and cheese, and place the thin escalopes on top. Continue in this fashion until all the ingredients are used up, ending with layer of lasagne covered with sauce and grated cheese. Bake in a moderate oven for approximately 30 minutes. Serve very hot.

This delicious and substantial dish is a satisfying meal in itself.

Pizza Calabrese
Calabrian Pizza

⅓ c/4 oz/100 g black olives
2 Tbsp/2 oz/50 g anchovy fillets
½ c/4 oz/100 g canned tuna fish (drained
    of oil)
6 Tbsp/4 Tbsp/4 Tbsp oil
1¼ lb/1¼ lb/600 g ripe, firm tomatoes
salt
1 lb/1 lb/500 g pizza dough (see recipe
    for Pizza Romana, page 135)
4 Tbsp/2 oz/50 g shortening (lard or
    margarine)
freshly ground pepper
1 Tbsp capers

Pit (stone) the olives and cut in half. Chop the anchovies and flake the tuna. Pour ¼ cup (3 Tbsp/3 Tbsp) olive oil into a large pan; add the skinned, seeded, and chopped tomatoes and a little salt. Reduce over a high heat for 15 minutes but make sure that the tomatoes do not turn to mush—the object is to reduce the juice. Grease a high-sided cake pan 10–11 inches (26–28 cm) in diameter. Place the risen dough on a board, open it up and insert the shortening, a pinch of salt, and a good pinch of pepper into the middle. Knead until the shortening is well worked into the dough. Divide the dough into two unequal pieces with one being about twice the size of the other, and roll out into two sheets. Line the cake pan (bottom and sides) with the larger sheet, and arrange the tomatoes, anchovies, tuna, olives and capers evenly in layers inside. Cover with the smaller sheet of dough. Fold the edges of the larger sheet over the top sheet and pinch together to seal as tightly as possible. Brush the top with oil and bake in a preheated oven at about 350°F (180°C/mk 4) for 1 hour. When the pizza is well browned, it is ready to serve. It is also delicious cold.

Morseddu
Calabrian Variety Meat (Offal) Pie

1¼ c/10½ oz/300 g pig's (or calf) liver
scant 1 c/7 oz/200 g pig's (or calf) heart
  (chopped)
1 Tbsp pork fat or lard
1⅓ c/10½ oz/300 g ripe tomatoes
2 cloves garlic
1 piece of red chili pepper
salt
1 lb/1 lb/500 g pizza dough (see recipe
  for Pizza Romana, page 135)
a little oil

Cut the liver into very thin strips and chop the heart finely. Heat the pork fat in a pan and sauté the heart and liver lightly; add the skinned, seeded, and chopped tomatoes and the very finely chopped garlic and chili pepper. Add salt to taste, cover, and braise for 30 minutes, stirring from time to time. The mixture should be of a fairly thick consistency; if it is too liquid, turn up the heat, remove the lid, and reduce while stirring.

Divide the bread dough into two portions, one twice the size of the other. Roll the larger portion out into a sheet about ½ inch (1 cm) thick and line the base and sides of an oiled cake pan (see illustration, right). Fill the lined pan

Right: Preparing Morseddu (Calabrian Variety Meat (Offal) Pie).

with the meat mixture, level out and cover with the second, smaller sheet of dough rolled out to a circle to fit snugly inside the top of the cake pan. Pinch the edges of the two dough sheets together. Bake in a preheated oven at 350°F (180°C/mk 4) for about 30 minutes.

Involtini alla Calabrese
Calabrian Pork, Ham, and Cheese Rolls

4 prime pork fillets
4 slices pancetta (fat bacon)
1 very fresh Mozzarella cheese
4 slices spicy salami
salt
freshly ground pepper
a little oil

Pound the pork fillets with a mallet, the flat blade of a meat cleaver, or a skillet until they are large and thin. Place a slice of pancetta (bacon) on each, then a few strips of Mozzarella and a finely chopped slice of salami; season with a little salt and pepper and roll up, securing with a cocktail stick. Brush the meat rolls with a little oil and cook under a preheated broiler (grill) turning frequently so that they brown evenly. When they are cooked, arrange them on a serving platter and sprinkle with a little sea salt. Serve immediately.

Costolette d'Agnello alla Cosentina
Lamb Chops Cosenza Style

¾ c/7 fl oz/2 dl oil
4 lamb chops (weighing about ¼–½ lb each)
1 lb/1 lb/500 g ripe tomatoes
2 large green peppers
3 Tbsp/2 Tbsp/2 Tbsp green olives
1 onion
2 cloves garlic
1 bunch parsley
salt
freshly ground pepper

Heat 6 tablespoons (4 Tbsp/4 Tbsp) oil in a skillet and fry the chops, turning to brown and cook them evenly on both sides. Pour the rest of the oil into a saucepan, add the skinned, seeded, and chopped tomatoes; the green peppers (seeds and membrane removed) cut into thin strips; the pitted (stoned) and halved olives; and the chopped onion, garlic, and parsley. Season with salt and pepper (a chopped piece of chili pepper goes very well with this dish) and simmer slowly for 15 minutes. Place the chops in the sauce and heat through, turning several times to coat thoroughly. Serve without delay.

Tortiera di Alici
Baked Anchovies

1¾ lb/1¾lb/800 g fresh anchovies
⅔ c/4 oz/100 g fine bread crumbs
3 Tbsp/2 Tbsp/2 Tbsp grated Pecorino cheese
1 Tbsp capers
1 small bunch parsley
1 clove garlic
salt
oregano
oil
2 ripe, firm tomatoes

Clean the anchovies, remove the backbone without separating the 2 halves of the fish, wash and dry. In a bowl, mix the bread crumbs (reserve 1½ tablespoons) with the grated Pecorino and the chopped capers, parsley, and garlic. Season with a little salt and a pinch of oregano and add ⅓ cup (3½ fl oz/1 dl) oil. Blend well. Oil a cake pan or baking dish generously and sprinkle with the reserved bread crumbs, line the bottom with a layer of anchovies (opened out flat), sprinkle with salt and a little of the bread crumb, cheese and herb mixture. Repeat the anchovy layer and continue until all the ingredients are used up. Top with the skinned, seeded and sliced tomatoes, sprinkle generously with oil, and bake in a preheated oven at 350°F (180°C/mk 4) for 30 minutes. This dish may be eaten warm or cold.

Stoccafisso alla Cosentina
Stockfish Cosenza Style

1¾ lb/1¾ lb/800 g presoaked stockfish (if unavailable, substitute salt cod)
scant 1 lb/14 oz/400 g potatoes
1 onion
1 bunch parsley
a few fresh basil leaves
¾ c/7 fl oz/2 dl oil
1 lb/1 lb/500 g very ripe tomatoes (put through a food mill or sieve)
salt
freshly ground pepper

Wash and skin the fish, remove any bones, and cut into pieces. Peel the potatoes and cut them into thick slices. Slice the onion and coarsely chop the parsley and basil. Place the oil and onion in a heavy pan or cooking pot and sauté, stirring constantly until the onion is soft. Add the tomatoes, season with salt and pepper, and simmer over a low heat for a few minutes. Place the pieces of fish side by side in the sauce, cover with the potato slices, and spread the chopped parsley and basil on top. Cover and simmer very gently for about 45 minutes, shaking the pan every now and then. Add a little water during cooking if necessary.

Sarde Aromatiche
Marinated Sardines with Fresh Mint

1½ lb/1½ lb/700 g fresh sardines
flour
oil
salt
7 Tbsp/5 Tbsp/5 Tbsp bread crumbs
1 sprig of fresh mint
2 cloves garlic
⅓ c/3½ fl oz/1 dl vinegar

Trim and gut the sardines and wash them thoroughly, then pat them dry and coat them with flour. Heat plenty of oil in a large pan and, when very hot, fry the sardines, turning frequently. When they are well browned, remove and drain on paper towels, then sprinkle with a little salt. Choose a deep, round non-metallic serving dish, arrange the fish in a circle, their tails meeting at the center, and sprinkle them with bread crumbs. Heat 6 tablespoons (4 Tbsp/4 Tbsp) oil in a small saucepan. Add the chopped mint leaves and chopped garlic. When the garlic starts to color, pour in the vinegar, add salt, and simmer for a few minutes, then pour through a strainer (sieve) onto the fish. The sardines should be served cold and are at their best after a couple of days.

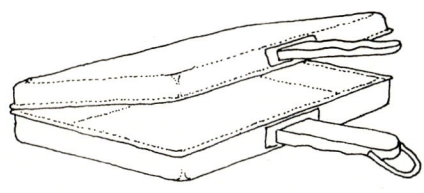

Pomodori Ripieni
Stuffed Tomatoes

8 large, ripe, firm tomatoes
10 Tbsp/8 Tbsp/8 Tbsp cooked small
    pasta (see page 18, illustrations
    26–41)
6 Tbsp/4 Tbsp/4 Tbsp oil
salt
freshly ground pepper
3 Tbsp/2 Tbsp/2 Tbsp grated Pecorino
    cheese
1 clove garlic
1 bunch parsley
1 sprig of fresh mint or ½ tsp dried mint

Wash and dry the tomatoes and slice them horizontally just above the middle to form a cup with a lid. Scoop out the pulp with a teaspoon, and sprinkle with salt. Turn them upside down to drain for 30 minutes. Place the cooked pasta in a bowl with ¼ cup (3 Tbsp/3 Tbsp) oil, a little salt, pepper, the Pecorino, and the very finely chopped garlic, parsley, and mint leaves. Mix well and stuff the tomatoes, covering each tomato with its lid. Place in an oiled baking dish and bake in a preheated moderate oven (about 325°F/170°C/mk 3) for 30 to 40 minutes. Serve hot or cold.

Peperoni alla Calabrese
Peppers Calabria Style

1¼ lb/1¼ lb/600 g fleshy, firm peppers
¼ c/2 oz/50 g oil
1 Tbsp grated Pecorino cheese
1 Tbsp capers
salt
freshly ground pepper
1 Tbsp bread crumbs

Wash the peppers, remove the seeds and membrane, and cut into pieces. Heat the oil in a pan and add the peppers; sauté until tender. Add the Pecorino cheese (or substitute Parmesan if Pecorino is too strong), the capers, a pinch of salt, pepper to taste, and the bread crumbs. Mix well and cook gently over a moderate heat to blend all the flavors. Serve very hot.

Ciambrotta
Calabrian "Ratatouille"

2 eggplants (aubergines)
2 potatoes
2 ripe, firm tomatoes
2 large, firm, fleshy peppers
1 onion
2 cloves garlic
⅓ c/3½ fl oz/1 dl oil
salt
freshly ground pepper

Peel and slice the eggplants (aubergines), sprinkle them with salt, and drain them in a colander covered with a weighted plate. Leave for 1 hour, then wash and dry. Peel, wash, and dice the potatoes. Skin, seed, and chop the tomatoes. Wash the peppers, remove seeds and membrane, and cut into thin strips. Slice the onion into rings and chop the garlic. Pour the oil into a pan, add the prepared vegetables, season with salt and pepper (use a piece of chili pepper instead of ground pepper if you prefer a spicier taste) and heat from cold. Simmer with the lid on over a moderate heat, stirring frequently, and

add a little water when needed (the vegetable mixture should not be too moist when cooked, however). Serve very hot as an excellent accompaniment to a wide variety of meats and poultry.

Mostaccioli
Aniseed Liqueur Cookies

2½ c/10½ oz/300 g all-purpose (plain)
    flour
scant 1 c/10½ oz/300 g clear honey
1 Tbsp aniseed liqueur, such as Sambuca
butter

Sift the flour into a mound on a pastry board, make a well in the center, and pour in the honey and liqueur. Work well to form a smooth dough the consistency of bread dough. Roll out into a sheet about ½ inch (1 cm) thick and cut out various shapes with a fluted pastry wheel. Butter a cookie (baking) sheet, arrange the cookies on it, and bake in a preheated oven at 300°F (150°C/mk 2) until the mostaccioli are golden brown. Remove the cookie (baking) sheet from the oven and let it cool. These cookies are best eaten a few days after they are made—they will then be moist and melt in the mouth. Mostaccioli keep well for long periods. If you prefer, you may substitute a different flavored liqueur.

SICILY

TRAPANI

PALERMO

MESSINA

ENNA

CALTANISSETTA

CATANIA

AGRIGENTO

SYRACUSE

RAGUSA

Spaghetti alla Siracusana

1 Tbsp capers
2 anchovy fillets
⅓ c/3½ fl oz/1 dl olive oil
1 clove garlic
1 lb/1 lb/500 g ripe tomatoes
1 red or yellow pepper
salt
freshly ground pepper
¾ lb/¾ lb/350 g spaghetti
¼ c/2 oz/50 g grated Pecorino cheese

Drain the capers or rinse and pat dry if you are using the salted variety. Chop the anchovy fillets. Pour the olive oil into a saucepan, add the finely chopped garlic and the skinned and seeded tomatoes (do not chop them, simply tear them roughly into pieces by hand). Simmer without a lid for 10 minutes, then add the anchovy fillets, the capers, and the pepper, cut into thin strips (seeds and membrane removed). Season with salt and freshly ground pepper and cook over a moderate heat until the sauce has reduced and thickened.

Cook the spaghetti in plenty of boiling salted water, drain when tender but still firm and turn into a heated serving bowl. Add the sauce and sprinkle with the grated Pecorino cheese; mix gently but thoroughly and serve immediately.

Trionfo della Marescialla
Spaghetti in Wine and Onion Sauce

1 large onion
1 clove garlic
1 small bunch parsley
4 Tbsp/2 oz/50 g butter
1 Tbsp all-purpose (plain) flour
¾ c/7 fl oz/2 dl dry white wine
1 tsp meat extract
salt
freshly ground pepper
10 oz/10 oz/300 g spaghetti

Chop the onion, garlic, and parsley finely and sauté in the butter in a heavy saucepan. When the onion starts to color, add the flour and cook, stirring constantly, over a fairly high heat until the flour turns a nut brown color. Pour in the wine, mixing well, and allow to evaporate; add some stock made from the meat extract dissolved in approximately ⅓ cup (3½ fl oz/1 dl) boiling water, season with salt and freshly ground pepper and simmer gently for 1 hour, stirring from time to time and adding a little water if necessary.

Cook the spaghetti in plenty of salted boiling water and drain when al dente. Turn into a deep, heated serving dish and top with the sauce. Serve at once without any grated cheese.

Pasta a "Picchi-Pacchi"
Spaghetti with Fresh Tomato and Basil Sauce

6 anchovy fillets
1 large onion
1 clove garlic
1 small bunch of fresh basil
3 large ripe tomatoes
6 Tbsp/4 Tbsp/4 Tbsp olive oil
salt
freshly ground pepper

Chop the anchovies and finely chop the onion with the garlic and the basil. Skin, seed, and chop the tomatoes coarsely. Sauté the chopped onion, garlic, and basil gently in the oil; add the anchovies and work them into the oil with a fork so that they dissolve into a thin paste; and then stir in the tomatoes. Reduce the heat and season with salt and freshly ground pepper. Simmer until the sauce has reduced and thickened to a smooth, creamy consistency.

Cook the spaghetti in a large pan of boiling salted water, drain when al dente, and turn into a heated serving dish. Add the sauce, mix quickly, and serve while still piping hot. No grated cheese should be served with this dish.

Pasta all'Aglio e Olio del Duca
Spaghetti with Mild Creamy Garlic Sauce

6 cloves garlic
¾ c/7 fl oz/2 dl milk
2 Tbsp/1 oz/25 g butter
¼ c/1 oz/25 g all-purpose (plain) flour
salt
freshly ground pepper
¾ lb/¾ lb/350 g spaghetti
⅓ c/3½ fl oz/1 dl olive oil

Bring 2 cups (18 fl oz/½ liter) water to a boil, add the 6 cloves of garlic, and simmer for about 2 hours.

Make a white sauce as follows: Bring the milk to the boiling point and keep it hot. Melt the butter in a small saucepan and, when it begins to color, add the flour and cook the roux for just under a minute while stirring continuously. Add the hot milk, mixing thoroughly, and season with salt and pepper. Cook over a low heat for about 20 minutes, stirring all the time. Remove from the heat and set aside but remember to stir at frequent intervals to prevent a skin from forming.

Cook the spaghetti in plenty of boiling salted water. While it is cooking, put the boiled garlic cloves and their cooking liquid through a fine strainer (sieve) and return to the saucepan. Add the oil and cook over a gentle heat to reduce a little more. When the spaghetti is al dente drain it and turn it into a heated serving bowl. Add the white sauce and then the garlic mixture, mixing quickly but thoroughly with two forks so that the spaghetti is well coated with the sauce.

Surprising as it may seem, this dish has only the most subtle flavor and aroma of garlic. Simmering the garlic cloves in water reduces their strength.

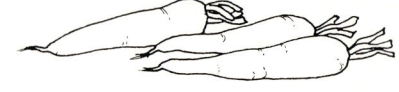

Spaghetti con la Mollica Fritta e l'Uva Passa

Spaghetti with Fried Bread Crumbs and White Raisins (Sultanas)

⅓ c/2 oz/50 g seedless white raisins (sultanas)
¾ lb/¾ lb/350 g spaghetti
1 clove garlic
6 Tbsp/4 Tbsp/4 Tbsp olive oil
⅔ c/2 oz/50 g very fine stale bread crumbs
salt
freshly ground pepper
1 small bunch parsley

Soak the raisins (sultanas) in lukewarm water for 30 minutes, then drain and dry on paper towels. Put the spaghetti in a large pan of boiling, salted water and, while it is cooking, prepare the sauce: Sauté the garlic clove, crushed with the flat of a knife blade, in the oil until it starts to color and then discard it. Add the very fine stale bread crumbs to the oil, season with salt and pepper and cook until the bread crumbs are golden brown. When the spaghetti is al dente, drain, and transfer to a heated serving dish. Stir in the bread-crumb mixture, the drained white raisins (sultanas) and a sprinkling of finely chopped parsley and serve hot. Cheese is not served with the spaghetti.

Spaghetti alla Norma

Spaghetti with Eggplants (Aubergines) and Tomato Sauce

3 eggplants (aubergines)
salt
2 c/14 oz/400 g ripe (or canned) tomatoes
⅔ c/¼ pt/150 ml olive oil
1 small bunch of fresh basil
2 cloves garlic
freshly ground pepper
¾ lb/¾ lb/350 g spaghetti
⅓ c/3 oz/80 g matured, hard ricotta cheese (grated), if unavailable, substitute Parmesan cheese

This delicious dish comes from Catania, the birthplace of the famous composer Vincenzo Bellini, and is named after his opera *Norma*.

Slice the eggplants (aubergines) thinly, sprinkle with salt, and place in a colander with a plate and a weight on top to drain for about 1 hour. Blanch and skin the tomatoes, remove the seeds and chop finely (if canned tomatoes are used, put them through a food mill or sieve). Heat ¼ cup (3 Tbsp/3 Tbsp) olive oil in a saucepan, add the tomatoes and the finely chopped basil and garlic. Season with salt and freshly ground pepper and simmer over a moderate heat until the sauce has reduced and thickened. Heat the rest of the oil in a large frying pan. Rinse the drained eggplant (aubergine) slices, pat dry with paper towels, and fry in the hot oil until golden brown on both sides. Remove with a fork and drain on paper towels, sprinkling with salt and pepper.

Cook the spaghetti in a large quantity of boiling salted water until tender but firm, drain, and place in a heated serving dish. Arrange the eggplants (aubergines) on top, cover with the tomato sauce, and sprinkle with the grated ricotta cheese.

Pasta con le Melanzane

Spaghetti with Eggplants (Aubergines) and Chili Pepper

2 large, firm eggplants (aubergines)
salt
1 piece of red chili pepper
1 clove garlic
olive oil
¾ lb/¾ lb/350 g spaghetti (or vermicelli)
1 small bunch parsley

Peel and dice the eggplants (aubergines), sprinkle with salt, and leave them in a colander with a plate and a weight on top for 2 hours to drain. Then rinse and dry.

Sauté the piece of chili pepper and the garlic clove in some olive oil over a low heat; when the garlic has turned brown, discard it and fry the diced eggplants (aubergines) in the oil. When golden brown and crisp, remove and drain on paper towels.

Cook the spaghetti or other pasta in plenty of boiling salted water until al dente; drain and turn into a heated serving dish. Drizzle a little olive oil over the spaghetti, sprinkle with chopped parsley, mix well, and top with the fried eggplants (aubergines). No cheese is served with this dish.

Pasta coi Broccoli "Arriminata"

Pasta with Broccoli and Pine Nuts

4 anchovy fillets
⅓ c/2 oz/50 g white seedless raisins (sultanas)
1 large head of broccoli or a small cauliflower
1 small onion
⅓ c/3½ fl oz/1 dl olive oil
2 c/14 oz/400 g ripe (or canned) tomatoes
freshly ground pepper
salt
½ c/2 oz/50 g pine nuts
¾ lb/¾ lb/350 g macaroni or penne
¼ c/2 oz/50 g grated Pecorino cheese
3 fresh basil leaves

Chop the anchovy fillets very finely. Soak the raisins in warm water for 20 minutes. Steam the broccoli or cauliflower cut into florets in a little salted water until tender but still firm. Keep it warm. Slice the onion into fine rings and sauté until translucent in 6 tablespoons (4 Tbsp/4 Tbsp) olive oil in a saucepan; add the skinned, seeded and chopped tomatoes (if canned tomatoes are used, put them through a food mill or sieve), and simmer for a few minutes. Add the broccoli or cauliflower, cover and keep warm over a very low heat. Using a fork, mash the anchovy fillets into a paste in a small saucepan over a low heat with a tablespoon of oil. Add to the tomato sauce, stir gently, and then add pepper and adjust the salt to taste. Add the drained raisins (sultanas) and the pine nuts and mix carefully so as not to break up the broccoli or cauliflower.

Cook the pasta in plenty of boiling salted water. When it is al dente transfer to a heated dish, add the sauce, and sprinkle with the grated Pecorino cheese mixed with the chopped basil leaves. Serve very hot.

Maccheroncelli col Cavolfiore
Macaroni with Cauliflower

1 medium cauliflower
1 clove garlic
4 anchovy fillets
½ c/2 oz/50 g pine nuts
¾ c/3½ fl oz/1 dl olive oil
salt
freshly ground pepper
10 oz/10 oz/300 g macaroni

Place the cauliflower in a little salted water, stalk downwards, cover, and steam. Meanwhile, chop the garlic, anchovies, and pine nuts finely and sauté them in the oil in a large saucepan for a few minutes. When the cauliflower is just tender but still quite firm, drain well, cut into florets, discarding the thicker, lower stalk, and add the florets to the flavored oil. Season with a little salt and pepper, turn and mix gently so that the cauliflower is coated with the mixture, then remove from the heat, cover, and keep warm.

Boil the macaroni in plenty of salted water and drain when it still has plenty of bite. Pour into the saucepan containing the oil and cauliflower and mix delicately so as not to break up the cauliflower florets. Serve very hot without any grated cheese.

For the best timing, begin cooking the macaroni as soon as you have drained the steamed cauliflower.

Pasta con le Sarde I
Macaroni with Sardines and Tomato Sauce I

1½ Tbsp/1 oz/25 g seedless white raisins (sultanas)
¼ c/1 oz/25 g pine nuts
½ lb/½ lb/225 g very fresh sardines
1 medium onion
2 anchovy fillets
6 Tbsp/4 Tbsp/4 Tbsp olive oil
2 c/14 oz/400 g very ripe (or canned) tomatoes (put through a food mill or sieve)
freshly ground pepper
salt
10 oz/10 oz/300 g macaroni or bucatini

Soak the raisins (sultanas) in lukewarm water for 20 to 30 minutes. Chop the pine nuts finely. Cut off the heads of the sardines; clean the fish and split open down the belly; remove backbone and entrails, and fillet. Sauté the chopped onion in a large pan with the oil until translucent. Add the chopped anchovy fillets and, using a fork, work into a thin paste with the oil and onion. Stir in the tomatoes, raisins (sultanas), and chopped pine nuts and simmer for a few minutes. Add the sardines, season with pepper and a little salt (remember the anchovies are very salty). Cover and cook slowly, stirring gently from time to time. Be careful not to overcook the sardines or they will break up when they are mixed with the macaroni.

Cook the pasta in plenty of boiling, salted water, drain when still quite firm and turn into a heated serving dish. Pour the sardines and sauce onto the spaghetti and mix carefully. Allow to stand for a couple of minutes before serving.

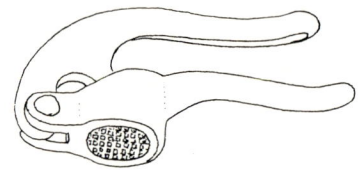

Pasta con le Sarde II
Macaroni with Sardines and Tomato Sauce II

1–2 Tbsp/1 oz/25 g seedless white raisins (sultanas)
¼ c/1 oz/25 g pine nuts
½ lb/½ lb/225 g wild fennel or the fresh or dried feathery leaves from cultivated fennel
½ lb/½ lb/225 g very fresh sardines
1 Tbsp all-purpose (plain) flour
salt
1 medium onion
olive oil
2 anchovy fillets
saffron
freshly ground pepper
10 oz/10 oz/300 g macaroni

Soak the raisins (sultanas) in lukewarm water for 20 minutes. Toast the pine nuts in a moderate oven until they turn pale golden brown. Wash the fennel very thoroughly, trim off any tough parts and soak in salted water (if only the feathery leaves are used, wash and then soak in salted water). The water in which the fennel has soaked should be reserved since the pasta will be boiled in it later.

Clean and gut the sardines as directed in the previous recipe, but do not separate the fillets. Coat lightly with flour and fry in a little hot oil—do not overcook or allow to become crisp. Drain on paper towels and sprinkle with a little salt. Chop the onion finely and sauté in 6 tablespoons (4 Tbsp/4 Tbsp) oil in a large skillet until transparent. Add the chopped anchovy fillets and work with a fork into a thin paste over a low heat. Then add the drained raisins (sultanas), the pine nuts, the wild fennel (or fennel leaves), a pinch of saffron, and a generous pinch of freshly ground pepper. Mix well and remove from the heat.

Boil the macaroni in a large pan of salted water until tender but firm, turn into a heated bowl and pour on the sauce, add the sardines and mix gently to avoid breaking up the sardines. This recipe comes from Palermo and is delightfully subtle in flavor, needing no grated cheese to complement it.

Pasta con le Zucchine
Pasta with Zucchini (Courgettes)

¾ lb/¾ lb/350 g any pasta of your choice
3 firm, fresh zucchini (courgettes)
6 Tbsp/4 Tbsp/4 Tbsp olive oil
salt
freshly ground pepper

While the pasta is cooking in ample boiling salted water, wash, dry and thinly slice the zucchini (courgettes). Fry in hot oil and season with salt and pepper, stirring constantly to keep from burning. When the pasta is al dente, drain and place in a heated bowl and mix in the zucchini (courgettes) and the oil in which they were cooked. Serve at once without any grated cheese.

Vermicelli alla Siciliana
Vermicelli Sicilian Style

4 very ripe (or canned) tomatoes
1 Tbsp butter
salt
freshly ground pepper
4 very fresh sardines
⅓ c/3½ fl oz/1 dl olive oil
¾ lb/¾ lb/350 g vermicelli

Put the tomatoes through a food mill or sieve and heat with the butter, a little salt and some freshly ground pepper to make a fairly thick sauce. Clean, gut and fillet the sardines, as directed in Pasta con le Sarde I on page 186, and fry two in 3 tablespoons (2 Tbsp/2 Tbsp) of the oil until crisp and browned. Drain on paper towels and sprinkle with a little salt. Chop the other two filleted sardines and add to the remaining oil in a large pan, working them into a paste with the oil and a little salt and pepper (if the paste is too thick add a tablespoon of milk).
Cook the vermicelli until tender but

very firm in plenty of boiling salted water; then drain and add to the sardine paste in the large pan. Pour in the tomato sauce, stirring continuously over a low heat to complete the cooking of the vermicelli, serve into individual heated plates, and top each serving with half a fried sardine.

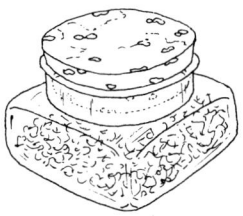

Maccheroni Incaciati al Sugo di Pesce
Macaroni with Herb, Tomato, and Fish Sauce

2 c/14 oz/400 g very ripe (or canned) tomatoes
1 onion
6 Tbsp/4 Tbsp/4 Tbsp olive oil
2 medium-sized whiting weighing about ½ lb/½ lb/225 g each
1 small bunch of fresh basil
salt
freshly ground pepper
1 small bunch parsley
¾ lb/¾ lb/350 g macaroni

Blanch and peel the tomatoes. Cut them in half and remove the seeds and squeeze them by hand to get rid of excess juice (if canned put through a food mill or sieve). Cut the onion into thin slices and sauté in the oil until translucent. Add the cleaned, trimmed, and filleted whiting, fry for a few minutes, turning once, and then add the chopped basil leaves and the tomatoes. Season with salt and pepper. Cover and simmer until the sauce has thickened, stirring now and again to prevent its sticking to the pan and burning. Shortly before removing the pan from the heat, stir in the finely chopped parsley.
Cook the macaroni in a large pan of boiling salted water and drain when tender. Turn onto a heated serving platter and top with the fish sauce.

Pasta Incaciata
Macaroni and Eggplant (Aubergine) Mold

2 eggplants (aubergines)
salt
olive oil
1 egg
1 clove garlic
1 small bunch of fresh basil
⅓ c/2 oz/50 g Mozzarella cheese
2 c/14 oz/400 g ripe fresh (or canned) tomatoes (put through a food mill or sieve)
¼ c/2 oz/50 g ground (minced) lean veal
½ c/2 oz/50 g fresh shelled (or frozen) peas
freshly ground pepper
2 chicken livers
10 oz/10 oz/300 g macaroni
¼ c/2 oz/50 g grated Pecorino or Parmesan cheese

Wash and slice the eggplants (aubergines), sprinkle with salt, and leave in a colander with a weighted plate for an hour to drain. Rinse them, pat them dry, fry in hot oil, and drain on paper towels. Hard-boil the egg, shell it, and slice it. Chop the garlic and basil leaves very finely and thinly slice the Mozzarella cheese. Pour 6 tablespoons (4 Tbsp/4 Tbsp) of oil into a large heavy pan, add the tomatoes, ground (minced) veal, and peas and season with salt and pepper. Bring these ingredients to the boiling point and then cover and simmer slowly for about 30 minutes, adding the washed, trimmed, and finely chopped chicken livers 5 minutes before the sauce is ready.
Cook the macaroni in plenty of boiling salted water and drain when tender but firm. Oil a deep baking dish and line the base and sides with the slices of fried eggplant (aubergine); place half the macaroni in the dish; and cover with half the Mozzarella slices, all the egg slices, and a third of the sauce. Follow with the remaining macaroni, then another third of the sauce, and the rest of the cheese slices and sprinkle with the grated Pecorino or Parmesan cheese. Press the contents of the baking dish

down gently with the flat of a wooden spoon, so that the dish will unmold more easily when cooked. Bake in a preheated oven at about 400°F (200°C/mk 6) for approximately 20 minutes. Remove from the oven, cover with a serving platter, and then invert the macaroni and eggplant (aubergine) mold onto it with a quick motion. Coat with the remaining sauce, which should be very hot, and sprinkle with a little more grated Pecorino or Parmesan. Serve without delay.

Cuscusu
Sicilian Style Couscous

For the couscous:
1 c/5 oz/150 g finely ground semolina
1 c/5 oz/150 g coarsely ground semolina
2 Tbsp olive oil

For the accompanying ghiotta di pesce or fish stew:
1 garlic clove
1 onion
1 bunch parsley
¾ c/3½ fl oz/1 dl olive oil
1 large tomato
2–2¼ lb/2–2¼ lb/1 kg assorted fish (see instructions)
salt
freshly ground pepper
nutmeg

There are many versions of this dish throughout the Mediterranean. In North Africa, its home, it is served with meat, fish, or vegetables and sometimes as a sweet dish, while the Sicilian version is made with excellent local fresh fish. Ideally, special utensils and equipment should be used in its preparation but it is possible to improvise satisfactorily with everyday kitchen tools.

In Sicily, the selection of fish for this dish would usually include a scorpion fish and a dentex. Porgy (gilt-head

Left: How to make Cuscusu, the Sicilian version of the North African dish, couscous.

bream) can be substituted for the latter and in addition a wide variety of other fish and seafood can be used: red snapper, turbot, halibut, sea perch, sole, gray mullet, cod, lobster, clams, shrimps (prawns), etc.

Preparation of the couscous:

Mix the two types of semolina in a wide, flat-bottomed wooden or earthenware bowl (in Sicily a specially designed earthenware dish called a *mafaradda* is used). Sprinkle with a little water in which the saffron has been dissolved. Use only enough water to moisten the semolina. Gently rake through the semolina with the fingertips, delving down to the bottom of the dish in order to evenly moisten the semolina and make tiny semolina balls, about the size of peppercorns. When quite a few of these have been made, place the semolina in a colander over another bowl, so that the little pellets will remain in the colander to be set aside to dry on a pastry cloth. Return the rest of the semolina to the original bowl and sprinkle with more saffron water, repeating the operation until all the semolina has formed into tiny balls. If the mixture becomes too wet at any stage, add a little more semolina. See the illustration of how to prepare couscous opposite.

(The *pignata di cuscusu* is the special two-tiered vessel in which the semolina is cooked in Sicily. The liquid from the fish stew is cooked in the lower part of the steamer, and the semolina pellets are steamed in the upper section. An ordinary steamer can be used instead, but a fine mesh metal strainer should be placed in the top half or the pellets may drop through the holes into the liquid below.)

While the couscous pellets are drying, prepare the fish stew as directed below. Then sprinkle the couscous pellets with about 2 tablespoons of olive oil and then mix very gently to distribute the oil evenly. Place them in the upper section above the simmering liquid and steam as described below.

Preparation of the fish stew:

While the semolina pellets are drying on a clean cloth, sauté the chopped garlic, onion, and parsley in the olive oil until the onion is translucent. Add the peeled and chopped tomato and simmer for a few minutes. Then add the prepared selection of fish cut into medium-sized pieces. Pour in about 1½ quarts (2½ pt/1½ liters) water and season with pepper and salt. Stir gently. When the fish is just cooked but still firm, strain off the liquid very carefully and keep the pieces of fish warm in a covered dish. Set aside approximately 1 pint (18 fl oz/½ liter) of the cooking liquid. Place the remainder in the bottom half of the steamer, topping up with warm water to make 1½ quarts (2½ pt/1½ liters) of liquid. Bring to a boil and then gently simmer and cover with the top part of the steamer with the semolina pellets in it. Place a damp cloth round the joint between the two halves to ensure a perfect seal. Place a lid tightly on top of the couscous and cook for about 1½ hours. The semolina can be stirred gently with the handle of a wooden spoon if it is cooking unevenly or clogging the holes in the steamer. When the semolina is cooked (about 30 minutes), transfer to a heated earthenware dish. If some of the pellets have stuck to one another, separate with a fork. Sprinkle the couscous with a little of the reserved cooking liquid, adding only a little so the semolina will absorb it evenly and not become mushy. Cover the earthenware dish and keep it warm. Then sprinkle again with a little of the reserved liquid. Repeat until all the liquid is used. It can take up to 1 hour, for the semolina must absorb all the reserved liquid in this manner. Finally, turn the semolina or couscous into a large serving dish and top with the fish pieces, removing as many of the bones as possible without allowing the fish to become cold. Add a little grated nutmeg, if desired, and some freshly ground pepper. Serve very hot.

Pasta con la Carne "Capuliata"
Baked Pasta with Meat and Cheese

1 onion
1 clove garlic
1 small bunch parsley
2 fresh basil leaves
4 Tbsp/2 oz/50 g butter
1¼ c/10½ oz/300 g ground (minced) beef
⅓ c/3½ fl oz/1 dl dry red wine
4 ripe (or canned) tomatoes (put through a food mill or sieve)
salt
freshly ground pepper
10 oz/10 oz/300 g any pasta of your choice
¼ c/2 oz/50 g grated Parmesan or Pecorino cheese
¼ lb/¼ lb/100 g mature Caciocavallo or Provolone cheese

Chop the onion, garlic, parsley, and basil very finely. Reserve 1 tablespoon butter and heat the rest in a pan until it starts to foam. Add the chopped onion and herbs, and sauté for a few minutes. Add the ground (minced) beef and fry, mixing well, for 3 to 4 minutes. Pour in the wine, increase the heat, and cook until the wine has evaporated. Add the peeled, seeded and chopped tomatoes and season with salt and pepper to taste. Cover and simmer over a low heat for about 30 minutes, stirring from time to time and adding a little hot water if necessary.

Cook the pasta in plenty of boiling salted water, drain while still very firm and pour into a heated bowl. Add the sauce and the grated Parmesan or Pecorino cheese and mix well (Pecorino is a stronger, sharper cheese than Parmesan). Grease a baking dish with the reserved butter and place a layer of pasta and sauce in the bottom, cover with a layer of Caciocavallo or Provolone cheese, previously sliced, followed by another layer of pasta and sauce and so on; continue layering the ingredients until they are all used up, ending with a layer of cheese. Bake in a moderate oven (325°F/170°C/mk 3) for about 20 minutes and serve hot.

Scaloppe di Maiale al Marsala

Escalopes of Pork with Marsala Wine Sauce

1 clove garlic
3 Tbsp/2 Tbsp/2 Tbsp olive oil
1 lb/1 lb/500 g fillet of pork (cut into thin
*   escalopes and flattened)*
1–2 tsp pounded pork fat or lard
salt
freshly ground pepper
6 Tbsp/4 Tbsp/4 Tbsp dry Marsala wine
1 tsp all-purpose (plain) flour

Crush the garlic clove with the flat of a knife blade and sauté in the oil and pork fat until it starts to color; then discard it. Add the pork escalopes to the fat, season with salt and pepper, and sauté briskly for about 4 minutes on each side. Remove the pork escalopes and keep them warm on a serving dish in a very slow oven. Deglaze the pan in which the pork was cooked by pouring in the Marsala and scraping the sides and bottom with a wooden spoon, then, stirring rapidly, add the flour mixed with 1–2 tablespoons of cold water. Simmer while stirring for 4 to 5 minutes and then pour the sauce over the meat and serve at once.

Bistecche alla Siciliana

Steak Sicilian Style

2 Tbsp/2 oz/50 g black olives
4 ripe (or canned) tomatoes
2 Tbsp/2 oz/50 g pickled chili peppers
1 stalk celery
2 cloves garlic
¼ c/3½ fl oz/1 dl olive oil
4 fillet steaks
1 Tbsp/2 oz/50 g capers
salt
freshly ground pepper
oregano

Pit (stone) the olives and cut in half. Skin, seed, and chop the tomatoes (put canned tomatoes through a food mill or sieve). Cut the peppers lengthwise in half and remove the seeds. Finely dice the celery. Crush the garlic cloves with the blade of a knife, sauté in the oil in a skillet, and when the cloves begin to turn brown, discard them. Sear the steaks in the hot, flavored oil, giving them 1–2 minutes on each side. Remove them from the pan and keep them warm. Fry the chopped celery, olives, peppers, capers and tomatoes in the oil and cooking juices, season with salt and pepper, and add a pinch of oregano. Simmer and reduce the sauce over a moderate heat for a short while, stirring gently. Return the steaks to the pan, turn them once or twice, and then serve immediately onto individual heated plates.

Pollo Ripieno

Stuffed Boned Chicken

1 chicken weighing about 3–3½ lb/
*   3–3½ lb/1.5 kg*
1 c/7 oz/200 g ground (minced) lean veal
¼ c/2 oz/50 g prosciutto (raw ham) or
*   sausage meat*
1 c/3 oz/90 g bread crumbs from stale
*   bread*
a few tablespoons milk
salt
freshly ground pepper
nutmeg (optional)
2 egg yolks
oil

Pluck, draw, and wash the chicken well, reserving the giblets. If the chicken is not already dressed, trim off the wing tips and feet (when boning a chicken, it is preferable to buy a bird which is not already dressed, due to the careless way in which the cavity and neck openings are usually cut). Bone the chicken as follows: Place the bird breast down on the board and make an incision the entire length of the spine, through both skin and flesh. Using a sharp boning knife, cut as close to the frame as you can. Push the skin and flesh back as you work. Work first towards the ball and socket joint of the leg, sever sinews and remove bone. Take great care not to break the skin, especially when the breast bone is reached as the skin is very close to the bone at this point (see the illustration opposite). Reserve bones for stock, if desired. Remove any tendons or veins and tie off securely at the neck, wing ends, and legs. Sew up the vent and neck ends.

Prepare the stuffing by mixing the ground (minced) veal with the finely chopped prosciutto (raw ham) and the bread crumbs which have been soaked in milk and squeezed free of excess moisture. Season with salt and pepper and, if desired, a pinch of grated nutmeg. Add the two egg yolks and blend very well. Stuff the chicken with this mixture through the incision in the back and sew up the opening. Never stuff a boned chicken too full or the skin may burst during cooking as the stuffing swells. Wrap securely in a piece of cheesecloth (muslin) and tie with string. Place on a rack, seam side down, in a large poaching kettle or saucepan and cover with water. Simmer gently for about 2 hours and then untie the cheesecloth (muslin) and remove the chicken. Reserve liquid for stock, if desired.

Heat some oil in a large skillet or frying pan and brown the chicken lightly on all sides. Carefully remove the string from the chicken. Serve immediately with fresh vegetables.

A delicious stock can be made by adding an onion, carrot and celery to the reserved bones and cooking liquid.

Stoccafisso alla Siciliana

Stockfish Sicilian Style

2 lb/2 lb/1 kg presoaked stockfish (if
*   unavailable, substitute salt cod)*
¼ c/3½ fl oz/1 dl olive oil
1 onion
5 ripe (or canned) tomatoes
1½ Tbsp/2 oz/50 g capers
2 Tbsp/2 oz/50 g black olives
1 Tbsp pine nuts

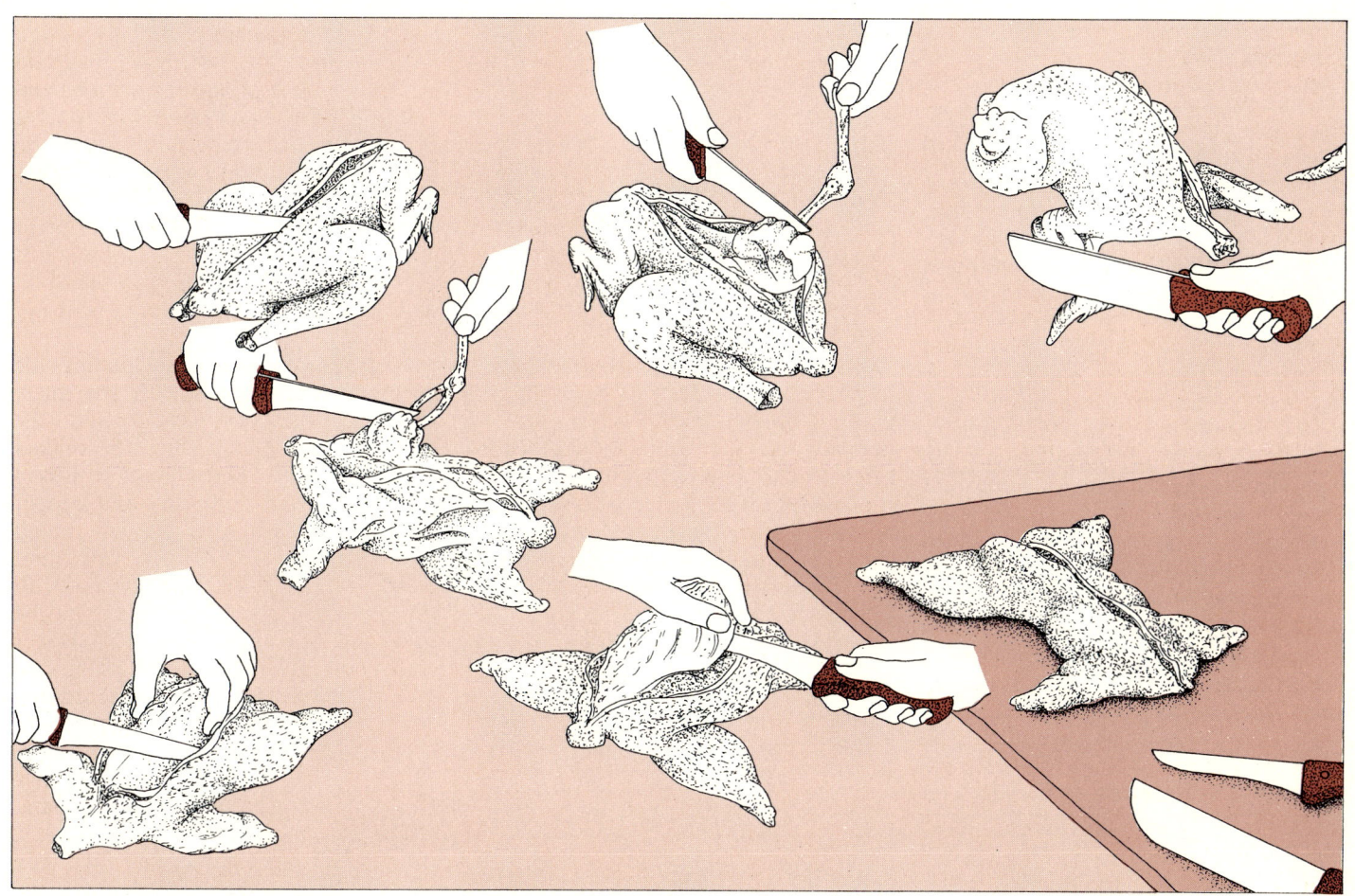

2 large potatoes
salt
freshly ground pepper
¾ c/7 fl oz/2 dl dry white wine

Cut the stockfish into slices about ½ inch (1 cm) thick. In a large earthenware cooking pot or non-metallic pan, heat the oil and sauté the thinly sliced onion until transparent. Add the skinned, seeded and chopped tomatoes (put canned tomatoes through a food mill or sieve). Simmer for a few minutes and then place the slices of fish side by side in the pan and sprinkle with the capers, the pitted (stoned) and halved olives, and the pine nuts and cover with a layer of finely sliced potatoes. Season with salt and pepper and pour in the white wine. Place in a preheated oven at 325°F (170°C/mk 3) and cook for one hour. Serve very hot.

Sarde Fritte alla Siciliana
Marinated Fried Sardines

1¾ lb/1¾ lb/800 g fresh sardines
¾ c/7 fl oz/2 dl good quality wine vinegar
all-purpose (plain) flour
oil
salt

Cut the heads, tails, and fins off the sardines, slit them down the belly and remove the guts. Remove the backbone without breaking the fish into two halves. Wash the fish and pat them dry. Place them in an earthenware or non-metallic dish, cover with the vinegar and leave them to marinate for 24 hours. Drain, coat with flour, and deep fry. Remove with a slotted spatula (fish slice) and drain on paper towels. Trans-

Above: How to bone a chicken, keeping the skin and flesh as intact as possible.

fer to a serving platter, sprinkle with salt (preferably coarse sea salt), and serve.

Tonno alla Siciliana
Marinated and Grilled Fresh Tuna Steaks

1¼ lb/1¼ lb/600 g fresh tuna (ventresca or belly cut is the best of all)
1 c/8 fl oz/¼ l dry white wine
juice of 1 lemon
1 sprig of fresh rosemary or a pinch of dried rosemary
1 clove garlic
salt

freshly ground pepper
6 anchovy fillets
⅓ c/3½ fl oz/1 dl oil

Start to prepare the dish at least 12 hours in advance by washing the tuna in plenty of running water, cutting it into steaks and marinating it in a non-metallic dish in the wine, lemon juice, rosemary, crushed garlic, and a pinch of salt and pepper. The following day, drain the slices of fish and broil (grill) them gently, basting frequently with the marinade. When the fish steaks are well done on both sides, place them side by side in a shallow dish and keep them warm (cover the fish with foil to prevent their drying out).

Using a fork, work the chopped anchovy fillets into a thin paste with the oil in a small pan over a low heat. Pour over the tuna and serve without delay.

Acciughe al Gusto di Finocchio

Anchovies with Fennel

2 cloves garlic
¼ c/2 fl oz/60 ml olive oil
8 large, fresh anchovies
salt
freshly ground pepper
1 tsp fennel seeds
⅓ c/3½ fl oz/1 dl dry white wine

Sauté the chopped garlic in the oil in a large skillet or fireproof earthenware dish and, as it begins to color, place the anchovies side by side in the pan and sprinkle with salt, pepper, and fennel seeds. Pour in the wine and simmer over a low heat for about 5 minutes. Turn the anchovies over carefully and cook for a further 5 minutes. Serve very hot.

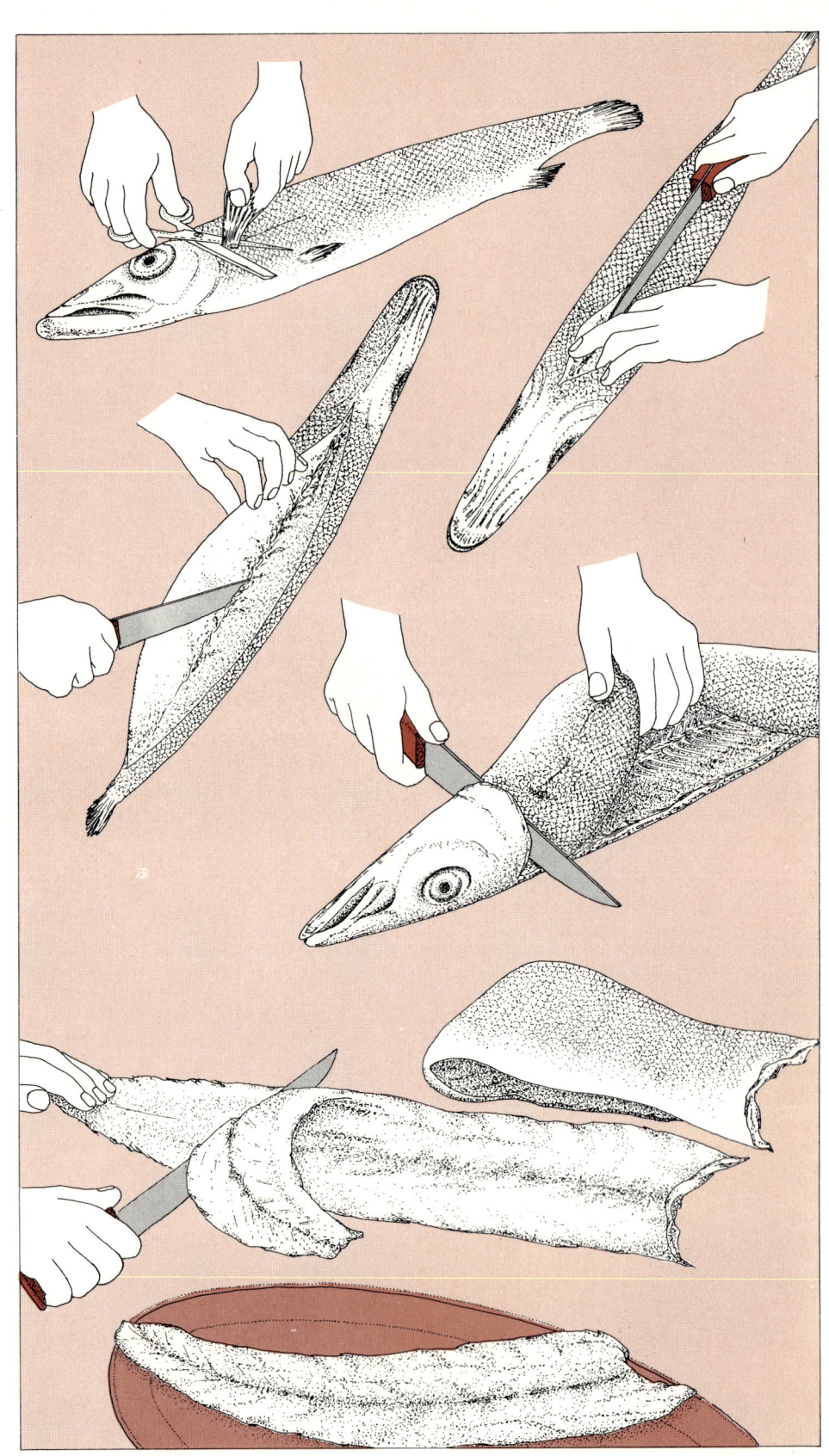

Right: Trimming, gutting, and skinning hake, as in the recipe for Nasello alla Palermitana (Hake Palermo Style).

Nasello alla Palermitana
Hake Palermo Style

olive oil
6 anchovy fillets
1 sprig of fresh rosemary or ¼ tsp dried
    rosemary
1½–1¾ lb/1½b–1¾ lb/700 g–800 g hake
    (cod or whiting can be substituted)
salt
freshly ground pepper
3 Tbsp/2 Tbsp/2 Tbsp bread crumbs
½ lemon
toasted bread

Pour 2–3 tablespoons olive oil into a small pan and mash the anchovy fillets into the oil with a fork over a low heat. Chop some of the rosemary leaves very finely. Prepare the fish by removing the fins, tail, and head, slitting it down the belly, and gutting it. Then carefully remove the backbone, taking care to keep the fish as intact as possible. Sprinkle the inside of the fish with salt and pepper and then smear with a teaspoon of the anchovy paste and add a pinch of chopped rosemary leaves. Place the fish flat in a large rectangular or oval baking dish and pour a generous quantity of oil over it so that it will not dry out or stick to the bottom of the dish. Smear the remaining anchovy paste over the fish and then sprinkle with the rest of the chopped rosemary and the bread crumbs. Place in a preheated oven at 325°F–350°F (170°C–180°C/mk 3–4) and bake for 30 minutes. If the fish seems at all dry, add a little more oil. When the fish is done, remove it from the oven, moisten with the juice of half a lemon, and serve at once in the baking dish, garnished with slices of crisp, toasted bread.

Alici all'Agro
Savory Anchovies

1¾ lb/1¾ lb/800 g fresh anchovies
3 ripe firm tomatoes
1 clove garlic
1 lemon
1 small bunch parsley
salt
freshly ground pepper
⅓ c/3½ fl oz/1 dl olive oil

Trim the anchovies, cut off their heads, gut them, and wash them well. Blanch, peel, seed and slice the tomatoes. Chop the garlic and parsley very finely. Cut the lemon into very thin slices. Arrange the anchovies in a circular ovenproof dish (preferably earthenware), in a circle, their tails meeting at the center, cover with the tomato slices and sprinkle with the chopped garlic and parsley. Season with salt and pepper and cover with the lemon slices. Pour over the oil and moisten with about ⅓ cup (3½ fl oz/1 dl) water. Bake in a preheated oven at 325°F (170°C/mk 3) for 30 minutes. Do not stir at all during cooking; simply move the dish sharply from side to side once or twice to prevent the fish from sticking to the bottom.

Although other varieties of small round fish can be cooked in this way, none has the distinctive flavor of anchovies.

Braciole di Pesce Spada
Stuffed Swordfish Steaks

1 lb/1 lb/500 g fresh swordfish
⅓ c/2 oz/50 g very fresh Mozzarella
    cheese
¼ c/2 fl oz/60 ml olive oil
1 onion
salt
freshly ground pepper
2 Tbsp/1 fl oz/3 cl brandy
¼ c/3 Tbsp/3 Tbsp bread crumbs
1 small bunch of fresh basil
thyme
1 lemon

Cut the Mozzarella into 8 slices and the swordfish into 8 thin steaks. (Fresh tuna, turbot, halibut, or other meaty fish can be used instead.) Heat the oil in a heavy pan and add the chopped onion and any trimmings from the fish (not the bones or skin), season with salt and pepper, and fry gently, moistening with the brandy. When the mixture has reduced, remove it from the heat and stir in the bread crumbs.

Place a slice of Mozzarella on each fish steak, top with the bread crumb mixture, 2 or 3 basil leaves, and a pinch of thyme. Roll up each steak and fasten with a cocktail stick. Broil (grill) the fish, turning occasionally, until golden brown and cooked through (about 15 minutes). Then arrange on a serving platter, garnish with lemon wedges, and serve immediately. Salmoriglio Sauce (see recipe, page 194) can be served with the swordfish steaks instead of the lemon.

Broccoletti alla Siciliana
Broccoli Sicilian Style

1¾ lb/1¾ lb/800 g young broccoli (Cape
    broccoli or Calabrese broccoli)
6 anchovy fillets
2 oz/2 oz/50 g mature, strong
    Caciocavallo cheese
1 medium onion
2 Tbsp/2 oz/50 g black olives
olive oil
salt
¾ c/7 fl oz/2 dl red wine
8–10 slices of coarse white bread

Trim any hard skin from the stalks and strip off any limp leaves; divide into three bunches. Chop the anchovies and cut the cheese into thin slices. Slice the onion into fine rings and pit (stone) and chop the olives. Pour 2–3 tablespoons of oil into a fireproof earthenware dish or heavy lidded pan and scatter some of the onion and chopped anchovies over the bottom of the dish; cover with a layer of broccoli spears, using ⅓ of the total quantity; follow with a layer of cheese slices, another sprinkling of onion slices, a little salt, and some chopped anchovies. Sprinkle a little olive oil over the ingredients and continue to arrange in layers until they have all been used up. Drizzle a little oil over the top layer and pour in the red wine. Cover tightly and cook very slowly over a very low heat for 1 to 1½ hours without stirring or lifting the lid at all; simply shake the dish from time to time to prevent the contents from sticking. When the dish is cooked, the wine will have been absorbed and the vegetables will be tender and very tasty. Arrange in the center of a heated serving platter and surround by thick slices of hot toasted bread. Young, fresh turnip tops can also be cooked in this way.

Melanzane "a Quaglie"
Eggplant (Aubergine) "Tassels"

4–8 small, long eggplants (aubergines)
salt
olive oil

Small, long eggplants (aubergines) are the ideal for this dish. If the skin of the eggplants (aubergines) is at all tough, peel but leave about 1 inch (2½ cm) unpeeled around the stalk. Working from the broad end of the eggplant (aubergine) towards the stalk, cut ¼-inch (½ cm) strips, stopping 1 inch (2½ cm) from the end. Then turn the eggplant (aubergine) 90° (i.e. on its side) and still working from the broad to the narrow end cut lengthwise through the original slices. The result should be a number of strips ¼ inch (½ cm) square joined at the stalk end, rather like a tassle. Sprinkle with a generous amount of salt, spreading the strips apart so that the salt will penetrate the entire eggplant (aubergine). Place in a colander and drain for an hour, with a weighted plate on top so that the bitter juices drain away, then rinse and pat completely dry with paper towels.

Deep fry the eggplants (aubergines) in very hot, but not smoking, oil (in two batches if necessary) until they are crisp and golden. Drain on paper towels,

sprinkle with a little salt, and arrange on a hot serving platter. Eat while still very hot and crisp.

Carote al Marsala
Carrots with Marsala Wine

¾–1 lb/¾–1 lb/400 g young, tender carrots
4 Tbsp/2 oz/50 g butter
2 Tbsp/1 fl oz/3 cl dry Marsala wine
salt
freshly ground pepper

Wash and scrape the carrots and slice them finely. Melt the butter in a pan and, when it starts to foam, add the carrots and fry over a fairly high heat for a few minutes. Pour in the Marsala, add a pinch of salt, cover and cook over a low heat until the carrots have absorbed all the butter and wine and are tender. Grind a little fresh pepper over the carrots before serving.

The carrots must be sliced very thinly and very evenly. If possible, use a food processor or vegetable slicer.

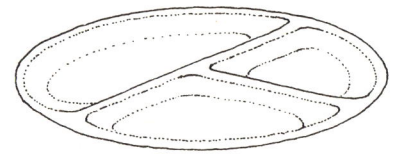

Salsa Sammurigghiu ("Salmoriglio")
Salmoriglio Sauce

½ c/4 fl oz/150 ml best quality olive oil
juice of 1 lemon
1 small bunch parsley
salt
oregano

This sauce is excellent with a variety of roasted and broiled (grilled) meats and is used a great deal in Sicilian cooking

Pour the oil into a bowl and beat energetically with a wire whisk.

Continue beating while adding two or three tablespoons hot water and then adding the lemon juice a very little at a time. Finally beat in the very finely chopped parsley, salt to taste, and the oregano and continue to whisk until the sauce becomes smooth and creamy.

Caponata
Sweet and Sour Eggplants (Aubergines)

1 Tbsp seedless white raisins (sultanas)
2 Tbsp/2 oz/50 g pitted (stoned) green olives
1¼ lb/1¼ lb/600 g eggplants (aubergines)
salt
oil
1 head of celery blanched
1 onion
4 ripe tomatoes
1 Tbsp pine nuts
1 Tbsp capers in brine
½ Tbsp granulated sugar
⅓ c/3½ fl oz/1 dl red wine vinegar
freshly ground pepper

Soak the raisins (sultanas) in warm water for 20 minutes, then drain. Chop the olives. Wash the eggplants (aubergines), dice without peeling, sprinkle with salt, and leave to drain for about 30 minutes in a plastic colander. When the bitter juices have drained away, rinse well in cold water and dry with paper towels. Deep fry in hot oil, turning frequently until the hot eggplants (aubergines) are golden brown and quite crisp. Drain on paper towels. Select the whitest, most tender stalks of the celery, cut them into strips 1¼–1½ inches (3–4 cm) long, wash and dry, and fry until golden brown and crisp.

Heat 3–4 tablespoons fresh oil in a skillet or frying pan and sauté the thinly sliced onion until it starts to color. Then add the skinned and seeded tomatoes, cut into strips. Cook for a few minutes, mixing gently but thoroughly. Then stir in the rest of the ingredients and season with a little salt and pepper. Simmer for 15 minutes over a low heat and then turn into a serving dish and leave to cool. This dish is usually eaten cold.

A Maltese variation is to add green peppers. These should also be blanched, and their seeds and membrane removed; they should then be cut into strips, deep fried, and added to the tomatoes with the other ingredients.

Arancini di Riso
Savory Fried Rice Balls

3 Tbsp/1½ oz/40 g butter
olive oil
½ small onion or 1 shallot
½ c/4 oz/100 g ground (minced) lean
    meat—a mixture of veal, pork and
    beef
scant ½ lb/7 oz/200 g freshly picked
    young peas or frozen petit pois
salt
freshly ground pepper
2 ripe tomatoes (put through a food mill
    or sieve)
1 c/7 oz/200 g Arborio rice
stock
grated Parmesan or Pecorino cheese
bread crumbs
2 eggs

Heat half the butter and 3 tablespoons (2 Tbsp/2 Tbsp) oil in a pan. When it starts to foam, add the very finely chopped onion and sauté until it starts to color. Add the meat and the peas, season with salt and pepper, and then stir in the tomatoes. Cover and simmer, stirring frequently, until the mixture has thickened considerably.

Boil the rice in a little lightly salted stock, adding more liquid as the rice absorbs the moisture. Draw aside from the heat while still al dente and stir in the remaining butter quickly, followed by a couple of tablespoonfuls of grated Parmesan cheese or, if preferred, a mixture of Pecorino and Parmesan cheese. Add an egg to bind the mixture together.

Shape the rice mixture into balls the size of small oranges, then tunnel into each ball with your index finger and fill it with a little of the meat and pea mixture. Then close up, smooth over, and roll it into an even ball. When all the rice balls have been filled, beat the remaining egg in a shallow dish, coat each ball with egg, and then roll it in the bread crumbs. Deep fry the rice balls in very hot oil (375°F/190°C) and then drain on paper towels. Serve very hot and accompany, if desired, with a little fresh tomato sauce: put the tomatoes through a food mill or sieve, simmer and reduce with a little butter and a pinch of salt.

Crispelle di Riso alla Benedettina
Sweet Fried Rice Balls

1½ c/12 fl oz/4 dl milk
salt
1 c/7 oz/200 g Arborio (or pudding) rice
finely grated rind of 1 small orange
¼ tsp baking powder
all-purpose (plain) flour
oil
1 Tbsp confectioners' (icing) sugar
a pinch of cinnamon

Pour the milk into a heavy saucepan, add a pinch of salt and dilute with 2 cups (18 fl oz/½ liter) water. Bring to a boil, add the rice, and cook slowly, stirring frequently. The rice should absorb all the liquid and be very soft and tender. Allow the rice to cool a little and then add the grated orange rind and the baking powder. Let the mixture stand for 30 minutes. Then, taking about a teaspoonful at a time, shape into little balls about the size of walnuts, roll in the flour, and deep fry in very hot oil until golden brown and crisp on the outside. Remove the rice balls from the oil with a slotted spoon and drain on paper towels. Transfer to a serving dish and dust with confectioners' (icing) sugar mixed with a very little powdered cinnamon. Serve at once.

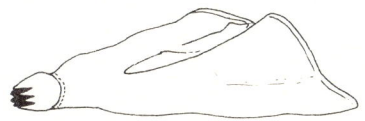

Pignolata Siciliana
"Snow on the Mountain" Sicilian Dessert

3½ c/14 oz/400 g cake flour (very fine
    flour)
2 c/14 oz/400 g superfine (caster) sugar
1 Tbsp/1 Tbsp/20 g brandy
10 eggs
1 Tbsp/scant 1 Tbsp/scant 1 Tbsp
    shortening (lard)
1 lemon
oil

Sift the flour into a mound on a pastry board, and make a well in the center. Reserving two egg whites, place 8 whole eggs and the 2 yolks in the well with the softened shortening (lard). Work slowly into the flour and then add the brandy, a few drops at a time and knead until the dough is smooth and homogeneous. Roll the dough into little sausages about the thickness of a little finger and cut into 1¼-inch (3 cm) lengths. Heat plenty of oil in a heavy pot or deep fryer and fry the cookies until they are golden brown. Remove them from the oil with a slotted spoon or the fryer basket and drain well on paper towels. Transfer them to a dish. Heat half the sugar in a heavy saucepan stirring constantly in the same direction until it caramelizes and then quickly pour over the fried cookies and shape into a mound with a wooden spoon—it is vital to work quickly as the caramel will set rapidly. Beat the two remaining egg whites until stiff but not dry. Heat the rest of the sugar in a saucepan until the sugar crystals have dissolved and just started to turn color. Remove from the heat, add the egg whites and the grated lemon rind and mix quickly and vigorously so that the mixture does not cook. Turn out on to the top of the caramel and cookie "mountain," so that the meringue looks like snow on the peak and upper slopes, and serve while still hot.

SARDINIA

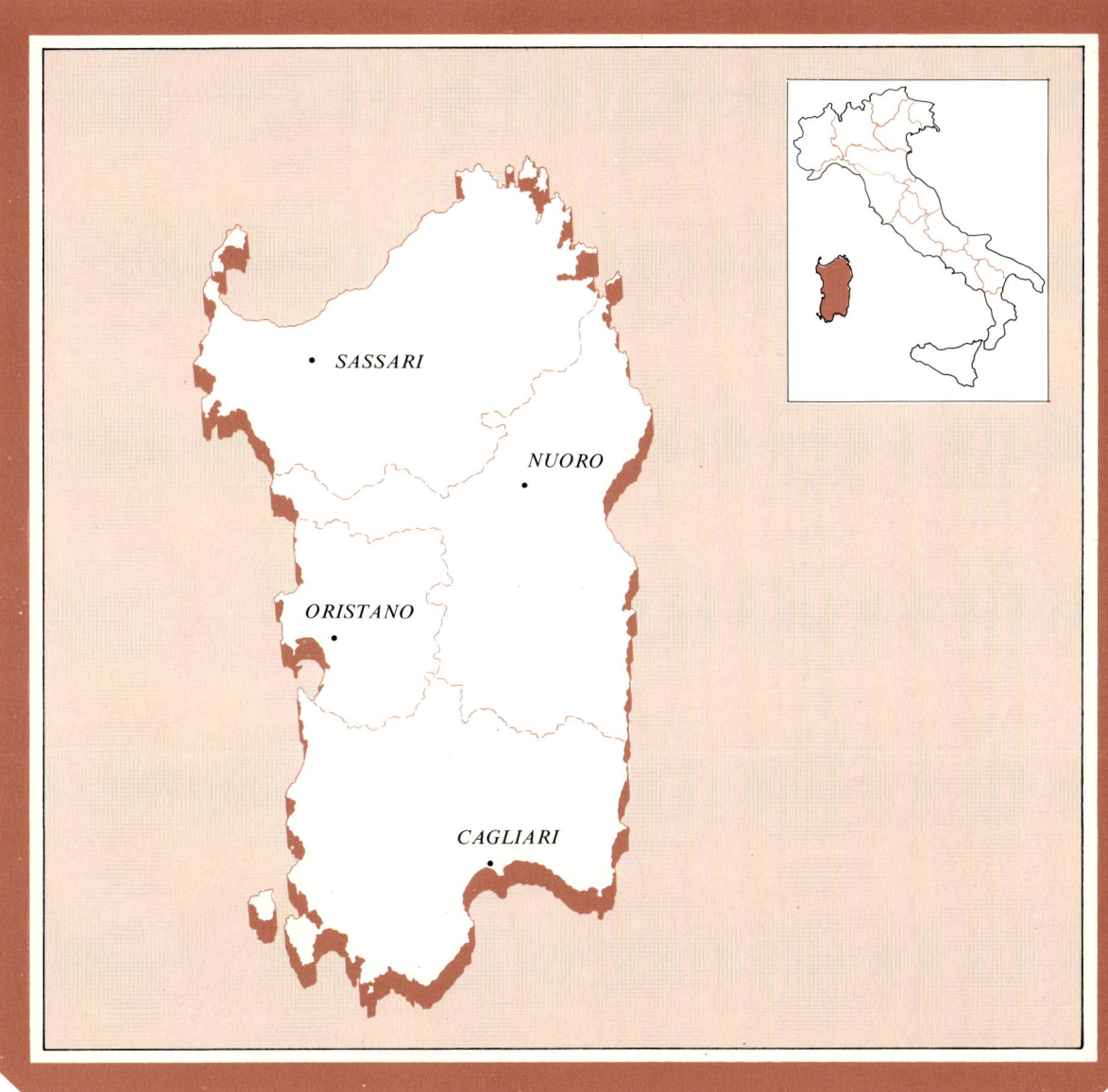

SASSARI

NUORO

ORISTANO

CAGLIARI

Malloreddus
Sardinian Gnocchi with Tomato Sauce

1½ c/10½ oz/300 g finely ground durum
    wheat flour
salt
saffron
a little all-purpose (plain) flour
1 onion
1 clove garlic
2–3 fresh basil leaves
6 Tbsp/4 Tbsp/4 Tbsp olive oil
1 lb/1 lb/500 g ripe (or canned)
    tomatoes (put through a food mill or
    sieve)
freshly ground pepper
1 tsp meat extract
¼ lb/¼ lb/100 g chopped sausage or
    ground (minced) meat (optional)

You should always prepare these delicious little gnocchi the day before they are needed.

Make the dough with the durum wheat flour, a pinch of salt, and a little lukewarm water with the saffron dissolved in it. Knead the dough very well until it is firm and smooth. Roll out small cylinders about the size of a pencil and cut them into approximately ½-inch (1 cm) lengths. Dredge each piece very lightly with flour to keep it from sticking and press it against the prongs of a fork, a strainer, or a concave grater (see page 55) to form a curled shell shape. Spread the gnocchi out on a cloth to dry.

Chop the onion, garlic, and basil and sauté them in the oil for a few minutes. (The flavor of the sauce can be enriched by adding chopped sausage meat or ground (minced) meat at this stage.) Add the tomatoes, season with salt and freshly ground pepper and add the meat extract diluted in a tablespoon of hot water. Simmer without the lid on until the sauce reduces and thickens.

Boil the malloreddus in a large pan of boiling salted water and remove them with a slotted spoon as they rise to the surface, place them in individual heated dishes and top them with a few spoonfuls of the tomato sauce. Serve the grated Pecorino cheese separately.

Frégula
Pasta for Soup

1½ c/10½ oz/300 g coarsely ground
    durum wheat flour
salt
saffron

Place the flour in a flat-bottomed bowl. Add ½–¾ cup (4–6 fl oz/1.2–2 dl) of cold, slightly salted water in which the saffron has been dissolved to the flour and gently work in with the finger tips in order to separate the grains and moisten them evenly. Rake the flour with the left hand and with the right roll it between the fingers to form small pellets or balls—the smallest should be about the size of peppercorns; some will be larger. Put these into a sieve and shake it to remove any loose grains of flour that have not been worked into pellets. Put the pellets on a clean cloth and let them dry out in the sun or in the oven at 225°F (110°C/mk ¼) until firm. They can then be stored successfully without becoming moldy or sticking to one another. Sort the pellets into larger and smaller sizes. The former can be used in substantial soups such as Minestrone and Cassóla (see the recipe below), and the latter in broths.

Culingiones
Sardinian Stuffed Pasta

½ lb/½ lb/225 g spinach
4 Tbsp/2 oz/50 g butter
salt
5 eggs
¼ c/2 oz/50 g mature Sardinian Pecorino
    cheese (grated)
nutmeg
freshly ground pepper
1–1½ Tbsp all-purpose (plain) flour
1½ c/10½ oz/300 g finely ground durum
    wheat flour
1 lb/1 lb/500 g ripe (or canned)
    tomatoes
1½ c/10½ oz/300 g young Sardinian
    Pecorino cheese

Pick over and wash the spinach thoroughly in several changes of water. Steam for 5 to 10 minutes in the water that remains on the leaves, drain, squeeze out as much liquid as possible, and then chop very finely. Sauté for a couple of minutes in a small pan with 1 tablespoon butter and a pinch of salt. Place the spinach in a bowl, adding 2 eggs, the crumbled young Pecorino cheese, a pinch of nutmeg, salt, pepper, and a tablespoon of flour, if needed, to bind the mixture together. Mix thoroughly with a wooden spoon to obtain a firm, smooth mixture.

Make the dough with the durum wheat flour, 3 eggs, and a pinch of salt and, following the directions on page 11 and the illustration opposite, stuff with the spinach and cheese mixture (culingiones are the Sardinian version of ravioli). Just before cooking the culingiones, make a sauce with the remaining butter, the tomatoes, and a pinch of salt. Simmer and reduce it over a moderate heat until it is fairly thick. Cook the culingiones in plenty of boiling salted water, drain, and transfer to a heated deep serving dish. Pour over the tomato sauce. Serve grated mature Pecorino cheese separately.

If a milder dish is preferred, serve grated Parmesan instead of Pecorino and dress the culingiones with melted butter instead of tomato sauce.

Cassóla
Fisherman's Stew

3 lb/3 lb/1.5 kg assorted fish (see
    instructions)
salt
⅓ c/3½ fl oz/1 dl oil
1 onion
1 clove garlic
1 bunch parsley
½ red chili pepper
4 ripe tomatoes
⅓ c/3½ fl oz/1 dl dry white wine
8 thick slices of bread

In Sardinia the fishermen themselves carefully choose an assortment of fish

Above: Preparing Culingiones (Sardinian Stuffed Pasta).

for Cassóla, since at least ten different species should be used for this stew. Suggested varieties are: squid, octopus, turbot, red mullet, fresh tuna, eel, sole, porgy (gilt-head bream) John Dory, skate, crab, crayfish or lobster.

Clean the fish well, gutting them, and removing the fins etc. Cut the larger fish into steaks or large pieces. Chop the crayfish or lobster tail into small pieces and cut the main part of the body in two. Reserve the heads and trimmings of the fish, and make a fumet with 2½ cups (1 pt/½ liter) lightly salted water. Heat the oil in a large cooking pot and sauté the finely chopped onion, garlic, and parsley until the onion and garlic start to color. Add a little crumbled chili pepper (more or less according to taste) and the skinned, seeded, and chopped tomatoes; simmer for a few minutes then add the wine and reduce. Add the tougher, firmer fish such as the squid and octopus (chopped), and then, after 15 minutes, the relatively firm fish (such as tuna, red mullet, etc.) followed by the more delicate fish (sole) and, last of all, the crayfish or lobster. Add a little fish fumet, cover, and continue to simmer over a low heat for 15 minutes after the last fish has been added. There should be plenty of broth to accompany the fish. Serve into individual dishes, with a thick slice of toasted bread placed in the bottom of each.

If desired, some of the larger pieces of fish can be removed from the soup and kept warm for use as a second course. As another variation, the broth of the soup can be strained and brought to a boil separately. Two to three tablespoons of Frégula (see the recipe above) are then added and cooked in the broth until tender.

Maccheroni col Ragù
Macaroni with Meat Sauce

½ lb/½ lb/225 g rib of beef
1 clove garlic
6 Tbsp/4 Tbsp/4 Tbsp olive oil
scant 1 lb/14 oz/400 g ripe (or canned) tomatoes
1 tsp meat extract
1 small bunch of fresh basil
salt
freshly ground pepper
¾ lb/¾ lb/350 g macaroni

Dice the meat. Crush the garlic clove with the blade of a knife and sauté gently in the oil. When it starts to turn brown, discard. Add the meat and brown on all sides, stirring frequently. Then mix in the blanched and skinned tomatoes (squeeze them gently to get rid of the seeds and excess juice). If canned tomatoes are used, put through a food mill or sieve. Simmer for a while and then add a cup of boiling water in which the meat extract has been dissolved. Add the chopped basil, season with salt and pepper, and simmer without the lid for a further 30 minutes or so, over a moderate heat.

Boil the macaroni in plenty of salted water until al dente, drain, and turn into a deep preheated serving dish. Top with the sauce and serve grated Parmesan or Pecorino cheese on the side.

Torta di Piselli
Cheese, Egg, and Pea Mold

1 very small onion or shallot
⅓ c/3½ fl oz/1 dl oil
1 lb/1 lb/500 g small tender young peas (fresh shelled or frozen)
4 eggs
salt
freshly ground pepper
¼ c/2 oz/50 g mild Pecorino cheese
1 c/3 oz/scant 100 g freshly grated bread crumbs
⅓ c/3½ fl oz/1 dl milk
2 Tbsp/1 oz/25 g butter

Cut the onion into thin rings and sauté in the oil. Add the peas just before the onion starts to color. Add a few spoonfuls of hot water every so often, so that the peas cook slowly without burning. Break the eggs into a bowl, add a pinch of salt, some freshly ground pepper, and the grated Pecorino cheese and mix well. Let stand for a little while. Place the fresh bread crumbs in a bowl or large cup and moisten with a little milk. When the bread crumbs have soaked up the milk, add them to the egg and cheese

mixture, stirring until a smooth, creamy blend is achieved. Remove the peas and onions with a slotted spoon and add to the egg mixture. Grease a baking dish with butter, fill with the mixture and bake in the oven at 275°F–300°F (140°C–150°C/mk 1–2) for 25 to 30 minutes.

Risotto alla Sarda

¼ lb/¼ lb/100 g lean pork
¼ lb/¼ lb/100 g lean veal
4 Tbsp/2 oz/50 g pork fat or
   ⅓ c/3½ fl oz/1 dl oil
½ onion
⅓ c/3½ fl oz/1 dl dry red wine
½ lb/½ lb/225 g ripe tomatoes
saffron
salt
freshly ground pepper
1 Tbsp butter
¾ lb/¾ lb/350 g Arborio rice
4½ c/1¾ pt/1 l homemade stock or
   1 bouillon cube and ½ teaspoon meat
   extract dissolved in the same quantity
   of hot water
¼ c/2 oz/50 g grated Pecorino cheese

Chop the meat finely (do not grind or mince it since this will not give the same consistency). Pound the pork fat (if used) and slice the onion into thin rings. Heat the fat or oil with the onion and sauté until light golden brown, then add the meat and brown it, stirring it frequently for a few minutes. Pour in the wine and reduce. Peel and seed the tomatoes, tear into large pieces and add to the meat together with the saffron, a little salt and a generous pinch of pepper. Cover the pan and reduce the sauce over a moderate heat until it thickens.

    Heat the butter in a separate pan and when it starts to foam, add the rice. Stir well with a wooden spoon and cook gently for 3 to 4 minutes, so that each grain is coated with butter, then add the meat sauce. Cook without the lid on,

Left: The traditional Sardinian method of spit-roasting a suckling pig, Porceddu. It is served on a bed of myrtle leaves.

adding a cupful of hot stock from time to time when needed, stirring very frequently, until the rice is very nearly done. Turn off the heat, add the grated cheese (if Pecorino has too sharp a taste, substitute Parmesan) and a little more pepper. Stir well once more and serve without delay.

Spezzatino d'Agnello
Lamb with Piquant Egg Sauce

1 onion
3 Tbsp/2 Tbsp/2 Tbsp oil
1¾ lb/1¼ lb/800 g leg of lamb, cut into
    small pieces
salt
3 Tbsp/2 Tbsp/2 Tbsp white wine
    vinegar + 3 egg yolks or
    juice of 1 lemon + 3 whole eggs

Fry the very finely sliced onion in the oil in a large pan and, when it begins to color, add the lamb, season with salt, and brown on both sides. Cook slowly for about 20 minutes. Remove from heat. Beat the egg yolks with the vinegar (or the whole eggs with the lemon juice) and pour onto the lamb, and mix well.

This lamb dish also makes a delicious filling for lasagne. Cook 10 ounces (10 oz/300 g) lasagne in plenty of boiling salted water for 10 to 15 minutes or until al dente. Drain, and arrange on a cloth. Cover the bottom of a well-buttered fireproof dish with a layer of lasagne, then a layer of lamb, and repeat until the ingredients are used up, ending with a layer of lasagne. Sprinkle with grated Pecorino cheese and dot with butter. Bake in the oven at 400°F (200°C/mk 6) for 20 to 25 minutes. Serve very hot.

Porceddu
Spit-Roasted Suckling Pig

About 10–12 servings
1 suckling pig weighing not more than
    10½–12¾ lb/10½–12¾ lb/5–6 kg
a large piece of pork fat
myrtle leaves (optional)

Spit-roasted suckling pig is a traditional Sardinian dish. Shepherds roast the pigs on makeshift spits made out of poles stuck in the ground about 2 feet (½ meter) from the fire, but they can also be roasted on automatic spits. Porceddu should always be cooked by the heat of a wood fire, preferably aromatic wood, which will impart a subtle flavor to the meat.

As shown in the illustration opposite, two short cross-pieces of wood are fastened near the tip of the wooden spit to facilitate turning the pole for even cooking. Another two pieces of wood are fixed below the pig to keep it from slipping down the pole as it roasts.

Clean the pig, scrape it and singe off any bristles; remove the entrails, dry the pig, and then split it lengthwise in half, mounting each half on a spit. Roast the rib side (the inside) first and baste by rubbing the piece of pork fat up and down the piglet. The fat will melt and cover the meat with a thin film. Turn when the first side is brown and continue to turn and baste from time to time. The piglet must be well done with the skin crackly and crisp. It will take 3 to 4 hours or longer. When it is done, cut into slices and arrange on a bed of myrtle leaves, if available. The whole pig, skin, ears and all, can be eaten, and, although it is probably best hot, it can also be eaten cold. (For automatic spits or barbecues the piglet may have to be quartered.)

Filetto alla Sarda
Fillet of Beef Sardinia Style

1½ lb/1½ lb/700 g fillet of beef
2 c/¾ pt/4 dl dry white wine
1 clove garlic
1 small bunch parsley
salt
freshly ground pepper
⅓ c/3½ fl oz/1 dl oil
4 anchovy fillets
juice of 1 lemon

Place the fillet of beef in an earthenware or cast-iron casserole with the wine, the crushed garlic clove, the small bunch of parsley (not chopped), and a generous pinch of salt and pepper if desired. Let it marinate for at least two hours, turning the meat frequently to allow it to absorb the marinade.

Once the meat has been marinated, add the oil, cover the casserole dish, and cook over a very low heat. Add a little hot water when necessary. The meat should be extremely tender when done. Take the meat out of the pot and set it aside to cool a little so that it can be thinly sliced. Arrange the slices overlapping one another slightly on a serving platter. Strain the cooking liquid and return it to the cooking pot, add the mashed anchovy fillets and the lemon juice, and heat for 1 minute, stirring thoroughly. Cover the slices of meat with this sauce and serve at once.

Involtini di Maiale al Forno
Roast Stuffed Pork Rolls

1¼ lb/1¼ lb/600 g loin of pork
1 clove garlic
1 small bunch parsley
4 Tbsp/2 oz/50 g pork fat
¼ lb/¼ lb/100 g pig's liver
1 c/4 oz/100 g bread crumbs from stale
    bread
¼ c/2 fl oz/60 ml milk
1 egg
salt
freshly ground pepper
4 thick slices of bread, browned in the
    oven
⅓ c/3½ fl oz/1 dl oil

Cut the pork into 8 slices of equal size and beat them with a mallet, the side of a cleaver or a skillet to an even thinness. Chop the garlic, parsley, pork fat and liver finely. Place them all in a bowl and add the bread crumbs which have been soaked in the milk and then squeezed to remove excess milk. Finally, mix in the egg and season with salt and pepper. Mix these ingredients well and spread them evenly on the flattened pork slices, stopping just short of the edges. Roll up the slices of meat and sew the ends with kitchen thread or string so that the filling does not escape during cooking. Thread on to 4 skewers (metal or wood) sandwiching a slice of bread between each pair of meat rolls. Place the 4 skewers in a roasting pan large enough to hold them all lying flat, sprinkle them with the oil, and cook in a preheated oven at about 300°F (150°C/mk 2) for 30 minutes. Remove the thread or string and serve at once.

Aragosta al Forno
Baked Lobster

4 1¼–1¾ lb/1¼–1¾ lb/600–800 g cooked
    lobsters
salt
1 bunch parsley
bread crumbs
oil
juice of 4 lemons

Break the claws off the lobsters, crack and remove meat. Split the lobsters in half lengthwise. Remove the flesh including the (greenish) liver and the coral (red roe), and reserve. Discard the stomach sac, which lies in the head and the intestinal vein. Place the lobster meat in a baking dish, add a little salt, sprinkle with chopped parsley and bread crumbs and drizzle with the oil. Bake in a preheated oven at about 350°F (180°C/mk 4) for 15 minutes. Remove from the oven, sprinkle with the lemon juice and return to the oven for a few minutes. Serve from the baking dish.

Trote alla Vernaccia
Trout in White Wine Sauce

4 trout of equal size
3 Tbsp/2 Tbsp/2 Tbsp oil
1 clove garlic
1 small bunch parsley
a sprig of fresh rosemary or dried
half a carrot
freshly ground pepper
salt

2½ c/1 pt/¾ l Vernaccia (Sardinian
    medium dry white wine)

Gut and trim the trout. Wash them well and pat them dry. Heat the oil in a large pan and sauté the very finely chopped garlic, parsley, rosemary leaves, and carrot. When they have softened a little lay the trout flat in the pan and season with pepper and salt. Turn the fish so that they brown evenly on both sides and then pour in enough wine to cover completely. Cover the pan and simmer over a low heat for about 20 minutes. By the time the fish is cooked, the wine should have reduced considerably. Serve.

Pollo "a Pienu"
Stuffed Chicken

1 chicken weighing about 3 lb/3 lb/1.5 kg
olive oil
1 c/4 oz/100 g bread crumbs from stale
    white bread
2 hard-boiled eggs
⅓ c/3½ fl oz/1 dl heavy (double) cream
1 Tbsp tomato paste
freshly ground pepper
salt

Clean the chicken thoroughly and reserve the heart and liver. Heat a little oil in a frying pan and brown the bread crumbs. Remove from the heat and add the finely chopped chicken liver and heart. Add the yolks of the hard-boiled eggs together with the cream and tomato paste and season with pepper and salt. Stir very thoroughly with a wooden spoon so that all the ingredients blend together into a smooth thick mixture. If it is too stiff, add a little more cream; if too thin, add more bread crumbs. Fill the chicken with this stuffing and sew up both openings. Place in a well-oiled, non-stick roasting pan and roast for about 1 hour in a preheated oven at 300°F–350°F (150°C–180°C/mk 2–4) turning the chicken if necessary. Test with a sharp knife or skewer. When the juices run completely clear the chicken is done.

Acciughe Ripiene alla Sarda
Stuffed Anchovies Sardinia Style

1¼ lb/1¼ lb/700 g large, very fresh
    anchovies
1 c/5 oz/150 g young, semi-hard cheese
canned anchovy fillets (one for each
    fresh anchovy used)
salt
all-purpose (plain) flour
2 eggs
bread crumbs
oil
2 lemons

Clean the fresh anchovies, cut off their heads, slit their bellies, and carefully remove their backbones without separating the fillets (see illustration opposite). Wash in running water and pat dry. Cut the cheese into thin strips and stuff each fish with an anchovy fillet and a strip of cheese. Close the fish, roll it in the flour, dip carefully in the beaten eggs and then coat with bread crumbs. Heat plenty of oil in a skillet until it is very hot (375°F/190°C). Fry the stuffed anchovies a few at a time until they are well browned on both sides. Drain on paper towels, sprinkle with salt, and serve on a heated platter garnished with lemon wedges.

Uova alla Sarda
Sardinian Eggs

4 eggs
salt
3 Tbsp/2 Tbsp/2 Tbsp oil
1 Tbsp vinegar
1 clove garlic
1 small bunch of parsley
1½ Tbsp bread crumbs

Hard boil the eggs for 7 minutes in salted water, place under cold running water for 2 minutes and then shell. Cut them in half lengthwise and place them in a skillet in a single layer. Sprinkle with a little salt and the oil and vinegar. Cook over a very low heat for a few minutes

until the vinegar has evaporated.
Remove the eggs with a spoon and place
them on a serving platter with the yolks
facing upward. Return the frying pan to
the heat, add the finely chopped garlic
and parsley and cook until soft, then stir
in the bread crumbs and cook until they
are golden brown. Spread the mixture
on the eggs and serve.

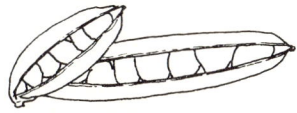

Polenta Condita
Layered Polenta

1¾ c/10½ oz/300 g coarse cornmeal
    (maize flour)
salt
½ *onion*
1 bunch parsley
a few leaves of fresh basil
⅓ c/3½ fl oz/1 dl oil
4 large ripe (or canned) tomatoes put
    through a food mill or sieve
½ lb/½ lb/225g small Sardinian sausages
    (thin, firm sausages rather like
    Spanish chorizo or kabanos)
¼ lb/¼ lb/100 g mature Sardinian
    Pecorino cheese
1 Tbsp butter

Prepare the polenta in advance, using
about 1½ quarts (2½ pt/1½ liters) of salted
water and the cornmeal (maize flour)
(see the instructions on page 16). When
the polenta is cooked, turn it out on a
polenta board or plate, allow it to cool,
then cut it into slices.

Sauté the chopped onion, parsley and
basil in the oil in a large pan until the
onion is translucent. Add the tomatoes
and the skinned Sardinian sausages cut
into thin rounds. Reduce over a
moderate heat. Butter a wide baking
dish, cover the bottom with a layer of
polenta slices, sprinkle with grated
cheese, and cover with a generous
amount of the sausage and tomato
sauce. Repeat this process until all the

*Right: Preparation of Acciughe Ripiene alla Sarda
(Stuffed Anchovies Sardinian Style).*

ingredients are used up, ending with a layer of polenta slices sprinkled with grated cheese. Dot the surface with small pieces of butter and place in a preheated oven at about 325°F (170°C/mk 3). When the top is crisp and golden brown, take from the oven and serve.

Torta di Albicocche
Apricot Cake

For the cake:
scant 1 cup/3½ oz/100 g cake flour (very fine flour)
⅔ c/scant 3 oz/80 g potato flour
6 eggs (separated)
1¼ c/7 oz/200 g confectioners' (icing) sugar
1 tsp baking powder
a few drops of vanilla extract (essence)
a little butter

Glazing and decoration:
1 lb/1 lb/500 g apricot jam
8–10 canned apricot halves in syrup
1 lb/1 lb/500 g apricot jelly
chopped almonds

Sift the cake (very fine) flour with the potato flour into a bowl. Beat the egg yolks with the sugar, the baking powder, and a few drops of vanilla extract (essence). In another bowl beat the egg whites until stiff. Add the egg yolk mixture to the whites and fold in gently. Pour into the bowl containing the flour, stirring continuously with a wooden spoon until you have a thick creamy

Above: Filling and glazing a Torta di Albicocche (Apricot Cake).

batter. Pour into a buttered cake pan and bake in a preheated oven at about 400°F (200°C/mk 6) for about 20 minutes or until a cake tester comes out clean.

When the cake has cooled, slice it very carefully horizontally into 2 or 3 layers. Spread a small quantity of jam evenly over one of the layers, place the next layer carefully on top of it. If the cake has been cut into 3 layers, spread the top of the second layer with jam and then cover it with the top layer. Spread this top layer with jam as well and arrange the well-drained apricots, rounded side up, on top of the jam (see illustration above). With a large pastry brush glaze the top and sides of the cake with the warmed apricot jelly. Press the chopped almonds onto the jelly on the sides of the cake.

Turta de Faiscedda
Bean Fritter

*1¼ c/14 oz/400 g shelled very tender fava
    (broad) beans
4 eggs
1 c/7 oz/200 g sugar
3 Tbsp/2 Tbsp/2 Tbsp bread crumbs
⅓ c/3½ fl oz/1 dl oil*

Place the shelled beans in a mixing bowl, (remove the inner skins as well). Add the eggs, the sugar and the bread crumbs. Stir well so that the ingredients are thoroughly blended. Heat the oil in a heavy iron skillet. When it is very hot, pour in the mixture and fry briskly on both sides.

Pardoline Dolci
Cheese Tartlets

*1 lb/1 lb/500 g fresh ricotta cheese
rind of 2 oranges
rind of 2 lemons
2 eggs
a pinch of saffron
6 Tbsp/4 Tbsp/4 Tbsp granulated sugar
¼ c/3 Tbsp/3 Tbsp finely ground durum
    wheat flour (or strong plain flour)
1¾ c/7 oz/200 g semolina
salt
4 Tbsp/2 oz/50 g shortening (lard)
a little all-purpose (plain) flour*

Push the ricotta cheese through a strainer or sieve); place it in a bowl; and add the grated rinds of the oranges and lemons, the two eggs, the saffron dissolved in a tablespoon of lukewarm water, 4 tablespoons (3 Tbsp/3 Tbsp) sugar, and the flour. Mix thoroughly until you have a smooth, blended mixture. Break off small pieces and roll them into little balls about the size of walnuts.

Mix a soft but fairly firm dough with the semolina, a pinch of salt, the softened (not melted) shortening (lard) and a little lukewarm water. Roll it out into a thin sheet and cut into circles about 4 inches (10 cm) in diameter with a pastry cutter. Place a little cheese ball in the center of each pastry circle, damp the edges of the circle with a finger dipped in water and enclose the ball in the circle to form a tartlet, pinching the edges together to form five evenly-spaced pleats or points. Dredge the cookie (baking) sheet with plenty of flour, space the pardoline out evenly, and bake in a preheated oven at 325°F–350°F (170°C–180°C/mk 3–4) for 30 minutes. When the pastries are golden brown, remove them from the oven. Sprinkle the tops at once with a little water and dust with the remaining sugar. Allow them to cool before serving.

Torta alle Mandorle
Almond Cake

*4 eggs (separated)
¾ c/5 oz/150 g granulated sugar
½ c/2 oz/50 g cake flour (very fine flour)
1 c/4 oz/100 g almonds
1 tsp baking powder
rind of 1 lemon
a few drops of vanilla extract (essence)
1 Tbsp butter
confectioners' (icing) sugar*

Beat the egg yolks with the sugar until the mixture is thick and creamy. Add the sifted flour, the peeled and finely chopped almonds, the baking powder, grated lemon rind, and vanilla extract (essence). Beat the egg whites in a separate bowl until stiff but not dry, then fold into the cake batter gently with a metal spoon.

Butter a cake pan, dredge lightly with a little flour and pour in the cake batter. Bake in a preheated oven (325°F–350°F/170°C–180°C/mk 3–4) for about 1 hour or until a cake tester comes out clean. When the cake is done, remove it from the oven and allow it to cool in the pan. Turn the cake out onto a serving plate and dust the top with confectioners' (icing) sugar.

Beef

The most concentrated sources of proteins, containing the vital amino acids that man must have in his diet, are provided by fish, poultry, game, eggs, dairy products, and meat. Beef has come to symbolize protein-rich food, and its rate of consumption is often used as one of the indices in determining the standard of living and prosperity of a country—along with the number of cars and television sets per capita.

Italy has, historically, been a relatively poor country, and it is only in the recent past that nearly all sections of society have been able to afford to eat beef several times a week. In fact, the Italians have now overtaken many of the other developed nations in the quantity of beef consumed per capita, particularly as regards the choicer cuts of prime beef and veal. This has brought about an absurd, and wasteful, state of affairs. Italy now has to import quantities of those cuts of beef that are most in demand; and young, immature animals are being slaughtered. If allowed to grow and fatten, they would produce far more meat per carcass (the best beef comes from young steers 4 to 5 years old). The "better" cuts of beef have no higher nutritional value than the less-sought-after parts of the animal, and, in fact, veal has a lower protein content than beef.

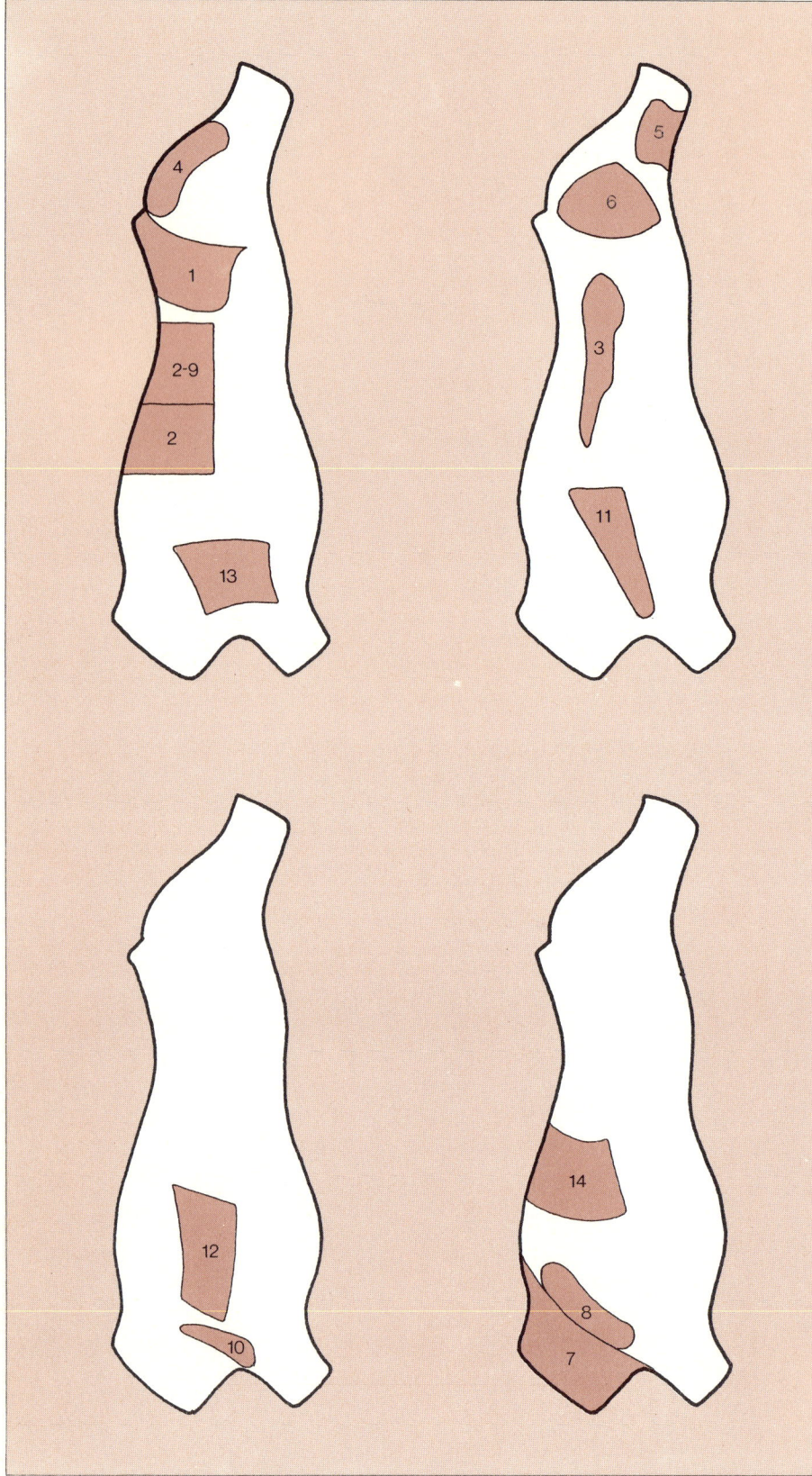

The illustrations on this page and opposite show the best-known Italian cuts of beef and the parts of the animal from which they come. Overleaf is a chart giving the nearest American and British equivalents and the type of cooking suitable to the cut of meat.

1 *scamone*
2 *lombata*
3 *filetto*
4 *girello*
5 *geretto*
6 *fesa interna*
7 *collo*
8 *girello di spalla*
9 *fiorentina*
10 *muscolo di spalla*
11 *copertina*
12 *taglio reale*
13 *fiocco*
14 *braciola*

Steaks, fillet steaks and escalopes are, more often than not, simply grilled or fried and eaten with a little salt. Much of their attraction lies in the fact that they are quick to prepare and involve little or no effort. This time saving, however, means a great deal less flavor. Eating habits show an increasing, depressing sameness—an unattractive facet of industrial society. Other cuts of beef often have a far more interesting taste, especially since meat is seldom aged for as long as it should be (from 2 to 6 weeks).

Yet there does seem to be some reversal to this trend. There is growing concern in the United States and elsewhere about the health hazards of eating too much red meat. Links between blood-cholesterol levels and heart disease, strokes, and other arterial diseases have made people more conscious of the amounts of high-cholesterol foods they eat. The suspicion that saturated-fat intake may be connected to other serious diseases has also made many people limit the amount of red meat they consume.

Throwing a steak on the grill or popping a roast in the oven may be a convenience and the number of times a week such meals appear on the table may be a status symbol, but they may not after all be the healthy meals we once assumed they were.

From a culinary point of view, this may lead to more adventurous eating with more emphasis being placed on a wider variety of foods: fish, grains, and vegetables, as well as combination dishes in which meat is only one ingredient. Ironically, many of the traditional regional dishes described in this book were developed by people who were too poor to have much meat in their diets. Where meat was available, it was usually used as a flavoring or served in small portions as one course among several at a meal. Yet these may be the very sort of foods that are best for our health. People who can well afford meat at every meal may be choosing pastas with interesting sauces, fish dishes, and stews and casseroles. It is to be hoped that they will also rediscover the tasty delights of a more diversified diet.

In this book, recipes are given that go a long way toward proving that the old ways were often the best where cooking is concerned, especially when the benefits of modern utensils and ovens can be employed to take much of the tedium out of the more repetitive processes and ensure even temperatures. One has only to try these traditional dishes to rediscover the pleasures of the table.

Continental methods of grading and butchering meats differ from American and British methods. Continental butchers usually cut their meats according to the natural muscle separations, whereas American meats, and British to a certain extent, are cut across the grain. Every effort has been made in this book to recommend the closest equivalent—or a suitable alternative—to the Italian cut that would be used for a particular recipe. For many of these recipes, which make very good use of the less-prized cuts of meat, it would be positively wrong to substitute a better cut or quality of meat. Such methods as braising or stewing will tenderize cuts with more connective tissue, which are the cuts that have the stronger flavor; and this more pronounced taste will withstand slow simmering and complement added herbs, vegetables, wine, and so forth. An expensive cut of prime beef will be disappointingly dry and lacking in flavor if simmered for hours in a stew.

The chart below shows the nearest American equivalents for Italian cuts of beef (and in brackets the closest British cut) and gives some indication of the uses to which they are best suited.

scamone	sirloin (rump)	Very good for roasts and broiled (grilled) steaks with or without a sauce. Sliced thin, it can be rolled around a filling.
lombata	rib merging into short loin (fore rib merging into sirloin)	This is the cut which provides Bistecca alla Fiorentina (T-bone steak). Boned, this cut makes excellent roasts.
filetto	tenderloin or fillet	This is the tastiest, most tender cut of beef. It can be prepared in a wide variety of ways from the simplest to the most elaborate. Fillet steaks include filet mignon and chateaubriand.
girello	rump and top round (topside and silverside)	Outstanding for stews and pot roasts, the meat from this section of the animal can also be cut into steaks in America.

geretto	hind shank (leg of beef)	Since this cut comes from the muscular part of the thigh, it needs long, slow stewing or braising.
fesa interna	rump merging into bottom round and tip steak or roast (topside and silverside)	This cut comes from the inside of the animal under the hip bone. In America, it is very popular for steaks, cutlets, and roasts.
collo	neck	Neck is ideal in stews, casseroles, and one-pot meals. Ground (minced), it can be used for stuffings, meatballs, or meat loaf.
girello di spalla	shoulder, arm steak or arm pot roast (clod merging into top rib)	This is a less-expensive cut than girello but has much the same qualities. It can be used for steaks or escalopes and is also excellent in braised dishes.
fiorentina	porterhouse steak	A very popular cut that can best be described as lombata with bone connected to the opposite fillet.
muscolo di spalla	rolled shoulder, arm steak or arm pot roast and brisket (shoulder)	This cut is ideal for pot roasting, braising and boiling.
copertina	chuck and shoulder (shoulder and rib)	An outstanding cut for pot roasts (beef braised in Barolo wine) and for casseroles. Cut thin, it can be used for pan-broiled (dry fried) steaks. It can also be ground (minced).
taglio reale	shoulder or English cut and short ribs (shoulder and rib)	This meat should be used for stews and braised dishes.
fiocco	rib steak or rolled shoulder (brisket and rib)	Composed of muscle and a good deal of fat meat, this cut should be used in stews and for boiled beef. It makes excellent stock.
braciola	rib	Braciola makes good pot roasts and stews. Steaks can be broiled (grilled) or pan-broiled (dry-fried).

Italian Cured Meats and Sausages

Two different types of meat product come under the Italian heading of salume. *Both are preserved partly or wholly by salting but cured meats involve the treatment of a whole joint or portion of meat, such as ham, which can be brined or dry-cured and may then be smoked to keep it in an edible condition for a considerable length of time, with or without refrigeration. Pork is the meat which best lends itself to salting and smoking and is therefore the most commonly chosen for this purpose. Such cuts as pancetta (belly of pork) (though in cooking fat bacon is a better substitute) or spalla (shoulder), positively improve with this treatment, while capocollo (collared head) and culatello (meat from the rump) make delicious cooked meats. The exquisite, painstakingly aged dry-cured prosciutto (ham), is ready to eat with no further preparation or cooking. Then there are the myriad sausages and salamis, encased in natural casings made from gut or intestine* (budelli) *or synthetic casings to keep them moist and help preserve the sausage meat. These products are made from pork or a mixture of meats with spices and fat, some coarsely cut, others fine in texture. Italian law sets standards and states that the types of meat used in these products shall be clearly displayed; so a seal must be affixed to the string tying the sausage. On one side is stamped the name of the region where the product originated and the manufacturer's name. On the other side letters indicate what meat is contained in the sausage: S stands for* carne suina *(pork); B for carne bovina (beef); O for carne ovina (mutton or lamb) and E for carne equina (horsemeat). Thus SB would mean a mixture of pork and beef. In this section a few examples of a wide and varied production have been selected and described in some detail.*

Bresaola

In the Canton of Grison in the Swiss Alps and in the Valtellina district in Italy, beef is cured by salting and air drying. The high altitude and the cold dry air lend themselves to preserving meats which would quickly deteriorate in other regions. The fillet or loin is usually cured, since the meat must be very lean; and any fat or connective tissue (where putrefaction tends to set in first) is carefully cut away. Bresaola is cut in very thin, almost wafer-like slices and eaten as an antipasto or appetizer with a dressing of olive oil, lemon, and pepper. The dried beef is usually ma-chine cut to ensure even slices but care must be taken not to cut it too far in advance or expose it to the air for any length of time before serving, since it tends to discolor and turn dark fairly rapidly after being sliced.

The name bresaola has been related by some etymologists to the verb *brasare*—to cook slowly, since in the early stages of curing the meat used sometimes to be lightly smoked and warmed through over a wood fire before being hung up to dry.

Salame di Milano

This has long been one of the most widely-produced sausages in the Po Valley. It is now manufactured on an industrial scale but has retained its basic characteristics. It is a rather large sausage made from finely ground (minced) pork (or sometimes a mixture of pork and beef), taken from the ham or leg, the neck, and the shoulder. The fat content is low in relation to the lean meat used, and the sausage meat is subjected to several processings which result in a thorough blending of the fat and lean meat into a smooth-grained, even-textured sausage.

Salame di Milano is aged for 3 to 4 months before it is ready to eat. It is widely available abroad.

Salame Varzi

Now that Salame Varzi is commercially produced, it has changed considerably from the farmhouse product of the village of that name. It is made from 70 percent lean pork and 30 percent pancetta or fat bacon. Sometimes a little garlic, pounded and mixed with white wine, is added. The ingredients go through a lengthy series of processes to achieve an evenly blended sausage. Varzi sausage usually measures about 12 inches (30 cm) in length and needs to mature for 2 to 3 months.

Speck

This is a specialty of Alto Adige. The main cuts of pork used to make it are the belly and leg. If the belly is used the result is like a smoked pancetta, and if the rear quarter or ham is used, the result is like a leaner smoked bacon. The pork is first soaked in brine with spices and seasonings, and the part which is not covered by rind is impregnated by the solution which flavors and preserves it. After a few weeks the speck is hung in a smoking room where extremely strict traditional methods are observed: the resinous and aromatic smoke from a large fire of a special variety of spruce tree, pine logs, and juniper wood, puts the final touch to the preservation of the meat.

The speck is then matured in a very dry, airy atmosphere, away from the light if possible. Sometimes a white mold forms on the outside of the meat, but if this is just a surface mold, it can be brushed off and does not alter the quality of the meat. Speck is sliced thinly, like prosciutto. The leaner parts are eaten as a first course and the fatter cuts are used in the preparation of soups and meat dishes, to which the speck imparts a delicious, subtle smokey flavor.

Pancetta Arrotolata or Veneta

Pancetta Arrotolata (rolled pancetta) can be prepared one of two ways. It can be stretched out flat and salted, in which case the result is quite moist, streaked with bands of fat and lean. This type of pancetta is used to lard roasting meats. It is wrapped around the meat to protect it from drying out. It is also frequently added to meat and other dishes for flavor. If the pancetta is leaner, with a high proportion of lean meat to fat, it is rolled up, seasoned with spices, and wrapped in a thin casing of gut. After ageing for a few months the pancetta is sliced and may be used in sandwiches. It can be said to be the poor relation of prosciutto; but, once aged, it has a very pleasing, delicate flavor, and the quality improves greatly if it is expertly matured.

Coppa

This is a very popular cured meat, and there are almost as many different ways of eating coppa as there are devotees. The meat which comes from the neck and shoulder (hand) or loin of the pig, is salted and then matured for a short period. Various places lay claim to producing the best coppa, one of the most famous being Carpaneto in Piacentino. Given the right conditions, coppa will keep very well, but, since it is lean, it tends to lose its moisture and harden if kept in a hot, dry atmosphere. Coppa which has started to dry out can in most cases be rescued by wrapping it in a linen cloth soaked in dry white wine and allowing the wine gradually to penetrate the coppa and moisten it. This will also alleviate the excessive saltiness which the meat acquires when it has dried out. When coppa is of the best quality, it is one of the finest cured meats available, and some connoisseurs even prefer it to Prosciutto di Parma.

Culatello is prepared in the same way as coppa but it is taken from the rump of the pig, and is a specialty of the province of Parma. Secret formulae and well-guarded traditions govern the preparation of this lean, ham-like cured meat, which should be moist with a very good aroma and flavor.

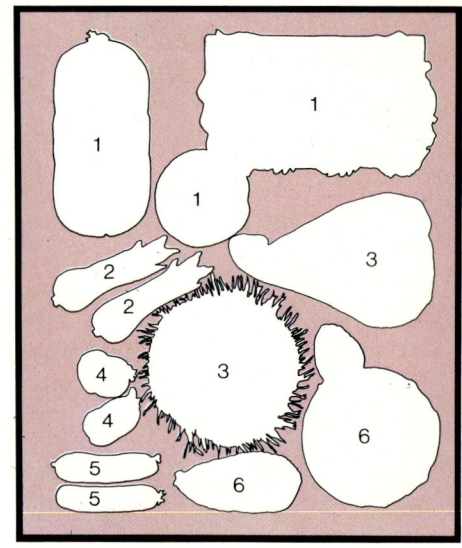

1 *Mortadella di Bologna*
2 *Zampone*
3 *Prosciutto di Parma*
4 *Salama da Sugo*
5 *Cotechino*
6 *Coppa*

Sopressa Veneta

Sopressa is a kind of pressed loaf of cooked meats, about $\frac{3}{4}$ of which are taken from the leg, neck and shoulder (hand) of the pig and the remainder from the belly. The meat is rather coarsely chopped but is evenly blended as to fat and lean by lengthy mixing. It is encased in an outer skin of intestine or sometimes a synthetic substitute. Farmhouse sopressa sausages used to be enclosed in lengths of the large intestine. Before the sopressa is aged it is pressed to expel any remaining air pockets, and it is from this operation that it got its name. Pressing is particularly necessary for sopressa because of its large diameter. It makes the sausage firmer and easier to cut and adds to its keeping qualities. Peasants often used to add a glass or two of grappa (a white spirit or rough brandy made from the skins and stalks of grapes) to the sausage mixture. This held up the ageing and hardening of the meat inside its casing, giving

sopressa its characteristic softness. Sopressa is eaten as an antipasto, as a snack, or in sandwiches and can be broiled (grilled).

Lugànega

The name lugànega which is still used today in the Marca Trevigiana to mean sausage in general, derives from the Latin word for sausage *lucanica*, so named because in Roman times the best ones were made in Lucania.

Cuts from the neck and cheek are used for these sausages. They are encased in lengths of the small intestine, either in one long thin length *salsiccia a metro* or in short links. The flavor of this sausage will vary according to the amount and type of spices used. However, generally speaking, modern taste prefers a milder sausage than that produced 50 or more years ago when more spices were used, tending to prevent the full flavor of the meat being brought out.

Prosciutto di San Daniele

San Daniele prosciutto should be cut from the bone shortly before it is eaten, and good Italian specialty shops will adhere to this principle. Each ham should weigh at least 19 pounds (9.5 kg). Only the best quality hams are selected for Prosciutto di San Daniele. The pigs are butchered and bled under rigorously hygienic conditions. The salting process is carried out in the period from October 1 to March 31, and the prosciutto must be allowed to mature for at least 9 months after salting. Only natural ageing processes are allowed, and the fresh hams must never be deep frozen before they are salted.

The ham has a characteristic guitar shape with the pig's foot or trotter still attached and stretched straight out. The shape of the joint is determined by a very precise and carefully executed method of butchering, which details which gluteal muscles must be severed and at what angle, how to sever the sinews and

connective tissue holding the joints and bones to the flesh, and which sections must be cut transversely (in general Italian butchers follow the European practice of cutting meats according to natural muscle separations, while American butchers, and British though to a lesser extent, cut meat across the grain).

The prosciutto is tested to see that the meat is tender. The fat must be pure white and in the correct proportion to the rose-colored lean meat. The ham should be mild and quite sweet (San Daniele is leaner but less sweet than Prosciutto di Parma); and the aroma must correspond to the length of time allowed for ageing.

Cotechino

Cotechino is a fresh pork sausage, made from lean meat from the head and neck of the pig mixed with chopped, salted pork rind. It should be cooked soon after buying and must be simmered gently for 2 to 3 hours. The sausage casing should be pierced with a needle or fine skewer in several places before cooking as the stuffing tends to swell and expand when heated and can burst the enclosing skin. Sometimes the strings fastening the sausage are undone, and it is wrapped in a piece of cheesecloth or muslin for cooking. A good-quality, correctly cooked cotechino will be moist with a slightly gelatinous consistency. It is usually served with lentils, boiled beans, or creamed potatoes.

Mortadella di Bologna

The name *mortadella*, which Italians use to designate a variety of large, smooth sausages and especially Mortadella di Bologna, comes from the Latin *myrtatella*, the Roman designation for all sausages flavored with myrtle berries. This seasoning was superseded by peppercorns when they were introduced to Europe from the East.

The famous Bologna version of mortadella is made from the less highly

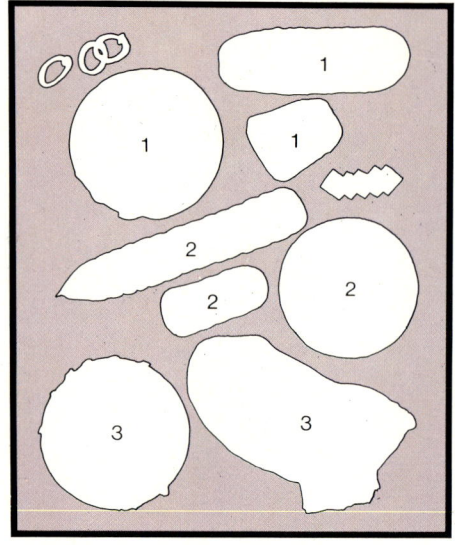

1 *Bresaola*
2 *Salame di Milano*
3 *Speck*

prized utility cuts of pork, together with pork fat, seasoning, and spices and is cooked in an oven at approximately 210°F (100°C). When made with pure pork only, the Mortadella bears the indication "P.S." If made from a mixture of beef and pork, it will be marked "S.B." Both of these varieties are graded according to quality: "Extra," "Super," and "Normale." These quality standards simply indicate the proportion of lean to fat meat. Mortadella is often sliced very thinly but its flavor comes out far more fully if it is cut in fairly thick slices and then diced (into $\frac{3}{4}$-inch (2 cm) squares and eaten as an antipasto or appetizer. Mortadella is also used in cooking.

Prosciutto di Parma

The production of this ham is closely controlled by the Consortium of Producers of Prosciutto di Parma and only the best quality hams from young

healthy pigs, reared on special farms in Emilia-Romagna, Lombardy, the Veneto, and Piedmont, and fed on very high-protein diets are used. Except for normal, light refrigeration, the meat must undergo no preserving process other than the classic curing and must never be deep frozen.

Prosciutto di Parma is sold either boned and sliced or still on the bone. In the latter case the ham is rather rounded and is sold without the pig's foot or trotter. The excess fat will have been trimmed off the underside of the ham and part of the skin and underlying fat will also have been removed, as will some of the tendons linking the femoral ball and socket joint. The hams should weigh about 16½–17½ pounds (8–9 kg) and never less than 14½ pounds (7 kg). The color of the ham when sliced should be between pink and red with a very light marbling of fat. The flavor is mild, delicately sweet, and not particularly salty—an unmistakable taste produced by the ageing of the ham. Prosciutto di Parma is never smoked. When sold boned the ham should be in pieces weighing not less than 11 pounds (5.5 kg). The shape will vary.

The age of a ham is calculated from the time it is salted. It varies according to its weight and the conditions under which the ham is matured, but it should not be less than 10 months for hams weighing 14½–18½ pounds (7–9 kg) and not less than one year for hams weighing over 18½ pounds (9 kg).

Zampone

In gastronomy, as elsewhere, necessity is the mother of invention, and many products have a curious history. The story, apocryphal or not, is told of a small town under siege in the Po valley where the inhabitants ran out of gut casings for sausage and turned to pork skin or rind and then, in desperation, to pig's forefeet (trotters), emptied of meat, leaving only the tips of the feet and hollow skin.

Modena is famous for these stuffed pig's feet (trotters), the filling being made of very finely chopped rind,

shoulder (hand), cheek, and hind shank (shin), pounded together until smooth and homogeneous. Salt, pepper and spices are added, and then the feet (trotters) are stuffed with this filling. Zampone takes longer to mature than cotechino and a good zampone which is properly aged is recognizable by its reddish or russet-brown skin. As with cotechino, it is vital to cook a zampone correctly. It must be soaked at least overnight in cold water and should then have its skin pricked in several places with a large needle or thin skewer. The zampone is then cooked in water which must come to a boil slowly and then simmer gently for about 3 hours. Zamponi are also available ready-cooked. They are called *zampone lampo* (lightning zampone), and they eliminate the inconvenience of cooking from scratch. They need only be heated just before serving. Zampone is usually eaten with creamed potatoes, lentils, boiled beans, or other hot vegetables.

Salama da Sugo

This sausage comes from Ferrara and is said to date from the times of the Este family, the princely rulers of Ferrara. The sausage is made from lean pork and pig's tongue, ground (minced) and mixed with spices and red wine and then encased in a pig's bladder or a wide piece of large intestine. It is oval or round in shape. The old-fashioned farmhouse process of maturing the sausage began with burying the sausage in the ashes of a wood fire, where it would absorb the aroma of the wood. It was then hung up in a cool, airy room to mature for 6 to 8 months. It is eaten hot with creamed potatoes.

This sausage is particularly moist and flavorsome, hence its name *da sugo* (juices).

Finocchiona

This large, broad pork-and-beef sausage is very much a Tuscan specialty. The proportion of fat to lean is quite high,

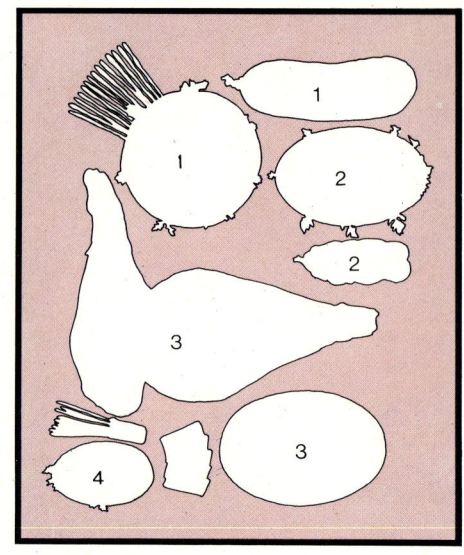

1 *Finocchiona*
2 *Capocollo Umbro*
3 *Prosciutto Toscano*
4 *Salamini or Salsicce di Cinghiale*

varying from 45 percent to 55 percent.

Finocchiona gets its name from the practice of adding a few fennel (*finocchio*) seeds to the sausage mixture. They permeate the meat with a distinctive and subtle flavor.

Prosciutto Toscano

Prosciutto Toscano has to mature in less favorable conditions than the Parma and San Daniele prosciuttos, but it is nonetheless very good and much appreciated. Since the atmospheric conditions in which it is aged are not optimum, it is more salted than other prosciuttos.

Prosciutto Toscano still comes mainly from farmhouse and small-scale producers and the majority are made from the meat of open range pigs, the best coming from the provinces of Casentino, Siena, and Grosseto. Hams with darker meat from cross-bred pigs (the

result of mating domestic sows with wild boar) are also processed.

Salamini or Salsicce di Cinghiale

These little sausages are made from wild boar's meat and are produced in the flat Maremma district of Tuscany, which is still very marshy and wild in places. Mainly lean meat is used, and the sausage has a strong, very distinctive flavor. These sausages dry out as they mature, and they are therefore often seen in Italian food stores in jars, preserved in oil. This not only keeps them moist, but also preserves the taste of the meat.

Capocollo Umbro

This Umbrian specialty consists of a roughly rectangular piece of meat cut from the loin of the pig, which is trimmed, seasoned with garlic and pepper, and soaked in brine for about 20 days. It is then washed with dry white wine and wrapped in greaseproof or waxed paper, left open at each end. After 8 to 10 days this wrapping is removed and the ham is completely wrapped in special unwaxed paper made from straw in order that the ham may breathe. It is then tied up with string, and hung in a cool atmosphere to mature for at least 3 months. The quality of the ham is excellent if lean pork is used and if the pig is suitably fed in the weeks leading up to slaughtering.

Salsiccia della Basilicata

In their works both Cicero and Martial made mention of *lucanica*, a sausage originating from Lower Italy, once the territory of the Lucani tribe. The modern region corresponding to ancient Lucania is southern Campania and central Basilicata.

Basilicata sausages are mainly made from lean pork, which is seasoned and

flavored with black pepper and small sweet or red chili peppers. These sausages can be eaten uncooked, broiled (grilled), or they can be lightly smoked and kept for a while.

Sopressata della Basilicata

Another well-known product from the same region is sopressata della Basilicata, made from 80 percent lean pork and 20 percent pork fat, seasoned with salt and black peppercorns and then encased in pig's gut. The sausage is pressed, i.e., weighted and squeezed to force out air bubbles and produce a closer, firmer texture. It is then matured for a brief period in rooms or sheds with a good flow of air. It is rarely smoked.

Even today these sausages are to be seen hanging by the hearth in farmhouses, where the flow of air and smoke help to mature and preserve the meat.

Capocollo Pugliese

Apulian capocollo, or cured meat, is prepared in much the same way as its Calabrian counterpart (see Capocollo Calabrese, below), but is usually smaller and subjected to more prolonged smoking. The smoke is produced by burning fresh oak boughs, and the meat is engulfed in cold smoke (away from the source of heat) during the early stages of maturing. The meat is aged for 5 to 6 months. To keep it from drying out in the very hot, dry summers of this area, the capocollo is often immersed in olive oil in earthenware pots or jars.

Capocollo Pugliese is often made much more spicy by the addition of powdered chili pepper to the flavorings and spices used to season the meat.

Capocollo Calabrese

Calabrian capocollo also comes from the loin of the pig. The pieces of meat are cut to more or less uniform dimensions and are soaked in brine. When taken from the brine they are thoroughly

1 Capocollo Pugliese (spicy)
2 Sopressata della Basilicata
3 Salsiccia della Basilicata
4 Capocollo Pugliese
5 Sopressata Calabrese
6 Capocollo Calabrese
7 Salsiccia Siciliana

rinsed with red wine, covered in very finely ground pepper and put in a natural casing. To ensure that they age evenly and successfully, they are tied between pieces of cane to keep them straight. They are then hung up so that the air and smoke can circulate freely around them to dry and mature them. The supporting canes are then removed and the capocollo is tied and hung up with string like other cured meats for storage.

Sopressata Calabrese

This sausage is made of lean pork mixed with fatter cuts and pancetta or pork fat in a proportion of 70 percent lean to 30 percent fat. The mixture is coarsely chopped with a knife and seasoned with salt, pepper or chili pepper, and a little red wine. Since a very rich red color is desirable, pig's blood or sweet paprika is added. After being encased in gut, the sausage is weighted and pressed to avoid the formation of air bubbles and elimi-

nate any already present. The sopressata is then lightly smoked above an open fire and can be eaten after 2 to 3 months' maturing in cool, well-ventilated storage rooms.

Salsiccia Siciliana

This Sicilian sausage is made of 80 percent pure, lean pork mixed with 20 percent pork fat. Its preparation differs little from that of small, fresh sausages of other regions. There is one variety, however, which is also flavored with parsley, fennel seeds, mature Caciocavallo cheese diced very small, and little pieces of tomato. This fresh sausage is most often broiled (grilled), and sometimes the sausage meat is removed from its casing and used as a delicious stuffing for poultry, meat, and vegetables.

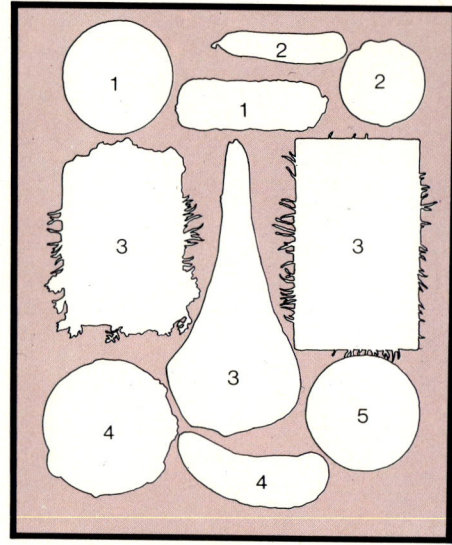

1 Pancetta Arrotolata or Veneto
2 Salame Varzi
3 Prosciutto di San Daniele
4 Sopressa Veneta
5 Lugànega (Treviso) sausages

Italian Cheeses

Although some Italian cheeses are world famous, a great many others which deserve to be more widely known are not exported and have remained local specialties. In some cases this is explained by the need for special ingredients which are not found elsewhere, and sometimes the method of preparation precludes mass production. Italian cheeses are conventionally classified according to their fat content. Full-fat cheeses are those which contain more than 45 percent butterfat; medium-fat cheeses have 25 percent to 45 percent butterfat; and those with less than 25 percent fat are known as low-fat cheeses. A cheese's texture and consistency is determined by the quality of its ingredients, the method of its preparation, and also by its age. Some cheeses are only at their best when matured for a considerable time. In Italian cuisine, cheese has for centuries been the basic dish of the poorest tables. Many cheeses have retained the status of everyday food, because their flavors go so well with bread and polenta.

The following is a list of some Italian cheeses with descriptions of their characteristics and contents.

Fontina

This cheese has become synonymous with the Aosta Valley region and is said to have originated from the Alpine region of Fontin. This attribution is disputed, however, since other localities also claim to be the birthplace of Fontina. In any case, Fontina has been well known since ancient times and its denomination is registered and protected.

Fontina is made with whole cow's milk, and there are two distinct types: one is made in the summer months when the cows are milked in the high Alpine pastures, the other when they are in their cow sheds for the winter. Fontina is a round wheel-shaped cheese, 18–22 inches (45– 55 cm) in diameter, with slightly bulging sides which are usually 3–4 inches (8–10 cm) high. A cheese can weigh from $17\frac{1}{2}$–40 pounds (8–18 kg) and the color of the rind varies from russet gold to dark brown. The color of the cheese inside varies from white to straw yellow, and it is rather like a rich, creamy Gruyère in texture with very few, small holes. Fontina has a delicate, buttery taste, which is more pronounced in the cheeses produced during the summer.

Fontina is a full-cream cheese which is dry-salted and aged from 90 to 100 days. Besides being a table cheese, it is also used in cooking and is in fact an important ingredient in a number of recipes (see for example Fonduta, page 20).

Toma

The name Toma usually refers to a type of hard cheese, which is produced throughout the Alpine and sub-Alpine regions of Piedmont and Lombardy. However, the name is not exclusive to this area. Cheeses which differ greatly from one another are produced in the Apennines and as far south as Sicily, where a cheese known as *tuma* is produced.

Besides the classic Toma there is a much smaller version, Tometta, which is also round and straight-sided, but while Toma can weigh up to $17\frac{1}{2}$–$19\frac{1}{2}$ pounds (8–9 kg), Tometta never exceeds $4\frac{1}{2}$ pounds (2 kg) in weight.

Another relative, Tomino is a soft, fresh creamy little cheese, cylindrical in shape, which usually weighs only about

7 ounces (200 g) and has a rather sharp taste.

Most of these cheeses are made from cow's milk mixed with goat's milk or ewe's milk. The pure white of the fresh cheese turns yellow as the cheese ripens and matures. Toma is mild tasting when eaten fresh and gets stronger tasting with age. The mature cheese is used in cooking to add flavor to polenta or as a grating cheese. Tometta can also be matured and its texture changes from the soft, creamy fresh cheese to a more pungent cheese with small holes. Tomino is only eaten fresh, often with a sauce or with tomatoes or small sweet peppers. This cheese is often preserved in herb-flavored oil.

Grana Padano

Grana Padano comes from the Lombardy plain, from the region north of the River Po. It is a medium-fat, hard cheese and, as its name suggests, granular in texture. It is made of partially skimmed milk from cows which are fed on fresh pasture or dried fodder, and the winter cheeses are not as good as those made from summer milk. Because of this variation in the quality of the milk, the cheese is considered by some to be unreliable.

Grana Padano is cylindrical in shape with slightly convex sides. It is 14–18 inches (35–45 cm) in diameter, 7–10 inches (18–25 cm) high, and weighs from $52\frac{1}{2}$–88 pounds (24–40 kg). It is light straw colored (yellower than Parmesan) with an aroma and flavor resembling Parmesan but somewhat sharper. The rind is $\frac{1}{8}$ to $\frac{1}{4}$ inch (4–8 mm) thick and the cheese is slow to mature, taking up to two years at temperatures varying between 50°–68°F (15°–22°C).

The main production zones are the provinces of Alessandria, Asti, Cuneo, Novara, Turin, Vercelli, Bergamo, Brescia, Como, Cremona, Mantua (left bank of the Po), Milan, Pavia, Sondrio, Varese, Padua, Rovigo, Treviso, Venice, Vicenza, Bologna (right bank of the River Reno), Ferrara, Forlì, Piacenza, and Ravenna.

The cheese is described, according to the season in which it was produced: *Vernengo* or *invernengo* is produced from December to March; *di testa* is produced from April to June; and *tardivo* or *terzolo* is produced from October to November. Not surprisingly *di testa*, made from the milk of cows pastured on late spring and early summer grass, is the best.

Gorgonzola

Gorgonzola is a famous and time-honored Italian blue-veined cheese. The mold *penicillium glaucum*, which is introduced early in cheesemaking and develops during the ripening of the cheese, gives it its characteristic greenish or blueish streaks.

Tradition has it that Gorgonzola was first produced in 879 A.D.; but even this venerable record is beaten by the French cheese Roquefort, which, according to legend, was given to the Emperor Charlemagne to eat on one of his long journeys by a pious hermit 8 years earlier.

Gorgonzola is made from whole cow's milk. The straight-sided cylindrical wheels are 6–8 inches (16–20 cm) high and 10–12 inches (25–30 cm) in diameter. Each wheel weighs about 15–33 pounds (7–13 kg). The cheese has a high fat content (about 50 percent). After the curd is formed, it is salted and pricked so that air can reach the inside of the cheese to speed up the development of the mold. The cheese is then matured for 5 to 6 months. A mature cheese has quite a pungent taste. Recently Gorgonzola production has allowed for varying degrees of milder and sharper cheeses — dependant largely on the fat content and the length of time the cheese is allowed to mature. If the cheese is not pricked to enable the mold to develop the resulting unveined cheese is called Panerone.

Robiola (Robbiole)

The name Robiola is said by some to come from the name of the place, Robbio in Lomellina; others maintain it

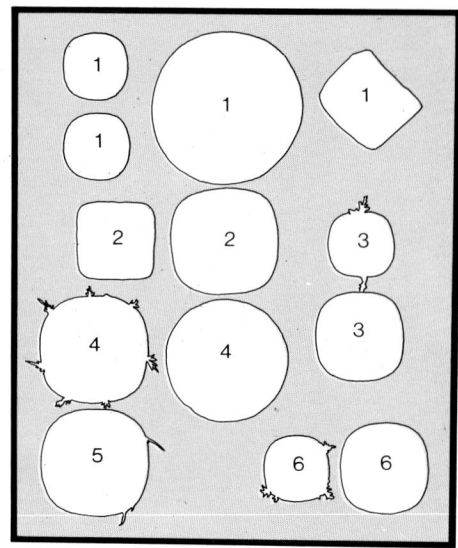

1 *Grana Padano*
2 *Taleggio*
3 *Crescenza (Stracchino)*
4 *Bitto*
5 *Mascarpone*
6 *Robiola*

derives from the Latin *rubeus* meaning red, and refers to a red covering in which the cheese was formerly encased.

Robiola is a small, soft, full-fat cow's milk cheese which is usually eaten fresh. Occasionally it is made from a mixture of cow's and ewe's or goat's milk. It can be ripened in 8 to 15 days, in which case it is classified, together with Crescenza, under the general heading of *Stracchini*. If, however, it is matured, Robiola acquires a sharper and more distinctive flavor. The Robiolas produced in the Valsassina, at Ballabio, Introbio, and Pasturo are all Stracchino-type cheeses. Very like Taleggio, but smaller, they are soft, smooth, and melting with a delicate flavor. Other highly prized Robiolas include Bec from the Langhe district which is made with milk taken from nanny goats around the time they mate (*becco*, in Piedmontese dialect, is the Italian word for billy goat). The cheeses produced in Roccaverano, Cevo, Bossolasco and Monferrato are also sought after. Some of these cheeses are pre-

served in oil with herbs, pepper, etc., in glass jars.

Crescenza

Some of the best examples of this medium-fat Lombard cheese come from the countryside around Milan. It is made with fresh, untreated whole milk; and, since it does not keep well, it is eaten fresh. The cheese is rindless and usually prepared in square form, about 6 inches (15 cm) square and 1½–2 inches (4–5 cm) high. Smaller cheeses are also made, varying from 7 ounces (200 g) to just over 1 pound (500 g) in weight.

The color is white to creamy, and the cheese is smooth in texture. If left in a warm atmosphere, it expands, almost as if it were rising like dough, and develops small holes in its body (its name is said to derive from this activity—*Crescenza* means "growth"). The fat content varies depending on the time of year when the cheese is made, falling in winter and rising in the summer. There are many smaller cheeses whose texture and taste resemble the soft, buttery, delicate Crescenza; they are known as *crescenzine*.

Crescenza is one of the *Stracchino* cheeses, a term denoting a wide variety of fresh rindless cheeses produced in the Lombardy plain, whose curd is not cooked during the cheesemaking process. The word *stracchino* derives from the dialect term *stracco* from the Italian *stanco* meaning "tired," because the best cheese was believed to come from the evening's milk (mixed with cream) from cows "tired" after long grazing in good pastures.

Modern methods of large-scale production of Crescenza come close to reproducing farmhouse quality despite the fact that traditions have been abandoned.

Bitto

A product of the Bitto valley in Valtellina, Bitto has an old established reputation, especially as a cheese used in famous local specialties, such as Pizzoccheri della Valtellina (see page 30) and Polenta Taragna (see page 36). Nowadays made from whole cow's milk, it used to be made from a mixture of cow's milk and goat's or ewe's milk.

The shape varies and the weight can be anything from 17½–22 pounds (8–10 kg) to weights greater than some Parmesan cheeses. Bitto ripens and matures slowly; about 6 months elapse before it is ready to eat. It is a rather fat, hard cheese with tiny holes. When it has aged for one or two years, it becomes sharper, firmer, and more aromatic, and crumbly like Parmesan when very mature. The color also changes over time.

Panerone

This cheese is typical of the Lombardy plain and in particular of the Lodi plain. A fat cheese made with whole cow's milk, it is cylindrical in shape with straight sides about 8 inches (20 cm) high and a diameter which varies from 10½–12 inches (26–30 cm). The body of the cheese has tiny evenly distributed holes and is a creamy white, sometimes shading into a pale straw yellow. It is, in fact, an unveined version of Gorgonzola. It is unsalted and is matured for no longer than two months. Its taste is very faintly and pleasingly bitter, and it has a fairly strong aroma.

Taleggio

Well known in Lombardy and, to a lesser extent, throughout Italy, Taleggio originally comes from the Alpine foothills near Bergamo.

It is made from whole cow's milk; is salted; has a smooth, soft, and creamy texture; and ripens for 40 to 50 days. The cheese is square and squat with straight sides. It weighs about 4¼ pounds (2 kg) and has a thin, soft crust or rind and a bland flavor with a faint tang which becomes stronger and almost sour with age. The body of the cheese has no holes in it to speak of and is

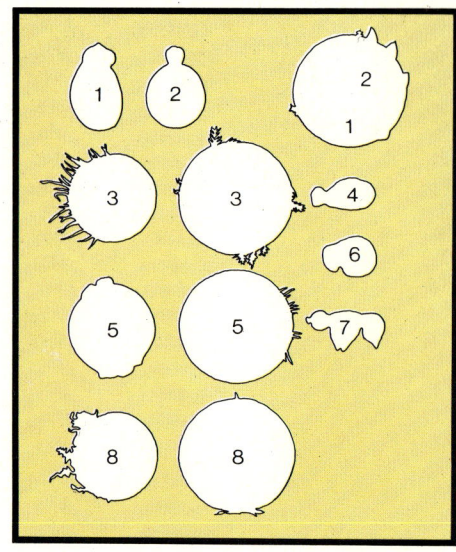

1 *Caciocavallo Pugliese*
2 *Caciocavallo della Basilicata*
3 *Provola*
4 *Scamorza Calabrese*
5 *Mozzarella*
6 *Scamorza Pugliese*
7 *Scamorza a Maialino (piglet-shaped)*
8 *Burrata*

whitish tending to pale straw in color.

Mascarpone

The name of this fresh, snow-white cream cheese is said to have originated when a Spanish high official in the seventeenth century (at the time parts of Italy were under Spanish rule) tasted the cheese and exclaimed "Màs que bueno!"—literally, "better than good!" or "delicious!"—whence Mascarpone. But it is also said to be a corruption of the Lombard dialect name for ricotta: *mascherpa* or *mascherpin*.

The Lodi plain was the original home of this double-cream cheese, but it is now so popular that it is made all over Italy.

The cream is made to coagulate by the addition of citric acid. Mascarpone has a very high butterfat content and is like very heavy, whipped cream in texture

and taste. It must be eaten soon after it is made, since it spoils quickly. For this reason, it is only produced during the autumn and winter months. Besides being eaten as a very soft or spreading cheese, Mascarpone is also mixed with chocolate, ground coffee or various liqueurs and brandy and used in cakes and desserts. It is also substituted for butter or cream in delicious delicately flavored pasta dishes. It may also be mixed with Gorgonzola or spread between layers of Provolone.

Fontal

Fontal belongs to a family of cheeses which includes Fontina and Montasio. It is produced from whole milk in the Alpine region of northern Italy.

The cheese is straw yellow, with some regularly spaced minute holes. It is wheel shaped, about 16 inches (40 cm) in diameter and has slightly convex sides approximately 4 inches (10 cm) high. Like Fontina, it is both a good table cheese and a good cooking cheese. It approaches Emmenthal in flavor and is therefore very versatile. It is particularly delicious in rice salad.

Morlacco

This cheese is said to originate from Morlacca in Yugoslavia from which it takes its name. Nowadays it is made throughout the area north of the province of Vicenza. At one time, Morlacco was known as "the poor man's cheese," because peasants relied on it as a staple food which was high in proteins, vitamins, and minerals and cheap to make or buy.

The cheese is made from partly skimmed cow's milk and is white and slightly salty, with a few very small holes. Its flavor becomes stronger as it matures, and it has a tendency to develop a blueish-green mold which gives it an unusual taste. The wheel-shaped cheese varies from 10–12 inches (25–30 cm) in diameter and has slightly bulging sides 4–6 inches (10–15 cm) high.

Asiago

Asiago is a semi-fat, hard cheese made from whole cow's milk, which is usually dry-salted or immersed in a weak brine and which is ready for eating as a table cheese after 4 or 5 months. When matured for over a year, it can be used as a grating cheese.

Asiago is cylindrical, 12–16 inches (30–40 cm) in diameter with slightly convex sides about 4 inches (10 cm) high. It usually weighs 22–30 pounds (10–14 kg). It is a pale straw color with a few fairly evenly distributed small and medium-sized holes. When eaten young, the cheese has a very delicate flavor, which grows quite sharp when the cheese is matured.

A type of Asiago produced on the Vezzena plateau is much stronger in taste and is usually matured for a year or even longer. It is a bright yellow color and has numerous holes regularly distributed throughout its body. The inhabitants of the Vezzena plateau usually eat this cheese with polenta.

Montasio

Typical of the cheeses made in the eastern Alpine region of Italy, Montasio is now widely produced in many other districts. The whole milk from which it is made comes from cows milked in the high Alpine pastures where they spend the summer. A winter cheese made from partly skimmed milk with a lower butterfat content also bears the name of Montasio, but it is always eaten young.

Montasio is wheel shaped, about 4 inches (10 cm) high and 14–16 inches (35–40 cm) in diameter and usually weighs less than 22 pounds (10 kg). This semi-fat cheese has a firm texture with quite a few smallish holes. It is salted by immersion in a weak brine solution. It can also be dry-salted. The taste is mild before the cheese has matured for any length of time but becomes stronger after it has aged for about a year. Because of its pungent taste, mature Montasio came to be called Pecorino even though it contains no ewe's milk

1 Asiago
2 Caciofiore Umbro
3 Montasio
4 Fontal

(*pecorino* means little sheep in Italian). The cheeses are subjected to rigorous quality control during the ageing process. Any which have too many holes or a faulty rind are discarded; only the best are left to mature.

The first people to make this cheese were the monks of Moggio abbey, whose cheese production has been traced back to late medieval times.

Formaggetta

This name covers a whole host of small fresh cheeses made in the Ligurian region of the Apennines. Sizes and shapes vary, but the cheeses are usually made from a mixture of goat's and cow's milk, although farmhouse production includes some cheeses made with all-goat's or all-cow's milk. These cheeses are nearly always eaten young; few are ever matured for keeping. They are more often preserved in oil which

heightens and increases their distinctive flavor.

When Formaggetta, especially goat's milk Formaggetta, is matured, it makes very good grating cheese which can be substituted for mature Pecorino cheese in Ligurian dishes, and others if desired. The cheeses which come from the Ligurian–Tuscan border are encased in a brownish rind and have a more pronounced flavor than their counterparts from the east.

Parmigiano Reggiano

One of Italy's oldest cheeses, Parmesan is said to have evolved from an Etruscan recipe, and is considered to be one of the world's finest cheeses both as a table cheese and as a grating cheese. The main areas of production include the provinces of Parma, Reggio Emilia, and Modena in their entirety, Mantua on the right bank of the River Po, and Bologna on the left bank of the River Reno.

Classic Parmesan is a hard cheese of medium butterfat content made from the milk of cows fed on fresh pastures. The yield of two successive milkings (evening and the following morning), after resting and partial skimming, is used for each batch. The production season begins on April 1 and ends on November 11. Within a few days of the curd being formed the cheese is salted in brine for 20 to 30 days. The method of maturing the cheese is entirely natural and lasts at least 2 years and usually longer. Parmesan has a very distinctive squat, cylindrical, barrel-like shape with slightly convex sides. It is 14–18 inches (35–45 cm) in diameter, 7–9$\frac{1}{2}$ inches (18–24 cm) high, and the minimum weight for an individual cheese is 52$\frac{1}{2}$ pounds (24 kg). The color is light straw yellow and the flavor and aroma of the cheese are pronounced but never sharp or pungent. The texture is minutely granulated and rather crumbly with tiny, barely visible holes. The rind is about $\frac{1}{4}$ inch (6 mm) thick and the origin of the cheese is certified by a special indelible stamping of "Parmigiano-Reggiano" all over the convex side of the cheese;

production and marketing are rigorously supervised by special inspectors under the auspices of a producers' consortium. When buying Parmesan, it is important to ensure that the rind is unbroken and the texture evenly granulated.

Pecorino Senese

This cheese from the province of Siena belongs to a large group of small ewe's milk cheeses or *caciotte di pecora*, but it has a distinctive aroma and flavor, which distinguishes it from other pecorino cheeses. Even when mature, it is fairly mild but has a faintly sour taste due to the type of pasture on which the sheep graze. The spring production is particularly good when the young grass is at its sweetest and most tender. Pecorino Senese is wheel shaped with slightly convex sides and weighs from 2–4$\frac{1}{4}$ pounds (1–2 kg). The province of Siena has, for centuries, been renowned for the quality and quantity of its production, particularly its matured cheeses.

Caciotta Toscana

The term *caciotta* is used to refer to a virtually boundless variety of cheeses made from cow's or ewe's milk or a mixture of both in the hills of Tuscany, Latium, the Marches, and Umbria. One might almost say that there are as many different types of *caciotta* as there are flocks grazing in the area, and the quality and character of the cheese depends on which farmhouse has produced it. Caciotta Toscana is probably one of the most widely known. It is made from cow's milk and can be eaten young or matured. The cheese is usually a smallish, flat, cylindrical shape with sides that are sometimes straight, sometimes slightly bulging. Among the many famous Tuscan *caciotte*, the best are those from San Gimignano, Pienza, Monte Amiata, the Maremma, and Casentino (those made in Casentino sometimes also contain ewe's milk).

1 *Pecorino Siciliano*
2 *Pecorino Sardo*
3 *Ragusano*

Marzolino

Formerly production of Marzolino—a ewe's milk cheese, which was much sought after throughout Tuscany and which even rates a mention or two in Italian literature—would get under way in the Val di Chiana in March. Nowadays, the cheese is becoming rarer, and production is declining.

Marzolino is roughly oval in shape, measuring 5 inches (12 cm) at its longest. The cheeses, which are to be eaten young have a whitish crust, while those to be aged are colored red. Sheep's blood used to be rubbed into the rind to give it color, but today, tomato is used. The texture of the cheese is firm with a few holes. When aged, Marzolino is white with a slight orangy cast and can be eaten as a table cheese or used as a grating cheese.

Caciofiore Umbro

In the past this cheese was produced on a large scale throughout Latium. Now it is confined to the Pian di Chiavano near Cascia. Made from the whey of cow's milk (*cacio* means "cheese" and *fior di latte* means "whey" in Italian), it is a soft cheese and is eaten fresh or when matured for only a short time. The taste is mild with a delicate aroma due to the type of pasture on which the cows graze. Cylindrical in shape, Caciofiore Umbro weighs just over 2 pounds (1 kg).

Ricotta Stagionata

Ricotta Stagionata (mature Ricotta), a salted hard cheese with a rind, is a specialty of certain regions of Sicily. These little cheeses are dried in the sun and make good grating cheese. In the Norcia district the local Ricotta Stagionata has a far higher fat content than usual and is widely used instead of Parmesan to dress simple pasta dishes. The flavor is delicate and milky and complements pasta extremely well. A similar cheese *Ricotta Schianta* is produced in Apulia in mainland Italy. It is a mature strong cheese, which requires longer processing than Ricotta Stagionata but which is also grated onto pasta dishes. Another method of preserving Ricotta is smoking which gives it a distinctive robust flavor.

Pecorino Romano

Pecorino Romano, a Roman ewe's milk cheese, is a hard, sharp, medium-fat cheese for which there is great demand both in Italy and abroad. Half the production is exported, mainly to the United States. Pecorino Romano is made from whole sheep's milk during a season lasting from March to June. During its preparation any residual whey is quickly drained from the curd as soon as it is put in the mold by a special process. The cheese is dry-salted over a period of about 90 days, washed at frequent intervals, and sometimes pierced so that the salt will penetrate more readily. Pecorino is ready to eat after 8 months. It is cylindrical in shape, 5½–8½ inches (14–22 cm) high, weighs from 17–44 pounds (8–20 kg), and is white or grayish white in color with a strong, sharp, salty taste. This type of Pecorino is produced in the provinces of Cagliari, Frosinone, Grosseto, Latina, Rome, Sassari, Nuoro, and Viterbo.

Caciotta Romana

This is a farmhouse cheese made on a small scale by individual producers in the hills around Rome and also at Nepi and Riano. This cheese is usually made with a mixture of ewe's and cow's milk, occasionally with all ewe's or all cow's milk. Although this cheese is not produced in such great quantities as in the early nineteenth century, when it attracted the praise of famous writers and poets, it still figures fairly prominently in Latium's cheese production. The cheeses are small, round, and straight-sided and weigh just over 2 pounds (1 kg). They are usually eaten young, although they can also be successfully used in cooking. In Rome they are often broiled (grilled) like Scamorza or fried with a very little oil.

Fior di Latte Abruzzese

Originally production of this cheese was limited to parts of Campania, but it has now spread over a wide area, the most important region being the Abruzzi. It is a poor relation of the true buffalo milk Mozzarella, since it is made with cow's milk which lacks the flavor of buffalo milk. In appearance it is very similar to Mozzarella, but it is not produced according to the method known as *pasta filata* (plastic curd or stretched curd) which consists of shaping the thickened milk mixture into elastic lengths. The color is milk white rather than the pure chalky white of Mozzarella. Fior di Latte Abruzzese is eaten fresh and is cooked in many regional dishes.

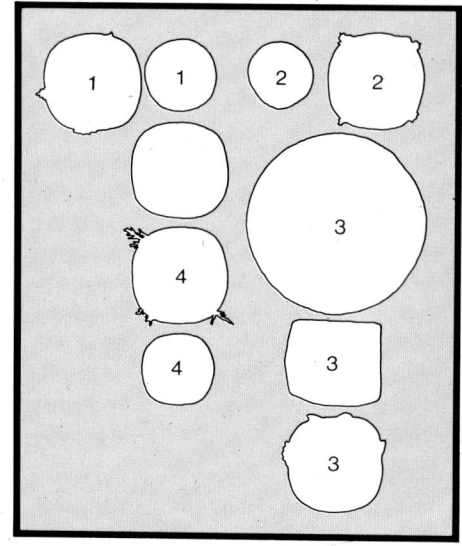

1 *Pecorino Senese*
2 *Caciotta Toscana*
3 *Parmigiano Reggiano*
4 *Marzolino*

Mozzarella

This famous cheese, which should be eaten soon after it is made, owes its name to the process by which it is made. The cheese is shaped into lengths (*pasta filata*) which are cut (*mozzata*) into small pieces as they are prepared.

This cheese dates back many centuries and used always to be made from buffalo milk. Buffalo are becoming rare in Italy, and increased demand means that Mozzarella is also commercially produced with cow's milk; but the superior buffalo Mozzarella can still be found, although it is more expensive. The centers of production for buffalo Mozzarella include the Battipaglia plain in the province of Salerno and the area around the River Volturno. Mozzarella should be the purest white, soft but solid with a mild fresh aroma. It may be round or oval and is sometimes very small (almost bite size). Ideally it should be eaten the day after it has been made. It is a very digestible, fairly low-fat

cheese (especially the cow's milk variety). Used in many southern Italian dishes, Mozzarella is a principal ingredient in pizza toppings.

Scamorza

This is another typical southern and central Italian cheese, rather like a small pear-shaped Caciocavallo in appearance. Made of buffalo milk and also, nowadays, from cow's milk, the best Scamorza cheeses come from Calabria (more elongated in shape), and Apulia (a foreshortened, fatter shape); Apulia also produces this cheese shaped to look just like a small pig. Like Caciocavallo and Mozzarella, Scamorza is widely used in cooking and is also eaten broiled (grilled), dressed with oil and pepper; baked in the oven on bread; or substituted for Mozzarella in Mozzarella in Carrozza (see page 158).

Provola

This cheese comes from central and southern Italy and, like Mozzarella, was once made exclusively with buffalo milk but is now also made from cow's milk. Buffalo milk Provola is becoming much rarer. It is made by the *pasta filata* or plastic curd method and the cheeses are small and roundish, weighing about $1\frac{1}{2}$–2 pounds (700–800 g). Four types of Provola are marketed: young, mature, smoked young, and smoked mature. The young cheeses taste like Mozzarella, when mature they resemble Caciocavallo. Commercially produced Provolas are covered with an outer coating of wax to keep the cheese soft and moist.

Provolone

The production of Provolone is controlled by standards officially drawn up to protect the quality of this classic cheese. However, it is thought by some to be similar to Caciocavallo. Made from cow's milk, it comes in varying shapes and sizes. This soft, slightly fat cheese can be pear-shaped, conical, or shaped like a melon or an elongated cylinder. The cone shape with rounded base and top is the most common. It is usually 14–18 inches (35–45 cm) high and weighs 2–13 pounds (1–6 kg); but often it is produced in gigantic sizes well over 3 feet (1 meter) high. The cheeses are strung up and suspended in pairs, like Caciocavallo. The color is white or pale straw and when matured can develop moist or weeping holes. Three qualities are produced: mild, sharp (aged), and smoked.

Caciocavallo

These hard, uncooked cheeses are produced commercially on a very large scale. They are made by the *pasta filata*, or plastic curd, method, kneaded in warm water, and traditionally shaped by hand into a distorted figure eight, the upper part forming a small knob so that the cheeses can be linked in pairs by braids of straw. They then pass through a salt bath, and are then slung over poles to dry, which would explain the name Caciocavallo—*caccio a cavallo*—"cheese on horseback." Others, however, claim that its name suggests that the cheese may once have been made from mare's milk.

The weight of Caciocavallo is usually around 2–4 pounds (1–2 kg), and the cheese is sometimes smoked. Table cheeses ripen for 2 to 4 months and those to be used for grating from 6 months to a year. The body of the cheese is smooth and firm, especially in less mature cheeses, and white or very pale yellow in color. The flavor of young cheeses is mild and delicate; when aged the taste becomes sharper and more pungent. The main producers are in southern Italy and the cheese is widely exported.

Burrata

Burrata is a specialty of Apulia and, at first sight, looks just like a large 1-pound

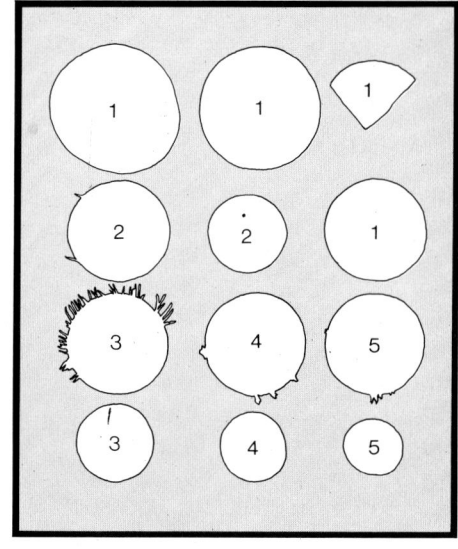

1 Pecorino Romano
2 Caciotta Romana
3 Fior di Latte Abruzzese
4 Caciofiore Umbro
5 Ricotta Stagionata di Norcia

(500 g) Mozzarella. Once it was made from buffalo milk; but now it is made from cow's milk and has a higher butterfat content than Mozzarella. Perhaps this accounts for its name which means "buttered." The creamy cheese is enclosed in a soft, edible crust.

Some consider Burrata to be one of the best *latticini*, or small soft cheeses, in the world and, excessive local pride apart, it is certainly delicious.

Pecorino Siciliano

In the first stages of the preparation of this cheese, Sicilian pecorino curd is placed in special reed or wicker baskets or *canestri*, and this has led to the cheese's other name, *canestrato*.

Pecorino Siciliano is a hard cheese made from whole ewe's milk during the period from October to June, and it must mature for at least 4 months. It is dry-salted and cylindrical in shape, weighing $8\frac{1}{2}$–$25\frac{1}{2}$ pounds (4–12 kg). The

rind is whitish-yellow and is marked by the basket in which the cheese was ripened. The body of the cheese is firm with a few holes, and it is sometimes flavored with a few peppercorns in which case it is called Pecorino Pepato or Maiorchino.

Ragusano

Ragusano is a Sicilian hard cheese from Ragusa which is made from whole cow's milk by the *pasta filata* (or plastic curd) method and is salted in brine. It is sometimes smoked. The cheeses are matured in pairs, tied together, and slung over poles. Ragusano can be eaten as a table cheese after 6 months. When aged further, it makes a good grating cheese. Ragusano is formed into a straight-sided oblong with rounded corners. The cords used to hold the cheese while it is ripening leave their mark on the thin, straw yellow rind which turns chestnut-brown with age. The body of the cheese has a few holes and is white when fresh, tending towards straw yellow when matured. The taste of of the young cheese is mild and delicate, becoming sharper later.

Pecorino Sardo or Fiore Sardo

This is the typical hard ewe's milk cheese of Sardinia. Its characteristic shape is like a round cake with sloping sides and it may weigh from 3–8½ pounds (1½–4 kg). The cheese is shaped in special conical molds which are placed broad base against broad base, an arrangement called *a schiena d'asino*—literally "hump-backed."

The cheese is first salted in brine, then dry-salted, and is eaten as a table cheese when less than three months old. After this it is better used grated. The rind is yellow when the cheese is young and almost black when aged. The cheese itself is white with a pleasantly sharp taste, growing stronger with age.

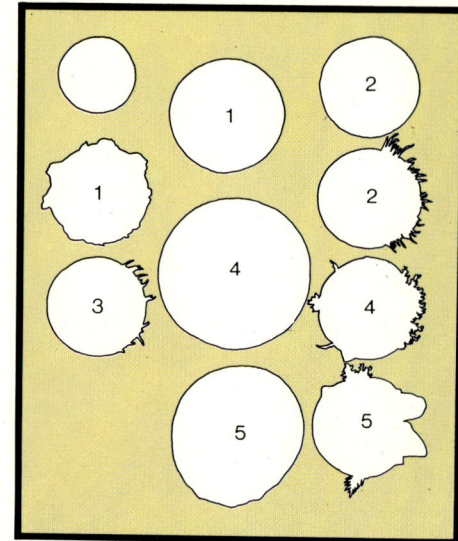

1 *Gorgonzola*
2 *Toma*
3 *Formaggetta*
4 *Fontina*
5 *Panerone*

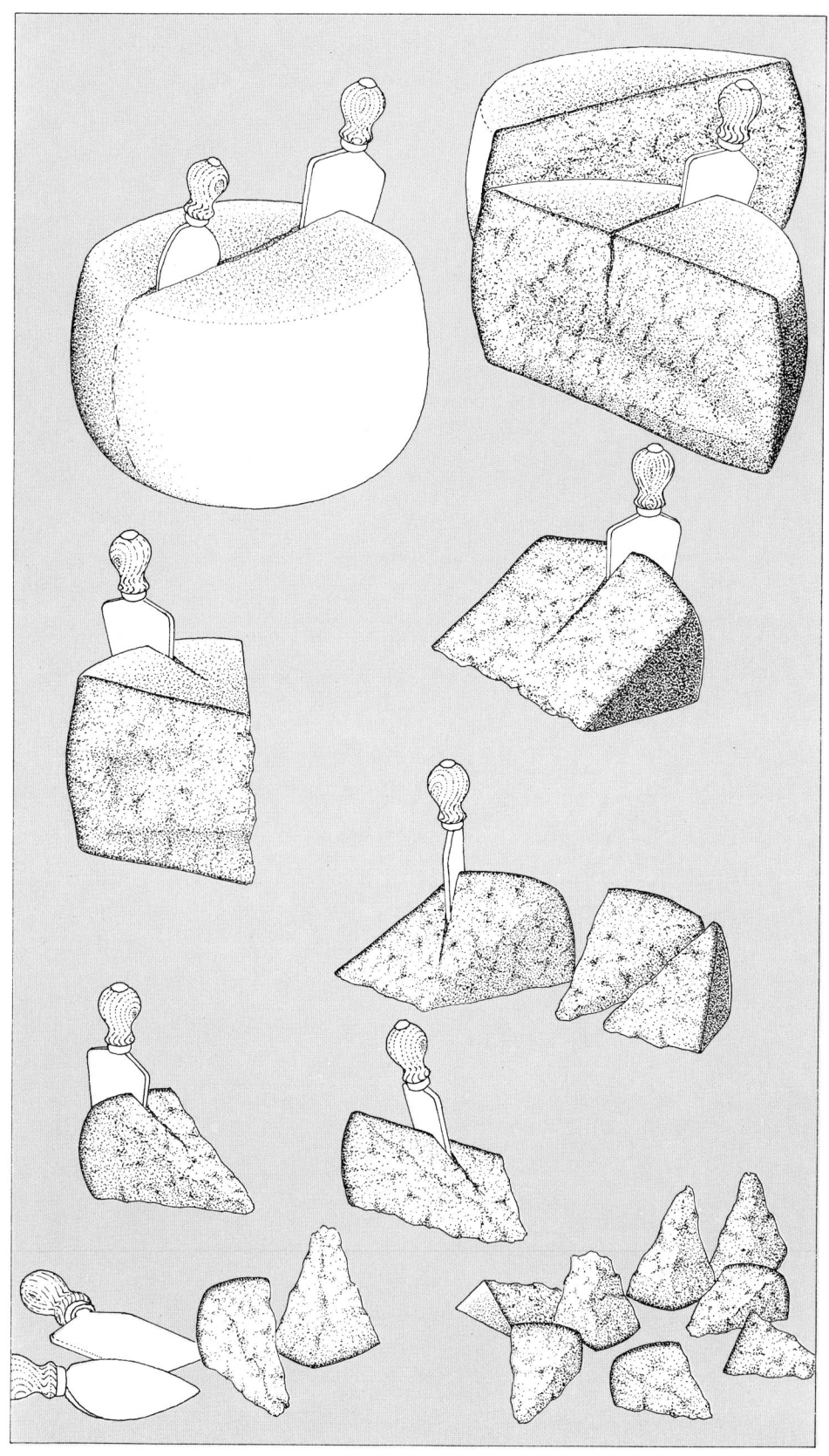

Left: How Parmigiano Reggiano and Grana Padano are cut using a special short, wide-bladed cutter.

Glossary

The following is a brief selection of cooking terms, utensils, foods, and ingredients used in traditional and modern Italian regional cooking.

Abbacchio

Very young, unweaned, milk-fed lamb. The lamb is killed by a blow on the head when it is only one month old, and this method of slaughtering may have given rise to its name, since *abbacchiare* means "to pole axe" or "knock down." Others, however, trace the name to the Latin term *ad baculum* meaning "tethered to a stake."

Lamb of such a tender age is not available in American markets, but one can buy what is known as "hothouse lamb" from certain butchers. "Hothouse lambs" are 2 to 3 months old and completely milk fed.

Agnolotti

Little squares or disks of stuffed egg pasta which were originally specialties of Piedmont, Lombardy, and Tuscany but are now widely popular.

Agnolotti may be stuffed with meat, cheese, or vegetables, or with a mixture of these.

Agresto

A sauce made from unripened grapes or verjuice used to flavor certain sauces. It must be used with care, since it has a very strong, bitter taste.

Ajada

A thick, paste-like sauce made by pounding garlic, nuts, bread crumbs, and olive oil in a mortar. At one time, it was used as a sauce for a lasagne dish eaten on meatless days, such as Fridays.

Amatriciana

A sauce used on pasta dishes, in particular Bucatini all' Amatriciana (See recipe, page 133).

The recipe comes from the town of Amatrice in Latium, and its creation is celebrated by a festival held every year on the first Sunday after the Feast of the Assumption (August 15).

Àola

A fresh-water fish, belonging to the Actinopterygii subclass. It is also called *alborella* in parts of Italy. It lies in shoals and is plentiful in Lake Garda.

Aranzada

A typical Sardinian dessert, a torrone or nougat, which has small slivers of orange peel cooked in honey and toasted almonds mixed into it.

Arista

Loin or saddle of pork, usually roasted on a spit. Mention is made of this roast being served as long ago as the early Renaissance.

Baccalà

Dried cod.

Baci di Dama (Lady's Kisses)

Little candies made of almonds, flour, butter, sugar, liqueur, and vanilla sugar mixed together with chocolate. They are a specialty of Sanremo, Novi Ligure, and Tortona.

Bagna Cauda

A specialty of Piedmont, *bagna cauda* is a dip made of anchovies, garlic, oil, butter, and cream. It is kept hot in an earthenware bowl over a spirit lamp on the table and is used as a dip for raw vegetables such as cardoons (edible thistles), celery, fennel, and Jerusalem artichokes. Truffles are often added to the sauce. (See recipe, page 20.)

Bagòss

A cheese produced in Bagolino (from which it takes its name) in Val Sabbia in the foothills of the Alps in Lombardy. It is a very strong cheese, made from cow's milk and is eaten on slices of bread crisped and browned over the embers of a fire. This cheese was once credited with aphrodisiac powers and was therefore also known as "the love cheese."

Bain-Marie

Originally a large version of the double boiler, a *bain-marie* is a hot water bath which allows for immersion of a cooking pan in boiling water. The term is also used to indicate this method of cooking (*au bain-marie*). A large container holding hot water is placed in the oven or on top of the stove, and smaller dishes or pans are partially immersed in it. The hot water provides insulation from direct heat and gives a slow, even heat. It is used when gentle cooking is needed for such dishes as egg custards, crème brulée, sauces, and molded soufflés. Various unconvincing hypotheses have been suggested to explain the name, including one that the method was invented by a legendary sister of Moses called Mary, who is said to have dabbled in alchemy in Egypt.

Bandiera (The Flag)

A dish made with ingredients which correspond to the colors of the Italian national flag: white onions, red tomatoes, and green peppers. The ingredients are sautéed together in olive oil until they are tender and their juices have formed a thick sauce. A good *Bandiera* must not be overcooked or mushy.

Battuto

This is a very useful term, which crops up over and over again in Italian recipes. It means, quite simply, a chopped mixture. When the instructions in a recipe direct the cook to chop a number of ingredients finely, these are from then on referred to as the *battuto*. The ingredients are chopped with the *mezzaluna* or half-moon cutter and often include parsley, celery, garlic, carrot, onion, pork fat, etc.

Bìgoli

In the Veneto region these large, fat spaghetti made from soft wheat flour and eggs are formed by pushing the dough through a special utensil called a *bigolaro*. If the pasta is made from whole-wheat (wholemeal) flour they are called *bigoli mati* (false bigoli) and are

served with a sauce made of oil and sardines. (See recipes on pages 48 and 49.)

Blend

To combine ingredients until they are smoothly and evenly mixed. This may be done either by stirring very thoroughly, pounding in a mortar with a pestle or, more commonly nowadays, by using a blender or food processor.

Bomba di Riso (Rice Timbale or Mold)

This dish figures prominently in the cooking of Emilia but has its equivalent in the Piedmontese *goffa* and the Neapolitan *sartù*. Cooked rice is used to line the base and sides of a mold, cooked meats in sauce are placed in the center and more rice is then placed in a layer on top. The mold is then baked in the oven.

Bóndola

The Venetian dialect name for a large, round pork (or mixed pork and beef) sausage, which is enclosed in part of the large intestine of a steer. Like the Lombard *bondiana* and the Emilian *bondeina*, this name is a variation of the Italian *bondiola*.

Botarga

This could be called Venetian caviar. The roe of large gray mullet are dried in the sun or air-dried and then thinly sliced and served as an antipasto with oil, lemon juice, and sometimes pepper.

Boudin

A type of sausage or black pudding from the Val d'Aosta. It is made from boiled pig's blood, pork fat, and pepper and is fried or boiled before serving. It is also sometimes called *sanguinaccio* (blood sausage).

Brasato

This term comes from the northern Italian word for hot glowing embers. It

is a method of cooking meats very slowly by burying the pot containing the meat in hot embers. Peasants would leave meat to cook in this way in the remains of their fires when they went out to work in the fields early in the morning. Often the meat would be variety meats (offal) or cheaper and less desirable cuts, but by the time the peasants came home in the evening, the meat would be tender and ready to eat after its long braising. In France the term *daube* describes a dish cooked in this way.

Brodetto

Fish soups or stews, various versions of which are found all along the Adriatic coast of Italy. In Venice this soup is called *broeto*.

Brovada

In Friuli turnips are matured in vinegar in special wooden tubs or vats for about three months. These brovada are then sliced into narrow strips and used to make *jota*, a rather sharp tasting soup (see recipe, page 63). Brovada are also boiled or braised with pork fat and served with pork dishes.

Burrielli

Bite-sized Mozzarella cheeses which the Neapolitans store in clay vessels or amphoræ called *lancelle*. The Italian word for butter is *burro* and the name given to these cheeses derives from the fact that they have a higher butterfat content than ordinary Mozzarella.

Büsêca

This name for tripe is said by some to derive from an obsolete Spanish word, by others from the colorful word for belly—*buzzo*. Whatever its origins, in Milan the inhabitants' fondness for this dish has earned them the nickname of *büsecón* (great tripe eaters) just as the Venetians are nicknamed *polenton* because they are supposed to eat so much polenta. (See the recipe for Büsêca on page 32.)

Bussolani or Bussolai
This is the name used in the Po Valley for cookie or sweet bread rings. The ingredients vary from place to place but the shape remains the same.

Cacciucco
This word comes from a Turkish word for small fish. In Leghorn it has come to mean a substantial fish soup or stew. The Leghorn *cacciucco* is a meal in itself and should not be confused with ordinary fish soup, both because of the care and attention paid to the choice of fish used and the meticulous preparation of the dish. (See recipe, page 103.)

Caciuni
A stuffed pasta like large ravioli, but instead of being made with egg noodle dough this pasta is made from bread dough. The filling is made of a mixture of young Pecorino and mature Pecorino cheeses in varying proportions depending on how strong a taste of cheese is desired. Egg yolks, sugar, and grated lemon rind are also used in the filling.

Calzone
This is a Neapolitan specialty which could be described as a turnover made from pizza dough. The dough is cut into circles, filled, and then folded over to form a stuffed half-moon. The most common ingredients for the filling are Mozzarella, Ricotta, or other cheeses, and prosciutto (raw ham). In other regions of central and southern Italy different fillings are used depending on what ingredients are most readily available locally—sometimes vegetables are used. At one time *calzoni* were fried rather than baked like pizza.

Candelaos or Gueffos
Sardinian candies made with ground almonds and sugar, and flavored with orange liqueur.

Cannelloni
Pasta tubes approximately $\frac{3}{4}$ inch (2 cm) in diameter. *Cannelloni* are boiled, stuffed with a meat or vegetable ragu, and then baked in the oven. The word *cannelloni* can also be used to describe pancakes rolled round a meat filling and then cooked in the oven.

Cannòli
Cannòli means "pipes," and these Sicilian pastries take their name from the round metal tubes or pipes around which they are rolled before being fried in deep fat, until crisp. The sweet pastry is then filled with sweetened Ricotta cheese and candied fruit and dredged with vanilla-flavored confectioners' (icing) sugar.

Caponata
Caponata is a traditional dish of southern Italy. It is made of a variety of fresh vegetables whose juices are allowed to soak into bread. Most commonly used are fresh tomatoes, onions, basil, garlic, green peppers, and olives which are dressed with oil, vinegar, anchovies, salt, and freshly ground pepper. (See recipe, page 194.)

The Tuscan version of this dish is called *panzanella*. The Sicilians have their own, very distinctive version which is known as *caponatina di melanzane*, and is made with eggplants (aubergines) fried with celery, onions, capers, olives, and tomatoes. The addition of pears, sugar, and white wine vinegar gives a sweet and sour taste.

Cappelletto
A kind of encased pork sausage (the same sausage meat as used in zampone) which is eaten boiled. Its three-cornered shape looks somewhat like a priest's hat (*cappello da prete*) which explains its name. *Cappelletto* is of course also the stuffed pasta sometimes known as *tortellino*.

Caramelization
The transformation which sugar undergoes at a temperature of 375°F–400°F (190°C–200°C). Usually a little boiling water is added once the sugar has dissolved and begun to brown. The resulting caramel is used in desserts. However, burnt caramel or Black Jack (400°F/200°C and over) is used to brown sauces and soups.

Carbonade
A traditional dish of Piedmont and Val d'Aosta using salt beef (one of the ways of preserving meat before the days of refrigeration). To reduce the extreme saltiness of the meat, an equal weight of onions was added in cooking. With the arrival of refrigeration, salting fell into disuse, but this dish still survives in many restaurants. It is similar to ordinary braised pork or beef and onions. *Carbone* means coal or charcoal in Italian, and the name may have arisen from the fact that this dish used to be cooked over charcoal fires, or from its very dark color, for not only was the preserved meat dark, it was also cooked with red wine.

Carta da Musica
"Music paper" is a type of very thin unleavened bread, made from hard or durum wheat flour, water, and salt mixed and rolled out into thin disks 8–10 inches (20–25 cm) in diameter and baked for a few minutes in a fairly cool oven. This bread was then sometimes boiled in a large pan of water and served with fresh tomato sauce and cheese with a poached egg on top. In this case it was called *pane frattau*. This bread is still eaten a great deal in Sardinia. (See illustration, page 160.)

Cartoccio
The method of cooking fish, meat, and some other foods in waxed (grease-proof) paper oiled or greased with butter has been adapted effectively to aluminum foil. The seasoned raw food is placed inside, and the wrapping is folded over and pleated to form an envelope or sealed bag. This method preserves the juices of the food and helps flavors to mingle. Besides meat and fish, vegetables and pasta dishes can be cooked in this way.

Casonsèi

In the districts surrounding Brescia and Bergamo *casonsei* are large ravioli stuffed with salami, spinach, seedless white raisins (sultanas), almond macaroons, bread crumbs, and cheese and dressed with melted butter and sage. The dish can be traced back to antiquity and some etymologists maintain that the name derives from the original Latin word for cheese, *caseus*, which of course is one of the ingredients in the filling. (See recipe, page 30.)

Cassata

An extremely popular Sicilian Easter dessert, which is so delicious that it is eaten all year round. Originally it was made of sponge cake filled with very fresh Ricotta cheese flavored with vanilla or chocolate, or sometimes other flavors. *Cassata* may well be another name which derives from the Latin *caseus* or cheese. For a long time *cassata* was made by the nuns of various convents in Sicily. In time, similar desserts came to be made with layers of fruit ice cream and from these was born *cassata gelata* or frozen *cassata*, which is now produced by the ice-cream industry.

Cassoeula (Casserole)

A favorite winter dish in Lombardy, cassoeula was originally made with pig's feet (trotters), sausages, pork rind, carrots, celery, tomatoes, and cabbage. There are many versions of the basic dish which vary from place to place: Milan, Como, Pavia, and Novara. The word for the dish or recipe comes by extension from the container in which it is cooked, an earthenware vessel designed for slow cooking of meat or game.

Cassóla

In the parts of Italy which came under Spanish domination, the word *cassola* has persisted. It denotes any dish which was originally cooked in a covered earthenware dish (see *Cassoeula*, above). In Sardinia, for example, Cassóla is a substantial fish soup. (See recipe, page 198).

Cecenielli

This is a Neapolitan word for the tiny young anchovies which are sprinkled on top of pizzas to give them added flavor. They can also be mixed with beaten eggs and made into a frittata.

Cenci

Cenci is Italian for rags. In Tuscany it is also the name of little cookies made with sugar, flour, eggs, and sweet wine. The dough is cut into ribbons and fried in boiling oil or fat (lard) (see recipe, page 111). The cookies are similar to Venetian *galani* (see recipe, page 60), *sfrappole* from Bologna, *donzelline, nastrini di monaca*, and *chiacchiere*.

Certosina (Charterhouse Style)

This term is used to describe a particular type of risotto said to have first been invented in the Charterhouse of Pavia. The risotto included peas, fresh-water shrimps, mushrooms, garlic, and olive oil.

Chitarra

A special cutting tool used to make *maccheroni alla chitarra* or "guitar" macaroni, a specialty of Abruzzi (see recipe, page 144). A series of steel cords are stretched over a board, just like the strings of a guitar, and the sheet of egg pasta dough is pressed down onto the wires with a rolling pin. When the strings are "played" by running the fingers over them, the square macaroni noodles fall down onto the board below. (See illustration, page 144.)

Cicerchiata

A dessert made in Abruzzi at carnival time. It consists of small cubes of sweet pastry fried in oil. These are then mixed with honey and shaped into rings or hearts.

Cieche

Tiny elvers, the blind young of the eel. Throughout the Mediterranean basin various countries have their own ways of cooking these new-born eels. In Pisa they are fried with sage and garlic; elsewhere they are mixed with beaten eggs and made into a frittata with cheese and bread crumbs to which sage, pepper, and lemon juice are usually added.

Cima

Cima ripiena is a typical dish of the Ligurian coast but it is found in many other regions under other names, the most common of which is *tasca ripiena* (a full pocket). Breast of veal is cut so that it can be stuffed and rolled. The stuffing usually consists of eggs, brains, calf or beef marrow, cooked peas, parsley, and a generous quantity of grated Parmesan cheese.

There are many variations on this basic theme and the stuffed breast of veal can be served hot or cold.

Ciriole

These are small eels, so called because they are wax-colored and candle-shaped (from the Latin *cereus*: wax-like or a wax taper). They are cooked with garlic, capers, anchovies, chili peppers, and white wine. In Umbria *ciriole* are also small, rather fat homemade spaghetti which are usually mixed with garlic, oil, and chili peppers.

Civét

A rich ragout of game prepared in the Val d'Aosta. Hare, roe-deer, and chamois are cut up, marinated in red wine with herbs and seasonings, and then fried and sprinkled with rough brandy or *grappa*.

Connìta

The Abruzzi dialect word for *condita* (seasoned or, for salads, etc., dressed). It is a soup made of pancetta (bacon) stock to which eggs beaten with Parmesan cheese and semolina are then added. It is really a more robust version of *Stracciatella alla Romana*.

Coppietto

A specialty of the Maremma district of Tuscany, where it was once very popular among the shepherds. It is prepared by cutting the lean meat of wild boars (or pork or beef) into thin strips, salting it, and seasoning it with ginger. The meat strips are dried and then smoked, folded, and tied together.

Crauti

Alto Adige's equivalent of the German sauerkraut. It is eaten with various dishes which usually include pork. This sour cabbage is made with hard white cabbage, sliced thinly, salted, seasoned with spices, and arranged in layers in special tubs. After two to three months the cabbage ferments. The *crauti* is then cooked with pork fat or lard in a heavy cooking pot or boiled and served as a vegetable.

In the Veneto *crauti* is prepared by adding white wine vinegar to the cabbage but without leaving it to ferment.

Crema Pasticcera (Pastry Cream/Confectioners' Custard)

A very popular egg-custard filling made as follows: Beat $\frac{3}{4}$ cup (scant 6 oz/180 g) sugar with 6 egg yolks until pale and fluffy and then slowly add $\frac{1}{3}$ cup (scant $1\frac{1}{2}$ oz/45 g) flour and a pinch of salt. Scald 2 cups ($\frac{3}{4}$ pt/4 dl) of milk containing a vanilla bean (pod) and stir into the egg mixture. Transfer to a heavy saucepan, place over a low heat, and stir constantly until the mixture begins to bubble gently. Turn down the heat as low as possible and continue stirring for about 3 minutes. Remove from the heat and discard vanilla bean (pod). (If a vanilla bean (pod) was not used, add vanilla extract (essence) at this stage.) Pour into a bowl and continue stirring until the mixture is cool so that a skin cannot form. Place in the refrigerator and chill. This quantity should yield about 3 cups (1 pt/$\frac{1}{2}$ liter).

Cren

A strongly piquant, peppery hot sauce made by grating the astringent root of horseradish (*Armoracia rusticana*). In some areas vinegar and bread crumbs are added to the sauce to make it slightly milder.

Crostini

Crostini are some of the most popular and traditional appetizers in Italian, and more particularly Tuscan, cooking. Coarse homemade bread slices are fried in butter and then spread with a soft, smooth mixture of calf's spleen, chicken livers simmered with onions, anchovies, and capers. In other regions different ingredients are used for the spread. In Spoleto truffles are pounded together with butter and anchovies.

Crostoni

Large, thick slices of homemade bread fried in oil and butter or simply crisped and browned in the oven. Regional cooking today includes a more modern version, in which soft or processed cheese is spread onto the bread slices and then baked in the oven for a few minutes. Gorgonzola is a great favorite and particularly good for this snack.

Crumiri

These little baton-shaped cookies come from Piedmont. They are made with cornmeal (maize flour), all-purpose (plain) flour, eggs, and sugar. They originated at Casale Monferrato.

Cubbàita

This Sicilian candy is probably a legacy of the time when Sicily was occupied by the Saracens who passed on a great deal of their skill in making sweetmeats to the indigenous population. *Cubbàita* are, however, sometimes traced back to the sweet cakes which were made for celebrating festivals in honor of the gods of plenty and fertility in the cities of the ancient Greek colonies in the south of Italy. Today's *cubbàita* is a special nougat made with honey, sesame seeds, and almonds.

Cuscusu

This dish, known in English as couscous, is widely eaten throughout the Mediterranean in such countries as Libya, Tunisia, Algeria, and Morocco. The Sicilian name for it has changed little from the Arab word *kuskus*. Pellets the size of peppercorns are formed from moistened semolina and are then steamed. The accompaniment eaten with the couscous changes from country to country. In Algeria this nearly always consists of meat or vegetables with a hot, piquant sauce, whereas in the Trapani region of Sicily it is eaten with a selection of fish.

Cuticùsu

This is a very old dish which comes from Macerata in the Marches. Beans are boiled and drained, mixed with a dressing of oil, vinegar, and anchovy fillets, and seasoned with marjoram and garlic which have been pounded in a mortar.

Dragoncello (Tarragon)

An aromatic herb sometimes called *erba serpentaria* in Italian. The true tarragon for culinary use is *Artemisia dracunculus*, a plant with long, narrow leaves which are bright green when the plant is very young and then turn a soft graygreen. It is widely used for flavoring chicken dishes, vinegar, salads, and sauces.

Extract

A concentrated meat or vegetable soup which is reduced by evaporation to a paste. It is used to heighten the flavor of various foods. Today there are commercially produced extracts and bouillon cubes containing monosodium glutamate.

Facciuni di Santa Chiara

In the convent of Saint Clare in Noto, Sicily, the nuns followed a very old tradition of making small sweet almond cakes with citron jam and orange marmalade which were coated with chocolate. These little cakes were called *facciuni* because a little angel's face (*faccetta*) was depicted on the top of each of them.

Farce or Stuffing

A variety of ground (minced) and chopped foods, mixed with spices and bread crumbs and usually bound together with egg. A farce adds flavor as well as helping keep fish, chicken, or meat moist. Pasta is also stuffed, and sweet fillings are used for certain cakes.

Farsumagru

A kind of meat loaf somewhat like the Genoese dish *Cima*. A piece of breast (usually veal) is laid out flat, pounded well, and then layered with eggs, cheese, pork sausage, etc. The veal is then rolled up, tied at each end rather like a large salami, and cooked in a large cooking pot. Like *Cima*, it is cut into thin slices and can be eaten warm or cold.

Favata

This soup is famous all over Sardinia. Its composition changes from place to place, but the basis is always dried beans, which have been soaked overnight in warm water and then cooked the following day in stock (usually pork stock) together with a piece of salt pork or pork fat.

Fave dei Morti (Dead Men's Beans)

These candies are traditionally eaten on All Souls' Day, November 2. They are made from a mixture of sugar, almonds, pine nuts, egg whites, and flour. They are a specialty of Lombardy but are popular throughout the Po Valley.

Fiandoléin

A foamy cream or custard made by beating whole milk, or cream, with egg yolks, sugar, and rum flavored with the zest of an orange—in other words, a milk zabaglione. The ingredients must be placed in a double boiler or bain-marie and beaten continuously over a gentle heat. This dessert is a specialty of the Val d'Aosta and is served with toasted rye bread.

Finanziera

Although this dish only became fashionable when it reached the court of Charles Emmanuel I, Duke of Savoy, it was for many years a traditional Piedmontese specialty. It consists of layers of veal, escalopes, sweetbreads, and mushrooms which were placed on top of fried slices of bread.

Foiólo

A Milanese expression for the section of beef tripe which is normally referred to in Italian as *centopelle* or honeycomb tripe.

Fondüa

A famous hot cheese sauce, the most delicious Italian version of which is made with Fontina cheese melted with eggs, cream, salt, pepper, and butter and finished with a garnish of slivers of fresh white truffles. It is often served with plain boiled rice. This dish is typical of the area of Piedmont near the foothills of the Alps. The original name has been Italianized to *fonduta*. (See recipe, page 20.)

Frégula

A Sardinian preparation made from semolina which is moistened and raked over with the hands to form little pellets the size of peppercorns. It is made in much the same way as the Sicilian cuscusu; however, in the Sardinian version these pellets are allowed to dry and are then cooked in stock with plenty of grated cheese. This dish is widely eaten by the Arabs in North Africa and must have been brought to Sardinia and Sicily centuries ago when these islands were invaded and ruled by North African conquerors. (See recipe, page 198.)

Fritto Misto (Mixed Fry)

Bolognese mixed fry includes the most astonishing variety of meat, vegetables, and fruit. Artichokes, tomatoes, apples, chicken, brains, zucchini (courgettes), oranges, bananas, and semolina gnocchi are among the foods which are coated in a batter made of eggs, milk, and flour and then fried in hot sunflower seed or vegetable oil until crisp and golden. The Florentines also have a mixed fry which includes brain croquettes, sweetbreads, artichokes, zucchini (courgettes), and lamb. In the mixed fry made in Ascoli, enormous olives filled with ground (minced) veal or beef stuffing are also used.

Frutti della Martorana or Frutti di Pasta Reale

These candies were once made in the convent of Martorana at Palermo in Sicily. They are made from almond paste and are skillfully shaped and colored in convincing imitations of all kinds of fruit. The almond paste is made with equal quantities of almonds and sugar pounded in a mortar and then mixed with a sweet liqueur and spiced lightly with cinnamon. It is rendered smoother and more workable by heating it in a heavy copper pan while mixing continuously. Pieces of the paste are broken off, modelled into the shape of fruits, and then painted with natural colorings and cooked in a warm oven as if they were pieces of painted pottery.

Fumét

In Italian this term has had a slightly different meaning from its French and English counterparts. In these languages it means a fish or game stock. The old-fashioned Italian method of making a meat stock was described as preparing a *fumét* and involved boiling various bones and trimmings of veal and beef with butter, pepper, herbs, and water for a considerable length of time. The resulting stock is stronger than the classic brown stock and used to be reduced until it formed a kind of meat extract which was then strained and stored in sterilized jars until needed.

Fusilli

Spiral-shaped spaghetti, Fusilli can be made at home with pasta dough made from durum or hard wheat flour and water or with egg pasta dough. The dough is cut into thin strips and wound around a skewer. Once they are dry they keep their shape well and remain spiral-shaped when boiled. Fusilli are also commercially produced by a special machine (see illustrations, page 17). One finds this type of pasta in Abruzzi, Latium, Campania, Apulia, Calabria, and Basilicata.

Garmugia

A very popular soup in the area around Lucca. Thinly sliced veal is sautéed in olive oil, together with pancetta, a few onions, peas, fresh beans, artichoke hearts and asparagus tips. After all these ingredients have been sautéed, plenty of water is added, and the soup is simmered until the vegetables are done. Served with crisp, brown slices of bread.

Genepì

A spirit or liqueur made from Alpine mugwort or wormwood. Genepì is a relation or perhaps the forerunner of the infamous absinthe which was finally banned in France when its harmful effects became clear towards the end of the nineteenth century. Usually green or colorless, Genepì is said to have been first distilled from Alpine plants by the herbalist Genepin in the second half of the fourteenth century.

Ghiotta

The word probably derives from an Arab word *ghatta* which means a highly spiced sauce or dressing. When a dish is described as being *alla ghiotta* this implies that it is accompanied by a special sauce or gravy.

Giardiniera (Garden Style)

A vegetable soup which does not include beans among its ingredients. The same word is also used for a mixture of vegetables such as carrots, celery, small onions, etc. pickled in vinegar and usually stored or sold in jars.

Giuliana (Julienne)

The term used originally by the French to describe a garnish of vegetables cut into shreds about 1½ inches (3½ cm) long. It is also the name of a clear vegetable soup made from consommé to which a selection of finely shredded vegetables is added. Finally it also describes a method of cutting other foods into thin strips or matchstick lengths. For example, it is used to describe meats, such as breast of chicken, prosciutto (raw ham), or pickled tongue used in mixed salads.

Goffa

See *Bomba di Riso*.

Guazzetto

A cooking term, used particularly in the Veneto, to describe a method of poaching, almost braising, foods by sautéing them and then adding a certain amount of stock, so that they are moist and tender.

Gubana

This is a dessert from Friuli which is rolled up like a strudel and then twisted round into a spiral. The pastry casing is often made of egg pasta dough, but many people prefer to use sweetened bread dough rolled out into a very thin sheet. The filling consists of walnuts, seedless white raisins (sultanas), pine nuts, plums or prunes, dried figs, candied orange and citron peel, and cocoa, moistened with rum or a very sweet wine. The name of the dessert probably comes from the Friuli dialect word *bubana* which means Cockaigne or land of plenty. The making of this confection used to be one of the "ceremonies" associated with Easter. It was regarded almost as a votive offering for a good season of growth and harvest.

Infarinata

In Garfagnana and Versilia, where this bean soup is traditional, it is also called *intruglia*. It is actually more like a very thin polenta. Cornmeal (maize flour) is cooked with beans, red cabbage, tomato paste and rosemary and complemented by fatty cuts of pork or sausage. It may be eaten hot or cold. Once it has chilled and set, it can be sliced and reheated by frying or placing under the broiler (grill).

Infiammare (Flamber or to Flame)

This process is seldom used in traditional Italian cuisine. It has more to do with aesthetics than with actually modifying the taste of the food. Brandy or sherry is heated to make it volatile and then set alight and poured flaming over meat, game, pancakes, etc. Food treated in this way is described as *flambé*.

Jota

This dish is typical of Friuli and Venezia Giulia. However, its preparation is different in each region. In Friuli, beans, cornmeal (maize flour), fermented turnips, and milk are the main ingredients; whereas in Venezia Giulia, beans, potatoes, sauerkraut, and small pieces of smoked pancetta or streaky bacon are used. (See recipe, page 63.)

Lampascioni

In Apulia this is the name for the wild onion (*Muscari comosum*) which belongs to the lily family. Only the bulb of these onions is eaten, boiled, in salads, or broiled (grilled), and they have a very strong diuretic action. Their pleasantly sharp and slightly bitter taste, which they retain even after cooking, makes them very popular.

La Pigneti

A method of cooking which has come by extension to mean a regional dish. In Basilicata lamb is cut into pieces and placed in an earthenware pot or jar with potatoes, onions, tomatoes, small sweet or hot peppers, Pecorino cheese, a piece of sausage, and water to cover. The jar is then sealed with clay and placed in an oven in which bread has just been baked. The meat cooks as the oven cools. This long, slow cooking was at one time very common all over Europe, and sometimes all the inhabitants of a village would take their cooking pots to the village baker to be cooked in the large oven.

To Lard

When a roast is very lean (such as certain cuts of veal and beef, notably the fillet), strips of seasoned fat are sewn into the flesh by means of a special larding needle. The strips of fat, or lardons are usually about 1½ inches (3–4 cm) long and ¼ inch (½ cm) wide and thick. They are cut from a slice of larding bacon. The bacon is solid fat which is specially cured without the use of saltpeter (so that the meat does not discolor). Larding fat can be difficult to obtain, although a variety called spik can be bought at specialty (especially Polish) food stores. Pork fat is a good substitute.

Lattaiolo

A delicious delicately flavored and digestible baked egg custard. It is made with cream or whole milk, egg yolks, and sugar, and is often flavored with rum or Alchermes, a red, rose water and spice liqueur. It is baked in a bain-marie and is not glazed with sugar like many custards.

Lepudrida

This word derives from the Catalan *olla podrida* (*olla* is a cooking pot, usually earthenware, and *olla podrida* is the term for a stew). In the region of Cagliari a substantial vegetable soup called *lepudrida* is prepared by cooking vegetables together with beef or pork. The Sardinian language includes many Catalan words.

Maccu

One of the oldest soups known to central-southern Italy. Dried beans with their thin inner skins removed are soaked overnight and then boiled in water flavored with wild fennel and oil. The beans are then sieved and various types of pasta are cooked in the thick soup.

Mandolino (Mandolin)

Usually a rectangular piece of wood, aluminum, or stainless steel across which a sharp blade of plain or fluted steel is fixed. The blade can be adjusted by a screw at the side to regulate the thickness of the slice. Vegetables to be sliced are rubbed briskly up and down the mandolin. In Italian the special utensil used for peeling potatoes is also referred to as a *mandolino*.

Mandorlato

A candy made from almonds which have been toasted in the oven and mixed with honey and other ingredients.

Martinsec

In the eastern Alpine region and more particularly in the Val d'Aosta, little pears with tough, textured, reddish skins and white sharpish-sweet flesh are called *martinsec*. They are cooked gently and slowly in red wine with sugar and a few cloves and then eaten cold.

Mazzafegati

The pig's liver sausages which go under this name are made throughout central Italy. Sometimes seedless white raisins (sultanas), sugar, and pine nuts are mixed with the pig's liver for a mild or sweet sausage. Piquant *mazzafegati* sausages are made by adding hot, peppery types of sausage meat to the basic ingredient. *Mazzafegati* are cooked in the oven or skewered and roasted on a spit.

Mazzancolle

In Rome and the surrounding regions, the large, succulent shrimp or scampi, known as *gamberoni* in other parts of Italy are called *mazzancolle*. They are usually broiled (grilled) in their shells or removed from their shells, lightly coated with flour, dipped in beaten egg, and fried.

Messicani

A regional dish which consists of rolls of lean veal stuffed with sausage meat, chicken livers, grated cheese, and nutmeg and then fried in butter. Why this dish, which gathered popularity between the two World Wars, should be called "Mexicans" no one seems to know. It is especially hard to understand, since in international cookery *mexicaine* means a mayonnaise flavored with anchovy paste and decorated with red and green peppers.

Mestecanza or Mesticanza

The term means "mixed up together" and is usually applied to mixed salads including red radicchio (red chicory), chicory (endive), escarole (scarole), watercress, and other fresh salad vegetables dressed with olive oil.

Morseddu

A Calabrian dish made either from pig's liver and heart in the home, or, more popularly in *trattorie* from pig's tripe. The word *morseddu* is said to derive from the Spanish *almuerzo*, formerly meaning breakfast but today lunch. In the "popular" recipe the tripe is cooked with tomatoes and other variety meats (offal) and very highly seasoned with chili peppers. In some restaurants *morseddu* is served inside a pita, making a substantial sandwich, albeit an extremely peppery one.

Mósa

A creamy soup which is eaten in Trentino-Alto Adige and some parts of the Veneto. White flour and cornmeal (maize flour) are cooked together in milk, and the mixture is finished by adding butter towards the end of the cooking.

Mostaccìòli

Little cakes made with flour and, as the name suggests (mosto means wine must) must or unfermented new wine. They are popular throughout southern Italy. The version found in Abruzzi is much more elaborate. The ingredients include almonds, honey, grated orange rind, and cinnamon, and they are often decorated with chocolate frosting.

Mostarda (Mustard)

A condiment made from the seeds of various plants which are pounded with vinegar or verjuice and seasoned with pepper and other spices. In Italy, Cremona mustard is made of candied fruits—pears, cherries, figs, plums, apricots, little oranges, and slices of melon and pumpkin, preserved in sugar syrup flavored with mustard oil. It is eaten with cold boiled meats. Also called *mostarda* is a Sicilian dessert made with unfermented grape juice.

Muscoli

A regional dialect word for mussels, which are also called *cozze* or *mitili*.

Mùstica

Another name for the tiny, young anchovies which are also called *bianchetti*, or little white fish, because of their lack of color and markings when they are this young. They are salted and stored in oil in earthenware or glass jars and are a specialty of the cuisine of the Ionian coast. The name *mùstica* probably derives from the terracotta jars in which they are kept.

Nocino

A liqueur made from steeping unshelled, green walnuts in aquavite. After one month the spirit is passed through a paper filter and sugar is added. The best walnuts for this purpose are grown in Emilia. This liqueur is now manufactured on a large scale.

Olla

An earthenware vessel used for cooking or storing food.

Pabassinas

These are Sardinian candies made with raisins (the Sardinian word for raisins is *pabassa*). Flour, toasted almonds, walnuts, and sugar are mixed with the raisins.

Paiolo

A round cooking kettle, usually made of copper. It was a very efficient cooking vessel because of the high conductivity of the copper. It used to hang from a chain at the end of a swivelling arm and could be swiftly swung over or away from the fire. Polenta was traditionally cooked in one of these copper pots.

Pan de Mej

The Milanese dialect word for the millet bread which used to be eaten with heavy (double) cream, making a pleasing, complementary combination of the crispy, rough bread and the smooth cream. Nowadays, *Pan de Mej* is a well-known dessert, made with cornmeal, (maize flour), white flour, butter, sugar, and yeast. (See recipe, page 38.)

Pandoro

A classic Christmas specialty which originated in Verona. It is often assumed that the name comes from *pan d'oro* or golden bread, but this attribution is mistaken. The real source is the archaic Veronese dialect word *pandòlo*, which was the name of a local dessert. The Veronese cake shop, Melegatti, was already selling this cake towards the end of the nineteenth century. It is a soft, melting mixture of flour, eggs, plenty of butter, and yeast, baked in a star-shaped mold and dredged with confectioners' (icing) sugar.

Pane Frattau

Another name for *carta da musica*. See the entry under that name.

Panforte

This rich and spicy cake which comes from Siena was already well known in Dante's time. But its origins go back even farther to thirteenth-century Tuscan sweet breads made with honey and pepper. The modern *panforte* is produced commercially and contains flour, sugar, a considerable quantity of candied fruits, almonds, and a variety of spices.

Paniscia or Panissa

As long ago as medieval times this was the name of a thick soup based on millet flour or chick peas. The soup has gradually changed, and today *panissa* is a thick soup made with rice and beans.

Pansoòti

Ligurian ravioli stuffed with a mixture of vegetables, cheese, and eggs, and topped with walnut sauce. (See recipe, page 72.) Pansoòti used to be served with a sauce made from walnuts, oil, egg yolks, and newly-curdled cheese (*prescinsoeua*).

Panzanella

This dish used to be very popular in Tuscany. Slices of homemade bread were soaked in water with anchovy fillets, onions, tomatoes, oil, vinegar, salt, and pepper. The history of the name of this dish is uncertain but it might derive from the Venetian dialect term *pan moiéta* (soaked bread). Eaten either hot or cold, *panzanelle* was a basic dish in the diet of Italian peasants all over the country, since it was a good way in which to use up stale, but precious, bread.

Paparèle

See the entry for *pappardelle* below.

Pappardelle

Very wide lasagne made of egg pasta dough which come from Tuscany. They are the equivalent of the Venetian *paparèle* and can be served with a variety of sauces. The most famous of these is prepared with hare in Arezzo and other parts of Tuscany. (See recipes, page 100.)

Passatelli
Passatelli noodles are made of eggs, Parmesan cheese, and bread crumbs and are formed into short, thick, cylindrical strands about 1–1¼ inch (3–4 cm) long by pressing the mixture through a special utensil, the *passatello*. A food mill can be used if the mesh with the largest holes is inserted. Passatelli are a specialty of Romagna and are pressed directly into a pan of boiling, homemade beef stock. (See recipe, page 84).

Peòci
The Venetians call their mussels by this name, a dialect form of the word *pidocchi* or lice, implying that the mussel is a form of sea parasite.

Pepatelli or Pepatille
A dessert made from bran or whole-wheat (wholemeal) flour, honey, chopped almonds, and plenty of freshly ground pepper.

Pepper, Cayenne
When the dried pods of the *Capsicum frutescens*—the small red, or chili, pepper is ground, it produces this very hot spice so popular in some regions of Italy.

Perciatelli
A type of spaghetti with a hole running through it. Another term for this type of pasta is *bucatini* (little holes).

Pesto
The famous Ligurian sauce used to dress pasta dishes and flavor soups. Fresh basil leaves are pounded in a mortar with pine nuts, garlic, and plenty of grated Pecorino cheese; then olive oil is gradually added. (See recipe for Pesto alla Genovese, page 77.)

Piada
See the entry for *schizzòti*.

Piatto Elefante
In the Alto Adige region this is the term used to describe a meal consisting of a very wide and abundant variety of meats and sausages served as one dish. A restaurant in Bressanone, which takes its name from the *Elefante* of the dish, is famous for preparing this specialty.

Piccagge
Very wide lasagne made mainly in Genoa. (See recipe, page 68.)

Piccellati
A specialty of Molise in southern Italy, *piccellati* are cakes made with a filling of bread crumbs, walnuts, almonds, grated orange rind, and honey or concentrated grape juice.

Pillotto
A good-sized piece of pork fat, which is speared on the end of a metal rod with a wooden handle and rubbed over the flesh of meats while they are cooking on a spit. The pork fat melts on contact with the hot meat and continually bastes it. This term is used in Umbrian cuisine. At one time, the pork fat was wrapped in a piece of paper which would catch fire when coming in contact with the heat of the flames and burn, dripping flaming hot drops of fat onto the meat roasting on the spit. This was a favorite way of cooking meat in central Italy. In Sardinia a similar way of roasting meat on a spit survives in the cooking of *porceddu* or suckling pigs. (See recipe, page 201.)

Pinne
Fan mussels. These molluscs are shaped like a ham and are up to 2½ feet (75 cm) long. The most remarkable feature of the fan mussel is its byssus, or projecting tuft of silky fibers, like the beard of the ordinary mussel but much finer. These were collected by fishermen in southern Italy, especially at Taranto, spun, and then woven into a fabric with a golden luster from which gloves and stockings were made. Today, along the Ionian coast, these mussels are eaten raw in salads, with olive oil, lemon juice, parsley, and pepper.

Pinza
In the eastern Alpine region *pinza* is the etymological equivalent of pizza, but its ingredients are very different. *Pinza* is a dessert made from stale bread soaked in milk, sugar, eggs, a little butter to help keep the mixture soft and creamy, pine nuts, and seedless raisins (sultanas). The resulting pudding is baked in the oven (see recipe, page 46). Other types of *pinza* are made with flour, sugar, and eggs in Friuli and Venezia Giulia at Easter time.

Pizza al Formaggio (Cheese Pizza)
Originally an Umbrian specialty, this pizza is also popular in the Marches, and usually starts off the Easter meal. It is made with eggs, Pecorino cheese, Grana cheese (similar to Parmesan), and olive oil, beaten together and then mixed with an equal quantity of bread dough. The ingredients are kneaded into a soft and pliable consistency. The dough is left to rise, then punched down, placed in a cake pan, and left to rise again before being baked in a hot oven. The dough should rise to double its original volume for a really good pizza.

Pizzoccheri
A specialty of the Valtellina district in northern Italy. These are wide tagliatelle or ribbon noodles, made from buckwheat mixed with all-purpose (plain) flour. The *pizzoccheri* are cooked with potatoes, cabbage, and other vegetables and then drained and mixed with melted butter, grated cheese, and a little garlic. (See recipe, page 30.)

Polenta di Patate

In some parts of Trentino and in the eastern region of the Alps polenta is not made with cornmeal (maize flour); it is made with mashed potatoes with a little buckwheat flour added to bind the mixture. The polenta is then topped with slices of soft cheese or slices of uncooked, cured sausage meat.

Polenta Taragna

A buckwheat flour polenta which is also sometimes called *furmentùn* made in roughly the same way as cornmeal (maize flour) polenta. When the buckwheat flour and water mixture is almost done, butter, and cheese are added to flavor and soften the polenta. The word *taragna* most probably derives from the verb *tarare*, to stir; and the utensil with which the polenta is stirred is called a *tarài*.

Potacchio or Potaggio

The term's most likely provenance is from the French *potage* which originally meant food cooked in a pot. In Italian cookery, this method of cooking is usually used for chicken, rabbit, or lamb.

Potìza

Putiza or *butiz* in Friulian dialect means belly, and *potìza* is a stuffed pastry, bulging with a filling of chocolate, milk, sugar, walnuts, plums, golden bread crumbs, dried figs, grated lemon rind, and spices such as cinnamon and nutmeg, all enveloped in a casing of a sweet dough made with flour, milk, eggs, and sugar. This dessert is a specialty of Gorizia.

Prèsniz

Like *potìza*, *prèsniz* is a stuffed pastry, but with a casing of sweetened puff pastry and with an even richer, more elaborate filling made of walnuts, almonds, fine bread crumbs fried in butter, sugar, chocolate, candied citron, seedless white raisins (sultanas), grated lemon rind, rum, vanilla extract (essence), and sometimes lemon juice.

Probusti

Garlicky little sausages made with lean pork and lean veal which are smoked lightly over a birch fire and then boiled and served with sauerkraut. These sausages originated in the Rovereto district of Trentino. They are now only produced on a very small scale.

Provatura

In some parts of Latium, Mozzarella is called *provatura,* since small Mozzarellas resemble the samples of cheese taken by the cheese testers to see whether the quality of the *pasta filata* or plastic curd is up to standard. *Provatura* means sample, or trial.

Pùddica

An Apulian-style pizza. The dough is rolled out to a thickness of $\frac{3}{4}$ inch (2 cm) and little hollows are scooped out with the fingers. The topping ingredients— strips of tomato, garlic, and oil—are placed in the hollows. Like pizza, *pùddica* should be served piping hot.

Puddighinos

Pullets or young cockerels stuffed with a filling of eggs, sautéed giblets, bread crumbs, cream, and tomatoes. These medium-sized chickens are bred and raised in Sardinia.

Puìna

In the Friuli-Venezia Giulia region and in many parts of the Veneto, this is the dialect word for Ricotta cheese. Often it refers to smoked Ricotta.

Puntarelle

These bitter endive (chicory) plants are often used in salads and are a specialty of Latium. The endive (chicory) is soaked in cold water so that it curls up and is then dried and dressed with oil, vinegar, and anchovy fillets.

Radicchio Arrosto

In the area round Treviso and in other parts of the Veneto, red Treviso chicory is broiled (grilled) and served with meat, etc. The tougher, outer leaves and the base are removed and the radicchio is then cut lengthwise in halves or quarters. It is sprinkled with oil and salt, placed under the broiler (grill), and turned very frequently so it does not burn on the outside. The vegetable is tender when it is cooked. It is served hot, flavored with a few drops of fresh lemon juice.

Ratafià

A liqueur made by macerating sour black cherries in sugar, and allowing them to stand in the sun for two months. Alcohol is then added, and the resulting liqueur usually has an alcoholic strength of 25 to 30 percent.

Ricciarelli

Sienese candies made with chopped almonds and sugar. *Ricciarelli* date back many hundreds of years and are now produced commercially.

Riso alla Pilota

In the areas where rice has been grown extensively for a long time many different ways of cooking it have been invented. In the plains of Verona and Mantua, a risotto is made which has fresh sausage meat (*tatassal*) in it. This recipe is called *alla pilota*, since its originators were the *piloti*, the men who worked in the rice fields winnowing the rice. Some people, however, maintain that the word *pilota* comes from the way in which the rice is cooked: *pilotato* or guided. Water is brought to a boil and the rice is poured carefully into the cooking pot so that it forms a cone covering the base of the receptacle and narrowing to a point just below the surface of the water. From geometry we know that a cone inscribed in a cylinder has $\frac{1}{3}$ the volume of the cylinder. Thus there will be 1 part rice to 2 parts water. With these proportions the rice will completely absorb the water by the time it is done. To prevent the rice's sticking to the bottom of the pan, it is advisable to cook it in the oven in a covered cooking pot.

Rosada

A type of pudding which used to be made in Trentino-Alto Adige for important dignitaries of the church. It is a particularly delicious dessert which can be generally described as a crème caramel with finely ground almonds.

Rôstida

In the Po Valley great use has always been made of such organs as the heart and lungs of pigs. *Rôstida*, or *rôstisciada*, refers to a method of preparing these organs and other cuts of pork by chopping them into small pieces and cooking them in butter. This is a winter dish, made when the pigs are slaughtered. (See recipe, page 26.)

Rôstisciada

See Rôstida above.

Salam d'la Düja

This is the typical *salame dell'olla*, pure pork sausage surrounded by pork fat and packed in little earthenware vessels or *olle*, which give the sausage its name. This sausage has a delicious full flavor and is tender and moist enough to be eaten only with a fork.

Saltimbocca

Thin slices of lean veal are covered with slices of prosciutto (raw ham) and sage leaves, secured with wooden cocktail sticks, and sautéed in butter. (See recipe, page 136.)

Sambuca

A liqueur made from aniseed and sugar in Latium. Historically, in the Campagna di Roma, the liqueur was made by infusing aniseed in alcohol and then adding sugar. Civitavecchia near Rome is renowned for its Sambuca.

Sanguinaccio

When a pig was killed, it was carefully bled so that the meat was pale pink, almost white in color. The blood was mixed with pork fat, bread crumbs, pine nuts, and sometimes a little sugar. It was then cooked and encased in gut, and the blood sausage (*sanguinaccio*) (or black pudding) was grilled or baked before eating. These sausages were prepared all over Italy with variations in the amount and type of seasoning used. Those were the days when farmers followed to the letter the old saying that the whole of a pig could be used for some purpose or other and that nothing need be thrown away.

Saór

A marinade in which sardines, previously floured and fried in plenty of oil, are immersed, usually for two or three days. The mixture of onions and wine vinegar used for marinating the fish is typical of Venetian cooking. (See recipe, page 57.)

Sartù

A rice dish which has been adopted by the Neapolitans in an area where spaghetti normally reigns supreme. It is in fact one of the outstanding recipes of the region, although nowadays it is not nearly so elaborate as it once was. The recipe given in this book is a simplified version of the complicated and very rich dish served in Naples in the nineteenth century. (See recipe, page 151.)

Sbira

The dock workers of the port of Genoa used to have a great fondness for this dish, and its name may originate from a habit of the police (*sbirri*) in the port: rather than sit down at mealtimes in the local *trattorie*, they would eat this dish standing up, presumably always on the lookout. *Sbira* is a substantial preparation of tripe and pieces of meat served on thick slices of coarse bread.

Sbrisolona

A pastry prepared in the Veneto made with large quantities of butter or fat. The consistency is therefore very crumbly, which is how the dessert came by its name (*sbriciolare* in Italian means to crumble).

Schizzòti

These very thin buns almost look as if they have been squashed flat; hence the name (*schiacciato* means crushed or squashed). Unleavened bread dough is mixed with pork lard. The flat bread used to be cooked in earthenware vessels buried in hot ashes. *Schizzòti* resemble the *piade* of Romagna and are folded over a filling and eaten like a sandwich. There is a sweet version, made with flour, sugar, eggs, and rum, flavored with rosemary, which is baked in the oven.

Sfogliatelle

Ring-shaped cakes made of short pastry or puff pastry. The latter are called *sfogliatelle ricce*. Some are twisted into rings, while others are filled with fresh Ricotta cheese and candied fruits and are eaten hot.

Smoking

One of the oldest ways of preserving meat and fish. Before being smoked, the meat or fish is usually immersed in a brine bath. It is then exposed to the drying action of the smoke in special smoking sheds or over wood fires. Like the salt brine, the smoke will preserve the meat, and it will also impart a pleasant flavor to it.

Sópa coada

This dish had very humble origins in the Veneto but has recently been brought into vogue by some very good restaurants. Two pieces of homemade bread enclose a layer of cheese and a layer of roasted pigeon. This sandwich is placed in a baking dish, covered with homemade stock and cooked in a slow oven for as long as 4 to 5 hours. Cooked so slowly, the bread absorbs all the moisture without burning and takes on the flavor of the stock, cheese, and meat. The name of this dish comes from this long cooking process. *Coada* is dialect for *covata*, or brooded over. In Treviso and in some other areas of the Veneto, tripe is used instead of pigeon.

Stoccafisso (Stockfish)
Sun-dried cod.

Stracciatella
A soup which is very popular in Latium. Eggs and Parmesan cheese are beaten with a fork, and poured into hot stock, and as the mixture sets it forms little shreds or strings. (See recipe, page 134.)

Sugna Piccante
A spread for toast or flavoring for vegetables popular in southern Italy especially in Basilicata. It is a mixture of fresh lard and plenty of red chili pepper. It is usually made at the time of year when the pigs are slaughtered. (See recipe, page 165.)

Surecilli
Surecilli is the Abruzzi dialect word for mice. It is also the name given to little gnocchi made with flour, water, and eggs. The gnocchi are boiled and then dressed with the juices from roast lamb or kid.

Taccozze
A type of pasta made in Umbria, the Marches, Abruzzi, Molise, and Campania. Egg noodle dough is rolled into a slightly thicker sheet than usual, then cut into pieces about 1–1¼ inches (3–4 cm) square. *Taccozze* are eaten with a sauce or are added to soup. In the latter case, the squares are made somewhat smaller. The name comes from *taccone*, a patch which is used to mend clothes, and in fact they have that shape.

Tajarin
Very narrow homemade tagliatelle, made with flour and eggs. This type of pasta is popular in Piedmont, especially in the area around Alba, where they are served with a sauce made of butter, onions, and chicken livers. (See recipe, page 22.)

Taralli
Ring-shaped cakes made throughout the south of Italy. They can be sweet or peppery. In order to make them very flaky, they are precooked in boiling water for a very short time and then browned by baking in a moderate oven.

Tarallucci
A diminutive form of *taralli*, these are little cookies in the shape of rings or disks which are also parboiled before being baked in the oven in order to make them flaky. This type of cake is associated with festivals since great numbers used to be sold from stalls when a village celebrated the festival of its patron saint.

Tarantello
A smoked and cured dish made with the choicest part of the tuna fish—the belly. The delicacy takes its name from the city of Taranto which was the oldest and most famous center of its production.

Tassa
In Molise *tassa* is a soup of bread and heated wine to which a generous amount of chili pepper is added in place of the usual spices. Farmers eat this food to warm themselves on the coldest days of the winter. It gets its name because it is eaten from a large cup (*tazza*) or bowl.

Testaroli
Small pancakes made with flour and water cooked in special shallow covered earthenware dishes called *testi*, which used to be placed in the hearth and covered with glowing embers and ashes. The pancakes were then cut into squares or wide ribbons, boiled for a few minutes, drained, and then dressed with oil, garlic, basil, and plenty of grated Pecorino cheese. (See recipe, page 98.)

Tiella
An Apulian specialty made with layers of potato, onion, and sliced mushroom, sprinkled with oil, salt, pepper, garlic, and parsley, arranged in a cooking pot or baking dish, topped with a layer of bread crumbs, and baked in the oven. The version eaten around Gaeta is made with two rounds of pizza dough, and may be either meat or fish based. The former filling consists of fresh cheese, eggs, sausage, and strips of tomato; the latter of seafood, tomatoes, pitted (stoned) olives, capers, and garlic. The "sandwich" is then fried in oil or shortening (lard).

Timballo (Timbale)
A dish consisting of a pastry crust filled with a mold of precooked food such as meat, mushrooms, macaroni, etc. It may also refer to the molded filling alone or to the mold in which it is made. The name of this dish probably comes from a semi-spherical drum, the *timballo*, whose shape is similar to that of a timbale mold.

Torrone (Nougat)
This candy is traditionally eaten during winter festivals in many parts of Italy. Toasted almonds are mixed with a blend of honey, sugar, and white of egg. There are many different types of nougat: some have hazelnuts, pine nuts, walnuts, or pistacchio nuts, and sometimes chocolate or figs are added to the basic mixture.

Tortelli
Small sweet or savory pancakes. A batter is made from eggs, milk, and flour to which mixed herbs or vegetables can be added. The mixture is tossed in oil or butter. The name *tortelli* is also used for larger forms of the stuffed pasta, *tortellini*.

Trofie
Very soft, tender gnocchi or dumplings made with a mixture of flour and mashed potato or with flour alone. They

are served with pesto or with a meat sauce. They are a Ligurian, in particular a Genoese, specialty.

To Thicken

This process is designed to give body to a liquid—be it a sauce, a soup, or meat juices. The thickening agent can be a roux (a cooked mixture of butter and flour), beurre manié (small pieces of butter worked together with flour into little balls), egg yolks, or cream. The result will be more or less creamy, depending on the method used.

Trussing

Before roasting or cooking a chicken on a spit, the legs and wings should be neatly folded against the sides of the bird and tied into place firmly with string. A trussed chicken will cook more evenly and be easier to baste, and there will be no protruding parts that could burn or stick to the pan.

Uccelletti di mare

Baby cuttlefish, tiny squid, and other seafoods are threaded on to skewers made of tamarisk wood, marinated in a special thick sauce made of bread crumbs, parsley, and oil, and then roasted over a wood fire.

Vaccinara

In Rome the men who slaughtered and butchered steers were known as *vaccinari*. Several Roman dishes, especially those made with less desirable cuts of beef, are prepared in a way which is called *alla vaccinara*, since they used to be served to these workers in *trattorie* near the slaughterhouses.

Vincisgrassi

An historic and traditional dish which is still a favorite in the Marches. It is made with lasagne, layered with a rich meat sauce and a white sauce and then baked in the oven (see recipe, page 120). The dish used to be a great deal more highly flavored and elaborate especially since it

used to contain sliced truffles.

Zabaione (Zabaglione)

Zabaione is often encountered in Piedmontese cuisine, in the Veneto, and in many other parts of Italy. One of the best known methods of making *zabaione* is as follows: Beat a rounded tablespoon of sugar with the yolk of an egg. When the mixture has become slightly frothy, half an eggshell full of Marsala wine is added. The mixture is beaten while being cooked in a bain-marie, and the *zabaione* is ready when it has increased in volume and become light and frothy. This recipe is for one portion, so it must be increased according to the number of people being served. *Zabaione* is delicious as a topping with puddings or other desserts or on its own with lady fingers (boudoir biscuits) or cookies.

Zelten

A classic dessert from Alto Adige. A rye bread dough is prepared, into which are worked plenty of dates, dried figs, seedless white raisins (sultanas), pine nuts, and walnuts, all of which have been moistened with brandy or rum. The dough is shaped into squares about $\frac{3}{4}$ inch (2 cm) high and topped with almonds and candied fruit. The cakes are baked and then sprinkled with a little honey and water.

Zeppole

Doughnuts or sweet pastry rings which are made in many regions of southern Italy. They are usually made of an egg and flour dough, boiled in water and then deep-fried and coated with honey. (See recipe, page 162.)

List of Recipes

Kitchen Equipment

Illustrated on this page and opposite are some of the utensils which are useful in any well-equipped kitchen and which are particularly necessary to Italian cooking.

1 Baking or cookie sheet
2 Round baking pan
3 Wire balloon whisk
4 Heavy copper saucepan (milk pan)
5 Mortar and pestle
6 Metal pastry decorating tube (forcing pipe)
7 Half-moon chopper
8 Paring knife
9 Cleaver (for cutting large pieces of meat and for flattening meat)
10 Cloth pastry bag with decorative tip (piping bag and nozzle)
11 Butcher's knife or all-purpose chef's knife
12 Poultry shears
13 Slicer (for cutting ham, cured meats and Italian salami)
14 Spatula (palette)
15 Serrated carving knife
16 Serrated knife for cutting bread and vegetables
17 Spatula (palette knife)
18 Ladle
19 Pancake turner or slotted spatula (fish slice)
20 Slotted spoon
21 Kitchen fork
22 Very large deep cooking pot or stock pot
23 Large cooking pot (preferably enameled cast iron)
24 Skillet or frying pan (preferably cast iron)
25 Small saucepan with pouring lip (for milk, sauces, stock, etc.) (milk pan)
26 Tall cooking pot (earthenware or enameled cast iron)
27 Small pan for frying or baking
28 Fine strainer or sieve
29 Colander
30 Fish steamer (kettle) (with detachable rack)
31 Gratin dish
32 Vegetable steamer
33 Copper kettle for polenta
34 Deep fryer
35 Springform cake pan (spring-release tin)